LANGUAGE AND LANGUAGE LEARNING

The Indispensable Foundation

LANGUAGE AND LANGUAGE LEARNING

General Editors: RONALD MACKIN *and* PETER STREVENS

1 Henry Sweet *The Practical Study of Languages*
2 J. R. Firth *The Tongues of Men* and *Speech*
3 Randolph Quirk and A. H. Smith *The Teaching of English*
4 Neile Osman *Modern English*
5 H. E. Palmer *The Principles of Language-Study*
6 N. E. Enkvist, J. Spencer and M. Gregory *Linguistics and Style*
7 H. E. Palmer *Curso Internacional de Inglés*
8 J. C. Catford *A Linguistic Theory of Translation*
9 Peter Strevens *Papers in Language and Language Teaching*
10 David Abercrombie *Studies in Phonetics and Linguistics*
11 *Five Inaugural Lectures* edited by Peter Strevens
12 Axel Wijk *Rules of Pronunciation for the English Language*
13 L. A. Hill *Selected Articles on the Teaching of English as a Foreign Language*
14 H. H. Stern *Foreign Languages in Primary Education*
15 Peter Ladefoged *Three Areas of Experimental Phonetics*
16 A. S. Hayes *Language Laboratory Facilities*
17 *Modern Language Teaching* edited by Hans Jalling
18 H. E. Palmer *The Scientific Study and Teaching of Languages*
19 *A Functional Language Examination* edited by H. S. Otter
20 J. Dakin, B. Tiffen and H. G. Widdowson *Language in Education*
21 *Language Testing Symposium* edited by Alan Davies
22 H. E. Palmer and H. V. Redman *This Language-Learning Business*
23 *An Annotated Bibliography on Modern Language Teaching: Books and Articles 1946–67* compiled by Janet O. Robinson
24 *Languages and the Young School Child* edited by H. H. Stern
25 *Prosodic Analysis* edited by F. R. Palmer
26 Edward M. Stack *The Language Laboratory and Modern Language Teaching*
27 *The Prague School of Linguistics and Language Teaching* edited by V. Fried
28 *The Indispensable Foundation: A selection from the writings of Henry Sweet* edited by E. J. A. Henderson
29 J. B. Pride *The Social Meaning of Language*
30 W. H. Mittins et al. *Attitudes to English Usage*
31 *Chomsky: Selected Readings* edited by J. P. B. Allen and P. van Buren
32 *Active Methods and Modern Aids in the Teaching of Foreign Languages* edited by R. Filipovic

The Indispensable Foundation

A Selection from the writings of HENRY SWEET

Edited by *EUGÉNIE J. A. HENDERSON*

'The importance of phonetics as the indispensable foundation of all study of language—whether that study be purely theoretical, or practical as well—is now generally admitted.'

Preface to *A Handbook of Phonetics*, 1877

London

OXFORD UNIVERSITY PRESS

1971

Oxford University Press, Ely House, London W. 1

GLASGOW NEW YORK TORONTO MELBOURNE WELLINGTON
CAPE TOWN SALISBURY IBADAN NAIROBI DAR ES SALAAM LUSAKA ADDIS ABABA
BOMBAY CALCUTTA MADRAS KARACHI LAHORE DACCA
KUALA LUMPUR SINGAPORE HONG KONG TOKYO

Library edition ISBN O 19 437113 1

Paperback edition ISBN O 19 437039 9

PRINTED IN GREAT BRITAIN

Contents

'The importance of phonetics as the indispensable foundation of all study of language—whether that study be purely theoretical, or practical as well—is now generally admitted. Without a knowledge of the laws of sound change scientific philology—whether comparative or historical—is impossible, and without phonetics their study degenerates into a mere mechanical enumeration of letter changes.'

Preface to *A Handbook of Phonetics*, 1877

'The truth is that phonology is not only the indispensable foundation of all philology, but also that no department, from the highest to the lowest, can be investigated fully without it, whether it be accidence, syntax, or prosody, or even that fundamental problem—the origin of language.'

Presidential address to the Philological Society, 1877

'The two main features of Storm's method are the prominence he gives to the living language, and his vindication of scientific phonetics as the indispensable foundation of all study of language, whether practical or theoretical.'

'The practical study of language', *Transactions of the Philological Society*, 1882–4

'It is now generally recognized, except in hopelessly obscurantist circles, that phonology is the indispensable foundation of all linguistic study, whether practical or scientific—above all, of historical grammar.'

Preface to *A New English Grammar*, 1891

Editor's Introduction

It might appear at first sight that a volume of selections from the writings on phonetics of a scholar whose first major work appeared almost a century ago could be of historical interest only, and that its publication must owe more to a sense of professional piety than to its practical applicability to the problems facing linguists and language teachers nowadays. This would be very far from the truth. The breadth and depth of Henry Sweet's linguistic outlook, no less than his accuracy of observation, lucidity of expression, and scrupulous attention to detail, are as valuable and pertinent today as ever they were, and no apology is needed for bringing them to the attention of students reared on later works that are often more pretentious but far less sound. As an 'all-round' linguist, Sweet has seldom been equalled and never surpassed. He was a brilliant phonetician, a highly distinguished comparative and historical linguist, a perspicacious grammarian, an eminent Anglicist, the inventor of an excellent system of shorthand, and a passionate advocate of spelling reform; and his work in any one of these fields was enriched through his knowledge of the others. His contribution to what he called 'living philology' is, indeed, the very antithesis of the fragmentation and over-specialization into which linguists are so often forced nowadays by the increasing complexities of their subject. To present an anthology of selected passages from the works of such a man, wrested from the contexts with which they are so thoroughly integrated, is in a sense to do violence to this quality of 'wholeness' which is the essence of Sweet's greatness, and it is on this score that some apology is perhaps called for.

The widespread current interest in linguistics as a discipline and in manifold applications is the fruit of the phenomenal growth of the subject during the last thirty or forty years. An inevitable but perhaps less unequivocally welcome legacy of this expansion has been the development of an elaborate professional jargon—of a great multitude and variety of technical terms which, while providing what may be thought of as a useful intellectual 'shorthand' for general linguists themselves, may for the inquiring novice frequently obscure rather than illuminate what is, after all, the very heart and soul of the matter—the nature of language itself. In my own teaching over the past twenty-five years I have been brought up sharply against the problems inherent in this situation by witnessing the struggles of students, and in particular of foreign students, to hack a path through the terminological jungle. Such students frequently come to the Universities of this country with very little, if any, formal linguistic training behind them, but eager to absorb as much as they can of the new ideas and approaches to language in the relatively short time at their disposal. They readily acquire a certain facility in the use of impressive-sounding technical jargon for linguistic description, and in the pursuit of formally laid down procedures for linguistic analysis, whilst at the same time exhibiting on occasion a startling lack of awareness of fundamentals. I have found myself constantly driven to seek some way of helping them to extricate themselves from the thorny thickets of theoretical elaboration and controversy and to exercise their own ears and minds directly upon language as a living experience, without the constraints and limitations imposed by current dogma. For this purpose, a carefully selected dose of Sweet has often proved a most successful prescription. After the somewhat turgid prose and closely reasoned argument of much recent writing on linguistics, Sweet's lucidity of style and thought, his originality and honest regard for first hand observation are like a gust of fresh air in a stuffy room. Unfortunately, many of his works are difficult of access and are not always to be found even in University libraries, so that I began some years ago to collect and prepare extracts for distribution to students who were unable to consult the originals. It is a selection from these extracts that, with the encouragement of my colleagues, is offered here.

The original collection of extracts included many passages which it has been necessary to omit from this book. With reluctance, I have had to excise many illuminating passages on the grammatical and historical aspects of language and have concentrated upon Sweet's writings on phonetics, especially in its more general aspects. A number of Sweet's important contributions to the study of English are still fairly readily available, so that I have not attempted to cover his writings on English in any detail in this work. The reissue as the first volume in this series of *The Practical Study of Languages*, which Professor Daniel Jones once aptly described as 'a work for all time', has made it possible to omit here the sections of the original collection devoted to the teaching and learning of languages. Space has been found for fairly lengthy sections on spelling reform and sound-notation, both topics to which Sweet himself attached great importance, and it has seemed particularly fitting, so soon after the centenary of the publication of Bell's *Visible Speech*, that Sweet's full and excellent critical account should provide a means of making Bell's system known to many who have no access to the original. Sweet's accounts of particular National Sound Systems have had to be excluded from the present volume for reasons of space, but it is hoped they may be presented separately in a later volume.

The extracts are arranged by topics, and within topics I have tried in the main to work from the general to the particular as far as possible. By and large, extracts relating to the same topic are presented in chronological order, except where this runs counter to the principle of presenting the general before the particular. The source and date of each extract is given at its foot. Inevitably, a number of passages relate to several topics and might well have been included in more than one section. To avoid unnecessary duplication they are entered in one section only but references to them will be found under all the relevant entries in the topic index on pp. 292–329. Where large portions of important works are the same except in small details—as for example certain passages in the *Handbook* and *Primer of Phonetics*, or in the *Sounds of English* and the article on 'Phonetics' in the 11th edition of the *Encyclopædia Britannica*—it has been thought useful to present these in the form of a single conflated extract, indicating both sources at its foot. Minor variations in style or punctuation and obvious misprints are not noted, but other differences between the texts are marked by the use of square brackets or sloping lines. These often seemingly small differences can be most revealing; sometimes it is clear that the later version represents an attempt at greater precision or clarity, at others it appears that the author has revised his earlier views upon the matter in hand. Probably the most striking example of the latter in these extracts is the expansion of the elementary vowel table in the later revised edition of the *Primer of Phonetics* from 36 to 72. A little-known paper of Sweet's on 'Mixed Vowels', which appeared in *Le Maître phonétique* in 1901, shows how this came about, and is included here as an interesting illustration of Sweet at work.

It has been my aim as editor to intrude as little as possible between reader and author. Editorial comments have therefore been kept to a minimum. With a few trivial exceptions, Sweet's own footnotes and 'Additional Notes' have been preserved and are presented within parentheses, headed either (*Fn.*:) or (*Additional note*:) respectively; they are incorporated in the running text in order to avoid confusion with the occasional footnotes of the editor. Page and paragraph references in the *Handbook* and elsewhere have usually been adapted to refer to relevant pages in the present volume; where this is inapplicable, they have been omitted. Sweet's original notation, including Visible Speech, has been preserved despite the superficial difficulties this may appear to set in the path of the reader to whom it is unfamiliar. So much of the history of phonetics is bound up with questions of notation, and so many of its problems are reflected therein, that it is an important part of the training of University students of the subject to acquaint themselves thoroughly with various systems of notation and to be able to slip without too much ado from one to another. This ability, combined with some knowledge of the history of symbols and of the changes in the conventions governing their use, provides a powerful corrective to the naïve reliance upon a given set of symbols which sometimes characterizes the outlook of the beginner in phonetics. Even an experienced phonetician, however, may be daunted at his first encounter with Visible Speech and Sweet's Organic Alphabet. A clear and simple introduction to the underlying principles will be found on pp. 256–9. To those in his own day who complained that some of the distinctions between symbols were so minute that they might escape a 'cursory reader', Sweet pointed out that such distinctions were not meant for cursory readers (p. 270). The unhurried reader will find mastery of the Organic Alphabet less difficult than anticipated and well worth the effort. It is hoped that the occasional inconvenience to the reader of switching notation systems from one extract to another will be mitigated by the index of symbols provided on pp. 287–91.

It should be made clear that this anthology does not claim to demonstrate exhaustively Sweet's views upon any of the topics included. This is a sampling only, and connoisseurs of Sweet's work will undoubtedly deplore the omission of many of their favourite passages. The extracts chosen and the sources from which they are derived bear the imprint of their beginnings—they were originally selected for the purposes described above, and the list of sources from which they are taken are in general those to which I myself have had ready access. That many treasures are missing may spur the reader to explore further for himself by going back to the originals. This is indeed the strongest justification for the present work—the introduction of the keen younger generation of linguists and phoneticians to the many excellences of Sweet and to the great insights into the nature of language that he can provide, in the firm belief that they will be eager to pursue and deepen the acquaintance on their own account.

EUGÉNIE HENDERSON

London 1970

I. Language and Languages in General

Language is essentially based on the dualism of form and meaning, and all attempts to reduce language to strict logical or psychological categories, by ignoring its formal side, have failed ignominiously. The form of language is its *sounds*. The science which teaches us to observe, analyse, and describe the sounds of language is phonology. Phonology is, therefore, the *science of linguistic observation*.

'On English Philology and Phonology', *Presidential Address to the Philological Society*, 1877, in *Collected Papers of Henry Sweet*, 1913, p. 85

Definition of language. Language is the expression of ideas by means of *speech-sounds* combined into *words*. Words are combined into *sentences*, this combination answering to that of ideas into thoughts. Thus in Latin the word *terra* expresses the idea 'the earth', and *rotunda* expresses the idea 'round', and these two words are combined together to form the sentence *terra rotunda*, which expresses the thought 'the earth is round'. Different languages have different sounds (sound-systems), and attach different meanings to the combinations of sounds into words, and of words into sentences.

Form and Meaning. There are, then, two sides to language—two ways of looking at it: there is the *formal* side, which is concerned with the outer form of words and sentences, and the *logical* side, which is concerned with their inner meaning. Thus the formal side of such a word as *man* is that it is made up of certain sounds standing in a certain relato one another—following one another in a certain order, etc. So also the form of such a sentence as *the man helped the boy* consists in its being composed of certain words following one another in a certain order, and standing in other relations to one another; and we can alter the form of a sentence by merely changing the order of the words of which it is made up, as in *the boy helped the man*. The study of the formal side of language is based on *phonetics*—the science of speech-sounds; the study of the logical side of language is based on *psychology*—the science of mind. But phonetics and psychology do not constitute the science of language, being only preparations for it: language and grammar are concerned not with form and meaning separately, but with the connections between them, these being the real phenomena of language.

A New English Grammar, 1891, pp. 6–7

Some languages, such as Chinese, show grammatical relations entirely by means of word-order and form-words. Others, such as Latin, rely mainly on inflections, though they use many form-words as well, with which, indeed, no language can dispense. We call such a language as Chinese an *isolating* language as distinguished from an *inflectional* language such as Latin. English is mainly an isolating language which has preserved a few inflections.

The classification of languages according to their structure, without regard to their relationship, is called the *morphological*, as opposed to the *genealogical* classification. English and Latin are genealogically related by being both members of the Arian family of languages, but they differ widely morphologically. English and Chinese, on the other hand, show great morphological resemblance without being in any way genealogically related.

A New English Grammar, 1891, p. 32

Difficulties of Language. The difficulties caused by the written form of the language, such as the complexity of its alphabet—which, again, may be the result of the writing being partly hieroglyphic—the ambiguity or unphonetic character of its orthography, are all purely external: Arabic is still Arabic when transcribed into Roman letters, nor is Japanese any the more Japanese for being written in a mixture of disguised hieroglyphs and syllabic alphabetic writing, both borrowed from China. No existing system of writing is anything but an external disguise borrowed from some other language: Arabic is disguised Syrian writing, and the Russian alphabet is Byzantine Greek.

. . . . .

All these considerations, if summed up impartially, lead us finally to the conclusion that, as regards ease of learning, all languages are intrinsically on a level—they are all equally easy or equally difficult; that is, of course, if we rigorously eliminate all external considerations, and disregard the special relations between individual languages.

But as it is practically impossible for any one who has not an equally perfect knowledge of all languages to test this by experience, it must remain an abstraction, like the dogma of the absolute regularity of sound-changes. We may also say of the dogma of the intrinsically equal difficulty of languages, as of that of the absolute regularity of sound-changes, that even if it is not true, it has a certain value as a corrective to one-sidedness and inaccurate reasoning.

. . . . .

From the admission that all languages are in themselves equally difficult, it does not necessarily follow that we are never to apply the word 'difficult' to languages. But it must be understood that when we say that one Oriental language is more difficult than another, we only imply that the external obstacles are greater, or that the structure of the language differs more from that of the average European language.

The Practical Study of Languages, 1899, pp. 54, 66, 69; L.A.L.L. Edn., pp. 53, 65–6, 68

It is a great mistake to suppose that any one nation has a special gift for acquiring sounds of foreign languages generally. Each nation has its special defects or advantages. . . . It cannot, of course, be denied that some languages are a worse preparation for the acquisition of foreign sounds than others, but a thorough training in general phonetics soon levels the inequality, and enables the learner to develop his special gifts independently of outward circumstances.

A Handbook of Phonetics, 1877, Preface, pp. xiii–xiv

Origin of Speech Sounds. It used to be generally assumed that primitive speech had a very limited range of sounds; but a little consideration will show that the opposite must have been the case. Language proper, which implies sound-groups (words) symbolizing ideas, and capable of being combined into sentences as freely as ideas are combined into thoughts, was preceded by a period of mixed gesture and imitation. Every object and phenomenon associated in nature with an imitable sound would naturally be named by an imitation of that sound: ɑʡɑʡ—or some such sound-group—meant 'cuckoo' from the beginning. The power of imitation was enormously developed through its use by hunters in decoying wild animals, where, of course, the best imitation would secure the best results. But gesture also helped to develop the power of forming sounds, while at the same time helping to lay the foundation of language proper. When men first expressed the idea of 'teeth', 'eat', or 'bite', it was by pointing to their teeth. If the interlocutor's back was turned, a cry for attention was necessary, which would naturally assume the form of the openest and clearest vowel **a**. Sympathetic lingual gesture would then accompany the hand-gesture, which later would then be dropped as superfluous, so that **ada** or, more emphatically, **ata** would mean 'teeth', or 'tooth', and 'bite' or 'eat', these different meanings being only gradually differentiated. We see that the primitive uninflected words or 'roots' of language were probably dissyllabic. So also the ideas of 'wind' and 'breath' were expressed by ꜿ + vowels, which is both an imitation of the sound of the wind and is at the same time one of the results of the action of breathing itself, 'blowing' being also expressed by ɔ. Now neither ꜿ nor ɔ forms part of the original Arian sound-system, as known to us by historical evidence. Not only isolated sounds like ꜿ were eliminated, but also whole classes of sounds. Primitive man must have expressed 'drinking' by an inbreathed c‹, and probably he expressed sensual enjoyment generally, as some of us still do by an inbreathed voiceless *l*—ω‹. These inconvenient inbreathers seem to have been eliminated everywhere in language, but the nearly-related suction-stops or 'clicks' still survive in many primitive languages, as in the South African Bushman and Hottentot, and in some Californian languages. These clicks were no doubt originally (as pointed out to me by Mr. J. Marshall, junr.) food-cries. Another class of sounds which have been eliminated in most languages is that of the throat-consonants or 'true gutturals', which still survive in Arabic, and also seem to have existed in parent Arian—at any rate, in Sanskrit. But the Sanskrit 'sonant *h*' may be a new formation, like the glottal stop in Danish. Clicks still survive as interjections in English.

History of English Sounds, 1888, pp. 50–2

Languages which are very rich in sounds, such as Sanskrit and Russian, generally owe it to assimilative influence. The difference between a poor and a rich sound-system is merely that the former utters the elements of such a group as ʒɷ] successively, while the latter utters the first two simultaneously—ʒ\] or ʟ], the former class of languages being generally more harmonious than the latter, which often have something 'sloppy' about them. We find, accordingly, that many of the Sanskrit sounds, such as ꜿʃ and ɷʃ, occur only in special sandhi-combinations. After what has been said about the richness of primitive sound-systems, it need hardly be repeated that extreme simplicity is no proof of the primitiveness of a sound-system, being, as often as not, the result of levelling, as in Gothic, where *e* and *o* were levelled under *i* and *u* respectively, or being only apparent—the result of a defective alphabet, as in the Old Persian of the cuneiform inscriptions. Languages spoken over a diversified linguistic area tend to simplify their sound-systems, as may be seen by comparing German and Italian with any of their dialects, most of which show complex sound-systems.

No language has an absolutely symmetrical sound-system, because every sound-system is the result partly of organic, partly of logical influences. The organic tendency is towards analogy and symmetry. Such organic changes as the unrounding of front vowels are generally carried out consistently: if we hear a German say **giitə** instead of *güte*, we expect him to say **ʃeen** instead of *schön*. There is also an organic tendency to carry out a uniform basis of articulation. Thus the English tendency is to flatten and broaden the tongue, which makes the vowels wide, and to hollow the fore part of it in forming such consonants as *l* and *t*, which tends to draw away the tongue from the teeth. If this tendency is exaggerated, it results in a general back-modification, which would end in making our concave *l* into a Russian ɛ. In E. there is also a tendency to keep the mouth half-shut, which is partly due to the climate, and is the first stop in the direction of rounding. A Frenchman, on the contrary, articulates with a convex tongue, either against the teeth, or as near them as possible, and opens his mouth widely. But the carrying out of a uniform basis of articulation would often lead to the loss of distinctive sounds. Thus the dentality of E. *þ* is quite inconsistent with the general character of its sound-system, but the conversion of *þ* into *s* or outer *t* has up to the present been successfully resisted by the logical principle of distinctness. But even without logical influences we find violations of the basis of articulation. Thus in Portuguese *t* and *d* are interdental, but *n* is the E. ʒ⊣ and *l* is ω⊣(, a sound which would seem to be totally opposed to Romance tendencies.

History of English Sounds, 1888, pp. 56–8

What is Language? Language may be defined as the expression of thought by means of speech-sounds. In other words, every sentence or word by which we express our ideas has a certain definite form of its own by virtue of the sounds of which it is made up, and has a more or less definite meaning.

The first thing in the study of language is to realize clearly this duality of form and meaning, constituting respectively the *formal* and the *logical* (or psychological) side of language.

Although language is inconceivable without this polarity of form and meaning, it is often convenient—and even necessary—to look at language from a more or less one-sidedly formal or logical point of view, as the case may be. The study of the formal side of language is based on *phonetics*—the science of speech-sounds; the study of the logical side of language is based on *psychology*—the science of mind.

But every expression of meaning by sound does not necessarily constitute language in the strict sense of the word.

Such sounds as *oh! ah! pah!* and the other interjections with which we express emotions, call for attention, utter commands, and so on, convey definite enough ideas, but by themselves they no more constitute language than the corresponding cries of animals do. Some of them indeed are excluded from the language of the speaker by their form. Thus we have interjections consisting entirely of consonants, such as the lengthened *sh!* with which we enjoin silence, and the *pst!* with which Germans call waiters in restaurants: we have to make *sh!* into *hush* before we can admit it into the English language.

What these sounds lack is 'articulation'—that is, logical articulation. From a formal point of view, such interjections as *pah!* or the cry of the cuckoo, or the bleat of the sheep, or the series of whistles with which a monkey expresses surprise or curiosity, are fairly articulate; but they are not logically articulate like the sentences of language proper, in which words are combined together to express corresponding combinations of ideas into thoughts. Such an interjection as *sh!* expresses the same ideas as the sentences *I wish you to be silent!*; *be silent!*; *don't make so much noise!*; but it expresses them vaguely: it is equivalent to a sentence, and yet is not a sentence. It is true that we can have sentences consisting of a single word, such as the imperative *come!* We regard *come* in itself as a word because we can freely combine it with other words to form sentences, which we cannot do with *sh!* till we have transformed it into a real word; it is therefore, as we have said, neither a word nor a sentence, but something between the two.

Language, then, implies the differentiation of *word* and *sentence*. It is evident that until it has reached this stage, it cannot claim to be an efficient expression or instrument of thought. This differentiation has not been attained by animals: they can express ideas by sounds, but they cannot combine these sounds together to express corresponding combinations of ideas. Thus they can make a sound which serves—whether intentionally or not—to warn their companions of danger; but they cannot, as far as we know, combine other sounds with it to indicate the nature of the danger; and if they indicate the source or locality of the danger, it is only by instinctive movements or glances.

There are other ways besides speech by which ideas may be communicated. One of these, as we have just seen, is *gesture*. When gestures, instead of being isolated, are consciously combined to show combinations of ideas, we have a true gesture-language, perfectly analogous to speech-language. Among the natives of North America the multiplicity of mutually unintelligible languages has led to the development of a common gesture-language in which conversations of some length can be carried on. A similar means of communication is often spontaneously developed among deaf-mutes in civilized countries. This natural language of deaf-mutes must be carefully distinguished from the artificial 'deaf-and-dumb-alphabet', which is a mere mechanical reproduction of the letters with which the words of the ordinary language are written.

. . . . .

Language, Imperfect and Traditional. In ordinary language or 'speech-language', on the other hand, the connection between form and meaning is much less direct. It is far easier to find appropriate gesture-symbols than it is to find appropriate and self-interpreting phonetic ones. It is true that it is easy enough to suggest such ideas as those of blowing and drinking by sound, and we can perceive a certain connection between the initial consonants of the English words *mouth* and *nose* and the things these words stand for; but the gesture-speaker has a much simpler and surer way of expressing them by merely pointing to them with his finger, and in the same way he can indicate other parts of the face, and find gestures to express such ideas as hearing and seeing, which cannot be directly suggested by any combination of sounds.

Of course, in a highly developed gesture-language the meaning of the gestures would not be always self-evident; but the number of self-interpreting signs is always infinitely greater than in speech-language. The consequence is, as regards the latter, that a fully developed speech-language has to be learnt from the beginning by each generation of its speakers; that is, it is kept up by tradition. This further implies permanent communities of some extent. The absence of these conditions among animals is alone enough to explain why they have not developed their interjectional cries into a genuine language.

The History of Language, 1900, pp. 1–4

II. Dialects, Styles, and Standards

Storm rightly blames the older German grammarians for confusing Tudor English, eighteenth- and nineteenth-century English in one chaotic mass, which is made the foundation of the practical study of the living language. With equal justice he protests against the tendency of grammarians to regard the spoken language as a corruption of the literary language; he maintains, on the contrary, that the spoken language is always the real source of the literary language. Indeed (as I remarked in my above-mentioned review) the spoken language is (with the exception of occasional abnormal artificialities) the *only* source of the literary language: every literary language arises from a more or less arbitrary mixture of spoken languages of different periods; such forms, for instance, as *thou lovest, he loveth*, which now only occur in the higher literature, were ordinary colloquialisms in Tudor English. Hence the general axiom—equally important for the practical and the scientific study of language—that the living spoken form of every language should be made the foundation of its study. This holds good, even if the ultimate object is the mastery of the literary language only, for the spoken is the only form of the language which is regular and definitely limited in the range of its grammar and vocabulary.

'The Practical Study of Language', *T.P.S.* 1882–4, in *Collected Papers of Henry Sweet*, 1913, pp. 35–6

Origin of Dialects. Language originates spontaneously in the individual, for the imitative and symbolic instinct is inherent in all intelligent beings, whether men or animals; but, like that of poetry and the arts, its development is social. Where there is free and uniform intercourse between all the members of a community the language will be uniform—that is, uniform in the sense of not splitting into dialects. Of course, every family, and every individual, will have their own peculiarities of speech, but there will be no local concentration of these peculiarities.

When the community is too large to permit of uniform communication throughout it, dialects begin. If we suppose a large plain, covered with villages of equal size and independence at equal distances, each village communicating directly only with its immediate neighbours, there will in a few generations be a distinctly different dialect in each village, and in course of time the dialects of the most northern, southern, eastern, and western villages will become mutually unintelligible to one another and to that of the central village. But there will be no lines of division: the dialects will shade insensibly into one another; the dialects of a village halfway between the most northern and the central village will partake so equally of the characteristics of the northern and central dialects that it will be impossible to assign it to either.

This overlapping of dialects—which always happens when there is no definite barrier—is due also to the fact that the separate changes which constitute difference of dialect or language do not follow the same boundary-lines, but cross one another to any extent. Thus in Old French the distinction between the 'Central French' or Parisian and the Norman dialect is generally fairly definite, but we find South Norman agreeing with its neighbour Parisian in changing Lat. *c* into *ch* [tʃ] before *a*, as in *chier* = Lat. *cārum* against the North Norman *kier*. This particular sound-change has, then, chosen an area of its own, regardless of the areas of the other changes which separate South as well as North Norman from Parisian.

But if such a territory is intersected by a range of mountains, a broad river, or any other obstacle to communication, running, say, east and west, then there will be a corresponding line of linguistic division: all the dialects north of the barrier will form a group with features in common distinct from those which unite the southern group of dialects; if the barrier is strong enough, the two nearest villages north and south of it will in time come to speak mutually unintelligible languages. Even the most trifling barrier—a narrow brook or strip of sandy heath—will be enough to mark off two groups of dialects.

Complete territorial separation through emigration is a self-evident cause of dialectal divergence: but in such cases there is always the possibility of the divergence having begun before the complete separation.

There are other factors which disturb the ideally uniform development of dialects. In real life, certain villages would be sure to gain some kind of ascendancy over those nearest them, and thus one or more centres of dialectal influence would be established: till at last, if centralization were strong enough, one dialect would be used as a means of expression all over the territory, as is now the case in England. If communication and education were made perfect, the standard dialect would entirely supplant the other dialects, and absolute uniformity of language would prevail.

In this way political development also tends to cause definite lines of division, for each linguistic centre swallows up the dialects nearest to it, till it comes in conflict with another centre, the line of division generally, though not necessarily, coinciding with some natural boundary. Hence, if we compare two standard languages of the same family, such as Dutch and German, we are struck by their fundamental difference, and have no hesitation in calling one Low, the other High German. But if we compare the dialects of the two languages, we shall find them shading off into one another by insensible degrees, there being many 'Middle German' dialects which carry out the change of *t* into ʊs, as in *zeit*, but leave initial *p* in its unaltered, Low German stage, as in *pund*, the present standard German being itself a dialect intermediate between High and Low.

It need hardly be said that the standard and the local dialects influence one another strongly. Standard E., which is mainly East Midland, has taken words and forms from almost every other dialect; *vat*, for instance, is Southern, *hale* (= *whole*) Northern.

Not only dialects influence one another, but also languages, even if they belong to totally distinct families. Thus Finnish is full of archaic Germanic and Lithuanian words, Persian is mixed with Arabic, and so on. Even sounds are borrowed. Thus the southern Bantu languages in Africa have borrowed the clicks from the Hottentots: Zulu has them, but they are wanting even in Bechuana. So also the peculiar 'choke-stops' of Armenian (ʊɿ, etc.) have been borrowed from the non-Arian languages of the Caucasus. Sanskrit, again, got its inverteds from the Dravidian languages of the South of India. English and Welsh too, with their **þ** and **ð** and their **w**, have much in common. There is no limit to the mixture of language in sounds, inflections, and syntax as well as in vocabulary. But the influence is never equal on both sides. Finnish has borrowed largely from Germanic, but there are very few common Germanic words of Finnish origin. So also the proportion of English words in spoken Welsh is about the same as that of French words in Chaucerian English, but there are very few Welsh words in English. In fact a very intimate mixture of two languages is always a prelude to the complete extinction of the weaker one, and this is why few, if any, of these thoroughly mixed languages become permanently fixed.

Dialects are not only local, but social, as in the distinction of polite and vulgar speech, vulgar speech being generally ahead in its development, as in the Cockney and dialectal dropping of **h** in English. There is also the important distinction of the literary and colloquial dialect, the former being mainly a written dialect, consisting of a mixture of living colloquialisms with the colloquialisms of earlier stages of the language, as when in poetry we use the fossilized colloquialism *thou hast* side by side with the living colloquialism *you have*. Of course, when the divergence amounts to unintelligibility, as when an Italian writes Latin, we have two distinct languages, a dead and a living, the latter being still liable to be influenced by the former, these influences spreading even to the vulgar dialect. Such languages as Latin and Sanskrit, when written and spoken by modern scholars and pundits, are commonly stigmatised as 'artificial'; but the artificiality is not in the languages themselves, but in the means by which they are preserved—in the case of Latin by written symbols, in that of Sanskrit by an uninterrupted oral tradition. This preservation of a dead language is, however, never perfect. In the first place, the process of fixing is always at first tentative and inconsistent —even Sanskrit embodying colloquial Prakrit forms—and secondly, it is impossible to fix the pronunciation as is again clearly shown in the present pronunciation of Sanskrit, in which some of the sounds, such as *sh* and *ç*, are confounded, and others much modified, partly by the influence of the living Gaurian languages, but apparently also by natural development of Sanskrit itself after it had ceased to be a colloquial language.

External circumstances not only have an influence on the development of dialects, but they also directly modify the sounds of a language. Climate has some, though a very slight influence. In cold countries there is less disposition to open the mouth widely. Hence that tendency to make *ā* into *ō* which is almost universal in the modern Germanic languages, but is quite absent from the Romance languages. The disposition of the speakers may also influence their pronunciation. The habit of speaking with a constant smile or grin unrounds the vowels, as in the Cockney **nau** = *no*. The refinement and effeminacy of large cities untrills the *r*. Even the caprices of fashion may have their effect, as is shown in the lisping pronunciation of those savages who knock out their front teeth.

A History of English Sounds, 1888, pp. 52–6

Change; Dialects and Cognate Languages. As soon as language became traditional, the connection between sound and meaning became practically arbitrary, so that not only was there a necessity of continually adding to the vocabulary and making the means of expression more precise, but there was nothing to check the natural tendency to change which we observe in all languages. Languages thus began to have histories.

Again, natural gesture-language is uniform everywhere. A traditional speech-language, on the other hand, requires uninterrupted intercourse between the whole body of its speakers to keep it uniform, and as this is difficult or even impossible beyond a certain area, all languages tend to split up first into a group of dialects and then into a group of cognate languages, as when Latin split up into an Italian, a Gaulish, a Spanish dialect, etc., and these dialects developed into the separate languages Italian, French, Spanish, which together form part of the Romance family of languages, whose common parent-language is Latin.

. . . . .

Periods. The first general effect of change in a language is that there comes a time when the earliest written documents of that language became obscure, and at last unintelligible, so that we are obliged to admit certain more or less definite periods in the language, such as Old English, Middle English, and Modern English, each of such periods admitting further subdivisions within itself.

Development of Dialects. The unity of a language can be kept up only by uniform intercourse between all its speakers; and if this is wanting, the language begins to split up into dialects.

If this development of differences of dialect is simply the result of the community being spread over too wide a tract of uniform country, the result will be an infinite number of dialects, each differing but slightly from the nearest one, but differing in course of time very considerably, from those furthest away from it. But there will be no definite lines of division, and the dialects will shade off insensibly one into another; so that any division, say, into a Northern, Central, and a Southern group of dialects, will necessarily be arbitrary in the case of those dialects which are exactly intermediate between the most marked Northern and Central or Central and Southern dialects. Even if we compare two languages, we find such dialects as some of the North Italian, which are exactly half-way between French and Italian. This overlapping of dialects is increased by the fact that any one of the numerous changes which cause differences of dialect may have different boundaries from those of the other changes. Thus a North-Central dialect may have a certain consonant change in common with the Northern group, or some of its sub-dialects, while in other respects following the changes of the other Central dialects.

If a dialect or group of dialects is sharply separated from the other dialects or groups by mountains, wide rivers, or other natural boundaries, or by differences of government or religion, it will correspondingly diverge from all the others and develop features of its own.

But when civilization brings with it the necessity of centralization, it becomes necessary to use one special dialect as a means of general communication throughout the country, especially if some of the dialects have become mutually unintelligible. If centralization goes on long enough, this common or standard dialect, after being influenced more or less by the local dialects, begins to supplant them, first in the speech of the educated, and then in that of the lower classes, till at last nothing remains of the original dialect but some peculiarities of speech and intonation, which last seems to survive longest. Thus it is that London English has not only become the educated speech of the whole kingdom, but has almost completely absorbed the rustic dialects of the home counties.

. . . . .

Strata: Literary and Colloquial. In most languages there are 'strata' or dialects which are non-local in the sense of never having had a definite locality, and which correspond to distinctions of class, culture, or occupation in the speakers of the language, the most important of these dialects being the results of the contrast of educated and vulgar, literary and colloquial speech. The distinction between educated or refined and vulgar is often a very fluctuating one; thus in English the present vulgarism *sparrow-grass* for *asparagus*, and such pronunciations as **forərd**, **piktər** for *forward*, *picture*, were considered perfectly correct two centuries ago.

As regards the distinction between literary and colloquial, it is important to observe that the literary peculiarities of any given period of a language are, for the most part, simply fossilized colloquialisms of an earlier period; thus the poetical and liturgical *thou hast* instead of *you have* was still a familiar colloquialism in the last century—so familiar, indeed, that it became vulgar and was dropped in polite speech, but was kept up in literature, mainly through the influence of the liturgical dialect of the Bible and Prayer-book.

It is now generally admitted that the only stratum of language which is natural in its development is the spoken language, of which the literary language is a more or less arbitrary and conscious modification, besides being, as already remarked, a mixture of colloquialisms of different periods, and therefore more or less of an anachronism. It is now an axiom of scientific philology that the real life of language is in many respects more clearly seen and better studied in dialects and colloquial forms of speech than in highly developed literary languages.

But although some of the latter—such as Homeric Greek and Spenserian English—are so mixed and arbitrary in their composition as to be simply monstrosities, we must be careful not to exaggerate the artificiality of literary dialects. The most far-fetched literary constructions and expressions are seldom arbitrary: they are generally founded on something in the spoken language of some period or other. . . . The importance of dialects may, on the other hand, be easily over-estimated, especially by half-taught enthusiasts, who, for instance, pick out a few conservative features in Lowland Scotch, and persuade themselves that it is the pure Anglian dialect of Old English preserved unchanged, in spite of the evident fact that it has diverged quite as much from Old English as the standard dialect has. Most of the present English dialects are so isolated in their development and so given over to disintegrating influences as to be, on the whole, less conservative than and generally inferior to the standard dialect. They throw little light on the development of English, which is more profitably dealt with by a combined study of the literary documents and the educated colloquial speech of each period as far as it is accessible to us.

. . . . .

It is necessary to observe that the distinction between literary and colloquial does not necessarily imply the existence of a written literature. The archaic language of the oldest Sanskrit hymns was faithfully preserved by oral tradition, together with the rules of grammar and pronunciation which alone made that faithful preservation possible, long before they were committed to writing.

. . . . .

Families of Languages. The difference between a group of dialects and a group or family of cognate languages is one of degree only, the most marked contrast being between a group of mutually intelligible dialects only one of which is the expression of national life, and a group of connected but mutually unintelligible languages, each of which is the expression of a distinct national life, culture, and literature. We can thus answer the question, Dialect or Language? either from a purely linguistic or a political point of view: from the latter point of view such languages as Spanish and Portuguese, Norwegian and Swedish, are unquestionably distinct languages, although linguistically speaking they are scarcely more than dialects of each other. In fact, the Galician dialect, though politically within Spain, is purely Portuguese, so that if it is a dialect of Spanish, Portuguese must be one also. Dialects frequently overlap political divisions in this way. Thus the Catalan dialect in Spain is Provençal, not Spanish, while the Provençal dialects, though for the most part politically French, are almost as distinct from French as French from Italian.

Mixed Languages. Whenever two dialects or languages come in contact, there is sure to be influence either on one side only or on both, the influence being generally much stronger on one side. The standard dialect may swallow up the local ones, but it is always liable to be influenced by them: every literary language is the result of mixture of dialects to some extent.

Families of languages do not admit 'a standard language', but nevertheless those languages of a family which have the greatest political, literary, or intellectual weight combined with the largest population, do practically exercise much the same influence as a standard dialect, especially if they are in a central position.

The History of Language, 1900, pp. 4, 72–3, 74–7

The object of this book is to give a faithful picture—a phonetic photograph—of educated spoken English as distinguished from vulgar and provincial English on the one hand, and literary English on the other hand. At the same time I must disclaim any intention of setting up a standard of spoken English. All I can do is to record those facts which are accessible to me—to describe that variety of spoken English of which I have a personal knowledge, that is, the educated speech of London and the district round it—the original home of Standard English both in its spoken and literary form. . . . After London English had become the official and literary language of the whole kingdom, it was natural that the same dialect in its spoken form should become the general speech of the educated classes, and that as centralization increased, it should preponderate more and more over the local dialects. But the unity of spoken English is still imperfect: it is still liable to be influenced by the local dialects—in London itself by the Cockney dialect, in Edinburgh by the Lothian Scotch dialect, and so on.

The comparative purity and correctness of the different varieties of spoken English is popularly estimated by the degree of approximation to the written language. But these comparisons are generally carried out in a one-sided and partial spirit. When an Englishman hears the distinct *r* and *gh* in the Broad Scotch *farther*, *night*, etc., he is apt to assume at once that Scotch English is more archaic than Southern English; but if he looks at the evidence on the other side, such forms as *ah ai oo* = *all one wool* will make him more inclined to believe what is the truth, namely that standard spoken English is, on the whole, quite as archaic, quite as correct and pure as any of its dialects—a truth which before the rise of modern philological dilettantism and dialect-sentimentality no one ever thought of disputing.

Still more caution is required in attempting to estimate the comparative beauty and ugliness of the different varieties of spoken English. Our impressions on this point are so entirely the result of association that it is hardly possible to argue about them. The Cockney dialect seems very ugly to an educated English man or woman because he—and still more she—lives in perpetual terror of being taken for a Cockney, and a perpetual struggle to preserve that *h* which has now been lost in most of the local dialects of England, both North and South. Northern speakers often reproach Londoners with 'mincing affectation'. But the London pronunciation of the present day, so far from being mincing, is characterized by openness and broadness, which are carried to an extreme in the Cockney pronunciation of such words as *father*, *ask*, *no*. A century ago, when this reproach was first levelled against the Cockneys, there was really some foundation for it, for at that time the broad *a* in *father*, *ask* was represented by the thinner vowel in *man* lengthened, the Northern *ask* and *man* being at that time pronounced with the short sound of the *a* in *father*. When the sugar-merchants of Liverpool began to 'speak fine' they eagerly adopted the thin Cockney *a* in *ask*, which many of their descendants keep, I believe, to the present day—long after this 'mincing' pronunciation has been discarded in the London dialect.

Another difficulty about setting up a standard of spoken English is that it changes from generation to generation, and is not absolutely uniform even among speakers of the same generation, living in the same place, and having the same social standing. Here, again, all I can do is to describe that form of the London dialect with which I am sufficiently familiar to enable me to deal with it satisfactorily. The only real familiarity we can have is with the language we speak ourselves. As soon as we go beyond that, and attempt to determine how other people speak—whether by observation or questioning—we make ourselves liable to fall into the grossest blunders. Of course, every self-observer has his personal equation, which he is bound to eliminate cautiously; and this I have done to the best of my power. Being partly of Scotch parentage—though I have lived most of my life near London—I have a few Scotticisms, such as *although* with sharp *th*, which sometimes crop up in rapid speech. Again, my pronunciation—like everyone else's—is in some cases more archaic, in others more advanced—more slovenly, more vulgar—than that of the majority of my contemporaries. When I pronounce *diphthong* with *p* instead of *f*, I have an impression that I am in the minority; and when I pronounce *either* and *neither* with the diphthong in *eye*, I have an impression that I am in the majority against those who pronounce these words with *ee*. But I have no means of proof that such is the case; and I know that if there were only one speaker in the world who said *eether*, he would probably assert confidently that this was the only pronunciation of the word—or at any rate the only 'correct' one. The fact is that the statements of ordinary educated people about their own pronunciation are generally not only valueless, but misleading. Thus I know as a fact that most educated speakers of southern English insert an *r* in *idea(r) of*, *India(r) office*, etc. in rapid speech, and I know that this habit, so far from dying out, is spreading to the Midlands; and yet they all obstinately deny it. The associations of the written language, and inability to deal with a phonetic notation, make most people incapable of recognizing a phonetic representation of their own pronunciation. When I showed my Elementarbuch to some English people, all of Northern extraction, they would not believe it represented my own pronunciation; they said it represented broad Cockney, of which they said there was not a trace in my own pronunciation.

I repeat then that this book is nothing but a contribution to our knowledge of spoken English—a knowledge which is still in its infancy and can be advanced only by a number of other trained observers giving similar descriptions of their own pronunciation. It is only on the basis of such individual investigations that we can hope to settle what are the actual facts of spoken English in Great Britain, America, and Australasia. Till we know how we actually do speak, we cannot deal with the question of how we ought to speak, and whether it is possible to reform our pronunciation, and take steps to preserve the unity of English speech all over the world.

Preface to *A Primer of Spoken English*, 1890, pp. v–ix

Differences of Pronunciation. Learn not only to recognize and tolerate differences of pronunciation, but to *expect* them. Remember that pronunciation is incessantly changing, and that differences of pronunciation between the older and the younger generation are not only *possible*, but *inevitable.*

Remember that language exists only in the individual, and that such a phrase as 'standard English pronunciation' expresses only an abstraction. Reflect that it is absurd to set up a standard of how English people *ought* to speak, before we know how they actually *do* speak—a knowledge which is still in its infancy, and can only be gained by careful observation of the speech of individuals, the only absolutely reliable observations being those made by a trained individual on himself.

Avoid, therefore, all dogmatism and hasty generalizations: be cautious in asserting that 'everybody speaks in such a way', or that 'no educated man pronounces so'. Do not appeal to the authority of an imaginary 'correct' or 'careful' speaker.

Confine yourself to plain statements of facts. If people tell you that spelling reform is a 'pestilent heresy', or that your London, Edinburgh or Dublin pronunciation is 'abominable', do not argue with them.

A Primer of Phonetics, 1890, p. 3

Varieties of Pronunciation. Phonetic notation does not necessarily imply phonetic spelling. If we found *picture* written in Broad Romic **piktjuə,** we should not admit this as a spelling of English as it actually exists: we should shrewdly suspect the speller of a burning desire to reform English spelling and English pronunciation at one blow. If our reformer were to go into the other extreme, and write **piktə**, we should admit the correctness of this spelling, but only for the vulgar dialect: we should refuse to admit any spelling but **piktʃə** as a representation of the educated spoken English of the present day.

Artificial Pronunciation. This use of a phonetic notation to represent imaginary and non-existing pronunciations is especially frequent in the case of 'gradations', such as **ðæt** demonstrative and **ðət** relative pronoun and conjunction, the tendency being to confound these two distinct words under the fuller form **ðæt.** So also those who wish to make phonetic spelling a protest against the natural development of the spoken language ignore such 'weak' or unemphatic forms as **im** pronoun and **kaant**, and insist on writing the 'strong' forms **him, kæn not** everywhere, regardless of distinctions of emphasis and position in the sentence. Even those who admit that the obscurer and shorter forms are under certain definite conditions of want of stress and emphasis universal in natural educated speech, maintain that the fuller forms are more 'correct' and elegant, and, at any rate, that foreigners ought to discard the weak forms, and thereby make their pronunciation more distinct, while at the same time setting a good example to the natives.

The answer to this is, that the first aim of foreigners who come to England is to understand the natives and make themselves understood by them. If the foreigner has never seen such a form as **kaant** written, he will not be able to understand it when he hears it spoken; while, on the other hand, even if he does not make himself unintelligible by saying **kæn not** under circumstances where every one else says **kaant**, it is in the end the simplest and best course to content himself with speaking as well as the average educated Englishman. In some German schools great care is taken to teach the pupils the correct English sounds by phonetic methods—and with remarkable success;

but when, as is too often the case, the weak forms, such as **ðət, ðə** = **ðɛə, ʃəl,** are ignored, and such words as *holiday*, *Oxford* are made to rhyme with *day* and *ford* instead of being pronounced **holidi, oksfəd,** the result is that the pupils speak a language which, though made up of English sounds, is as a whole quite un-English, so that when they come to England, they have to unlearn their pronunciation, and make the—generally unsuccessful—attempt to construct a new one on the basis of the laws of gradation. It is a pity their teachers do not realize that even so slight a change as that of **hau d ju duw** into **hau du ju duw** makes the sentence un-English, however perfect the individual sounds may be.

There is more excuse for teaching an artificial pronunciation of such languages as German and Italian, where the multiplicity of educated dialects resulting from want of centralization has made it difficult to settle which is the standard, or how a standard is to be formed. Nevertheless, the foreigners who adopt the so-called 'theatre-German' (*bühnendeutsch*) pronunciation would certainly make themselves ridiculous, as this well-meant attempt to set up a standard of pronunciation is not founded on any rational linguistic principle. Nothing, for instance, can be more monstrous than the recommendation to pronounce final *g* as a voice stop.

In all languages the pronunciation of the stage is merely a special development of the ordinary educated colloquial pronunciation. In such languages as French and English, where all educated people speak practically the same dialect, there need be but little separation between the colloquial and the oratorical pronunciation; and with us, at least, the stage has no authority in questions of pronunciation.

But in French and most other languages there is still a tendency—which may be observed in English also—to make the pronunciation not only of oratory but of mere reading aloud distinct from that of everyday life, as is shown very clearly in the *liaisons*. Thus, in reading aloud, a Frenchman would sound the **t** of the ending *-ment* before a vowel, but never in speaking.

Here the principle of association comes in. To a Frenchman the ending *-ment* suggests primarily the pronunciation **-mã** before a vowel as well as a consonant; but when he speaks or reads to an audience, he makes an effort to sound the **t** before a vowel; just as an Englishman in speaking slowly and solemnly may make **kaant** into **kæn not,** although in English there is no necessity felt for departing from the colloquial pronunciation. It is evident that the first and most immediate associations of the foreign learner ought to be with the colloquial forms. When he has learnt these, he will be on a level with the educated native, and, like him, can afterwards learn the more artificial pronunciation, and thus establish a series of secondary oratorical associations. If his associations are primarily with the oratorical forms, his ordinary conversation will be unnatural and offensive to the native ear.

Degrees of Colloquialism. But there are degrees of colloquialism. In all languages the pronunciation may vary according to the degree of familiarity between the speakers. Even in England a young man will sometimes unconsciously modify his pronunciation in speaking to a strange lady or an older man.

The mood of the speaker, too, may have an effect. Tension of mind—as in giving definite directions, explaining a difficulty, impatient command—is naturally accompanied by greater vigour of enunciation; while indifference and langour show themselves in half-finished consonants and curtailed sound-groups. We can hear in English the sharp snap of *what!* degenerate in the mouth of the same speaker into the languid **woh** or almost **waa**, which may further degenerate into a mere grunt.

Again, the pronunciation of the same person may vary according to the speed of utterance. This is very marked in French, where the elimination of the weak **ə** depends greatly on speed. In Passy's *Elementarbuch* the texts are given in the pronunciation of medium speed, a quicker and slower pronunciation being occasionally given in the notes. Thus to the normal **õ vjẽ d sɔne msjø** and **i j ãn a də tut le kulœœr** corresponds the slow **õ vjẽ də sɔne məsjø** and the quick **j ãn a d tut le kulœœr**, and to the medium **ɛstrɔrdinɛɛr, si vu plɛ**, the slow **ɛkstraɔrdinɛɛr** and the quick **sj u plɛ.**

It is evident that the foreigner should aim at what may be called a medium colloquial style of pronunciation. It is painful and incongruous to hear the rapid pronunciation of clipped speech reproduced in a slow, solemn, oratorical tempo. On the other hand, it is much more irrational to teach a foreigner pronunciations which never occur in the colloquial speech of natives. The best general advice is therefore: never be oratorical; be colloquial, but not too colloquial.

The revolt against artificial standards of pronunciation sometimes tempts phonetic enthusiasts into constructing colloquial monstrosities when dealing with a foreign language—they become more colloquial than the most slovenly native. Thus a foreigner who has learnt to obscure weak-stressed vowels in English—who has learnt to say **kæriktə**, **maaĝit**, **izri-əl** in spite of the associations of the written forms *character*, *Margate*, *Israel*—is apt to get reckless, and go too far in this direction, making perhaps **nɔ·wijdʒən næpsæk** into **nəwijdʒən næpsək**, pronunciations which I remember having seen actually given.

Vulgarisms should be avoided; not because they are in themselves ugly or less logical, or in any way more objectionable than the corresponding polite forms, but simply because they belong to a different dialect. But we must distinguish between real and theoretical vulgarisms: that is, between forms which, as a matter of fact, do not occur in educated speech, and those which are commonly called 'vulgar', and yet do occur in educated speech. Of theoretical vulgarisms, some are simply universal in educated speech, such as the loss of the consonant **r** in *lord* by which this word becomes identical in pronunciation with *laud*, others widely spread, such as the **r** in *idea*(*r*) *of*, *India*(*r*) *Office*. But as this latter colloquialism is not universal, the insertion of the **r** generally occurs only in rapid speech and in closely connected groups of words, so that its omission does not produce any effect of unreality or artificiality, it would be mere perversity in the foreigner to imitate it in his slow pronunciation. But while it is a real vulgarism to omit **h** in full-stressed words, it is a disagreeable affectation not to drop it in such collocations as *tell him*. This affectation is widely spread; but it is always artificial; so that the speakers who try to keep it up consistently are always liable to fail. For these reasons a foreigner should avoid it: that is, he should say **tel -im**, keeping the **h** for the emphatic **tel him not hәә.**

The statements of unphonetic natives about vulgarisms and other varieties of pronunciation are never reliable, and should be listened to with great caution. A foreigner once asked a learned Englishman which was right, **aast** or **aaskt**, as the preterite of *ask*; and was told that there was no such pronunciation as **aast**. A minute after the learned man was heard to say **sou ij aast im әn aast im әn aast im әgen.** On another occasion a well-known authority on the English language began in a mixed company to denounce the vulgarisms in my *Elementarbuch des gesprochenen Englisch*. A German pupil of mine who was present sent a whisper round the circle, telling them to listen carefully for these very vulgarisms in the authority's own pronunciation. The latter then began a lengthy harangue; and, to his surprise, was continually interrupted by bursts of laughter from his audience.

Standards of Pronunciation. As the educated pronunciation of a language is never absolutely uniform, the question arises, which is the standard? To the foreigner this is not a sentimental or aesthetic question, but a purely practical one.

As the literary languages of most countries are simply the fossilized dialects of their respective capitals—literary French being nothing but the written form of the older Parisian dialect, literary English of the older London dialect—there seems every reason why the dialect of the capital should be taken as the standard of the spoken language as well. Practical considerations point to the same view. First, there is the numerical preponderance of the speakers of the dialect of the capital. Secondly, foreigners naturally gravitate to the capital or, at any rate, make it their starting-point. Even in Germany, where there is much less centralization than in France and England, it is surely more practical for the foreigner to learn the educated speech of Berlin than that of some provincial town where on abstract grounds 'the best German' is said to be spoken.

Even within the narrowest limits there may be differences of pronunciation. Even in educated Southern English we sometimes find a word pronounced in several ways. When Dr. Johnson was asked by a lady whether he pronounced the word *neither* as **naiðər** or **niiðər**, he replied **neeðər, mædæm.** The last pronunciation is now extinct, but the other two still seem to be about equally frequent. The fluctuations of French pronunciation are even greater. In such cases the learner must select one pronunciation and keep to it. It follows, of course, that his text-books should, as far as possible, give a uniform pronunciation, no matter how arbitrary the selection may be.

The Practical Study of Languages, 1899, pp. 38–43; L.A.L.L. Edn, pp. 37–42

No language is perfectly uniform over the whole of its area. Just as languages differ from each other in phonetic structure—in their sounds and pronunciation—so also dialects of the same language differ from each other more or less. Thus the sound-system of Lowland Scotch, which was originally a mere variety of Northern English, differs considerably from that of Standard English.

Standard English itself was originally that mixture of the Midland and Southern dialects which was spoken in London during the Middle Ages, just as Standard French is the dialect of that district of which Paris is the centre.

Standard English, like Standard French, is now a class-dialect more than a local dialect: it is the language of the educated all over Great Britain. But although it has, to a great extent, supplanted the local dialects, it is still liable to be influenced by them; each speaker imports into it something of his own local form of speech, whether it be a rustic dialect or the vulgar cockney of London, Liverpool, or any other large town. The best speakers of Standard English are those whose pronunciation, and language generally, least betray their locality.

English, like all living languages, changes from generation to generation: slight and imperceptible as the differences in the pronunciation of father and son may appear to be, there is always some change under ordinary normal conditions. Hence pronunciations which are vulgar in one century may become fashionable in the next, sounds which are distinct in one generation may be confounded in another, and new distinctions may be made, new sounds may arise.

A spoken language is, therefore, a vague and floating entity. . . . A standard spoken language is, strictly speaking, an abstraction. No two speakers of Standard English pronounce exactly alike. And yet they all have something in common in almost every sound they utter. There are some peculiarities of pronunciation which pass unnoticed, while others, less considerable perhaps in themselves, are at once felt as archaisms, vulgarisms, provincialisms, or affectations, as the case may be, by the majority of educated speakers.

The Sounds of English, 1908, pp. 7–8

Correctness of pronunciation, on the other hand,[1] is, as we have seen, a specially phonetic, not an elocutionary question. And yet there is none on which elocutionists are more ready to dogmatize than on this. Most of them attach as much—or even more—importance to correcting what they assume to be defects of pronunciation in their pupils as to improving their voice-production.

They are seldom content with attacking vulgarisms and provincialisms; they make war on principle on all colloquialisms, although, of course, they find it impossible to get rid of them in practice. They ignore gradation and the obscuration of unstressed vowels; the general result of which is that the pupil is forced to acquire an artificial elocutionary language distinct from that of everyday life. . . . It has often been argued that by giving an artificial distinctness to weak sounds, as in the orthographic pronunciation of our dictionaries, we make the words more distinct. It is of course true that in themselves such words as **ænd, tuw, fɔə** are more sonorous, and in so far more distinct, than **n, tə, fə,** but it does not necessarily follow that the context is made more intelligible by substituting an unexpected strong form for the natural weak one. In fact, the contrary is so much the case that misunderstanding may arise from such substitutions. Thus in the sentence *I shall be at home from one to three* the substitution of **tuw** for **tə** at once suggests a confusion between the preposition and the numeral. So also by making **sɐndi** into **sɐndei** we only incur the risk of being understood to say that we will come some day instead of on Sunday. The truth is that we cannot make words more distinct by disguising them. Another

[1] i.e. as contrasted with 'distinctness of pronunciation' which is, according to Sweet, 'the common property of phonetics and elocution'. *Ed.*

disadvantage of this artificial pronunciation is that it often gives a false or exaggerated emphasis, as in **bred ænd batə**, which seems to imply 'bring me bread, and don't forget the butter!'

Another argument sometimes adduced in favour of artificialities of pronunciation is that they improve the language by making it more sonorous or more harmonious. There is no doubt something in this. Where the standard dialect admits a variety of pronunciations, it is not only allowable but desirable to select that one which is preferable either in itself or through its associations. Thus in singing, no one would hesitate in preferring monophthongic **ii** and **uu** to **ij** and **uw**, and reducing the diphthongization of **ei** and **ou** to a minimum, and in preferring the narrow to the wide pronunciation of their first elements; and the same applies also, though less stringently, in the case of elocution. And then we can go a step further, and restore an extinct, or introduce a dialectal pronunciation, as when the Germans insist on the point-trill **r** instead of the back sound, which is now universal in educated German speech. The German elocutionists follow the singers in theory, but not always in practice; in fact, the point-**r** is intolerable in any German declamation which is at all colloquial in subject. The difficulty with this is to know where to stop. If the elocutionists followed the singers in substituting the Italian **a** for **æ**, why not go a step further, and get rid of the still uglier vowel in *come* by returning to the older pronunciation and restoring the full **u**? If this kind of thing were carried out consistently, the result would be a language which in many respects would be better than the existing English—but it would no longer be English; it would hardly be intelligible. And even if the changes stopped far short of this, they would still give the impression of unreality and insincerity which always accompanies artificiality.

But we must not go to the other extreme of insisting on the retention of the colloquial pronunciation in all elocution without regard to differences of subject and style. It is not only in poetry that the retention of the shortened forms of colloquial speech is often impossible; these forms would often produce an equally jarring, incongruous, or even ludicrous effect in elevated prose, free as it is from the constraint of metre. . . .

We now have to consider the conditions, apart from poetical form, which make it necessary to substitute a higher for a lower style of pronunciation.

The most important of these is speed. Even in ordinary conversation, slow, deliberate speech necessitates, or at any rate allows of, a much freer use of strong forms such as **ænd** where they would be quite out of place in quick speech.

But it is not generally a mere question of speed. We feel also that weak and clipped forms are often incompatible with the gravity and dignity with which slow speech is naturally associated. Even in the most elevated poetry we may constantly drop the weak **h** in such words as *his* and *him*, and then we may come to a passage where there is no emphasis, ictus, or pause—perhaps not even a slackening of speed—to suggest the substitution of the strong form; and yet the artistic instinct may imperatively demand it. So also even in familiar prose such forms as *it's* and *can't* may jar on our ear so decidedly that we must perforce substitute the full forms, even when they sound stilted or even positively unnatural: we deliberately prefer this extreme to the other extreme of triviality and vulgarity.

The Sounds of English, 1908, pp. 77–9, 87–8

III. Phonetics

A. GENERAL

[In this section are assembled a number of Sweet's pronouncements upon the nature, aims, and methods of phonetics and its relationship to other branches of linguistic science. The reader's attention is drawn to Sweet's use of the word 'phonology', which in his presidential address to the Philological Society in 1877 (below) appears to be synonymous with 'phonetics', but in *The History of Language* in 1900 is distinguished from phonetics as embracing the 'whole science of speech-sounds' as contrasted with the 'analysis and classification of the actual sounds' which is the main concern of phonetics (p. 28). Later still, in 1911, we find him commenting that 'the originally synonymous [i.e. with "phonetics"] term "phonology" is now restricted to the history and theory of sound-changes' (p. 34). It is worth noting that for Sweet phonetics was 'an essential part of grammar itself' (p. 29), not an almost totally unrelated exercise as some of his successors have sought to maintain. *Ed.*]

The first requisite is a knowledge of phonetics, or the form of language. We must learn to regard language solely as consisting of groups of sounds, independently of the written symbols, which are always associated with all kinds of disturbing associations, chiefly historical.

'Words, Logic and Grammar', *T.P.S.* 1875–6, in *Collected Papers of Henry Sweet*, 1913, p. 3

The science which teaches us to observe, analyse, and describe the sounds of language is phonology. Phonology is, therefore, *the science of linguistic observation.* The purely antiquarian philologist, who deals only with dead languages, is apt to ignore these simple principles, and to look on phonetics and pronunciation as something purely subordinate, simply because he is never brought face to face with the ultimate facts of all linguistic investigation, viz: the living language. The truth is, that phonology is not only the indispensable foundation of all philology, but also that no department, from the highest to the lowest, can be investigated fully without it, whether it be accidence, syntax, or prosody, or even that fundamental problem—the origin of language.

Many, who admit the utility of phonetics, think that 'it ought not to be carried too far'. They say that phoneticians ought only to make broad distinctions, and to avoid that 'hair-splitting' which according to them is the besetting sin of the English school of phonetics founded by Messrs. Bell and Ellis. These critics forget that sound generalizations can only be based on a minute study of details, and that in all sciences the only way to arrive at trustworthy results is by pushing the observation of details as far as human faculties permit. Nor can any one tell *a priori* whether a given distinction, which to one observer appears almost inappreciable, may not to one who speaks a different language appear very marked. In fact, Nature itself, and not least as shown in language, is extremely given to hair-splitting and often paves the way for the most violent changes, as, for instance, diphthongization, by minute and almost inappreciable modifications, which it is the business of the trained phonetician to detect and analyse.

Presidential Address to the Philological Society, 1877, 'On English Philology and Phonology', *T.P.S.* 1877–9, in *Collected Papers of Henry Sweet*, 1913, pp. 85–6

The two main features of Storm's method are the prominence he gives to the living language, and his vindication of scientific phonetics as the indispensable foundation of all study of language, whether practical or theoretical.

'The Practical Study of Language', *T.P.S.* 1882–4, in *Collected Papers of Henry Sweet*, 1913, p. 35

It is now generally recognized, except in hopelessly obscurantist circles, that phonology is the indispensable foundation of all linguistic study, whether practical or scientific—above all, of historical grammar.

Preface to *A New English Grammar*, 1891, p. xii

Phonetics is the *science* of speech-sounds. From a practical point of view it is the *art* of producing speech-sounds and recognizing them by ear.

It describes the actions and positions of the vocal organs—throat, tongue, lips, etc.—by which speech-sounds are produced, and classifies sounds according to their organic formation. This is the *organic* side of phonetics. The *acoustic* study of speech-sounds classifies them according to their likeness to the ear, and explains how the acoustic effect of each sound is the necessary result of its organic formation.

A Primer of Phonetics, 1890, p. 1

The main axiom of living philology is that all study of language must be based on phonetics.

Phonetics is the science of speech-sounds, or, from a practical point of view, the art of pronunciation. Phonetics is to the science of language generally what mathematics is to astronomy and the physical sciences. Without it, we can neither observe nor record the simplest phenomena of language. It is equally necessary in the theoretical and in the practical study of language.

Phonetics not an Innovation. The necessity of phonetics has, indeed, always been tacitly recognized—even by its opponents. Even such a simple statement as that 'English nouns take *-es* instead of *-s* in the plural after a hiss-consonant' involves elementary facts of phonetics; the terms 'vowel' and 'consonant', 'hard' and 'soft', all imply phonetic analysis. What the reformers claim is not that phonetics should be introduced—for it is there already—but that its study should be made efficient by being put on a scientific basis.

In fact, phonetics is almost as old as civilization itself. The Alexandrian grammarians were not only phoneticians—they were spelling reformers! Few of those who mechanically learn the rules of Greek accentuation by way of gilding the refined gold of their scholarship have any idea that these to them unmeaning marks were invented by the Alexandrian grammarians solely for the purpose of making the pronunciation of Greek easier to foreigners. The Romans, too, were phoneticians: they learnt Greek on a phonetic basis, as far as their lights allowed them. The Sanskrit grammarians were still better phoneticians. It is the unphonetic, not the phonetic methods that are an innovation.

The Practical Study of Languages, 1899, p. 4; L.A.L.L. Edn., p. 4

The whole science of speech-sounds is included under *phonology*, which includes the history and theory of sound-changes; the term *phonetics* excludes this, being concerned mainly with the analysis and classification of the actual sound.

. . . . .

The first task of phonetics is to describe the shape and positions of the throat, tongue, lips, and the other organs of speech by which sounds are produced; this is the *organic* side of phonetics. The *acoustic* study of sounds classifies them according to their likeness to the ear, and explains how the acoustic effect of each sound is the necessary result of its organic formation. Thus the high pitch and clear sound which is common to the consonant **s** and the vowel **i** is the result of a narrow passage being formed in the fore part of the mouth between the fore part of the tongue and the palate; and this similarity of sound explains why in late Latin such words as *spiritu*(*s*) developed an **i** before the **s**, whence modern French **ɛspri** through **ispiritu*. (*Fn.*: The * is used to show that the form is hypothetical only.)

For scientific purposes it is necessary to have a general knowledge of the whole field of possible sounds, for in dealing with any one sound it is often necessary to know all the sounds it may have developed out of and all that it is liable to change into.

The History of Language, 1900, pp. 12–13

Phonetics is not merely an indirect strengthener of grammatical associations, it is an essential part of grammar itself. It enables us to state grammatical and philological laws with a brevity and definiteness which would be otherwise unattainable, as when we condense the information that under certain circumstances in a given language *d* becomes *t*, *g* becomes *k*, and *b* becomes *p*, into the simple statement that 'voice stops become breath'. In Eliot's *Finnish Grammar* (p. 11) we find the following statement: 'The final *e* of a dissyllabic stem disappears in nouns before terminations commencing with *t*, and in verbs before terminations beginning with *k* or *n*, provided that *e* is preceded by any simple consonant but *k*, *p*, *v*, *m*, or by a double consonant of which the last letter is *t* or *s* (except *ht*). Thus from the stem *une*, 'sleep', *vuore*, 'mountain', *vete*, 'water' (nominative *vesi*), come the forms *unta*, *vuorta*, *vettä*. . . .' If in this statement we substitute for the negative and purely abstract conception of 'any simple consonant but *k*, *p*, *v*, *m*,' the positive enumeration of the consonants left after this subtraction, namely *r*, *l*, *s*, *t*, *n*, we are able to simplify it still further by saying that in nouns *e* is dropped before *t* when the *e* is preceded by a forward consonant, the evident reason being that these consonants are formed in the same place as *t*.

A knowledge of sentence stress and intonation is not only an essential part of elocution and correct pronunciation, but is also an integral part of the syntax of many languages.

In short, there is no branch of the study of language which can afford to dispense with phonetics.

The Practical Study of Languages, 1899,
p. 49; L.A.L.L. Edn., p. 48

The importance of phonetics as the indispensable foundation of all study of language—whether that study be purely theoretical, or practical as well—is now generally admitted. Without a knowledge of the laws of sound-change, scientific philology—whether comparative or historical—is impossible, and without phonetics their study degenerates into a mere mechanical enumeration of letter-changes. And now that philologists are directing their attention more and more to the study of living dialects and savage languages, many of which have to be written down for the first time, the absolute necessity of a thorough practical as well as theoretical mastery of phonetics becomes more and more evident. Many instances might be quoted of the way in which important philological facts and laws have been passed over or misrepresented through the observer's want of phonetic training. Again, if our present wretched system of studying modern languages is ever to be reformed, it must be on the basis of a preliminary training in general phonetics, which would at the same time lay the foundation for a thorough practical study of the pronunciation and elocution of our own language—subjects which are totally ignored in our present scheme of education.

Preface to *A Handbook of Phonetics*, 1877, pp. v–vi

The importance of phonetics in the practical teaching of language is still very far from being recognized to its full extent. The first great step will be to discard the ordinary spelling entirely in teaching pronunciation, and substitute a purely phonetic one, giving a genuine and adequate representation of the actual language, not, as is too often the case, of an imaginary language, spoken by imaginary 'correct speakers'. To teach the pronunciation of such a language as modern French by means of an orthography which is really a very corrupt representation of the sixteenth century pronunciation, is as absurd as it would be to teach Dutch with a German grammar, or to explain the anatomy of a horse by a picture of a zebra or an ichthyosaurus. When the language is firmly fixed in the memory in its phonetic form, it will be time to study the older spelling in connexion with the historical study of the older stages of the language. Of course, the difficulty of the transition from the spoken to the literary language can never be fully overcome, but it is far easier than the unnatural process of basing the study of the spoken language on an imperfect mastery of the literary one. . . . But the gain of a phonetic grasp of language extends far beyond such special considerations [such as the acquisition of a good pronunciation without the necessity of going abroad; the ability to understand foreigners and make oneself understood by them, etc. *Ed.*]. A secure grasp of the sounds of a language is a great strengthening of the general mastery of its forms and meanings, and a minute discrimination of the phonetic differences between closely allied languages (as when the French and Italian *a*, the Dutch *u*, and German *ü* are kept apart) is the surest safeguard against otherwise inevitable confusions. Phonetics alone can breathe life into the dead mass of letters which constitute a written language: it alone can bring the rustic dialogues of our novels before every intelligent reader as living realities, and make us realize the living power and beauty of the ancient classical languages in prose and verse. Again, phonetics alone enables us to analyse and register the various phenomena of stress, intonation, and quantity, which are the foundation of word-division, sentence-structure, elocution, metre, and, in fact, enter into all the higher problems of language: a psychological study of language without phonetics is an impossibility.

'The Practical Study of Language', *T.P.S.* 1882–4; in *Collected Papers of Henry Sweet*, 1913, pp. 39–40

The proper way of studying phonetics is, of course, to go through a regular course under a competent teacher, for phonetics can no more be acquired by mere reading than music can. Those who have no teacher must begin with carefully analysing their own natural pronunciation, until they have some idea of its relation to the general scale of sounds. They can then proceed to deduce the pronunciation of unfamiliar sounds from their relations to known sounds, checking the results by a practical study of the languages in which the new sounds occur. A thorough study of French pronunciation under a native will do more than anything to free the student from one-sided English associations and habits. Nor let him delude himself with the idea that he has already acquired French pronunciation at school or elsewhere: in nine cases out of ten a little methodical study of sounds will convince him that he does not pronounce a single French sound correctly.

The student should not allow himself to be disheartened by the slowness of his progress and the obtuseness of his ear, for even the most highly gifted and best trained are often baffled for weeks and even months by some sound which another will find quite easy both to distinguish by ear and to pronounce. A great deal depends on the character of the native language, the learner naturally grafting peculiarities of his own language on his pronunciation of foreign ones, as when an Englishman diphthongises the long vowels in French and German; and, again, finding those sounds difficult which do not occur, or have no analogues, in his own pronunciation. It is a great mistake to suppose that any one nation has a special gift for acquiring sounds or foreign languages generally. Each nation has its special defects or advantages. The Russian pronunciation of German, for instance, is at once betrayed by the substitution of **ih** for the *ü* and by many other peculiarities: in fact those Russians and Poles who speak French and German perfectly are often unable to speak their own languages properly. The more civilized and influential a nation is the worse linguists are those who speak its language; but when Englishmen (and even Frenchmen) really devote themselves to the practical study of language, they prove quite equal to other nations, as, for instance, Dutchmen or Russians, who are obliged, the former by the smallness of their country, the latter by their barbarism, to learn a number of foreign languages. It cannot, of course, be denied that some languages are a worse preparation for the acquisition of foreign sounds than others, but a thorough training in general phonetics soon levels the inequality, and enables the learner to develop his special gifts independently of outward circumstances. It is on its value as the foundation of the practical study of language that the claims of phonetics to be considered an essential branch of education mainly rest.

Preface to *A Handbook of Phonetics*, 1877, pp. xii–xiv

The first business of phonetics is to describe the actions of the organs of speech by which sounds are produced, as when we describe the relative positions of tongue and palate by which **s** is produced. This is the *organic* side of phonetics. The *acoustic* investigation of speech-sounds, on the other hand, describes and classifies them according to their likeness to the ear, and explains how the acoustic effect of each sound is the necessary result of its organic formation, as when we call **s** a hiss-sound or sibilant, and explain why it has a higher pitch—a shriller hiss—than the allied hiss-consonant **ʃ** in *she*.

The Practical Study of Languages, 1899, p. 6; L.A.L.L. Edn., p. 6

Theoretically, of course, the organic study of phonetics is a branch of anatomy and physiology; while from the opposite point of view it is based on that branch of physical science known as acoustics, together with the anatomy and physiology of the organs of hearing.

Unfortunately, this basis is still so imperfect as regards the acoustic side of phonetics that it is not too much to say that from the physical science point of view there is as yet no science of phonetics at all. The principles of acoustics are well established, and much is known about the anatomy of the ear. But how the ear transmits to the brain the impressions of sound is still as great a mystery as ever. And although practical phonetics has made the mechanism of the vowels clear enough, there is still no generally received acoustic theory of their formation.

But phonetics considered as a branch of physical science is a subject of only secondary importance. The real function of phonetics is philological and literary: its true *raison d'être* is to serve as a basis for the study of languages. And if we regard phonetics as essentially a linguistic science, we shall find that the want of a rigorous scientific basis is not such a serious defect after all.

And where the basis exists it is often superfluous. This is especially the case with the anatomy and physiology of the organs of speech. Thus even the most advanced instrumental phonetician finds that, although he ought theoretically to have a thorough knowledge of the anatomy and functions of the muscles of the tongue, he can determine—or fail to determine—its positions quite as well without this knowledge.

The Sounds of English, 1908, pp. 104–5

It must be remembered, however, that instrumental phonetics is still in its infancy. Its methods are being continually improved and simplified, and it is impossible to say as yet what they may result in.

At present there is a natural—and indeed, unavoidable—antagonism between the practical linguistic phonetician and the physico-mathematical instrumental phonetician. The qualifications and training required on both sides are so opposed to each other, and each of these branches of research makes such imperious demands on the time and energy of its votaries, that it is difficult to see how any one investigator can combine them.

Although the conservative phoneticians of the older school may go too far in ignoring the results of instrumental phonetics, it is possible to go too far the other way also. Some of the younger generation seem to think that the instrumental methods have superseded the natural ones so completely that attending a course of 'phonétique expérimentale' at some holiday course in France makes the laborious training of the linguistic phonetician superfluous.

This assumption has had disastrous effects. It cannot be too often repeated that instrumental phonetics is, strictly speaking, not phonetics at all. It only supplies materials which are useless till they have been tested and accepted from the linguistic phonetician's point of view. The final arbiter in all phonetic questions is the trained ear of a practical phonetician. Differences which cannot be perceived by the ear—and many of the results of instrumental phonetics are of this character—must be ignored; and what contradicts a trained ear cannot be accepted.

And it must not be forgotten that the utility of instrumental phonetics as a means of research does not necessarily imply a corresponding utility as a help in acquiring a practical mastery of sounds—which, as we have seen, is the only sound foundation of the science. As yet, instrumental phonetics, so far from being a help in the practical study of sounds, has been rather a hindrance, by diverting the learner's attention from that patient cultivation of the organic and acoustic sense which is the indispensable basis.

The Sounds of English, 1908, pp. 109–10

Phonetics (Gr. φωνή voice), the science of speech-sounds and the art of pronunciation. In its widest sense it is the 'science of voice', dealing not only with articulate, but also with the inarticulate sounds of animals as well as men. The originally synonymous term, 'phonology', is now restricted to the history and theory of sound-changes. The most obvious of the practical applications of phonetics is to the acquisition of a correct pronunciation of foreign languages. But its applications to the study of the native language are not less important: it is only by the help of phonetics that it is possible to deal effectively with vulgarisms and provincialisms of pronunciation and secure uniformity of speech; and it is only on a phonetic basis that the deaf and dumb can be taught articulate speech. From a more theoretical point of view phonetics is, in the first place, the science of linguistic observation. Without phonetic training the dialectologist, and the missionary who is confronted with a hitherto unwritten language, can neither observe fully nor record accurately the phenomena with which they have to deal. These investigations have greatly widened the scope of the science of language. The modern philologist no longer despises colloquial and illiterate forms of speech. On the contrary, he considers that in them the life and growth of language is seen more clearly than in dead literary languages, on whose study the science of comparative philology was at first exclusively built up. It was not till philologists began to ask what were the real facts underlying the comparisons of the written words in Sanskrit, Greek, Latin and the other Indo-European languages, embodied in such generalizations as Grimm's Law, that 'letter-science' developed into 'sound-science' (phonology). The rise and decay of inflexions, and the development of grammatical forms generally, are, from the formal point of view, mainly phonetic problems; and phonetics enters more or less into every department of historical and comparative grammar.

Methods of Study and Investigation. Phonetics is the science of speech-sounds. But sounds may be considered from two opposite points of view—the *organic* and the *acoustic*. From the organic point of view a sound is the result of certain actions and positions of the organs of speech, as when we define *f* as a lip-teeth (dento-labial) consonant. This is the point of view of the speaker of a language. To the hearer, on the other hand, *f* is not a lip-teeth, but a hiss-consonant similar to that denoted by *th*. This is the acoustic point of view. Theoretically, the organic study of phonetics is a branch of anatomy and physiology, that part of these sciences which deals with the organs of speech and their functions; while, from the opposite point of view, the study of phonetics is based on that branch of physical science known as acoustics, together with the anatomy and physiology of the organs of hearing.

Unfortunately, this basis is still imperfect. The principles of acoustics are well established, and we know much about the anatomy of the ear. But how the ear transmits to the brain the impression of sound is still a mystery. Again, although the mechanism of the vowel is clear enough, there is still no generally received acoustic theory of their formation. In fact, from the physical science point of view there is as yet no science of phonetics.

The real function of phonetics is philological and literary. The only sound basis of a theoretical knowledge of phonetics is the practical mastery of a limited number of sounds—that is to say, of the sounds which are already familiar to the learner in his own language. It is evident that the more familiar a sound is, the easier it is to gain insight into its mechanism and to recognize it when heard. It is indispensable to cultivate both the organic and the acoustic sense. These processes we are continually carrying out in ordinary conversation. All, therefore, that we have to do in dealing with native sounds is to develop this unconscious organic and acoustic sense into a conscious and analytic one. The first step is to learn to isolate each sound: to pronounce it, as far as possible, apart from its context; and to preserve it unchanged through every variation of length and force and in every combination of sounds. The next step is to analyse its formation. Let the student, for instance, compare the two consonants in such a word as *five* by isolating and lengthening them till he can both hear and feel the voice-vibration in the second one. In the same way let him learn to feel the changes in the position of the tongue and lips in passing from one vowel to another.

When the native sounds have been thoroughly studied in this way, the learner will proceed to foreign sounds deducing each new sound from those which are already familiar to him.

The natural method of learning sounds is mainly a subjective one. We listen patiently till our ears are steeped, as it were, in the sound; and then, after repeated trials, we hit on the exact position of the organs of speech by which we can reproduce the sound to the speaker's satisfaction. But the natural method admits also of objective control and criticism of the movements of the lips and jaws by direct observation. The movements and positions of the tongue and soft palate, and other modifications of the mouth and throat passages are also more or less accessible to observation—in the case of self-observation with the help of a small mirror held in the hand. If the mirror is small enough to go into the mouth, and is fixed obliquely to a handle, so that it can be held against the back of the mouth at such an angle as to reflect a ray of light down the throat, we have the *laryngoscope*. Laryngoscopy has confirmed earlier results, and has also added to our knowledge of the throat sounds. But, on the other hand, it has been a fruitful source of error. There has been great discrepancy between the results obtained by different observers; and many results which were at first received with implicit confidence for their supposed rigorously scientific and objective character have been found to be worthless. It seemed at first as if Röntgen's discovery of the so-called X-rays would meet the want of a means of direct observation of the positions of the tongue, not lengthways but from the side, as also of the interior of the throat. But although the cheeks are, to a certain extent, transparent to these rays, the shadow of the tongue projected on the screen is too indistinct to be of any use.

But there are other methods besides those of direct observation by which the positions of the tongue may be objectively determined and measured with more or less accuracy. The interior of the mouth may be explored by the fingers. If the little finger is held against the gums during the articulation of the vowels in *it*, *ate*, *at*, the difference in the height of the tongue will at once become apparent: in the formation of the first vowel the tongue is pressed strongly against the artificial palate, while in that of the second it only just touches it, and in that of the third it does not touch at all.

Several forms of apparatus have been devised for a more accurate information of the positions of the tongue and the other movable organs of speech. The best results hitherto as regards the vowel-positions have been obtained by Grandgent, who uses disks of cardboard of various sizes fixed to silver wires. A full description of this and other methods will be found in Scripture's *Element of Experimental Phonetics*.

There are other methods, whose results are obtained only directly. The simplest of these are, the *palatographic*, by which are obtained 'palatograms' recording the contact of the tongue with the palate. The apparatus most generally used consists of a thin, shell-like artificial palate, which is covered with chalk and placed in the mouth; when the sound is made, the articulation of the tongue is inferred from the contact-marks on the palate. This method is evidently limited in its application. It, too, has the drawback of not being applicable to the sounds formed in the back of the mouth. The outlines of palatograms are much vaguer than they appear in the published drawings of them; and it is a question whether the thickness even of the thinnest plate does not modify the record.

The methods hitherto considered are all comparatively simple. They require no special knowledge or training, and are accessible to all. But there are more elaborate methods—with which the name 'experimental phonetics' is more specially connected—giving special training in practical and theoretical physics and mathematics, and requiring the help of often complicated and costly, and not easily accessible, apparatus. The investigation of the speech curves of phonograph and gramophone records is a typical example. Good examples of these methods are afforded by E. A. Meyer's investigations of vowel-quantity in English (*Englische Lautdauer*, Uppsala, 1903). Their characteristic feature is their delicacy and the minuteness of their distinctions, which often go beyond the range of the human ear. Although their results are often of value, they must always be received with caution: the sources of error are so numerous.

The claims of instrumental phonetics have been so prominently brought forward of late years that they can no longer be ignored, even by the conservative of the older generation of phoneticians. But it is possible to go too far the other way. Some of the younger generation seem to think that the instrumental methods have superseded the natural ones in the same way as the Arabic superseded the Roman numerals. This assumption has had disastrous results. It cannot be too often repeated that instrumental phonetics is, strictly speaking, not phonetics at all. It is only a help: it only supplies materials which are useless till they have been tested and accepted from the linguistic phonetician's point of view. The final arbiter in all phonetic questions is the trained ear of a practical phonetician: differences which cannot be perceived must—or at least may be—ignored; what contradicts the trained ear cannot be accepted.

'Phonetics', *Encyclopædia Britannica*, 11th Ed., 1911, pp. 458–9

B. THE ORGANS OF SPEECH

[The text of the first extract below is substantially the same in both the *Handbook* and the *Primer of Phonetics*. Passages in the *Handbook* which are not found in the *Primer* are enclosed in sloping lines, viz. / . . . /; passages exclusive to the *Primer* are enclosed in square brackets. Sweet's own footnotes are included in the text in parentheses, viz. (*Fn.*: . . .). *Ed.*]

The foundation of speech is breath expelled by the lungs and variously modified in the throat and mouth. (*Fn.* to *Handbook*: The exceptions to this general rule are very few. The most important are the 'clicks'.)

[Speech-sounds are generally formed with *out-breathing* or expiration >, rarely with *in-breathing* or inspiration <. The sounds known as *clicks* are formed by the air in the mouth without either out- or in-breathing.]

The breath passes from the lungs through the wind-pipe into the larynx / ('Adam's apple')/. Across the interior of the larynx are stretched two elastic ligaments, the 'vocal chords'. They are firmly inserted in the front of the larynx at one end, while at the other they are fixed to two movable cartilaginous bodies, the 'arytenoids', so that the space between them, the 'glottis', can be narrowed or closed at pleasure. The glottis is, as we see, twofold, consisting of the chord-glottis, or glottis proper, and the cartilage glottis. The two glottises can be narrowed or closed independently. The chords can also be lengthened or shortened, tightened or relaxed in various degrees by means of the muscles they contain.

Above the 'true' glottis, and still forming part of the larynx, comes the 'upper' or 'false' glottis, by which the passage can be narrowed or partially closed. On the top of the larynx is fixed a sort of valve, the 'epiglottis', which in swallowing and in the formation of certain sounds is pressed down so as to cover the opening of the larynx.

The cavity between the larynx and the mouth is called the 'pharynx'. It can be expanded and contracted in various ways.

The roof of the mouth consists of two parts, the soft and the hard palate. [The boundary between them may easily be found by pressing the forefinger on the palate and sliding it back till the palate yields to the pressure.] The lower pendulous extremity of the soft palate, the 'uvula', can be pressed backwards or forwards. / It is pressed back in closing the passage into the nose. When the pressure is relaxed, as in ordinary breathing without speech, the breath flows through the nose as well as the mouth /. [It is pressed back to close the passage into the nose in the formation of all non-nasal sounds, such as *ah*, *d*. When the pressure is relaxed the breath flows through the nose, as in ordinary breathing and in the formation of nasal sounds, such as *n*, or French *a* in *sang*.]

The other extremity of the palate is bounded by the teeth, of which we must distinguish the 'edges' and the 'rim', or place where they join the gums. The gums extend from the teeth-rim to the 'arch-rim', behind which comes the 'arch', whose front wall is formed by the 'teeth roots' (alveolars). [The middle part of the palate from the arch-rim to the beginning of the soft palate is called 'front'. The soft palate and the wall of the pharynx behind it constitute the 'back' of the mouth.]

Of the tongue we distinguish the 'back' [or root], the middle or 'front', and the tip or 'point', together with the ['rim' or edge of the tongue on both sides of the tip, and the] 'blade', which includes the upper surface of the tongue immediately behind the point. 'Lower blade' implies, of course, the lower, instead of the upper surface [of the tongue. Front, blade, and point are included under the common term 'fore'].

Besides the main positions indicated by these names, an indefinite number of intermediate ones are possible. The chief varieties are designated by the terms 'inner' and 'outer', inner implying nearer the back of the mouth, outer nearer the teeth. Thus the 'outer front' of the tongue is a place nearer the point than simple front, and is therefore an approximation to the 'blade' [position].

Sounds are also modified by the degree of separation of the jaws, and by the movements of the lips and cheeks.

A Handbook of Phonetics, 1877, pp. 1–2;
and *A Primer of Phonetics*, 1890, pp. 7–9

[Where it is necessary to distinguish Narrow from Broad Romic notation in the extract below, the former is enclosed in square brackets. *Ed.*]

Most speech-sounds are ultimately formed by the air expelled from the lungs (voice-bellows). This air passes through the two contractible bronchi, or bronchial tubes, into the also contractible trachea or windpipe, on the top of which is fixed the cartilaginous larynx (voice-box). Across the interior of the larynx are stretched two elastic ligaments, the 'vocal chords', which are inserted in the front of the larynx at one end, while at the other end they are attached to two movable cartilages, so that the passage between—the 'glottis'—can be closed, or narrowed in various degrees. The glottis is, therefore, twofold, consisting of the chord glottis and the cartilage glottis. The two can be narrowed or closed independently. The chords can also be lengthened or shortened, tightened or relaxed in various degrees and in different directions—lengthways or crossways.

When the whole glottis is wide open, no sound is produced by the outgoing breath except that caused by the friction of the air. This is the foundation of 'breath' sounds, such as **f**. In 'voiced' (voice) sounds, such as **v**, the cartilage glottis is more or less completely closed, and the chords are brought close enough together to be set in vibration by the air passing through them. Breath (voicelessness) is indicated when necessary by adding the breath-modifier [*h*] in Narrow Romic, which in Broad Romic is written simply **h**: [**l***h*] = **lh** = voiceless **l**.

If the glottis is narrowed without vibration, 'whisper' is produced. In the 'weak whisper' there is narrowing of the whole glottis; in the 'strong whisper', which is the usual form, the chord glottis is entirely closed, so that the breath passes only through the cartilage glottis. In what is popularly called whisper—that is, speaking without voice-vibration—the breath sounds remain unchanged, while the voice sounds substitute whisper in the phonetic sense for voice. Thus if the initial **f** of *feel* is pronounced by itself, the hearer cannot tell whether the word is spoken aloud or whispered; but if it is immediately followed by **iil** formed with vibration of the vocal chords, he knows that it is spoken; if by **iil** formed with only narrowing of the glottis, he knows that it is spoken in a whisper.

Whispered sounds may form integral elements of ordinary loud speech. Thus in English the final consonants of such words as *leaves*, *oblige* are whispered except when a voice sound follows without any pause, as in *obliging*. In such a word as *obliged* **əblaidʒd** before a pause or a breath sound the two last sounds are both formed with whisper. It will be observed that whisper in consonants has acoustically the effect of weak breath.

The contractible cavity between the larynx and the mouth is called the 'pharynx'.

We now come to the mouth. Its roof consists of the 'hard palate' in front, and the 'soft palate' behind. The inner boundary of the former may easily be found by pressing a finger against it and pushing the finger back till the palate suddenly yields to the pressure.

The lower pendulous extremity of the soft palate is the 'uvula' (throat-tongue, as it was appropriately called in Old English). In its passive state, as in ordinary breathing, it leaves the passage into the nose open; and this makes any accompanying mouth-sound into the corresponding 'nasal' or 'nasalized' sound. Nasality is indicated when necessary by adding the nasal modifier [*n*]. In the formation of non-nasal (oral) sounds, such as **b**, the uvula is pressed backwards and upwards, so as to close the passage from the pharynx into the nose. If **b** is pronounced with this passage opened by lowering the uvula, it becomes the corresponding nasal consonant **m** = [**b***n*].

The other extremity of the palate is bounded by the teeth, behind which are the gums, extending from the 'teeth-rim' to the 'arch-rim', formed by the projection of the teeth-roots or 'alveolars', behind which is the hollow called 'the arch'.

The tongue can articulate with various parts of its surface against various parts of the palate, the teeth, and the lips.

The lips can articulate against each other, and against the teeth. The passage between the lips can be closed or narrowed in various degrees. Sounds modified by lip-narrowing are called 'lip-modified' (labialized) or 'round' (rounded), the last term being specially applied to vowels.

The Sounds of English, 1908, pp. 19–21

Most speech-sounds are formed with air expelled from the lungs (voice-bellows), which passes through the two contractible bronchi or bronchial tubes into the also contractible windpipe or trachea, on the top of which is fixed the larynx (voice-box). Across the interior of the larynx are stretched two elastic ledges or cushions called 'the vocal chords'. They are inserted in front of the larynx at one end, and at the other they are fixed to the movable cartilaginous bodies 'the aretynoids', so that the passage between them—the glottis—can be narrowed or closed at pleasure. The glottis is, as we see, twofold, consisting of the chord glottis and the cartilage glottis. The two can be narrowed or closed independently. The chords can also be tightened or relaxed, lengthened and shortened in various degrees.

When the whole glottis is wide open, no sound is produced by the outgoing breath except that caused by the friction of the air. Sounds in whose formation the glottis is in this passive state are called 'breath' sounds. Thus **f** is the breath consonant corresponding to the 'voice' or 'voiced' consonant **v**. In the production of voice, the chords are brought close enough together to be set in vibration by the air passing between them. In the 'thick' register of the voice (chest voice) the chords vibrate in their whole length, in the 'thin' register or falsetto only in part of their length. If the glottis is narrowed without vibration, 'whisper' is the result. In the 'weak whisper' there is narrowing of the whole glottis; in the 'strong whisper', which is the ordinary form, the chord glottis is entirely closed, so that the breath passes only through the cartilage glottis. In what is popularly called 'whisper'—that is, speaking without voice—the breath sounds remain unchanged, while voiced sounds substitute whisper (in the phonetic sense) for voice. Thus in whispering such a word as *feel* the **f** remains unchanged, while the following vowel and consonant are formed with the glottis only half closed. Whispered sounds—both vowels and consonants—occur in ordinary loud speech in many languages. Thus the final consonants in such English words as *leaves*, *oblige* are whispered, except when following without a pause by a voiced sound, as in *obliging*, where the ʒ is fully voiced.

Above the glottis—still within the larynx—comes the 'upper' or 'false' glottis, by which the passage can be narrowed. On the top of the larynx is fixed a leaf-like body, the 'epiglottis', which in swallowing, and sometimes in speech, is pressed down over the opening of the larynx. The contractible cavity between the larynx and the mouth is called the 'pharynx'. The roof of the mouth consists of two parts, the 'soft' and the 'hard palate'. The lower pendulous extremity of the soft palate, the 'uvula', in its passive state leaves the passage into the nose open. In the formation of non-nasal sounds, such as **b**, the uvula is pressed up so as to close the passage from the pharynx into the nose. If **b** is formed with the passage open it becomes the corresponding nasal consonant **m**. The other extremity of the (hard) palate is bounded by the teeth, behind which are the gums, extending from the teeth-rim to the arch-rim—the projection of the teeth-roots or alveolars.

There is great diversity among phoneticians as regards the mapping out—the divisions—of the palate and tongue, and their names. Foreign phoneticians generally adopt very minute distinctions, to which they give Latin names. Bell in his *Visible Speech* makes a few broad fundamental divisions. In the arrangement adopted here (mainly based on his) sounds formed on the soft palate are called 'back', and are subdivided into 'inner' = nearer the throat, and 'outer' = nearer the teeth, further subdivisions being made by the terms 'innermost', 'outermost' the position exactly half-way between these two last being defined as 'intermediate back'. Sounds formed on the hard palate or teeth may be included under the common term 'forward', more accurately distinguished as 'teeth' (dental), 'gum', 'front' (palatal, afterwards called 'top' by Bell), which last is really equivalent to 'mid-palatal' including the whole of the hard palate behind the gums. All of these divisions are further subdivided into 'inner' etc., as with the back positions.

Of the tongue we distinguish the 'back' (root), 'front' or middle, 'point' (tip), and 'blade', which includes the point and the surface of the tongue immediately behind it. The tongue can also articulate against the lips, which, again, can articulate against the teeth. The lip passage can be closed or narrowed in various degrees. Sounds modified by lip-narrowing are called 'lip-modified' (labialized) or 'round' (rounded) the last being specially used in speaking of vowels.

'Phonetics', *Encyclopædia Britannica,* 11th Edn., 1911, p. 462

C. ANALYSIS AND SYNTHESIS

[One of the ways in which Sweet differed most strikingly from the great majority of the phoneticians and phonologists who followed him was in the emphasis he attached to the synthetic aspects of language study, which he regarded as fully as important as the analytic aspects. His prediction that his successors would necessarily concern themselves principally with synthesis proved false. The great bulk of phonetic and phonological research since his time has been strongly analytical in tendency and even Sweet's 'three general factors of synthesis', quantity, stress, and intonation, have by many linguists been forced into an analytical mould. The resultant impoverishment of linguistic research would probably have disappointed Sweet but would certainly not have surprised him. The modern techniques of acoustic phonetics are bringing home to phoneticians the linguistic importance of the glides and other synthetic features which Sweet felt so strongly, but in the main these have still to make their full impact upon general linguistic theory and practice. *Ed.*]

Although language is made up of words, we do not speak in words, but in sentences. From a practical, as well as a scientific point of view, the sentence is the unit of language, not the word. From a purely phonetic point of view words do not exist. As I have said in the *Primer of Phonetics*, 'No amount of study of the sounds only of a sentence will enable us to recognize the individual words of which it consists. We may write down every sound, every shade of (phonetic) synthesis, but we shall never be able to analyse the sentence into separate words till we know its meaning, and even then we shall find that word-division postulates much thought and comparison of sentences one with another'. Thus the sound-group **telə** may stand for the single word *teller* or the two words *tell her*, there being no more pause between the words of a sentence than between the syllables of a word. In French, where word-division is much less clearly marked by stress and other formal criteria than in English, it is still more difficult to mark off the divisions of words by ear only. Thus the title of Darmesteter's well-known popular book on etymology, *La vie des mots*, is pronounced **lavidemo** with practically equal stress on all the vowels, and nothing to show, as in English, whether the internal consonants form groups with the preceding or the following vowel, so that if we did not know what is meant, we might transcribe it into nomic spelling in half a dozen ways, especially if some unknown proper name entered into it: *la vie* . . . . ., *l'avis* . . . . ., *l'avide et* . . . . ., ... *des mots*, ... *dé maux*, *Lavy* . . . . ., ... *Maux*, ... *Desmaux*.

We see, then, that there are two ways of dealing with languages: (1) the synthetic, which starts from the sentence; (2) the analytic, which starts from the word.

From the point of view of the practical study of language the synthetic method implies that the analysis of the language is not carried further than, at the most, cutting it up into sentences, which are grasped and learnt as wholes, instead of being separated into words, and put together like pieces of mosaic, as on the analytic method.

As the division of sentences into words is an essential preliminary to grammatical study, the synthetic principle is as opposed to grammatical analysis as it is to the analysis of a sentence into words.

The great development of analytic methods in modern times is partly the result of our fixed word-division in writing and printing, partly of the increasing elaboration of grammars and dictionaries, and partly of the growth of minute scholarship, philology, and etymology.

These analytic methods are often carried to a monstrous and almost incredible extreme in the historical and 'scientific' study of dead languages, as elaborated in Germany, and now being imported into this country. On this system, the words of an Old English or any other text are taken word by word and discussed etymologically, each word being transliterated into the form it assumes, or ought to assume, in the other cognate languages. The result of such a method is that the students learn a good deal about words, but nothing about the language itself, the sense of whose individuality is completely lost amid the chaos of conflicting associations.

The Practical Study of Languages, 1899, pp. 98–9; L.A.L.L. Edn., pp. 97–8

Analysis regards each sound as a fixed, stationary point, synthesis as a momentary point in a stream of incessant change. Synthesis looks mainly at the beginning and end of each sound, as the points where it is linked on to other sounds, while analysis concerns itself only with the middle of the fully developed sound.

A Handbook of Phonetics, 1877, p. 56, and *A Primer of Phonetics*, 1890, p. 41

D. ANALYSIS

1. *Speech Sounds*

[This section overlaps to some extent the earlier section on 'The Organs of Speech' (pp. 38–42), and should be read in conjunction with it. The section deals with speech sounds in general, and with such broad categories of sound as what Sweet called throat-sounds and nasal sounds, and with the distinction between 'narrow' and 'wide'. In the passages extracted from the *Handbook* and the *Primer of Phonetics*, passages exclusive to the former are enclosed in sloping lines, /. . ./, passages exclusive to the latter in square brackets, except that it has not been felt necessary to enclose single Romic symbols—found in the *Handbook* but replaced by Organic symbols in the *Primer*—in sloping lines. For a detailed account of the development of Sweet's views upon the Arabic throat-sounds, see pp. 121–6.

The reader is referred to pp. 270–85 for an account of Sweet's use of the Organic Alphabet, symbols from which appear in some of the extracts below, and to the comprehensive Index of Symbols on pp. 287–91. *Ed.*]

The foundation of speech-sounds is breath expelled from the lungs, and variously modified by the vocal organs—throat, nose, mouth, lips. Each sound is the result of certain definite actions or positions of the vocal organs, by which the sound-passage assumes a certain definite shape.

Throat-Sounds: Breath and Voice. The first modification the breath undergoes is in the throat. If the vocal chords, which are stretched across the inside of the throat, are kept apart so that the air can pass through with but little hindrance, we have *breath*, as in ordinary breathing or sighing, and in the consonant **h**, as in *high*. If the chords are brought together so as to vibrate, we have *voice*, as in murmuring or in the word *err*.

Nasal Sounds. If the passage into the nose is left open, we have a *nasal* sound, such as **m** in *am*. In the formation of all sounds that are not nasal—non-nasal sounds—such as the **b** in *amber*, the nose-passage is closed by pressing back the uvula or soft palate.

Consonants. If the mouth passage is narrowed so as to cause audible friction—that is, a hissing or buzzing sound—a *consonant* is produced. Thus if we bring the lower lip against the upper teeth, and send out breath, we form the 'lip-teeth-breath', or, more briefly, the 'lip-teeth' consonant **f.** If we form an **f** with throat vibration, we get the corresponding 'lip-teeth-voice' consonant **v.** Breath or voiceless consonants are sometimes expressed by adding ***h*** to the symbol of the corresponding voice consonant, thus **w*h*** as in *why*, is the breath consonant corresponding to the voice consonant **w** as in *wine*. 'Stopped' consonants are formed with complete stoppage of the mouth-passage. Thus the 'lip-stop' consonant **p** is formed by bringing the lips together so as completely to stop the passage of air.

Vowels. If the mouth-passage is left so open as not to cause audible friction, and voiced breath is sent through it, we have a *vowel*, such as **aa** in *father*. Every alteration in the shape of the mouth produces a different vowel. Thus a slight alteration of the **aa**-position produces the vowel **æ** in *man*.

Vowel-like consonants. Some consonants have hardly any friction when voiced, and are called *vowel-like* consonants. Such consonants are **l**, as in *little* **litl**, and **m**.

A New English Grammar, 1891, pp. 226–7

Speech-sounds are generally formed with *out-breathing* or expiration ›, rarely with *in-breathing* or inspiration ‹. *Suction-stops* or clicks, as in the familiar *tut!* ʊ‹, are formed without either out- or in-breathing.

Throat Sounds. When the glottis is wide open, the air passing through it produces *breath* o; when the glottis is narrowed so as to make the vocal chords vibrate, *voice* ɪ is the result; if the chords are approximated without being allowed to vibrate, *whisper* ◊ is the result. If whisper is strengthened by contraction of the superglottal passage or 'false glottis', we get the *wheeze* ◊ʌ, as in the Arabic *Hha*, which can be voiced ɵ as in the Arabic *Ain*. The *Glottal stop* x is produced by a sudden shutting or opening of the glottis, as in a cough.

A History of English Sounds, 1888, p. 1

Throat Sounds. Breath, Voice and Whisper. When the glottis is wide open, no sound is produced by the outgoing breath, except that caused by the friction of the air in the throat, mouth, etc. This passive state of the glottis is called 'breath' **Hh** (*Fn*. to *Handbook*: The usual diacritic ʽ *before* the modified letter is also occasionally employed to denote breath)[1] [and is symbolized by o, pictorial of the open glottis, whence is formed the 'breath modifier' ː].

The most important 'active' states of the glottis are those which produce 'voice' and 'whisper'.

[1] Sweet later (1880) emended this footnote, adding: 'before a voice-symbol it denotes whisper, thus ʽg = whispered g'. *TPS* 1880–1.

Voice /ʌ (*Fn.*: ʌ = turned v = 'voice')/ is produced by the action of the breath on the vocal chords in two ways. (1) If the glottis is entirely closed by the chords so that the air can only pass through in a series of extremely rapid puffs, we have that most sonorous form of voice known as the 'chest' voice or 'thick register' of the voice. (2) If the chords are only brought close enough together to /enable/ [make] their edges /to/ vibrate, without /any/ [complete] closure of the glottis, that thinner quality of voice known as the 'head' voice or 'thin register' is produced which in its thinnest and shrillest form is called 'falsetto'. [The symbol of voice is ɪ, pictorial of the glottal chink. The 'voice-modifier' symbol is ;.]

/If the chords are approximated without being allowed to vibrate, whisper **ʌh**, 'ʌ, is produced./ [If the glottis is narrowed without vibration, 'whisper' is produced which is symbolized by o, as being intermediate between breath and voice. The 'whisper-modifier' ɒ is a curtailed o.] There are two degrees of whisper, the 'weak' and the 'medium'. (For 'strong' whisper see p. 49.) In the weak whisper /the whole glottis is narrowed/ [there is slight narrowing of the whole glottis]; in the medium, which is the ordinary form, the chord glottis is entirely closed, so that the breath passes only through the cartilage glottis.

/The distinctions of breath, voice, and whisper are the most general of all, for every sound must be uttered with the glottis either open, narrowed, or closed, and the same sound may be pronounced either breathed, voiced, or whispered. Thus, if we press the lower lip against the upper teeth edges, we have the position of the 'lip-teeth' consonant. If we drive the air from the lungs through the passage thus formed, leaving the glottis open, we obtain the 'lip-teeth breath' consonant **f**. If the chords are narrowed till voice is produced, we obtain the 'lip-teeth voice' consonant **v**. If the student prolongs an **f**, and then a **v**, without any vowel, he will soon see that in the case of **f** the sound is formed entirely in the teeth, while with **v** the sound is distinctly compound, the hiss in the teeth being accompanied by a murmur in the throat. If he presses his two first fingers firmly on the glottis, he will distinctly feel a vibration in the case of **v**, but not of **f**. There is the same distinction between **s** and **z**, **th** as in 'thin', and **dh** as in 'then'.

It is of great importance to acquire a clear feeling of the distinction between breath and voice, and the student should accustom himself to sound all consonants both with and without voice at will . . ./

The popular and the phonetic use of the term 'whisper' do not quite agree. Whisper in popular language simply means speech without voice. Phonetically speaking whisper implies not merely absence of voice, but a definite contraction of the glottis.

In ordinary whispering, as opposed to speaking aloud, what happens is this: Breathed /elements/ [sounds], being already /voiceless/ [without voice], remain unchanged. Voiced /elements/ [sounds] substitute whisper (in the phonetic sense) for voice. If we pronounce two such syllables as 'vee' and 'fee', first in an ordinary loud voice and then in a whisper, we shall find that in 'vee' both consonant and vowel are changed, while in 'fee' only the vowel is changed, the consonant remaining breathed as in loud speech. It must, therefore, be understood in phonetic discussions that whenever we talk of a whispered sound we mean one that is pronounced with a definite contraction of the glottis. Whether we talk of a 'whispered *f*' or a 'whispered *v*' is indifferent—both names signify the 'lip-teeth whisper' consonant **ʻv** [the latter implying however a *substitution* of whisper for voice]. (*Fn.* to *Handbook*: The ʻ, = 'breath', combined with **v**, which implies voice, suggests something intermediate to breath and voice, which is whisper.)

The acoustic distinction between breath and whisper is not very marked, but if we compare /**ʻv** with **f**/ [breathed and whispered *f*], we perceive clearly that /**ʻv** is, like **v**/ [the latter is, like the voiced *v*], a composite sound, /with a distinct friction in the larynx/, [being formed partly in the throat]. Whispered sounds are also feebler than breath ones, the force of the outgoing air being diminished by the glottis contraction.

Other /Larynx/ [Throat] Sounds. /Glottal Catch **x**/ [*Glottal Stop* ꭓ]. When the glottis is suddenly opened or closed on a passage of breath or voice, a percussive effect is produced, analogous to that of **k** or any other 'stopped' consonant. The most familiar example of this /'glottal catch'/ ['glottal stop'] is an ordinary cough. The student should carefully practise the glottal /catch/ [stop] in combination with vowels till he is able to produce **xa** [ꭓɈɨ] and **ax** [Ɉɨꭓ] as easily as **ka** and **ak**, taking care not to let any breath escape after the **x** in **xa** [ꭓ in ꭓɈɨ], as is the case in coughing. He should learn to shut and open the glottis silently, and to know by the muscular sensation alone whether it is open or shut. It is easy to test the closure of the glottis /by tapping on the throat above the larynx/ [by pressing the forefinger on the throat above the larynx and tapping on its nail] /which/, when the glottis is open, [the tapping] produces a dull sound, when shut, a clear and hollow one like the gurgling of water being poured into a bottle, and /its pitch/ [the pitch of this sound] can be raised or lowered at pleasure by retracting or advancing the tongue.

x [ꭓ] forms an essential element of some languages [such as Danish, where, for instance, *hund* ƍɪꭓɔ 'dog' is distinguished from *hun* ƍɪɔ 'she' solely by the 'stödtone' or x]. /It is common in Danish after vowels, and often distinguishes words which would otherwise be identical. Thus *hun* **hu'n** is 'she', but *hund* **hux'n** is 'dog', **kHɔ'm** is 'come', **kHɔx'm** is 'came', both written *kom*. According to Mr Bell it is used in the Glasgow pronunciation of Scotch as a substitute for the voiceless stops, as in **waxehr*r*** = 'water', **bɐxehr*r*** = 'butter'./[1]

Wheeze /**Rh**/. If we strongly exaggerate an ordinary whisper, we produce that hoarse, wheezy sound known as the 'stage whisper' [or 'strong whisper' ʘʌ]. In the formation of this sound there is not only the glottis narrowing of the ordinary medium whisper, but there is also contraction of /the superglottal passage or 'false glottis'/ [the upper glottis], /the opening being/ [and the opening may be] further narrowed by depression of the epiglottis. /The sound is a common variety of **r**, especially when it is voiced **R**. It is the regular sound in Danish, the laryngal action being combined with retraction of the tongue and rounding, so that the sound is really **R+ghw**. **R+gh** may also be heard in North Germany./ If there is 'trilling' or vibration of the upper part of the glottis, /the Arabic *Hha* **Rhr** and *Ain* **Rr** are formed/ [we have the Arabic *Hha* ʘʃ, the voiced form of which is the Arabic *Ain* ʘʃ].[2]

A Handbook of Phonetics, 1877, pp. 3–7, and
A Primer of Phonetics, 1890, pp. 9–12

Deep Throat-Sounds. If we narrow the passage below the glottis—apparently in the bronchial region (*Fn.*: See *Le Maître phonétique*, 1904, p. 36), we get a clear hiss not unlike that of a goose, and closely resembling the back-open-breath consonant c in Scotch *loch*. This sound o˔, the deep-open-breath consonant, is one of the 'Arabic gutturals'—that one which is transcribed *ḥ*, as in o˔]ɨ *ḥā* (the name of the letter), ɜ]o˔o˔[ʊ *waḥḥid* 'proclaim the unity of God!', ɷʃ[ɨo˔ *rīḥ* 'wind'.

Being formed independently of the glottis, this sound can be voiced and whispered. When voiced, it makes the vocal chords vibrate slowly and intermittently, giving that gruff, creaky quality of voice with which many speakers in all countries—especially Germany—exaggerate the effect of a deep bass voice. If we soften the creak by diminishing the throat-contraction, we get the *r*-like sound of the weak deep-open-voice consonant ɪ˔v, which is the other Arabic guttural in ɪ˔v[ɨɜ *'ēn* 'eye' (also the name of the letter), ɒ]·ɪ˔v[ɨʊ *ba'īd* 'distant'.

A Primer of Phonetics, 1906, pp. 12–13

[1] Sweet later corrected this: 'I was told by Mr Bell that in the Glasgow "water", etc. the oral stop is really formed simultaneously with the glottal stop, not suppressed, = ɜ]ʊx]ɷʃ', *TPS* 1880–1, p. 339. *Ed.*

[2] See Sweet's later discussion of these sounds on pp. 121–6. *Ed.*

Nasal Sounds. In ordinary breathing the uvula hangs loosely down, and the air passes behind it through the nose as well as the mouth. In forming all the non-nasal sounds the uvula is pressed up so as to cover the passage into the nose. If the passage is open the sound becomes nasal. Thus **b** and **m** are formed in exactly the same way except that with **b** the nasal passage is closed, with **m** it is open. Similarly, if in pronouncing the vowel **a** the uvula is lowered, we obtain the corresponding nasal vowel **a*n***.

The pure nasal vowels, which are common in many South German dialects, must be carefully distinguished from the French nasals, in which there is guttural compression as well as nasality, a combination which may be denoted by ***q***, thus **a*q*** is the French 'en', 'an', **o*q*** = 'on', **væ*q*** = 'vin', **œ*q*** = 'un'. (*Fn.*: The exact formation of the French nasals has long been a disputed question. The guttural element I believe to be some kind of lateral cheek (and, perhaps, pharynx) compression: it is somewhat vaguely described by Mr Bell as consisting in a 'semi-consonant contraction of the guttural passage'. *Later Additional Note* by author in Appendix: *French Nasals.* I now doubt the necessity of any guttural compression in the formation of the French nasals: their deep tone may be due simply to the greater lowering of the uvula than in South German and American nasality.)

There are various degrees of nasality, according as the nose passage is completely or only partially open. Many speakers pronounce all their vowels with imperfect closure of the nose passage, which gives their pronunciation the so-called 'nasal twang'. This nasality is so common in North America, especially in New England, as to constitute a characteristic feature of American pronunciation. It is, however, very frequent in London English also.

A Handbook of Phonetics, 1877, pp. 7–8, 211

Nasal Sounds are formed by depressing the uvula so as to let the breath pass through the nose. Nasality is denoted by ʅ.

A History of English Sounds, 1888, p. 1

Narrow and Wide. These are very important general modifications of all /sounds produced or modified in the mouth/ [vowels. The narrow vowels are symbolized by a 'dot-definer' ſ, the wide by a 'hook-definer' ʃ. The 'narrow-modifier' ⁁ and the 'wide-modifier' ⁘ are formed from ʌ and v]. The distinction depends [mainly] on the *shape* of the tongue. In forming narrow /sounds/ [vowels] there is a feeling of tenseness in that part of the tongue where the sound is formed, the surface of the tongue being made more convex than in its natural 'wide' shape, in which it is relaxed and flattened. This convexity of the tongue naturally narrows the passage—whence the name. /This narrowing is produced by raising, not the whole body of the tongue, but only that part of it which forms, or helps to form, the sound. Thus, starting from the mid-wide vowel ***e*** we may narrow the passage either by raising the whole body of the tongue to the high ***i*** position, or else by contracting the muscles in the front of the tongue so as to make it more convex without otherwise changing its height. We may then raise this narrow-mid **e** to the high **i** position. Although in **i** the tongue is nearer the palate than in the wide ***i***, we can never change ***i*** into **i** by simply raising the tongue: we must alter its shape at the same time from wide to narrow. If ***i*** is raised so high as to produce a distinct consonantal hiss, it will still remain wide in sound./ [The narrowing is the result not of raising the whole body of the tongue (with the help of the jaws), but of 'bunching up' that part of it with which the sound is formed. Hence if we take a low-wide vowel, such as the low front-wide ɿ in *man*, we can raise it through the ʗ in *men* to the high position of the ʃ in *it* without its ever running into the mid-front-narrow [in French *été*. So also ʃ may be raised till it becomes a consonantal buzz without ever passing into the high-front-narrow ſ in French *si*—that is, as long as the tongue retains the laxity and comparative flatness of a wide vowel.

[The distinction between narrow and wide is not so clear in the back vowels, where the convexity of the tongue seems to be accompanied by tension and consequent advancing of the uvula.

[It is, of course, possible for a vowel to be exactly half way between narrow and wide, which is symbolized by adding the wide modifier to the narrow vowel symbol, thus ſ˅ = half wide *i*, as in Norwegian *fisk*.]

/The distinction of narrow and wide applies to consonants, and not (as Mr Bell assumed) to vowels only./ [The distinction of narrow and wide applies to consonants as well as vowels, though in consonants it is less noticeable, and can generally be ignored. It is symbolized by the addition of the modifiers ˄ for narrow, ˅ for wide consonants.] The distinction between French and English **w** in 'oui' and 'we' is that the French **w** is narrow [ϿϿ˄], the English wide [Ͽ˅], the former being consonantized **u** [ɫ], the latter ***u*** [ɫ]. In English the hisses are generally wide, in French narrow. Narrow **s** may be heard in energetic hissing, wide **sh** in gentle hushing [sɫ˄, ʑɫ˅]. [Consonants seem to be generally wide in English, narrow in French.] /(*Fn.* to *Handbook*: Mr Bell, who first noticed the distinction of narrow and wide, explains it as due to tension and relaxation of the pharynx. I for a long time held to this view, imagining the tension of the tongue to be something secondary and merely sympathetic.

However I afterwards noticed that the sense of pharyngal and palatal tension was always concentrated on that part of the mouth where the sound was formed, in front sounds on the hard palate. This was a reductio ad absurdum, showing that the feeling was really imaginary. The relation was thus reversed: the tongue tension was shown to be the real cause of narrowness and wideness, and the other feeling to be imaginary and secondary. I do not believe that the shape of the pharynx, the approximation of the palatal arches, etc., have any effect in producing distinctive vowel sounds.)

/The distinction being a delicate one is not to be acquired practically without considerable training. Beginners are apt to confuse widening with lowering of the tongue, especially when the wide vowel is unfamiliar. The best way to avoid this is to run through a whole series from high to low, first narrow and then wide, taking, for instance, first **i**, **e**, **æ**, then ***i***, ***e***, ***æ***. In this way a clear idea of the distinction between changes in the *shape* and in the *position* of the tongue will be obtained.

/A narrow vowel may be widened by trying to utter it as lazily and listlessly as possible, without altering the position of the tongue./

A Handbook of Phonetics, 1877, pp. 8–10, and
A Primer of Phonetics, 1890, pp. 18–19, 29

Narrow and Wide. Narrow (˄˄) sounds are formed with tensity and convexity, wide (˅˅) with slackness and flatness of the tongue. There are various degrees of narrowness, and it is possible to produce a sound which is exactly half way; the Norwegian short *i* in *fisk* is an example, (ɪ˅˅).

A History of English Sounds, 1888, pp. 1–2

[The immediately following extract is substantially the same in *The Sounds of English* and the article on 'Phonetics' in the 1911 edition of the *Encyclopædia Britannica*. Passages exclusive to the former are enclosed in sloping lines, passages exclusive to the latter in square brackets. *Ed.*]

Speech Sounds: The most general test of a single sound as opposed to a /group of sounds (sound-combination, sound-group)/ [compound sound (sound-group)] is that it can be lengthened without change /as we see in lengthening a simple monophthongic as opposed to a diphthongic vowel/.

As regards the place of articulation, no sound is really simple: every sound is the result of the shape of the whole configurative passage from the lungs to the lips; and the ultimate sound-elements, such as /breath and/ voice, are never heard isolated. The most indistinct voice-murmur is as much the result of the shape of the superglottal passages as the [clearest and] most distinct of the other vowels, and its organic formation /(position)/ is as definite /and fixed/ as theirs is; the only difference being that while in what we regard as unmodified voice /-murmur/ all the organs except the vocal chords are in their passive /or/ neutral positions, /the other vowels are formed by actively modifying the shape of certain definite portions of the configurative passages. Thus if we pass from the neutral vowel-murmur to **i** we raise the front of the tongue close to the palate, the lips remaining neutral as before; while in forming **u** we narrow the lip-passage, and at the same time raise the back of the tongue/ [the other vowels are formed by actively modifying the shape of the superglottal passages—by raising the tongue towards the palate, narrowing the lips, etc.].

The Sounds of English, 1908, p. 22, and 'Phonetics', *Encyclopædia Britannica*, 11th Edn., 1911, p. 462

The changes in sounds which result from active narrowing of the passages admit of an important distinction as 'sound-modifying' and 'sound-colouring', although the distinction is not always definite. Nasality and rounding are examples of sound-modifying processes. Thus we hear a certain resemblance between **b** and **m**, **i** and **y**, but we regard all these four as distinct and practically independent sounds. Contraction of the pharynx, on the other hand, as also of the false glottis and windpipe, have only a sound-colouring effect: if a vowel is formed with such contractions its quality (timbre) is altered, but it still remains the same vowel. It follows from the definition of speech-sounds that they admit of a twofold classification: (1) organic and (2) acoustic. As already remarked, the older phoneticians used to classify the consonants organically, the vowels mainly from the acoustic point of view. The first to give an adequate organic classification of the vowels was the author of *Visible Speech*. Bell gave at the same time an independent acoustic classification of the consonants as well as the vowels. His acoustic classification consists simply in arranging the sounds in the order of their 'pitches' (tone-heights). The pitches of the breath consonants are absolutely fixed in each individual pronunciation, while those of spoken vowels can be varied indefinitely within the compass of each voice by tightening the vocal chords in various ways and shortening their vibrating portions: the tighter and shorter the vibrating body, the quicker its vibrations, and the higher the tone. But when a vowel is whispered or breathed nothing is heard but the resonance of the configurative passages, especially in the mouth, and the pitches of these resonant cavities are as fixed as those of the breath consonants; in other words, a whispered (or breathed) vowel cannot be sung. Although the absolute pitches of voiceless sounds may vary from individual to individual the *relations* of the pitches are constant: thus in all pronunciations **ç** and whispered **i** are the highest, breath **w** in *what* and whispered **u** nearly the lowest in pitch among consonants and vowels respectively.

If phonetics were an ideally perfect science there would be no occasion to discuss whether the acoustic or the organic study of the vowels and the other speech-sounds is the more important: a full description of each sound would necessarily imply (1) an exact determination of its organic formation, (2) an acoustic analysis of the sound itself, both from the objective physical point of view and from the subjective one of the impression received by ear, and (3) an explanation of how (2) is the necessary result of (1). Even this last question has already been solved to some extent. In fact, the connexion between the organic formation and the acoustic effect is often self-evident. It is evident, for instance, that **i** and **ç** owe their clear sound and high pitch to their being formed by short, narrow passages in the front of the mouth, while **u** owes its low pitch to being formed in exactly the opposite way, the sound being rather muffled and the pitch consequently still more lowered by the rounding.

One reason why it is impossible to classify the vowels exclusively on acoustic principles is that two vowels formed in quite different ways may have the same pitch. Thus the 'high-front-round' **y** and the 'high-mixed' **ï** have the same pitch, the tongue-retraction of the mixed position of the latter having the same effect as the rounding of the former. It is evident, therefore, that the fundamental classification of the vowels must, like that of the consonants, be purely organic. And although for practical purposes it is often convenient to classify sounds partly from the acoustic point of view, a full scientific treatment must keep the two points of view strictly apart, and make a special chapter of the relations between them.

'Phonetics', *Encyclopædia Britannica*, 11th Edn., 1911, p. 463

2. *The Distinction between Vowels and Consonants*

[In the second extract below, passages exclusive to the *Handbook* are enclosed in sloping lines, those exclusive to the *Primer of Phonetics* in square brackets. *Ed.*]

The main distinction between consonants and vowels is . . . that consonants are independent of voice, vowels not. All breath articulations are therefore *ipso facto* consonants. Voice articulations are easily tested by opening the glottis: if they yield a distinctly audible friction, they are consonants. The buzz caused by the friction is often audible without devocalisation as in the case of **z** and **dh**.

If an open vowel, such as **a** or **æh**, is submitted to this test, we obtain nothing but a sigh, which is inaudible except when pronounced forcibly. But if we take a high vowel, such as **i**, and devocalize it, we obtain a hiss which is quite distinct enough to stand for a weak **jh**. The same may be said of devocalized **u** = weak **wh**. This would justify us in regarding **i** and **u** themselves as weak **j** and **w**. In fact the boundary between vowel and consonant, like that between the different kingdoms of nature, cannot be drawn with absolute definiteness, and there are sounds which may belong to either.

In Scotch **iɪ** is often pronounced with a distinct buzz, and is then simply a held **j**. In French also the **i** is often pronounced, if not with a buzz, at least with a distinct consonantal squeeze, so that in such a word as 'guerrier' **gær˯je** it is difficult to know whether to call the *i* a vowel or a consonant. After a voiceless stop, where the **i** is devocalized there can be no doubt as to its consonantal sound, as in 'pied' **p˯jhe**. So also often finally, as in 'sympathie' **-t˯jhɪ**. Similarly with **y** in 'vécu' **vek˯jh*w*ɪ**.

On the other hand, there are many voice consonants which may be regarded as 'vowel-like' consonants. In fact, whenever a voice unshut consonant is pronounced without a distinct buzz, it is, to the ear at least, a vowel while being held. This applies especially to the voice nasals, which are, indeed, almost incapable of being buzzed. **l** also, though it can be buzzed, is generally vocalic in sound. Lastly, **gh** and **r** can both be relaxed into sounds which are almost entirely free from friction, although they then may almost be regarded as vowels. But the friction comes out distinctly when any one of these vowel-like consonants is devocalized, and if they are consonants when breathed, they must be equally so when voiced. In the case of **l** and the nasals, although they have a purely vowel effect while being held, they always end with a distinct flap when the contact is broken, which unmistakeably proclaims their consonant character.

A Handbook of Phonetics, 1877, pp. 51–2

The main distinction between vowels and consonants is that while in the vowels the mouth-configuration merely modifies the vocalized breath—which is therefore an essential element of the vowels—in consonants the narrowing or stopping of the /oral/ [mouth-] passage is the foundation of the sound, and the state of the glottis is something secondary. Consonants can therefore be breathed as well as voiced, the mouth-configuration alone being enough to produce a /distinct sound/ [distinction] without the help of voice. All consonants can be /formed with whisper/ [whispered].

A Handbook of Phonetics, 1877, p. 31, and
A Primer of Phonetics, 1890, p. 28

Vowels and Consonants. The two most important elements of speech-sounds are those which depend on the shape of the glottis on the one hand, and of the mouth- and lip-passages on the other.

It is on the relation between these two factors that the familiar distinction between vowel and consonant depends. In vowels the element of voice is the predominant one: a vowel is voice modified by the different shapes of the superglottal passages, especially the mouth and lips. In consonants, on the other hand, the state of the glottis is only a secondary element: a distinctively consonantal articulation is the result of narrowing some part of the configurative passages so as to produce audible friction, as in **f**, **v**, or of complete stoppage as in **p**, **b**. Vowels are characterized negatively by the absence of audible friction and of stoppage. If such a vowel as **i** is formed with the tongue so close to the palate as to cause distinct buzzing, it becomes, from the articulative point of view, a consonant, although we hardly feel it as such, because it still retains its syllabic function. Such half consonantal vowels are called 'constricted'.

There is no more difficulty in combining vowel-position with breath and whisper than there is with consonants. Whispered vowels occur as integral elements of loud speech in many languages; they may be heard in English in rapid speech in the initial weak syllables of such words as *together*, *September*, and in weak monosyllables such as *but*.

Breath or voiceless vowels may be heard in French at the end of words, as in *ainsi*, where the breath **i** sounds like a weak voiceless **j**. An open vowel such as **a** is much less distinct when formed with breath: it is little more than a sigh. This want of sonority is, of course, the reason why breath and whispered vowels are so much rarer than the corresponding classes of consonants.

The division between vowel and consonant is not an absolutely definite one. As we see, the closer a vowel is, the more it approaches a consonant; thus it may seem difficult to know whether to regard the English **j** as a very open or 'loose' consonant, or as a constricted un-syllabic vowel. But if it is lengthened, its consonantal buzz comes out clearly enough, showing that the former view is the correct one.

But there are some consonants which in their voiced forms have no more buzz than a vowel, even when lengthened, such as **l** and the nasals **ŋ**, **n**, **m**, which are accordingly called liquid, vowel-like, or 'soft' consonants, as opposed to the 'hard' consonants, which include the stops and the hisses **f**, **s**, etc., which when voiced, **v**, **z**, etc., are called 'buzzes'. **m**, indeed, is so much a vowel that it can be sung on: 'humming a tune' means singing it with the nose passage open and the mouth shut—that is, on a lengthened **m**. If we hum in this way, and then close the passage into the nose by retracting the uvula, the voice-murmur still has a purely vowel-like effect, although, of course, it cannot be held except for a short time. **b** itself, although formed with complete stoppage of the breath, is therefore acoustically a pure vowel—at least in the middle of its prolongation. It is only the audible percussion which accompanies its beginning, and still more its end, which proclaims it to be, after all, a consonant. The same percussive or flapping effect is heard, though in a less degree, at the end of **m**, **l** and the other soft consonants.

The Sounds of English, 1908, pp. 22–4

The most important elements of speech-sounds are those which are dependant on the shape of the glottis and of the mouth passage respectively. It is on the relation between these two factors that one of the oldest distinctions between sounds is based: that of *vowel* and *consonant*. In vowels the element of voice is the predominant one: a vowel is voice modified by the different shapes of the superglottal passages. In consonants on the other hand, the state of the glottis is only secondary. Consonants are generally the result of audible friction, as in **f**, or of complete stoppage, as in **p**. If the glottis is at the same time left open, as in **f**, **p**, the consonant is 'breath' or 'voiceless'—if it is narrowed enough to make the chords vibrate, as in **v**, **b**, the consonant is 'voice' or 'voiced'; intermediate positions producing the corresponding 'whispered' consonants. Vowels are characterized negatively by the absence of audible friction or stoppage: if an **i** is formed with the tongue so close to the palate as to cause buzzing, it becomes a variety of the front consonant **j**. There is, of course, no difficulty in forming a vowel with the glottis in the position for breath and whisper. Thus breath **i** may often be heard in French in such words as *ainsi* at the end of a sentence, the result being practically a weak form of the front-breath consonant **ç**. The division between vowel and consonant is not an absolutely definite one. As we see, the closer a vowel is—that is, the narrower its configurative passage is—the more like it is to a consonant, and the more natural it is to devocalize it. Some voice consonants, on the other hand, have so little buzz that acoustically they constitute a class between consonants and vowels—a class of 'vowel-like' or 'liquid' consonants, such as **n**, **m**, **l**.

'Phonetics', *Encyclopædia Britannica*, 11th Edn., 1911, p. 463

3. *Vowels*

[In this important section comparison between Sweet's accounts in the *Handbook* and in the first and revised editions of the *Primer of Phonetics* is particularly interesting. The principal difference is the expansion of the original thirty-six elementary vowels of the *Handbook* and the first edition of the *Primer* to seventy-two in the revised edition of the *Primer*, but the relatively minor differences between the *Handbook* and the first edition of the *Primer* are also instructive. For the reader's convenience, the vowel tables from the *Handbook* and the 1890 and 1906 editions of the *Primer* are presented together in Tables I–IV on pp. 66–9. Table I on p. 66 shows the thirty-six elementary vowels as they appear in the *Handbook*, accompanied by 'unambiguous key-words', whenever these could be given, from the 'better known languages', especially English (E.), Scotch (Sc.), French (F.), and German (G.); the English sounds are described as 'those of the educated southern pronunciation', the Scotch those of the Edinburgh pronunciation, and the German are distinguished as North (Hanoverian) German (N.G.), Middle (M.), and South (S.) German: 'occ.' signifies 'occasional'. Table II on p. 66 shows the thirty-six elementary vowels as they appear in the 1890 edition of the *Primer of Phonetics*, 'with key-words from English (E.), Scotch-English (Sc.), American-English (Amer.), French (Fr.), German (G.) and other languages'. Tables III and IV show the seventy-two elementary vowels as set out in the revised edition of the *Primer* in 1906. In his preface to this edition, Sweet describes this extension of the vowels as the 'most important innovation' to the original text, and refers the reader to his article on 'Mixed vowels' in *Le Maître phonétique*, December 1901, for an account of how the extension came about. The article in question is reprinted later in the section on pp. 79–82. In the original printed texts, the vowels are only numbered in the extended tables of the revised edition of the *Primer*, while the *Handbook* arranges narrow, narrow-round, wide, and wide-round vowels under separate headings. For convenience of comparison, vowels are numbered in all tables below and the presentation is uniform throughout.

It is perhaps worth recording that Paul Passy, in his review of the second edition of the *Primer of Phonetics* (in *Le Maître phonétique*, 1903, pp. 39 f.), while acknowledging that it was possible to pronounce vowels in the manner specified by Sweet for his 'shifted vowels', and that the consequent distinctions might enable one to classify certain nuances of vowel quality better than hitherto, expressed doubts as to whether they were sufficiently important to merit the status of 'elementary vowels' rather than that of special modifications of these. In his rejoinder (in *Le*

Maître phonétique, 1903, pp. 54 f.), Sweet pointed out that some of the 'shifted vowels' had already formed part of Bell's original table (see p. 258) 'under the disguise of mixed-round vowels', and that he had had to find a new place for them. He claimed, moreover, that 'such vowels as those in Norwegian *hus* and *der* compared with English *there* have as distinct a character of their own as any other vowel'.

The section closes with a brief reference to diphthongs and triphthongs. Involving as they do consideration of such matters as length, stress, syllabicity, and glides, diphthongs and triphthongs are treated by Sweet as features of synthesis, and extracts giving fuller accounts of these will be found in the sections below that deal with synthesis, especially pp. 155–9. *Ed.*]

A vowel may be defined as voice (voiced breath) modified by some definite configuration of the superglottal passages, but without audible friction [(which would make it into a consonant). The symbols of the different vowels are all formed by modifying the voice symbol ɪ]. (*Fn.* to *Handbook*: *Whispered* vowels occur as integral elements of ordinary loud speech, in some native American languages. See Haldeman, quoted by Ellis, E. E. P., 1914.)

/*Tongue Shape*: *Narrow and wide.* The most important general modifications are those which cause the distinction of narrow and wide, already described. Wide vowels are generally denoted by italics, thus ***i*** is the wide form of **i**./

Tongue positions. As each new position of the tongue produces a new vowel, and as the positions are infinite, it follows that the number of possible vowel sounds is infinite. It becomes necessary, therefore, to select certain definite positions as fixed points whence to measure the intermediate positions.

The movements of the tongue may be distinguished generally as *horizontal* and *vertical*—backwards and forwards, upwards and downwards. The horizontal movements produce two well-marked classes, (1) 'back' (guttural) vowels, [formed by the root] /in which the tongue is retracted as much as possible, such as **aː** in *father*, **uː** in *fool*/; and (2) 'front' (palatal) vowels, [formed by the forepart of the tongue] /such as **iː** in *see*, **æ** in *man*, in which the tongue is advanced. The former are formed by the back of the tongue only, the point being kept down, the latter by the front. The distinction is easily felt by pronouncing **aː** and **iː** in succession./ [In the formation of back vowels, such as ʃ in *father*, ɟ in *fall*, the back or root of the tongue is brought into prominence partly by retraction of the whole body of the tongue, partly by pressing down the forepart of the tongue, the latter element of the articulation being apparently the most essential. In the formation of front vowels, such as ſ in *it* and ɭ in *man*, the tongue is advanced so that its front comes into operation.] There is also a third class, the 'mixed' (gutturo-palatal) vowels, /which have an intermediate position, /[such as the ɪ in *err* where the whole tongue is allowed to sink into its natural flattened shape, in which neither back nor front articulation predominates] /such as the English **æhı** in *err*, the German **eh** in *gabe*. Mixed vowels are indicated by the diacritical **h**/.

The vertical movements of the tongue [which are mainly effected (1906 Edition: 'generally accompanied') by lowering and raising the jaw,] produce various degrees of 'height', or distance [of the tongue] from the palate. Thus in ***i*** ſ /as in *bit*/, the front of the tongue is raised as high and as close to the palate as possible without causing [audible] friction [or buzz]. [In [, as in *men*, it is somewhat lowered, and] in ***æ*** ɭ /as in *man*/ it is lowered as much as possible. From among the infinite degrees of height three are selected, 'high' [as in ſ], 'mid' [as in []], and 'low' [as in ɭ]. /***i*** is a high, ***æ*** a low vowel, while ***e*** as in *say* is a mid vowel./ These distinctions apply equally to back [and] mixed /and front/ vowels, so we have altogether nine cardinal vowel positions:

ɿ high-back	Ɪ high-mixed	ſ high-front
] mid-back	ʅ mid-mixed	[mid-front
ȷ low-back	ɪ low-mixed	ɭ low-front

[It will be observed that we place the back vowels on the left side of the table, because the direction of the stream of breath by which sounds are formed is supposed to move in the same direction as in our ordinary writing, viz. from left to right, so that 'left' corresponds to 'back' in all phonetic diagrams and symbolization. Hence the 'vowel-modifier' is turned to the left in the symbols of back vowels (]), and to the right in those of front vowels (ſ), mixed vowels combining the back and front modifiers (ɪ).]

/Each of these [i.e. cardinal. *Ed.*] positions yields a different vowel sound according as the tongue is in the 'narrow' and 'wide' shape.

/It is found that these nine positions correspond very nearly with the actual distinctions made in language, and that if we admit two intermediate positions between each of them, we practically reach the limit of discrimination by ear. The intermediate heights are distinguished as 'lowered' and 'raised', thus the 'lowered high-front' has a position below the 'high-front', and above the 'raised mid-front', which is above the simple 'mid-front'. Practically, however, the distinction between 'raised' and 'lowered' can hardly be carried out, and raised **e** and lowered **i** must generally both be assumed to represent the same half-way position. These vowels are written thus [**ei**]. Or exponents may be used, whenever accessible, eᴵ. Horizontal intermediates are defined as 'inner' and 'outer', and are indicated thus, ˏe, ˎeh, both indicating practically the same sound. The student should at first neglect these minutiae, and concentrate his attention on the elementary positions./

[In passing from ſ to ʗ and ʈ there is not only lowering of the tongue, but the point of greatest narrowing is also shifted back progressively, the size of the resonance-chamber in the front of the mouth being thus increased in both directions.

[Intermediate positions between the nine cardinal ones are marked by diacritics: ⊥ 'raiser', ⊤ 'lowerer', ⊣ 'retracter', ⊢ 'advancer', ⊣⊥ 'backward raiser', ⊢⊥ 'forward raiser', ⊣⊤ 'backward lowerer', ⊢⊤ 'forward lowerer'. Thus ſ⊤ and ʗ⊥ both denote a vowel intermediate between the *i* of *it* and the *e* of *men*, viz. the second vowel in *pity* ɒſʊſ⊤. So also]⊢⊤ and ɪ⊣⊥ both denote a vowel intermediate between the] in *but* and ɪ in *err*, as in the Irish and American pronunciation of *but*. (*The 1906 Edition omits the last sentence and carries on as follows:* Besides the nine cardinal positions there are nine other 'shifted' positions. We have seen that normal mixed vowels are characterized not only by 'mixed' position—that is, intermediate between back and front —but also by flatness of the tongue. These shifted positions are obtained by combining flatness of the tongue with back position, and the slopes of back and front vowels respectively with mixed position, giving the three series:

Ɪ⊣⊣ in-mixed	]⊢⊢ out-back	ſ⊣⊣ in-front
]⊣⊣	]⊢⊢	ʗ⊣⊣
ɪ⊣⊣	ɟ⊢⊢	ʈ⊣⊣

[The in-mixed or 'back-flat' vowels are obtained by retracting the positions of the mixed vowels into the corresponding back positions. Thus if we form ɪ, the low-mixed-narrow vowel in English *err*, *sir*, and then retract the tongue into the full back position, we get the low-in-mixed-narrow ɪ⊣⊣ which may be heard in the Irish pronunciation of *sir*. ɪ⊣⊣ is, therefore, simply an exaggeration of ɪ⊣, inner-low-mixed. So also ɟ⊢⊢ and ʈ⊣⊣ are exaggerations respectively of ɟ⊢ outer-low-back and ʈ⊣ inner-low-front. The vowels of the last two series are mixed in position, but retain the slope of the corresponding back and front vowels. It is not easy to distinguish between inner and in-front, but the in-mixed and the out-back vowels have a distinct acoustic character of their own by which they are sharply marked off from the corresponding back and mixed vowels.)]

/The height of the tongue is partly due to the action of the muscles of the tongue itself, but also in a great degree to the movements of the jaw.

Thus if we start from the high ***i*** position and lower the jaw, allowing the tongue to sink with it, we obtain first the mid ***e*** position and then the low ***æ*** one. Hence the partial closure of the mouth in forming high vowels.

/The question naturally arises, Which of the nine positions is the natural one when the organs are at rest? If we vocalize the breath as emitted in ordinary quiet breathing, without shifting the tongue in any way, we obtain an indistinct nasal murmur, which, if de-nasalized by closure of the nose passage, resolves itself into the mid-mixed (or the low-mixed vowel, if the mouth is opened as wide as possible). We see, then, that the two 'natural' or 'neutral' vowels are **eh** and ***e*h** both of which are widely distributed in actual language./

Rounding. /Rounding is a contraction of the mouth cavity by latera compression of the cheek passage and narrowing of the lip aperture, whence the older name of 'labialization'. (*Fn.* to *Handbook*: Mr Bell says that 'the mechanical cause of round quality commences in the superglottal passage.' I find, however, that this is not essential.)/ [Rounding (labialization) is a narrowing of the mouth-opening by approximation of the lips. It can, of course, be combined with all the tongue-positions described above. It is symbolized by a line drawn across the vowel stem—f = French *u* in *lune*.] There are three principal degrees of lip-narrowing, corresponding to the height of the tongue, high vowels having the narrowest, low the widest lip-aperture. This is easily seen by comparing [the vowels of such a series as] the high-back-round /**uː**, as in *who*,/ [ƚ in *good*,] the mid-back-round **oː** ʄ, as in *no*, and the low-back-round /**ɔː**, as in *law*/ [ɟ in *not*.] It will be seen that in **uː** the lips are contracted to a narrow chink, while in **oː** ʄ the opening is wider and broader, and in **ɔː** ɟ only the corners of the mouth are contracted.

/It will be observed that the action of rounding is always concentrated on that part of the mouth where the vowel is formed. In rounding front vowels, such as the high-front-round **y**, as in the French *lune*, the cheek compression is concentrated chiefly on the corners of the mouth and that part of the cheeks immediately behind them, while in back vowels, such as the high-back-round **u**, the chief compression is at the back of the cheeks.

/Lip-narrowing is, therefore, something secondary in back-rounded vowels, as it is possible to form them entirely with cheek-narrowing or 'inner rounding'. The absence of lip-rounding is, however, distinctly perceptible. According to Mr Bell inner rounding is practised by ventriloquists as a means of concealing the visible action of ordinary rounding./

[There are two kinds of rounding, *inner* and *outer*. In outer rounding—

with which front vowels are rounded—the lips are brought together vertically. If the lips are separated by a finger and thumb upwards and downwards, it will be found impossible to form a front-round vowel such as f—the result will be ſ—the French *i*. Back and mixed vowels, on the other hand, are rounded by lateral compression of the corners of the mouth and, apparently, of the cheeks as well. If a finger and thumb are put in the corners of the mouth so as to bear upon the cheeks about an inch inwards, and then expanded sideways, it will be found impossible to pronounce a back-round vowel such as ǂ—the result will be a muffled form of the ʝ in *father*. If, on the other hand, the lips are spread upwards and downwards during the utterance of such a vowel as ǂ, it will still retain much of its distinctive rounded character. The distinction between inner and outer rounding is taken for granted in the ordinary vowel-symbols, as in f, ƚ. Where necessary they are expressed by the modifiers) for outer, ɒ for inner rounding. Thus ʝ) is a muffled form of *a* in *father*, distinct from ǂ = ʝɒ.]

The effect of rounding may /on the other hand,/ be increased by projecting (pouting) the lips, /which of course practically lengthens the mouth channel by adding a resonance-chamber beyond the teeth/ [so as to form an additional resonance-chamber beyond the teeth]. This action is generally avoided in English, but may often be observed in the Scotch **u**, and generally in continental pronunciation [as in French and German. It is symbolized by adding the 'protruder' (ɔ), thus ɒƚɔɑ = Scotch *book*].

The influence of the lips may also be observed in the unrounded vowels. /In the formation of the low and mid vowels, such as **a**, the lips are in the 'neutral' position of rest, but in forming the high **i** the mouth is spread out at the corners, which makes the sound of the vowel clearer. (*Fn.* to *Handbook*: I had not noticed this until I read the remarks of Sievers (*Grundzüge der Lautphysiologie*, p. 39).) This lip-spreading may, of course, be applied to **a** and the other vowels as well. It may also be neglected elsewhere, as is frequently the case in English which dulls the effect of the high vowels.

/If back vowels are pronounced with lip-narrowing alone (without inner rounding as well) we do not obtain the corresponding round vowels, but simply muffled varieties of the ordinary sounds. Similarly, if a front vowel is pronounced with inner rounding only, the result is simply a muffled, gutturalized front vowel, not a front rounded vowel./ [In the formation of the high-front vowel ſ in *it*, the sound is made clearer by spreading out the corners of the lips. So also to a less degree with the mid- and low-front vowels. But in a back vowel such as the ʝ in *father* the lips tend to the neutral position of rest, although these vowels may also be made clearer by lip-spreading, which is symbolized by the addition of the 'spreader' ıı, as in ſıı = French *i*. In English the lips are less spread than in many other languages, such as French and German.]

Although there is a natural connection between the height of the tongue and the degree of lip-narrowing—it would evidently be a waste of sound to narrow the back of the mouth and then allow the sound to diffuse itself in the /front/ [forepart] of the mouth, or to widen the back part of the [voice] channel and then muffle the sound by over-narrowing of the mouth /channel/ [passage],—there are [many] cases of *abnormal* degrees of rounding in language. /Thus in Danish and Swedish **o**, as in *sol*, always has the same lip-narrowing as **u**, and **ɔ** as in *maane*, *måne*, has that of **o**, the lip-narrowing being thus in each case a degree above the height of the tongue./ [We must distinguish between 'under-rounding' and 'over-rounding'. Under-rounding implies a *less* degree of rounding than is normally associated with the vowel's height, as when a high vowel is formed with the rounding of a mid or low vowel; it is symbolized by adding the inner rounder ꝺ to the symbol of a back, the outer rounder) to the symbol of a front vowel. Thus 1ꝺ is a combination of the tongue position of the ɫ in *good* with the lip-position of the ɟ in *no*—a sound which seems to occur in the dialects of the North of England. Over-rounding implies a *greater* degree of rounding than normally belongs to the vowel's height; it is symbolized by adding the rounder to the symbol of the normal rounded vowel. Thus ƒ), as in German *über*, is the mid-front vowel with the rounding of the high front f; it is a compromise between the French vowels ƒ, as in *peu*, and f, as in *pur*. Degrees of abnormal rounding may be discriminated by the addition of the raiser and lowerer (see p. 61); thus 1ꝺ⊥ implying mid, and 1ꝺ⊤ low rounding.] /Every vowel, whether narrow or wide, is capable of rounding, which gives a total of thirty-six elementary vowel-sounds./

Tables of Vowels and General Remarks. The thirty-six [seventy-two—1906] elementary vowels are given in the annexed tables.

Names. In naming the vowels, 'height' comes first, and 'rounding' last—'high-back-narrow-round', etc.

/As regards the notation it may be remarked that all mixed vowels are indicated by adding the letter **h** in the case of unrounded mixed vowels to the corresponding front, in that of rounded mixed vowels to the corresponding back vowel symbol. Wide vowels are generally indicated by italics. The only exception is in the case of the back unrounded vowels, where the italics indicate widening of the mouth channel, not by relaxing, but by lowering the tongue. The narrow back unrounded vowels are indicated by the 'turned' letters of the corresponding wides. The relations of the front rounded and unrounded vowels are suggested by **ə**, being a turned **e**, and by the analogy of **œ** to **æ**. **ɔ** is assumed to be a turned **o**./ [In the 'narrow Romic' notation wide vowels are expressed by italics, mixed by dots.]

A Handbook of Phonetics, 1877, pp. 10–17, and *A Primer of Phonetics*, 1890, pp. 12–22; 1906, pp. 13–22

Nasal Vowels. In the formation of nasal vowels voiced breath flows through the nose as well as the mouth. If the nose passage is kept only slightly open, we get the 'nasal twang' of many American and some English speakers, which modifies all the vowels impartially, although, of course, it is more audible in the more open vowels than in the close high ones. In languages which distinguish between nasal and un-nasal vowels the nose-opening of the former is necessarily more marked than in a mere nasal twang. It is especially marked in French, where the nasal vowels in such words as SJʃ *sang*, ϶[ʃ *vin* are very sonorous. The nasality-modifier is supposed to be pictorial of the pendent uvula.

Other Modifications of Vowels. Vowels may be uttered simultaneously with several of the consonants. Thus, if we put the tongue in the **l**-position we shall find little difficulty in articulating almost any vowel, although, of course, the back vowels are the easiest. Most of these consonant-modified vowels are of little practical importance. But there are classes of *point-modified* vowels which deserve notice. They are symbolized by the addition of the 'point-modifier' ⌊. The English point-consonant ω in *starry* is in itself almost a vowel, and if we carry the raised tongue-point position by which it is formed into the preceding vowel, we make SƱ]ƚωſ˖ into SƱ]ƚ⌊˧ωſ˖. If the point is turned back or 'inverted', we get]ƚ⌊c with a peculiar 'snarling' effect, common to most of the dialects of the south-west of England, and heard in such words as *hard*, *sir*.

Breathed and Whispered Vowels. If an open vowel such as] is uttered with gentle breath instead of voice, we get a scarcely audible sigh, in which however the characteristic effect of the vowel is still audible. If we take a high vowel such as ſ in *bit*, the friction of the breath is clearly audible, and still more so in the narrow ʃ. So also with ɫ and ɫ, which, when devocalized, sound like a weak *wh*. In French this devocalization of high vowels is frequent, as in [ʃSſ: *ainsi*. Voiceless vowels are indicated by the addition of the breath-modifier **:**.

VOWEL TABLE I (*A Handbook of Phonetics*, 1877, p. 16)

1 **ʌ** high-back- narrow	7 **ih** high-mixed- narrow N. Welsh tag*u*	13 **i** high-front- narrow F. f*i*n*i*	19 **A** high-back- wide	25 ***i*h** high-mixed- wide Occ. E. pr*e*tty	31 ***i*** high-front- wide E. b*i*t
2 **ɐ** mid-back- narrow E. b*u*t	8 **eh** mid-mixed- narrow G. gab*e*	14 **e** mid-front- narrow F. *été*	20 **a** mid-back- wide E. f*a*ther	26 ***e*h** mid-mixed- wide E. *e*ye (***e*h**[***i*h**])	32 ***e*** mid-front- wide Danish tr*æ*
3 ***ɒ*** low-back- narrow Occ. Sc. b*u*t	9 **æh** low-mixed- narrow E. b*ir*d	15 **æ** low-front- narrow E. *ai*r	21 ***a*** low-back- wide Sc. f*a*ther	27 ***æ*h** low-mixed- wide E. h*o*w (***æ*h**[**oh**])	33 ***æ*** low-front- wide E. m*a*n
4 **u** high-back- narrow-round F. s*ou*	10 **uh** high-mixed- narrow-round Swedish h*u*s	16 **y** high-front- narrow-round F. l*u*ne	22 ***u*** high-back- wide-round E. f*u*ll	28 ***u*h** high-mixed- wide-round Swedish *u*pp	34 ***y*** high-front- wide-round G. sch*ü*tzen
5 **o** mid-back- narrow-round G. s*o*	11 **oh** mid-mixed- narrow-round	17 **ə** mid-front- narrow-round F. p*eu*	23 ***o*** mid-back- wide-round N.G. st*o*ck	29 ***o*h** mid-mixed- wide-round F. h*o*mme	35 ***ə*** mid-front- wide-round N.G. sch*ö*n
6 **ɔ** low-back- narrow-round E. s*aw*	12 **ɔh** low-mixed- narrow-round	18 **œ** low-front- narrow-round F. p*eu*r	24 ***ɔ*** low-back- wide-round E. n*o*t	30 ***ɔ*h** low-mixed- wide-round	36 ***œ*** low-front- wide-round

E. = English. F. = French. G. = German. N. = North. Occ. = Occasional. Sc. = Scotch.

1 high-back-narrow ʅ ʌ. Gael. l*aogh*.	7 high-mixed-narrow Ɪ ï. Welsh *un*.	13 high-front-narrow ʃ i. Fr. s*i*.	19 high-back-wide ʅ *ɑ*.	25 high-mixed-wide Ɪ *ï* pretty.	31 high-front-wide ʃ *i* b*i*t. *see* sʃ℧. ʃ⊤ pit*y*, f*ear*.
2 mid-back-narrow] a. b*u*t.	8 mid-mixed-narrow ʅ ë. G. gab*e*. Amer. *ear*th ʅɪ.	14 mid-front-narrow [e. G. s*ee*. Sc. s*ay*. [⊥ Dan. s*e*.	20 mid-back-wide] *a*. f*a*ther.]⊦ Dan. m*a*ne.	26 mid-mixed-wide ʅ *ë*. *e*ye. bett*er*.	32 mid-front-wide [*e*. m*e*n. *say* s[ʃ⊤.
3 low-back-narrow J ɐ. Cockney p*ar*k.	9 low-mixed-narrow I ä. s*ir*.	15 low-front-narrow ʅ æ Swed. l*ä*ra.	21 low-back-wide J *ɒ*. Swed. m*a*t.	27 low-mixed-wide I *ä* h*o*w. Port. c*a*m*a*.	33 low-front-wide ʅ *æ*. m*a*n.
4 high-back-narrow- round ǂ u. Fr. s*ou*. Sc. b*oo*k. ʅ) Swed. *u*pp.	10 high-mixed-narrow- round Ŧ ü. Norw. h*u*s. Ŧ⊦ Swed. h*u*s.	16 high-front-narrow- round ƒ y. Fr. l*u*ne.	22 high-back-wide- round ǂ *u*. p*u*t. *too* ℧ǂɘ.	28 high-mixed-wide- round Ŧ *ü*. val*ue*.	34 high-front-wide- round ƒ *y*.
5 mid-back-narrow- round ǂ o. G. s*o*. ǂ) Swed. s*o*l.	11 mid-mixed-narrow- round ǂ ö.	17 mid-front-narrow- round ƒ ə. Fr. p*eu*. ƒ) G. *ü*ber.	23 mid-back-wide- round ǂ *o*. G. st*o*ck. b*o*y. n*o* ꞁǂɘ).	29 mid-mixed-wide- round ǂ *ö*. Fr. h*o*mme. foll*ow* >Jωǂǂ).	35 mid-front-wide- round ƒ *ə*. Fr. p*eu*r.
6 low-back-narrow- round Ɉ ɔ. l*aw*. Ɉ) Swed. s*å*.	12 low-mixed-narrow- round Ɨ ɔ̈.	18 low-front-narrow- round ƒ œ. Swed. f*ö*r.	24 low-back-wide- round Ɉ *ɔ*. n*o*t.	30 low-mixed-wide- round Ɨ *ɔ̈*.	36 low-front-wide- round ƒ *œ*. ƒ) G. g*ö*tter.

VOWEL TABLE III (*A Primer of Phonetics*, 1906 Edition, p. 24)

1 high-back-narrow ʅ ʌ.	7 high-mixed-narrow I ï. Welsh *un*. I˧ Russ. synŭ.	13 high-front-narrow ſ i. Fr. *si*.	19 high-back-wide ʅ *ɑ*.	25 high-mixed-wide I *ï*.	31 high-front-wide ſ *i*. b*i*t. *see* Sſɷ. ſ˔ pit*y*, f*ear*.
2 mid-back-narrow] a. b*u*t.	8 mid-mixed-narrow ʅ ë. G. gab*e*. occ. Am. *ear*th ʅɪ.	14 mid-front-narrow [e. G. s*ee*. Sc. s*ay*. [˗ Dan. s*e*.	20 mid-back-wide] *a*. f*a*ther.	26 mid-mixed-wide ʅ *ë*. bett*er*.	32 mid-front-wide [*e*. m*e*n. *say* S[ſ˔.
3 low-back-narrow J ɐ. Cockney p*ar*k.	9 low-mixed-narrow I ä. s*ir*.	15 low-front-narrow [æ. *ai*r.	21 low-back-wide J *ɒ*. Norw. m*a*t.	27 low-mixed-wide I *ä*. h*ow*. Port. c*ama*.	33 low-front-wide [*æ*. m*a*n.
4 high-back-narrow-round ɟ u. G. g*u*t. ɟ˫ Sc. b*oo*k.	10 high-mixed-narrow-round Ŧ ü. Swed. h*u*s.	16 high-front-narrow-round f y. Fr. p*u*r.	22 high-back-wide-round ɟ *u*. p*u*t. *too* ƆɟƐ.	28 high-mixed-wide-round Ŧ *ü*.	34 high-front-wide-round f *y*.
5 mid-back-narrow-round } o. G. s*o*. }) Swed. s*o*l.	11 mid-mixed-narrow-round ɟ ö.	17 mid-front-narrow-round { ə. Fr. p*eu*. {) G. *ü*ber.	23 mid-back-wide-round } *o*. b*o*y. *no* Ɩ}}).	29 mid-mixed-wide-round ɟ ö. Du. bet*e*r.	35 mid-front-wide-round { *ə*.
6 low-back-narrow-round Ɉ ɔ. l*aw*. Ɉ) Swed. s*å*.	12 low-mixed-narrow-round ɟ ɔ̈.	18 low-front-narrow-round ɟ œ. Fr. p*eu*r.	24 low-back-wide-round Ɉ *ɔ*. n*o*t.	30 low-mixed-wide-round ɟ *ɔ̈*. Swed. *u*pp.	36 low-front-wide-round ɟ *œ*. ɟ) G. g*ö*tter.

VOWEL TABLE IV (*A Primer of Phonetics*, 1906 Edition, p. 25)

37 high-in-mixed- narrow $ï_2$. Gael. *ao*.	43 high-out-back- narrow $ʌ^2$.	49 high-in-front- narrow i_2.	55 high-in-mixed- wide $\textit{ï}_2$.	61 high-out-back- wide $\textit{ʌ}^2$.	67 high-in-front- wide $\textit{i}_2$. pretty.
38 mid-in-mixed- narrow $ë_2$.	44 mid-out-back- narrow a^2.	50 mid-in-front- narrow e_2.	56 mid-in-mixed- wide $\textit{ë}_2$.	62 mid-out-back- wide $\textit{a}^2$. *up*; *eye*.	68 mid-in-front- wide $\textit{e}_2$.
39 low-in-mixed- narrow $ä_2$. Ir. s*i*r.	45 low-out-back- narrow $ɐ^2$.	51 low-in-front- narrow $æ_2$. Swed. l*ä*r.	57 low-in-mixed- wide $\textit{ä}_2$.	63 low-out-back- wide $\textit{ɒ}^2$. Dan. m*a*ne.	69 low-in-front- wide $\textit{æ}_2$.
40 high-in-mixed- narrow-round $ü_2$.	46 high-out-back- narrow-round u^2. Norw. h*u*s.	52 high-in-front- narrow-round y_2.	58 high-in-mixed- wide-round $\textit{ü}_2$.	64 high-out-back- wide-round $\textit{u}^2$. val*ue*.	70 high-in-front- wide-round $\textit{y}_2$.
41 mid-in-mixed- narrow-round $ö_2$.	47 mid-out-back- narrow-round o^2.	53 mid-in-front- narrow-round $ə_2$. Sc. g*ui*d.	59 mid-in-mixed- wide-round $\textit{ö}_2$.	65 mid-out-back- wide-round $\textit{o}^2$. foll*ow*.	71 mid-in-front- wide-round $\textit{ə}_2$.
42 low-in-mixed- narrow-round $\ddot{ɔ}_2$.	48 low-out-back- narrow-round $ɔ^2$.	54 low-in-front- narrow-round $œ_2$. Swed. g*ö*r.	60 low-in-mixed- wide-round $\textit{ɔ̈}_2$.	66 low-out-back- wide-round $\textit{ɔ}^2$. *O*ctober.	72 low-in-front- wide-round $\textit{œ}_2$.

Whispered vowels, which are indicated by the addition of the whisper-modifier ᴅ, are common in some languages, such as Portuguese, where *Oporto* is pronounced ɪ·ɒ'ʃωʃʊ'ɪᴅ. They may sometimes be heard in unstressed syllables in English, as in ʊlᴅ·ɵʃvl *together*.

A Primer of Phonetics, 1890, p. 20

Vowels are voice modified by different configurations of the superglottal passages, but without audible friction. By position they are either *back* (guttural), *front* (palatal), or *mixed*, that is, formed by a position intermediate between back and front. They have three degrees of elevation of the tongue, *high*, *mid*, *low*. When the tongue is lowered from the high position, the place of narrowing is at the same time shifted back. So we have altogether nine positions:

high-back	high-mixed	high-front
mid-back	mid-mixed	mid-front
low-back	low-mixed	low-front.

Each of these positions yields a different vowel-sound according as the tongue has the narrow or the wide shape. Intermediate positions are: *retracted* (⊣) and *advanced* (⊢), *raised* (⊥) and *lowered* (⊤). Each vowel-position can be further modified by *rounding* (labialization). Front vowels are rounded by the lips only (outer rounding), mixed and back vowels more by the cheeks (inner rounding). There are three degrees of lip- and cheek-contraction in rounding, high vowels having the narrowest, low vowels the widest lip-opening. When a vowel has a higher degree of rounding than belongs to its height, as when a mid vowel is formed with the rounding of a high vowel, it is said to be *over-rounded*, which is denoted by adding the 'rounder', as in ʃ) = the Swedish close *o*. The opposite phenomenon of *under-rounding* is denoted by adding the 'rounder' to the symbol of a front vowel, the 'inner rounder' (ɒ) to that of a mixed or back vowel, as in ſ) = Swedish *y*, lɒ = Swedish short *u*. Vowels are also capable of *point*-modification (\), the tip of the tongue being raised while the vowel-position is maintained.

The thirty-six elementary vowels are given in the annexed table in their Organic and Romic symbols, together with key-words. [This table is identical with Table II on p. 67 from the *Primer of Phonetics*, except that the keyword 'Sc. *book*' is omitted. *Ed.*]

Acoustically considered, a vowel is voice modified by a resonance-chamber, viz. the mouth. Every time we alter the position of the tongue and lips, we create a new resonance-chamber, which moulds the voice into a different vowel. Each vowel has an inherent pitch, due to the shape and size of the resonance-chamber. The following is the order of some of the chief vowels in pitch, beginning with the lowest:

ɫ; ɫ; ɟ; ɟ; ɟ; ɟ; J;];]; ɪ, ɫ;], [; I, f; ɩ; ɩ; [; [; ſ; ſ.
u; ***u***; o; *o*; ɔ; *ɔ*; *ɒ*; a; *a*; ä, œ; ë, ə; ï, y; *æ*; æ; *e*; e; *i*; i.

Vowels separated only by a comma have the same pitch. It will be observed that vowels of distinct formation are often alike in pitch and consequently in sound.

A History of English Sounds, 1888, pp. 2–4

Acoustic Qualities of Vowels. We have hitherto entirely ignored the acoustic effects of the vowels. This has been done designedly. The first and indispensable qualification of the phonetician is a thorough practical knowledge of the formation of the vowels. Those who try to learn new sounds by ear alone, without any systematic training in the use of their vocal organs, generally succeeded only partially. /Even in those exceptional cases in which a naturally quick ear combined with favourable occasions for practice enables a linguist to acquire an accurate pronunciation of foreign languages by imitation alone, his knowledge is little better than that of a parrot, for he is unable to record the sounds he has learnt or to teach them to others, and the results of his labours perish with him. In the case of those who have only an average ear, and still more of those who have a defective ear, organic training is indispensable. There can be no question that flexible organs well trained together with only an average ear, will yield better results than even an exceptionally good ear without organic training. Nor must it be forgotten that fineness of ear is not necessarily accompanied by flexibility of the vocal organs. Indeed, what is commonly called 'an ear for sounds', that is, the power of imitating sounds, depends quite as much on organic flexibility as on fineness of ear./

The test of /'ear' by itself/ ['a good ear'] is the power of discriminating sounds. This is an indispensable qualification for those who wish to write down sounds /by ear/ [from hearing], and must be carefully cultivated [by all students of phonetics]. /To recognize a sound with certainty under the various differences of quantity, force, environment, etc., is no easy test, and requires long practice. The student should accustom himself to repeat the different vowels in a loud voice, and should compare those that are most like, till he is able to distinguish them. He should also, if possible, hear them pronounced by voices of different register and quality, the effects of which are often confusing, especially when a man's voice is contrasted with a woman's or child's./ [In learning foreign sounds the habit of patient listening should be cultivated before everything. No attempt at imitation should be made till the acoustic impression has been fixed. Otherwise the student hears his own imperfect imitation as much as the correct sounds. It is important to hear the same sound pronounced by different voices. Hence the advantage of learning sounds in the country where the language they occur in is spoken. In his daily practice of portions of the vowel-table, the student should sometimes whisper the vowels, sometimes utter them in a loud voice, and compare the sounds of those that are most like, till he can distinguish them.]

It will soon be observed that vowels whose formation is distinct are often very similar in sound. This will be better understood if we consider that a vowel is, acoustically speaking, voice modified by a resonance chamber, viz. the mouth /(the influence of the pharynx being for the present ignored)/. Every time we /change the position of the tongue/ [move the tongue and lips] we create in reality a new resonance chamber, which moulds the voice into a different vowel. Every vowel can have its pitch raised or lowered by varying the length of the vocal chords, as when /the scale/ [a scale or a chord] is sung on any one vowel. But each vowel has besides an inherent pitch of its own, due to the shape and size of /the/ [its] resonance chamber. Thus, if ſ **i**, ȷ **a**, and ƚ **u** are all sung to the same note, we hear how much deeper /the pitch of/ ƚ **u** is than /that of/ ȷ **a**, while ȷ **a** is /also/ much deeper than ſ **i**. The best way, however, of hearing the /natural pitch/ [inherent pitches] of the vowels is to whisper them, for the pitch of the whisper itself being invariable, the differences caused by the resonance are clearly heard. The connection between the size and shape of the resonance chamber and the pitch is self-evident. /**i** evidently owes its high pitch to its being formed by a narrow channel in the front of the mouth, while the pitch of **a** is lowered by the greater size of its resonance chamber, and that of **u** by the narrowing of the lip-aperture, both **a** and **u** being formed in the back of the mouth. The wide forms of the front and mixed vowels are lower in pitch than the narrow ones, because of the greater width of the mouth cavity, but in the case of back vowels the wides are higher than the narrows. Rounding naturally lowers the pitch./ [Thus ſ owes its high pitch to its being formed by a narrow channel in the front of the mouth, while the pitch of ȷ is lowered by the greater size of its resonance-chamber, and that of ƚ by the narrowing of the lip-aperture, both ȷ and ƚ being formed in the back of the mouth, which, of course, gives them a deeper and more hollow sound independently of other influences. The wide forms of the front and mixed vowels are lower in pitch than the narrow ones, because of the greater width of the mouth cavity in the case of the wide vowels; but in the case of the back vowels the narrows have the lower pitch, because they retract the tongue more.]

/The following is the order of the vowels in pitch, according to Mr Bell, beginning with the lowest:

u, ***u***; **o**, ***o***; **ɔ**, ***ɔ*** { ***ɒ***, ***a***; **ɐ**, **a**; **ᴧ**, **ᴀ**; ***æh***, **æh**; ***eh***, **eh**; ***ih***, **ih** / ***ɔh***, **ɔh**; **oh**, ***oh***; **uh**, ***uh***; ***œ***, **œ**; ***ə***, **ə**; ***y***, **y** }
æ, **æ**; ***e***, **e**; ***i***, **i**./

[The exact pitches of the vowels have not yet been determined; we have not even got so far as to arrange them in the order of their pitches. The following is Mr Bell's order of the pitches of some of the chief vowels, beginning with the lowest, vowels having the same pitch being bracketed together:

ƚ ƚ } } Ɉ Ɉ J]] { I l I / ŧ ƒ ƒ } ɩ ɩ [[ſ ſ.

The pitches of the back vowels offer the greatest difficulties, especially in the back-rounded vowels. Thus an increase in the *force* of the whisper will raise the pitch of ƚ from one to two tones, by throwing the sound forward to the lips. But if we whisper the last six front vowels, we can hear that they rise uniformly by a semitone, making a chromatic scale.]

It is evident from the table that the same pitch may be produced by /distinct/ [different] modifications of the same resonance chamber, /which agrees with the remark already made, that vowels whose formation is distinct are often very similar in sound/. Thus, starting from ſ **i**, we can lower its pitch either by retraction of the tongue, giving I **ih**, or by rounding, which gives ƒ **y**, and consequently I **ih** and ƒ **y** have the same pitch, [the retraction of one vowel being equivalent to the rounding of the other,] and they are so alike in sound that those who hear I **ih** for the first time generally imagine it to be a round vowel. /Again, English people who hear **œ** for the first time generally imitate it by their own **æh**, and German phoneticians still regard E. **æh** and **ɐ** as 'obscure' varieties of **œ** and **ə**. Hence also the English imitation of the French **oh** or ***oh*** in *bonne* by the English **ɐ** in *bun.*/ [Hence also the tendency to confuse English ɪ in *err* with an open sound of German *ö* or French *eu.*]

It is also important to observe that such pairs as ſ ***i*** and [**e**, ƚ ***u*** and } **o** are as near in sound as ſ **i** and ſ ***i***, ƚ **u** and ƚ ***u***, /which differ only in narrowness and wideness/ [the order of pitches being [, ſ, ſ and ƚ, ƚ, }]. The explanation is precisely analogous to that of the similarity of I **ih** and ƒ **y**, namely, that the pitch of ſ **i** /can be deepened either by widening into ***i*** or lowering to **e**, the result being nearly the same in both cases, as shown by the French imitation of English ***i*** by **e**/ [is deepened by increasing the distance between tongue and palate, and so enlarging the resonance-chamber, and that this can be effected either by flattening the surface of the tongue, as in ſ, or by lowering the whole body of the tongue, as in [. ſ and [are very similar in sound, and some foreign phoneticians still ignore the difference, denoting ſ and [etc., by the same sign. Raised [˔ has the same pitch as ſ, from which it can hardly be distinguished when short]. Hence we get the following pairs of vowels extremely alike in sound, and consequently very liable to be confounded:

ſ *i* and [e; [̦ *e* and ɩ æ
f *y* and ⨍ ə; ⨍̦ *ə* and ɟ œ
ɫ *u* and] o;]̦ *o* and ȷ ɔ.

The mixed and round pairs already exemplified are also very close:

Ɪ ih and f y; Ɪ̦ *ih* and f *y*
ʅ eh and ⨍ ə; ʅ̦ *eh* and ⨍̦ *ə*
ɪ æh and ɟ œ; ɪ̦ *æh* and ɟ̦ *œ*.

/It is interesting to observe that these pairs are often confounded even in vernacular speech. It very seldom happens that (*Fn.*: As in Danish.) three such sounds as e, *e*, and æ are kept distinct in a language, the general rule being that when the distinction of 'close' and 'open' *e* is made, e is the close sound, while the open one is represented by ***e*** or **æ** indifferently. This is the case in English, and it is impossible to determine whether ***e*** or **æ** is the commoner sound in such words as *head*, *then*, etc.

/As regards the acoustic relations of mixed vowels to their corresponding fronts and backs, it must be noted that unrounded mixed vowels resemble more their corresponding fronts, rounded their back vowels, as is indicated by the symbols. The rounded mixed vowels owe their 'back' quality to their retention of the inner rounding of the back rounded vowels./

A Handbook of Phonetics, 1877, pp. 20–5,
and *A Primer of Phonetics*, 1890, pp. 24–8

If we start from a high-wide vowel, such as ſ, we shall find that the nearest vowel in sound is not [̦, but the narrow-mid [, while the nearest in sound to [̦ is another narrow vowel, the low ɩ. This agrees with the pitches of these vowels, for while [̦ is a whole tone lower than ſ, there is a descent of only a semitone from ſ to [; in fact, the series ſ [[̦ ɩ ɩ̦ forms a descending chromatic scale. It also agrees with the height of the tongue, for the flattening of the tongue in ſ widens the passage more than with ſ but not so much as with [, where the whole body of the tongue is lowered. The same relations exist not only between the front-round, but also between the back-round vowels. The unrounded back vowels may be disregarded here. The following pairs of wide and narrow vowels are, therefore, very similar in sound:

ſ *i*	and	[e;	[*e*	and	ɩ æ
f *y*	and	{ ə;	{ *ə*	and	ɫ œ
ɫ *u*	and	} o;	} *o*	and	ɟ ɔ.

. . . . .

Again, we can lower the pitch of ſ either by rounding or retraction, and in the resulting f and Ɪ these modifications balance one another exactly, so that the two vowels have the same pitch, and are very similar in sound. This gives us the following pairs of acoustically similar unrounded mixed and front-round vowels of the same height:

Ɪ ï	and	f y;	Ɪ *ï*	and	f *y*
ɭ ë	and	{ ə;	ɭ *ë*	and	{ *ə*
ɪ ä	and	ɫ œ;	ɪ *ä*	and	ɫ *œ*.

A History of English Sounds, 1888, pp. 43–4

As every alteration in the shape of the mouth produces a different vowel, the number of vowels is infinite. Hence what we call the vowels, **a**, **i** etc., are really *groups* of an indefinite number of vowels differing very slightly from one another.

Rounding. The shape of the mouth-passage by which vowels are formed depends partly on the position of the tongue, partly on that of the lips. If the lip-opening is narrowed while the tongue is in a certain position, the resulting vowel is said to be *rounded*. Thus **y** in French *lune* is the *round* vowel corresponding to the unrounded **ii**, which is nearly the sound in English *he*, both vowels having the same tongue-position.

Tongue-Retraction. The tongue-positions depend partly on the degree of *retraction* of the tongue, partly on its *height* or distance from the palate.

If the root of the tongue is drawn back, we have a *back* vowel, such as the **aa** in *father*. If the forepart of the tongue is advanced, we have a *front* vowel, such as **ii**. If the tongue is left in its neutral position, intermediate between back and front, we have a *mixed* vowel, such as **əə**.

Tongue-Height. If the tongue is raised as close to the palate as is possible without making the vowel into a consonant, a *high* vowel is formed. Thus **i** is a high-front vowel, **u**, as in *full*, a high-back-round vowel. There are two other degrees of height, *mid* and *low*. For convenience we may include mid and low vowels under the common name 'un-high' vowels, distinguishing them as *close* and *open*, according to the degree of openness of the mouth-passage. We denote open vowels, when necessary, by italics. French *é* in *été* is the mid-front-close vowel, or, more briefly, the front-close vowel, for when a vowel is not expressly called high, we assume it to be un-high. English ***e*** in *men* is the corresponding mid-front-open vowel. The Scotch vowel in *men* is more open than the English, being a low-front vowel; but these English and Scotch vowels are so similar that we include them under the common name 'front-open'. Very open vowels are called *broad.* **æ** in *man* is a broad front vowel. The distinction of close and open applies also to the high vowels. Thus French **i** in *fini* is the close high front vowel, English ***i*** in *finny* is the open high front vowel.

Acoustic Qualities of Vowels. If we compare the acoustic qualities of the vowels—that is, the impression they make on the ear—we find that they differ in pitch and clearness, close **i** having the highest pitch and clearest sound, while **u** has the deepest sound. Tongue-retraction and lip-rounding both have the same effect of lowering the pitch and dulling the sound of the vowels. Thus the back and mixed vowels **aa, əə** are duller in sound than the front vowels **i, e, æ**, and the front round vowel **y** is duller than the corresponding unrounded vowel **i**. Hence vowels formed in quite different ways often have the same pitch, which makes them very similar in sound. Thus the English mixed vowel **əə** and the French front round vowel **œ** in *peur* are very similar in sound.

The Vowels in Detail. The following are the most important vowels:

(A) Unrounded vowels.

a 'clear back'. This vowel occurs only long in English, in such words as **faaðə** *father, farther,* **aamz** *alms, arms.* Short **a** occurs in French and German, and in many English dialects, as in the Yorkshire *man.*

ɐ 'dull back'. The English vowels in *son, sun, courage* **kɐridʒ.**

ə 'mixed' or 'neutral' vowel. **təən** *turn,* **bəəd** *bird.* The short **ə** in **məəmə** *murmur* is a weak vowel.

i 'high front'. Close **i** in French *fini*, the short E. ***i*** being always open. Weak open **i**—which, when necessary, we write **ĭ**—as in **petĭ** *petty* is opener than the strong **i** in *pit*, being really intermediate between ***i*** and ***e***. Long close **ii** is the older English sound in such words as *see, sea, receive, machine*, and this sound is still preserved in Scotland and the North of England. In the South of England it is diphthongized into ***i*** followed by very close **i**, which is nearly the sound of the consonant **j** in *you*, so we write **sij**, etc.

e 'front'. French *é* is close front. The English vowel in *men, bread, leopard* **lepəd** is open front ***e***. Before **ə**—with which it forms a diphthong

—it is still opener, as in **feə** *fare, fair,* **ðeə** *there, their.* The long close front **ee** is still preserved in Scotch in such words as *name, day* where Standard E. has the diphthong ***e*i.**

æ 'broad front'. The E. vowel in *man, thresh.*

(B) Round vowels.

u 'high back round'. Close in French *sou,* the E. short ***u*** in *full, good* being always open. The older close **uu** in such words as *moon, move, you* **juu** is still kept in Scotland and the North of England, but in the South of England it becomes ***u*w** with a distinct **w.** Weak open **u,** as in *value,* is the high mixed round vowel, which, when necessary, we write **ü—væljü.**

o 'back round'. Close in French *beau* **bo.** Close **oo** in Scotch *no, know,* where Standard E. has the diphthong ***o*u.** The **o** in the diphthong ***o*i,** as in *boy,* is the same open sound. Weak **o,** as in *October,* is the open mixed vowel, which, when necessary, we write **ö—öktoubə.** Weak **öu,** as in *fellow,* is hardly to be distinguished from **ö.**

ɔ 'broad back round'. This is the sound of the E. short vowels in *not, what.* The long broad vowel is heard in such words as *naught, fall.* For convenience we write the short vowel **o,** the long **ɔ** in Standard E.— **not, nɔt.**

y 'high front round' = rounded **i.** French *une.* German *über.*

œ 'front-round'. Close in French *peu,* whose vowel is a rounded French *é.* Open in French *peur.*

Nasal Vowels. If a vowel is formed with the nose-passage open, it is said to be *nasal,* which we mark by ***n*.** Thus we have nasal **a, æ** in French *sang, sans* **sa*n*,** *vin* **væ*n*.**

. . . . .

The following table will show the relations of the chief vowels more clearly. Those marked * do not occur in English:

high-back *ʌ	high-mixed *ï	high-front i
back a; ɐ	mixed ə	front e; æ
high-back-round u	high-mixed-round ü	high-front-round *y
back-round o, ɔ	mixed-round ö	front-round *œ

The relations of the English vowels may be shown thus:

Short:	**ɐ**	**ə**	**i**	**e, æ**	**u**	**o**
Long:	**aa**	**əə**				**ɔ**
Half diphthongs:			**ij**	**ei**	**uw**	**ou**
Full diphthongs:	**ai, au**					**oi**
Murmur diphthongs:			**iə**	**eə**	**uə**	**ɔə**

A New English Grammar, 1891, pp. 230–4

Vowels are the result of different shapes of the voice-passage, each of which moulds the neutral voice-murmur **ə** into a different vowel, mainly by different positions of the tongue and lips, but without narrowing the passage so much as to cause an audible hiss or buzz, which would make the vowel into a consonant. The number of possible vowels is as unlimited as the number of the organic positions which produce them. But if we select certain definite positions as fixed points, it is easy to determine intermediate positions.

If we pass from such a vowel as **i** in *pit* to **ɔɔ** in *fall*, we can feel that the root of the tongue is drawn back, while in **i** the fore-part of the tongue is raised towards the palate. We may therefore call **i** a *front* and **ɔ** a *back* vowel. In **ə** the tongue is in an intermediate position which we call *mixed*. Again, if we pass from **i** to **æ** in *man*, we can feel that the front of the tongue is lowered, so that we may call **æ** a *low* vowel as opposed to the *high* **i**, in which the tongue is brought as close to the palate as is possible without making the **i** into a consonant—a kind of **j**. If in passing from one to the other we stop half-way, we get the *mid* vowel **e** in *men*. If, again, we stop half-way between **i** and **e** we get the second vowel in *pity*, which we may define either as 'lowered high-front' or 'raised mid-front'.

Every vowel may be *rounded* by bringing the lips together. Thus, if we round **i**, we get the high-front-round **y**, which is the sound of French *u*.

We have, lastly, the difficult distinction of *narrow* and *wide*. Thus French **i** in *si* is the high-front-narrow vowel corresponding to the wide English ***i*** in *it*, wide vowels being distinguished when necessary by italics. So also ***u*** in English *good* is the wide of the Scotch **u** in *good*, which is the high-back-narrow-round vowel. In the formation of narrow vowels the tongue and flexible parts of the mouth are made tense and convex in shape, while in wide vowels they are relaxed and flattened.

Vowels of different formation often have the same, or nearly the same, pitch or inherent tone. Thus the high pitch and clear tone of **i** or ***i*** may be dulled either by rounding or retraction of the tongue towards the high-mixed position of ï in Welsh *dyn* or *ï* in English *pretty*, the result being that ï has the same pitch as y, *ï* has the same pitch as *y*. There is the same relation between the low-mixed-narrow **ää** in English *purr* and the low-front-round narrow œœ in French *peur*, which are very similar in tone though formed in totally different ways.

'Widening' a vowel flattens the tone and therefore has an effect similar to lowering the whole body of the tongue; hence the high-front-wide ***i*** is similar in sound to the mid-front-narrow **e** in French *été*. Mid-front-wide ***e*** in English *men* resembles the low-front-narrow **ɛ** in Scotch *men* and English *care* so closely that we can class the two together as 'open' varieties of the 'close' French **e**. So also the mid-back-wide-round ***o*** in German *stock* and the low-back-narrow-round **ɔ** in English *fall* form acoustic pairs.

The History of Language, 1899, pp. 15–16

Mixed Vowels. When, after a preliminary study of Bell's Visible Speech, I sought instruction in phonetics from the author himself, I was disappointed to find that when I rounded the mixed vowels, Bell would not recognize the result as genuine mixed-round vowels, but only as muffled varieties of the corresponding mixed vowels: his mixed round vowels had more of the character of the corresponding back-round vowels.

After a time I learnt to form my mixed-round vowels to Bell's satisfaction. But when I tested my command of them by passing from them to the corresponding mixed vowels, the result never seemed quite right: the tongue seemed to require a slight shifting each time. For a long time I did not suspect any flaw in Bell's system, but attributed my difficulties to want of control of the tongue on my part.

When I revised my pronunciation of Swedish last year with a native of Stockholm, I heard a pronunciation of the short *u* in *upp* quite different from that to which I had accustomed myself. This new sound was much nearer in acoustic effect to our English vowel in *up*. For a long time I could not find a place for it in the vowel system. At last I identified it as a rounded form of the low-mixed-narrow vowel in English *sir*.

A careful comparison of the new vowel with the one which I had hitherto, following Bell, been accustomed to regard as the normal low-mixed-narrow-round vowel, now showed that the latter was 'mixed' in position only: it was simply a back vowel formed with the whole body of the tongue advanced into the middle of the mouth. The real difference between it and the new vowel was not, as I was at first inclined to believe, the result of any difference in the rounding, but in the latter being formed with the tongue flat in the mouth while the former retained the slope of a back vowel.

The term mixed, in fact, was found to be ambiguous; it had hitherto been used to imply (1) position in the middle of the mouth half-way between back and front, and (2) flatness of the tongue as opposed to the slope of the normal back and front vowels. Bell's mixed vowels were, therefore, 'mixed' in both senses, while his mixed round vowels were mixed only in the former sense.

If a back vowel, that is, a 'back-slope' vowel, can be formed in the mixed position, there seems no reason why a flat vowel could not be formed in the back position. A few trials soon convinced me not only that it was quite easy to form such a mixed vowel as that in English '*sir*' with the tongue retracted to the back position, but that the resulting vowels had a distinct acoustic quality of their own.

Lastly, I found that it was possible to retract the front vowels into the mixed position, although this series had not so distinctive an acoustic effect as the others.

The general result was to add three new columns to Bell's vowel-square, thereby making it into an oblong, and raising the number of normal elementary vowels from 36 to 72 . . .

If we distinguish between 'mixed' position and 'flat' shape of the tongue, we should naturally call the three new series:

back-flat back-mixed front-mixed.

But this is confusing; and with a view to disturbing Bell's nomenclature as little as possible, and bearing in mind that Bell's mixed-round vowels (in the above terminology 'back-mixed-round') are merely back vowels advanced a step further in the mouth, I suggest using the term 'out' to imply that the position is so much 'outer' that the tongue is in the full mixed position. So also 'in' may be used to imply that a vowel is retracted into the mixed position. So I would substitute for the above names the following:

in-mixed out-back in-front.

In accordance with this nomenclature we can provisionally indicate the in-vowels by doubling the mark of retraction (thus ⊣⊣), and the out-vowels by doubling the mark of advancing (⊢⊢).

This extension of the vowel-scheme really simplifies it in some respects. Many vowels which before seemed anomalous or intermediate formations, now fall into their places as normal formations. The extension has not only led to a more correct analysis, but has provided places for some vowels that formerly would not fit in at all.

To the in-mixed series belongs undoubtedly the Scotch Gaelic vowel in *laogh*, which has more of the *u* quality than the genuine high-back-narrow vowel has. This *u*-quality is the natural result of the long narrow channel caused by the tongue being flattened instead of sloping downwards from root to tip.

If I form this Gaelic vowel and then lower the tongue from the high-in-mixed-narrow to the corresponding low-position, I get a vowel which is one of the vowels which in Irish-English are substitutes for the English vowel in *sir*, from which it differs only in having the flat tongue retracted from the mixed to the back position.

The in-mixed-round vowels have a most peculiar hollow sound, which I seem to have heard as individual substitutes for the ordinary back-round vowels.

To the out-back series belong most of the vowels that were formerly put under mixed-round, such as the Norwegian *u* in *hus*.

But the Swedish *u* in *hus* seems to be the same as the West-of-England vowel in *two*, which I long ago analysed as high-mixed-narrow with a rounding different from that of the Norwegian *u* in *hus*, of which I regarded the corresponding Swedish sound as simply an outer form. Now, of course, I explain the difference as the result of difference in the shape of the configurative passage. The Norwegian sound is, therefore, **u**⊦⊦, the Swedish genuine rounded ï. The short Swedish *u* is, as already stated, the genuine low-mixed-narrow-round.

The investigation of the non-round out-back vowels has yielded some interesting results.

I have for some time been puzzled by a wide variety of the English vowel in *up*, which I think now is my own natural pronunciation. It is not the low-mixed-wide vowel, which formerly was the only place I could find for it. I find now that this is the out form of the vowel in *father*, from which it is obtained by simply moving the tongue forward into the middle of the mouth while preserving the slope of the tongue. The first element of the diphthong in *eye* seems to be the same vowel.

The out-low-back-wide vowel is the sound which I formerly regarded as the outer form of the mid-back vowel in *father*. It is interesting to observe that Mr Eijkman, after careful measurements, has come to the conclusion that the long thin Dutch *a* is a low, not a mid vowel. I now agree with him.

To the in-front series belongs the English *e* in *pretty*, which is certainly not a flat vowel. If it were a genuine high-mixed vowel, English learners would not have such difficulty with the high-mixed position.

The Swedish and East-Norwegian sound in *der* is evidently the in-front vowel corresponding to the normal low-front-narrow vowel in English *there*. It will be observed that both in-front vowels are the result of *r*-influence.

Of course, these views are to some extent still only tentative, but as I cannot ignore them in my own teaching, I thought it best to make them known at once, without attempting the laborious task of finding out how far they have already been anticipated, or are implied in the systems of other phoneticians, some of which I have great difficulty in understanding. Meanwhile, all that I give here is the result of my own direct observation.

'Mixed Vowels', *Le Maître phonétique*, 1901, pp. 144–7

Tongue-Positions. As each new position of the tongue produces a new vowel, and as the number of possible positions is infinite, it follows that the number of possible vowel-sounds is also infinite. It is necessary therefore to select certain definite fixed points to serve as marks, as it were, of latitude and longitude, whence the intermediate positions can be measured and defined with more or less minuteness.

The horizontal movements of the tongue produce two well-marked classes of vowels: 'back', such as **aa**, **ɔ**, **u**, and 'front', such as **ii**, **e**, **æ**. In the former the tongue is retracted into the back of the mouth, and its forepart is pressed down, so that the tongue slopes down from the back to the front of the mouth. In the latter the front of the tongue is raised towards the front of the palate, as in the front open consonant **j**, so that the tongue slopes down from the front backwards. The retraction of the tongue in back vowels may be easily tested by putting the little finger inside the lower teeth while forming first the front vowel **æ** and then the back vowel **ɔ**. While the **æ**-position is being maintained the tip of the tongue presses on the finger. When the change is made to the **ɔ**-position, the tip of the tongue is drawn back quite clear of the finger. There is a third class of 'mixed' vowels, in which the tongue does not slope either way, and is neither retracted nor advanced, but lies flat in a neutral position; **əə** is a mixed vowel.

The vertical movements of the tongue, which are accompanied by, and partly depend on, the raising and lowering of the lower jaw, produce various degrees of height or distance of the tongue from the palate. In a 'high' vowel, such as **ii**, the tongue—in this case, the front of the tongue—is raised as high and as close to the palate as is possible without causing audible friction; while if it is lowered as much as possible from this position without otherwise altering the relative position of tongue and palate, we obtain the corresponding 'low' vowel. Thus **æ** is a low-front, **ɔ** a low-back, and **əə** a low-mixed vowel. If the tongue stops exactly half-way, we obtain the normal 'mid' position, as in the first elements of **ei** and **ou**, which are mid-front and mid-back respectively.

In this way the whole mouth may be mapped out schematically into nine squares:

high-back	high-mixed	high-front
mid-back	mid-mixed	mid-front
low-back	low-mixed	low-front

It follows from what has been said that each of these squares admits of further subdivisions. English **i** and **ii** are both high-front vowels; but if we isolate the beginning of the vowel in *eat* and compare it with the vowel in *it*, we shall find that the tongue is raised higher in the long than in the short vowel, and that the tongue can be raised even higher than it is in the long vowel without developing consonantal friction and becoming constricted.

It may here be remarked that vowels as they actually occur in speech are seldom raised or lowered to their extreme positions; which, therefore, can hardly be regarded as the normal ones. Nevertheless, in studying the vowel-system as a whole apart from any one language, it is important that the learner should get into the habit of always forming the high and low vowels in the extreme rather than in the less definite normal position—or rather, positions—so that the points from which he obtains the normal mid-position of each vowel may be as definite as possible.

If then we regard English **ii** as beginning with the normal high-front vowel, we can define any approximation to the high position as 'raised' **i˔**, while any position lower than normal can be distinguished as 'lowered' **i˕**. In Scotch pronunciation **i** is lowered still more; so much so indeed that it must be regarded rather as a raised mid-vowel—**e˔**.

If now we compare the English **æ** with the ideal low-front vowel, we shall find that in addition to not being fully lowered, it is not fully front: in our **æ** the tongue is slightly retracted. We define it therefore as 'inner', which we mark by adding the 'inner modifier', **æ⊣**, just as we defined the height of **i** by adding the 'raiser' ˔ and the 'lowerer' ˕. When a back vowel is advanced towards the front of the mouth, it is said to be in the 'outer' position; for which, again, an appropriate 'outer modifier' is provided. Thus **u⊢** is the English sound in *put*, **u⊣** the German sound in *mutter*.

It is, of course, possible to combine the vertical and horizontal modifiers, as in **æ⊣˔** = the English vowel in *man*. Such combinations as ⊣⊢, ˔˕ may be used to show expressly the normal positions implied generally by the absence of such modifiers.

In this way each of the nine squares may be again subdivided into nine smaller ones; thus with the front-vowel square:

i⊣⊥	**i**⊥	**i**⊢⊥
i⊣	**i**	**i**⊢
i⊣⊥	**i**⊤	**i**⊢⊤

Further subdivisions would go beyond the limits of appreciation of even the most sensitive and highly trained ear.

Narrow and Wide. This important distinction applies to all vowels: every vowel, whatever its position in the scale, must be either narrow (tense) or wide (lax). In the Narrow Romic notation wide vowels are distinguished by being put in italics. French **i** in *fini* and English **i** in *finny* are both high-front vowels, but the former is narrow [**i**], the latter wide [***i***]. In passing from [***i***] to [**i**] the passage between the front of the tongue and the palate is further narrowed, not by raising the whole body of the tongue, but by altering its shape: in a narrow vowel the tongue is bunched or made convex lengthways, and there is a feeling of tension or clenching; in wide vowels the tongue is relaxed and comparatively flattened. The change from wide to narrow may be illustrated by laying the hand loosely on the table, and then tightening its muscles so as to draw the finger-tips back a little, and raise the knuckles, so that the upper surface of the hand becomes more convex.

If we lower the tongue, starting from [**i**] and [***i***] respectively, we obtain the two parallel series:

high-front-narrow	[**i**]:	F. *si*	high-front-wide [***i***]:	*it*
mid-front-narrow	[**e**]:	F. *été*	mid-front-wide [***e***]:	*ate*
low-front-narrow	[**æ**]:	*air*	low-front-wide [***æ***]:	*at*

. . . . .

It will be observed that the three narrow vowels are quite distinct from one another in sound, and so also the three wide ones, but that certain narrow vowels are very similar to certain wide vowels. Thus [**æ**] and [***e***] are so alike in sound, especially when short, that they may from the 'broad' point of view be regarded as interchangeable representatives of the 'open' vowel corresponding to the 'close' [**e**]. It is only by careful and repeated hearing that we can observe that the low vowel is a little broader and more open in sound than the mid one. This broader sound of the **e** is frequent in English, especially in the North English and Scotch dialects.

To understand these relations it is necessary to realize that a vowel is, acoustically speaking, voice modified by a resonance-chamber or resonator, namely the mouth. Every time we move the tongue and lips we create a new resonance-chamber which moulds the voice into a new vowel.

The pitch of every spoken or sung vowel can be raised by tightening, and lowered by relaxing the vocal chords, as when a scale is sung on one vowel. But each vowel has, besides, an inherent pitch of its own, which is the result of the size and shape of its resonance-chamber. Thus if **i**, **a**, and **u** are all sung on the same note, it is easy to hear that the first is the highest, the third the lowest in pitch, that **u** is deeper than **a**, while **a** itself is deeper than **i**. The best way of hearing the inherent pitches of the vowels is to whisper them, for this gives the pitch of the resonance-chamber, which is invariable: a whispered vowel cannot be sung.

If, then, we whisper the three narrow front vowels in the order high, mid, low, we shall find that [**e**] is a tone lower than [**i**], and that [**æ**] is a tone lower than [**e**]. If we whisper the corresponding wide vowels in the same order, we shall observe the same relation between their pitches, each wide being a semitone lower than the corresponding narrow vowel, so that if we whisper all six in the order, [**i**, ***i***, **e**, ***e***, **æ**, ***æ***], the series will form a descending semitonic or chromatic scale.

The connexion between the size and shape of the resonance-chamber and the pitch is clear enough in the case of these vowels. [**i**] owes its high pitch to its being formed by a very narrow, short passage in the front of the mouth. In [*i*] the flattening of the tongue lengthens and widens the passage, and consequently dulls the sound. It is still more dulled in [e], in whose formation the whole body of the tongue is lowered. In fact, in the series [**i**, ***i***, e, *e*, æ, *æ*] there is progressive widening of the configurative passage. This may easily be tested experimentally by pressing the little finger against the palate, and trying to articulate the series against it; it will be observed that the strong pressure of the tongue against the finger in forming the first vowel is distinctly relaxed in the second, and still more in the third, and so on till the extreme [*æ*] is reached, in whose formation the tongue does not touch the finger at all.

Rounding. Rounding can, of course, be added to all the tongue-positions.

The degrees of rounding are infinite. As fixed points we distinguish three, corresponding to the three heights of the tongue, the general rule being that the higher the tongue-position of the round vowel, the narrower the lip-passage, as may be seen by comparing the back round vowels:

high-back-narrow-round	[**u**]: F. *sou*	h.-b.-wide-r.	[***u***]: *good*
mid-back-narrow-round	[**o**]: F. *beau*	m.-b.-w.-r.	[***o***]: *oil*
low-back-narrow-round	[**ɔ**]: *all*	l.-b.-w.-r.	[***ɔ***]: *not*

. . . . .

In going down either of these series it will be seen as well as felt that as the tongue is lowered from the high-back position, the lip-passage is progressively expanded. In 'high-rounding' the lip-passage is made as small as possible without causing friction, in 'mid-rounding' there is a wider opening of the lips, and in 'low-rounding' they are only drawn together a little at their corners.

But abnormal rounding also occurs. There is no difficulty, for instance, in combining mid position of the tongue with high rounding, as in the second element of **ou** in *no*, which differs from the first only in being formed with high instead of mid rounding, the position of the tongue remaining unchanged throughout the whole diphthong. This kind of abnormal rounding is called 'over-rounding', and is expressed by adding the 'rounder' to the symbol of the corresponding normally rounded vowel. Thus the Narrow Romic notation of English **ou** is [***oo***)].

It is also possible to under-round. The vowel in *good* is 'under-rounded' in the dialects of the North-West of England: the high position of the back of the tongue is retained, while the lips are relaxed almost to low rounding. Under-rounding is expressed by adding the rounder to the symbol of the corresponding un-round vowel; thus the vowel in question is written [***ɹ***)]. This vowel has to a Southern ear a sound intermediate between that of *put* and *putty*.

In comparing narrow and wide **u** it will be observed that there is a tendency to pout the lips more in the former. The same difference is observable, though in a less degree, in **o** and **ɔ**. This pouting is only a secondary phenomenon, which is the result of the strong general contraction in the back of the mouth, with which back vowels are made narrow. Lip-pouting does not sensibly modify the acoustic effect of a vowel: it only makes the rounding a little more marked.

. . . . .

It is, of course, just as easy to round front as back vowels, although front-round are not so frequent in languages as back-round vowels.

They do not occur in Standard English. But the student should now learn to round at least the narrow front vowels, by which he will obtain the following well-marked series of vowels, all of which occur in French:

high-front-narrow-round	[y]: F. *pur*
mid-front-narrow-round	[ə]: F. *peu*
low-front-narrow-round	[œ]: F. *peur*

What has been said of the relations between tongue height and rounding in the back-round applies equally to the front-round vowels. Here also we find occasional abnormal rounding. Thus if [ə] is over-rounded into [ə›] by exaggerating its mid into high rounding, we obtain the North German long vowel in *über*, which has a duller sound than that of the French *u*.

. . . . .

Back (*un-round*) *Vowels.* These are obtained by unrounding the back-round vowels already described:

high-back-narrow	[ʌ]	high-back-wide	[*ʌ*]
mid-back-narrow	[a]: *up*	mid-back-wide	[*a*]: *father*
low-back-narrow	[ɐ]: occ. F. *pas*	low-back-wide	[ɒ]: F. *pas*

. . . . .

Mixed Vowels. These are denoted in Broad Romic by two dots over the symbol of the front or back vowel of the same height, whichever is most convenient. The un-round mixed vowels are:

high-mixed-narrow	[ï]: N. Welsh u*n*	high-mixed-wide	[*ï*]
mid-mixed-narrow	[ë]: Sc. *better*	mid-mixed-wide	[*ë*]: *better* [ë˔]
low-mixed-narrow	[ä]: *sir*	low-mixed-wide	[*ä*]: *how*

. . . . .

From the acoustic point of view it is important to note that the mixed vowels have the same pitch as the corresponding front-round vowels. Thus [ï] has the same pitch as [y], and [ä] has the same as [œ], which explains why French *peur* sounds like *purr* to an English ear. Speaking acoustically, we may say that [ä] is the [æ] of *care*, obscured, not by rounding, as French [œ] is, but by flattening the tongue.

The round mixed vowels are not frequent in language, being mostly vague and indistinct in their acoustic character; their rounding is inner; outer rounding only muffles them:

h.-m.-n.-r.	[ü]: W.E. *two*	h.-m.-w.-r.	[*ü*]
m.-m.-n.-r.	[ö]	m.-m.-w.-r.	[*ö*]: Dutch *beter*
l.-m.-n.-r.	[ɔ̈]	l.-m.-w.-r.	[*ɔ̈*]: N. Ir., Swed. *full.*

Shifted Vowels. We have already seen that all back vowels do not have exactly the same degree of tongue-retraction: we distinguish between inner and outer back. It we start with the fully retracted [*u*˧] of German *mutter*, *und*, and shift the tongue progressively forward in the mouth, without otherwise altering its position relative to the palate, we at last move it right out into the middle of the mouth, into the position of a mixed vowel. This is called the 'out' position, and is denoted by the addition of the 'out-shifter': [*u*ɔ]. This is the vowel in the second—unstressed—syllable of **vælju** *value*, although many have only [*u*˫] for weak **u**. Narrow long [uɔ] is the N. Ir. vowel in *you*.

An out-back vowel is, therefore, one which, while retaining the slope of a back vowel, has the place of a mixed vowel. The round out-back vowels have nothing of the acoustic quality of the mixed vowels, and yet are quite distinct from the fully retracted back vowels: they are intermediate in sound between them and the corresponding front-round vowels; thus [uɔ] has a sound between that of [u] and [y].

[*o*] and [ɔ] are also shifted to the out-position in unstressed syllables in English, as in the last syllable of *solo* [oɔ*o*ɔ], and the first of *October* [ɔɔ].

By unrounding the former of these we obtain the mid-out-back-wide [*a*ɔ], which is the first element of E. **ai**, and is a frequent substitute for [a] in *come up*. This vowel has something of the acoustic effect of a mixed vowel.

By unrounding [ɔɔ] we obtain the low-out-back-wide, which is the thin French *a* in *la patte*, and a frequent substitute for æ in many English dialects. It has a clearer sound than [*a*ɔ], just as [*ä*] is clearer than [*ë*]; acoustically it is between [*a*] and [*æ*].

Just as a back vowel may be shifted forward into the out-position, so also a front vowel may be shifted back into the 'in' position, denoted by the 'in-shifter' [ꞓ], although the difference between in and inner front is not generally so marked as that between out and outer back. High-in- (or inner-) front-wide [*i*ꞓ] is frequent in such words as *pretty* and *prince*. Mid-in-front-narrow is one of the many pronunciations of the vowel written *ui* in Sc. in such words as *guid* 'good'.

Mixed vowels also have an in-position, obtained by retracting them into the full back position while keeping the tongue flat, instead of sloping it from back to front as in a genuine back vowel. If the [ä] of *sir* is treated in this way, we get the low-in-mixed-narrow [äc], heard in the Irish pronunciation of *come up, sir!* [ïc] is the most usual pronunciation of Scotch Gaelic *ao*, as in *gaoth*, 'breeze', where the *th* is silent.

Table of Vowels. The following tabulation of the vowels will be found convenient for reference, and practice in passing from one to the other:

1. ʌ	7. ï	13. i	19. *ʌ*	25. *ï*	31. *i*
2. a	8. ë	14. e	20. *a*	26. *ë*	32. *e*
3. ɐ	9. ä	15. æ	21. *ɒ*	27. *ä*	33. *æ*
4. u	10. ü	16. y	22. *u*	28. *ü*	34. *y*
5. o	11. ö	17. ə	23. *o*	29. *ö*	35. *ə*
6. ɔ	12. ɔ̈	18. œ	24. *ɔ*	30. *ɔ̈*	36. *œ*

37. ïc	43. ʌɔ	49. ic	55. *ïc*	61. *ʌɔ*	67. *ic*
38. ëc	44. aɔ	50. ec	56. *ëc*	62. *aɔ*	68. *ec*
39. äc	45. ɐɔ	51. æc	57. *äc*	63. *ɒɔ*	69. *æc*
40. üc	46. uɔ	52. yc	58. *üc*	64. *uɔ*	70. *yc*
41. öc	47. oɔ	53. əc	59. *öc*	65. *oɔ*	71. *əc*
42. ɔ̈c	48. ɔɔ	54. œc	60. *ɔ̈c*	66. *ɔɔ*	72. *œc*

The Sounds of English, 1908, pp. 24–39

Vowels. The most obvious distinction between vowels is that which depends on the share of the lips in their articulation. In such non-round vowels as **i** and **a** the lips are passive, or even separated and spread out at their corners, by which the vowels assume a clearer resonance. If, on the other hand, the lips are actively approximated, they become the round vowels **y** and 'open' **o** respectively.

Vowels are formed with different degrees of rounding. As a general rule, the narrowness of the lip-passage corresponds to the narrowness of the mouth-passage. Thus, in passing from the vowel of *too* to those of *no* and *saw* the back of the tongue is progressively lowered, and the rounding is diminished in the same proportion.

But there is also abnormal rounding. Thus, if we pronounce **o** with the lips in the position they have in forming **u**, the resulting 'over-rounded' vowel sounds half-way between **o** and **u**; the second element of the diphthong **ou** in *go* is formed in this way. Conversely, the **u** in *put* is 'under-rounded' in the North of England: the tongue position is kept, but the lips are only brought together a little at the corners, as in **ɔ**.

The mouth positions of the vowels are the result of two factors: (1) the height of the tongue—its nearness to the palate—and (2) the degree of its retraction. Bell distinguishes three degrees of height: in his system, **u** is 'high', the **o** of *boy* is 'mid', and the **ɔ** of *saw* 'low'. He also has three degrees of retraction: in 'back' vowels, such as **u**, the root of the tongue is drawn to the back of the mouth, and the whole tongue slopes down from back to front. In 'front' vowels, such as **i**, the front of the tongue is raised towards the hard palate, so that the tongue slopes down from front to back.

Most of these slope-positions yield vowels of a distinct and clear resonance. There is also a class of 'flat' vowels, such as **ə**, in which the tongue is in a more or less neutral position. If the tongue is raised from the low-flat position of **əə** in *bird* to the high position, we get the **ï** of North Welsh *dyn* 'man', which, as already observed, is acoustically similar to **y**.

The flat vowels were called 'mixed' by Bell, in accordance with his view that they are the result of combining back and front articulation. And although this view is now generally abandoned, the term 'mixed' is still retained by the English school of phoneticians.

In this way Bell mapped out the whole mouth by the following cardinal points:

high-back	high-mixed	high-front
mid-back	mid-mixed	mid-front
low-back	low-mixed	low-front.

In this arrangement 'high-back', etc., are fixed points like those of latitude and longitude. Thus normal 'high' means that the tongue is raised as close to the palate as is possible without causing consonantal friction, and 'back' implies retraction of the same kind. Intermediate positions are defined as 'raised', 'lowered', 'inner', 'outer'.

The most original and at the same time the most disputed part of Bell's vowel-scheme is his distinction of 'primary' and 'wide'. All vowels fall under one of these categories. Thus, the primary French **i** and the corresponding English wide ***i*** are both high-front vowels, and yet they are distinct in sound: the English vowel is a semitone lower in pitch. Bell explained the greater openness of the wide vowels as the result of greater expansion of the pharynx; and he considered the other class to be most nearly allied to the consonants—whence their name 'primary'—the voice-passages in the formation of primary vowels being expanded only so far as to remove all fricative quality. But alterations in the shape of the pharynx have only a sound-colouring, not a sound-modifying, effect; and Sweet showed that the distinction depends on the shape of the tongue, and accordingly substituted 'narrow' for Bell's 'primary'. He also showed that the distinction applies to consonants as well as vowels: thus the narrow French **w** in *oui* is a consonantization of the narrow French **u** in *sou*, while the English **w** preserves the wide quality of the ***u*** in *put*.

In forming narrow sounds there is a feeling of tension in that part of the tongue where the sound is formed, the tongue being clenched or bunched up lengthwise, so as to be more convex than in its relaxed or 'wide' condition.

The distinction between narrow and wide can often be ignored in practical phonetic writing, for it generally depends on quantity; length and narrowness, shortness and wideness going together. When the distinction is marked, wide vowels may be expressed by italics, as in German **biinə**, **b*i*n**.

Bell's category of 'mixed-round' vowels had from the beginning been a source of difficulty to students of *Visible Speech*. But it was not till 1901 that Sweet showed that they are only mixed as regards position: they are really the corresponding back-round vowels moved forward into the middle of the mouth while preserving the slope of the back vowels, instead of having the tongue flat as in the (unround) mixed vowels. They are 'out-back' vowels: there is an exaggeration of the outer back position of such a back-round vowel as the English ***u*** compared with the full back ***u*** in German *mutter*.

In the same way by moving the tongue backwards while forming a front vowel another series of 'in-front' vowels is obtained.

The 'in-mixed' vowels are obtained by shifting the neutral mixed positions into the full back position, keeping the tongue flat, so that these vowels might also be called 'back-flat'.

The out-back, in-front, and in-mixed vowels are included under the common designation of 'shifted', as opposed to 'normal' vowels.

There is a large number of other vowel-schemes, of which a survey will be found in W. Vietor's *Elemente der Phonetik*. Many of the older ones are in the form of triangles, with the three chief vowels *a*, *i*, *u* at the three corners, the other vowels being inserted between these extremes according to their acoustic relations. Since the appearance of *Visible Speech* many attempts have been made to fit his [*sic*. Ed.] new vowels into these older schemes.

Of all the vowel-schemes the one now most generally known is perhaps that of the International Phonetic Association already mentioned. In this scheme the distinction of narrow and wide, though admitted and occasionally marked, is not an integral part of the system, the vowels being classified first as 'velar' (back) and 'palatal' (front), and then according to openness as 'close', 'half-close', 'medium', 'half-open', and 'open'.

'Phonetics', *Encyclopædia Britannica*, 11th Edn., 1911, pp. 463–4

Diphthongs and Triphthongs. If two vowels are uttered with one impulse of stress, so as to form a single syllable, the combination is called a *diphthong*, such as **oi** in *oil.* Most diphthongs have the stress on the first element. If three vowels are combined in this way, we have a triphthong, as in **faiə** *fire.* A simple long vowel, such as **əə**, is called a *monophthong.*

. . . . .

We call **ei, ou**; **ij, uw** *half diphthongs*, because they are not very distinct, their two elements differing only in height.

Full diphthongs, on the other hand, such as **ai, au, oi** are made up of vowels as distinct as possible from one another. But in English as in many other languages, the elements of such diphthongs are not kept so distinct as they might be. Thus, while the diphthong in Italian *aura* is really a clear **a** followed by a high close **u**, the corresponding English diphthong in *house* begins with a mixed vowel resembling **æ**, and ends with an indistinct mixed **ö**, the English diphthong **ou** ending nearly in the same way. So also the English diphthong in *why, time* begins with a mixed vowel and ends in a sound between ***i*** and ***e***. The English **ei, oi** end in the same way. So by writing **haus, whai, taim** we merely indicate a movement from openness to closeness either of the mouth-passage or the lip-passage.

There is another class of *murmur diphthongs* ending in **ə**, as in *hear, here* **hiə**, *fare, fair* **feə**, *poor* **puə**, *pure* **pjuə**, *more* **mɔə.** There are also murmur triphthongs, as in *fire* **faiə**, *loyal* **loiəl.**

A New English Grammar, 1891, pp. 229–30, 233–4

4. *Consonants*

[The extracts in this section are arranged in the main so that the shorter more concise accounts appear after the detailed ones, concluding with the relevant passages in Sweet's article in the 1911 edition of the *Encyclopædia Britannica.* Sweet's papers on the Arabic throat-sounds follow as a tailpiece. These latter are not only valuable for the vivid picture they present of the great phonetician at work, but also because Sweet's excursion into Arabic modified his views about the articulation of certain consonants. This is reflected in the differing descriptions of the throat sounds (pp. 45 f., 49, 121–6), and in the changes in the symbols used for them in columns 1 and 11 on Table VII as contrasted with Table VI on p. 104. It also accounts for the expansion of the consonant classes by place from five (see pp. 94, 96, 99, 102) to six in the later editions of the *Primer of Phonetics* (see p. 99). In *The Sounds of English* (see p. 110) and in the *Encyclopædia* article (p. 119) these classes are further expanded to seven, by the separation of 'lip-teeth' and 'lip' consonants.

Of the tables on pages 103–5 it is further remarked that in order to facilitate comparison, numbers which do not appear in the original texts have been added to the columns in Tables V and VI, following the usage in the later editions of the *Primer of Phonetics*, as shown in Table VII. The table of consonants in *A History of English Sounds* is the same as that in the first edition of the *Primer* (i.e. Table VI), except that the *History* has the symbol **ɫ** where the *Primer* uses λ. It will be observed that the glottal stop, which in Table V appears among the voiced consonants, is transferred to the unvoiced consonants in Tables VI and VIII.—Note also the addition of 'Dutch *w*' to Table VII and Sweet's vacillation between the terms 'divided' and 'side' for one of the classes by form.

In the long passage beginning on p. 97 the differences in the texts of the first and revised editions of the *Primer of Phonetics* are shown by enclosing passages exclusive to the former in sloping lines, and passages exclusive to the latter in square brackets.

Other points of detail recommended to the reader's attention are the nice distinction Sweet draws between 'out-back **k**' and retracted **c** (p. 113); his insistence in the *Primer* that 'narrowness' and 'wideness' are not to be confused with 'tenseness' and 'looseness' (pp. 99, 110. But cf. p. 84 where 'narrow' and 'wide' appear to be equated with 'tense' and 'lax'); and his varying assessment of the acoustic qualities of **f** and **θ** (pp. 114, 116). *Ed.*]

A consonant is the result of audible friction, /squeezing/ or stopping of the breath in some part of the mouth /(or occasionally of the throat)/ [or throat]. The main distinction between vowels and consonants is that while in the former the mouth configuration merely modifies the vocalized breath, which is therefore an essential element of the vowels, in consonants the narrowing or stopping of the oral passage is the foundation of the sound, and the state of the glottis is something secondary. Consonants can therefore be breathed as well as voiced, the mouth configuration alone being enough to produce a distinct sound without the help of voice. /Consonants can all be formed with whisper/ [All consonants can be whispered].

A Handbook of Phonetics, 1877, p. 31; and
A Primer of Phonetics, 1890, p. 28

The friction of consonants may be varied by narrowing or widening the friction channel. The term 'hiss' implies audible friction of breath consonants, and 'buzz' of voice consonants.

Consonants admit of a twofold division (A) according to place, (B) to form.

(A) *Place*. By place there are five main classes:

(1) *Back* (guttural) formed by the root of the tongue and the soft palate. Examples are **k** as in *come*, **q** as in *sing*.

(2) *Front* (palatal) formed by the front (middle) of the tongue and the roof of the mouth. **j** as in *you*, **N** as in F. *Boulogne*.

(3) *Point* formed by the point of the tongue and (generally) the upper gums or teeth. This class is commonly called 'dental', but the point of the tongue is not necessarily brought against the teeth. Examples of point consonants are **t**, **n**, **l**.

(4) *Teeth*. Teeth consonants when formed by the point of the tongue may be considered as 'outer' (see below) varieties of point consonants. There is also a 'lip-teeth' consonant, **f**. When outer point (or 'point-teeth') consonants are formed by placing the point of the tongue between the teeth they are called 'interdental'.

(5) *Lip*. South German *w* in *wie*, *wo* is an example of a pure lip consonant. North German *w* = **v** is a 'lip-teeth' consonant.

Each of these positions admits of infinite subdivisions by shifting the tongue backwards and forwards, but it is amply sufficient to distinguish three varieties of each position, 'inner', 'outer', and 'medium', the last being assumed as the normal position. The inner variety is denoted thus, ˏ**t**, the outer being ˎ**t**.

There are two special tongue modifications that require notice, 'inversion' **t**† and 'protrusion' **t**⸸. In inversion the point is turned back towards the soft palate, so that the narrowing or stopping is formed between the lower edge of the tongue-point and the top of the arch. In protrusion the tip of the tongue is extended to the lips. Inverted consonants allow of the distinction of 'inner' and 'outer'.

Besides the simple positions there are 'mixed' or 'compound' consonants formed by narrowing, etc. the mouth channel in two or more places at once. Thus the English **w** is formed not only by lip-narrowing, but also by raising the back of the tongue towards the soft palate; it is therefore a 'lip-back' consonant.

(B) *Form*. By form there are also five classes:

(1) *Open* consonants are those in which the passage is simply narrowed without any contact, such as **kh** in German *ach* and Scotch *loch*,

s, th. The restriction as to contact applies only to the actual friction channel, and even then there may be slight contact, provided the current of breath is not impeded. Thus in forming **kh** the uvula often touches the back of the tongue, but without modifying the sound in any way, and even in **s** the tongue often comes into contact with the ridges of the gums without influencing the sound. In such a consonant as **f**, on the other hand, the contact of the lips and teeth has the effect of forcing the breath to seek a channel elsewhere, namely through the interstices of the teeth, which form the real friction-channel. It is, however, also possible to form an **f** between the lips and the teeth without any contact.

(2) *Divided* consonants are formed by stopping the middle of the passage, leaving it open at the sides. The commonest type of this class is the 'point-divided' **l**.

(3) *Stopped* (or shut) consonants are formed by complete closure of the mouth passage, as in **k**, **d**.

(4) *Nasal* consonants are formed by complete closure of the mouth passage, the nose passage being left open. If we take any stop, such as **b**, and allow the air to pass through the nose by lowering the soft palate, we obtain the corresponding nasal, in this case **m**.

When an unstopped (open or divided) consonant is pronounced with the nose passage open, it is said to be 'nasalized', which is denoted by ***n***. Thus **j*n*** is a nasalized **j**.

(5) *Trills* are a special variety of unstopped consonants. They result from the vibration of the flexible parts of the mouth, either against one another, as when the lips are trilled, or against some firm surface, as when the tip of the tongue trills against the gum in forming a trilled **r**. Their common character is due to the rapid periodic interruption of the breath by the contact of the vibrating body with that against which it is trilled, its elasticity (or, in the case of the uvula, its weight) causing it to resume its former non-contact, to be again driven back.

Trills are, therefore, intermediate between open (and divided) and shut consonants.

Trilling is indicated by ***r***, thus **r*r*** is the trilled **r**.

Table of Consonants. The table on p. 103 will give a general idea of the relations of the principal consonants and of their symbols. As regards the latter, it will be observed that **h** is used as a general diacritic, sometimes to denote open as opposed to shut consonants, sometimes to indicate devocalization. The front consonants, with the exception of **j**, are indicated by the capitals of the small letters which stand for the corresponding points. The back-divided is denoted by **ɿ**.

A Handbook of Phonetics, 1877, pp. 31–4

Consonants are the result of audible friction or stopping of the breath in the throat or mouth. But in many consonants the friction is not audible when they are uttered with voice. When the friction is audible in a voiced consonant, as in ꙅ **z**, ⋗ **v**, it is called a *buzz*, the corresponding breath consonants ꜱ **s**, > **f**, being called *hisses*. All consonants can be formed either with *breath*, *voice*, or *whisper*. The last are denoted by ▷: >▷ = whispered **f**. Consonants are either narrow (˄) or wide (˅); in E. they are wide, ɜ˅ *w* being equivalent to close ɫ *u*.

By form there are four classes of consonants: (1) *open*, such as ω **r**, ꜱ **s**. (2) *side*, such as ꞷ **l**, which is often *one-sided* or unilateral. (3) *stopped*, such as ɑ **k**, ϖ **d**. (4) *nasal*, formed with stoppage of the mouth passage, the nose passage being left open, as in ꞁ **n**, ꜰ **m**. When an unstopped (open or side) consonant is pronounced with the nose passage open, it is said to be 'nasalized', as in ɜʃ, which is nasalized **w**, or an **m** uttered with only partial lip-closure. *Trills* or 'rolled' consonants are a special variety of open consonants, and are denoted by ʃ; thus ωʃ is the Scotch **r**. All consonants may be pronounced with *tenseness* (∧) or 'closeness', or with *looseness* (∨), thus a loose **j** ɷ∨ is equivalent to the vowel ʃ **i**.

By place there are five main classes: (1) *back*, such as ɑ **k**, ꓘ **ŋ** (as in *sing*). (2) *front*, such as ɷ **j** (in *you*). (3) *point*, such as ʊ **t**, ꞷ **l**. (4) *blade* (formed by the surface of the tongue immediately behind the point), such as ꜱ **s**. (5) *lip*, such as ᴅ **p**, ꜰ **m**. Point and blade consonants are included under the general term 'forward'. Most of these admit also of 'inner' and 'outer' varieties, as in the case of the vowels. Point consonants admit of *inversion* (ᶜ), in which the point of the tongue is turned back, and *protrusion* (ᵓ), in which it is protruded to the lips. Thus ʊᶜ is an inverted or 'cerebral' *t*. Some consonants are formed by a combination of two positions. Thus ꙅ **ʃ** (as in *she*) is a *blade-point* consonant, > **f** a *lip-teeth* consonant, ᴗ **þ** (as in *thin*) a *point-teeth* consonant, which is really equivalent to 'outer point'. When the point of the tongue is put between the teeth, the sound is called 'interdental'. All consonants are liable to be modified by the back-open ((**x**), front-open ⸜ (**j**), point-open ⸝ (**r**), lip-open) (**v**) = 'outer rounding', and lip-back-open ɒ (**w**) = 'inner rounding' positions. c) = German *ch* in *auch* is for convenience written c̷, and ɔ(= English *wh* is written ɜ. Other combinations are expressed by + between the symbols of the two elements, as in ɑ+ᴅ = **k** and **p** uttered simultaneously, or by means of the *blade-* (ʂ), *stop-* (ı), *open-* (ıı), *side-* (ʜ), *unilateral* (ᶣ), *throat-stop-* (ʇ) modifiers. (*) is used as a general modifier, thus ᴗ* is any variety of **þ**.

A general table of the consonants is given on p. 104.[1]

A History of English Sounds, 1888, pp. 4–5

[1] See comment on this table on p. 93.

The friction of an 'open' consonant depends on the width of the organic passage. Consonants whose friction is distinctly audible both with breath and voice, such as **s** and **z**, **f** and **v**, are called 'hisses' when breathed or whispered, 'buzzes' when voiced. Some consonants are formed with so wide a passage as to be almost vowels when voiced, and consequently almost inaudible when breathed. Such 'vowel-like' consonants are **l**, the weak English **r**, and the nasals **n**, **m**, whose want of friction is due to the unimpeded flow of the breath through the nose. Breath 'stop' consonants, such as **t**, have no sound whatever in themselves, and are only rendered audible by the puff of breath or explosion that accompanies them. Voice stops, such as **d**, are practically vowels in themselves, and their consonantal character is only shown at the beginning or end of the stop. **l** and the nasals betray their consonantal character in the same way: when they are final, the consonantal flap is distinctly audible, as in *tell*, *ten*. Breath in consonants is left unsymbolized, voice being indicated by the incorporation of the voice-stroke, thus ʊ = **t**, ʊ̶ = **d**, ω = voiceless, ω̶ = voice **l**. Whisper is shown by the whisper-modifier; as in ωɒ = whispered **l**.

The distinction of narrow and wide applies to consonants as well as vowels, though in consonants it is less noticeable, and can generally be ignored. It is symbolized by the addition of the modifiers ᐱ for narrow, ᐯ for wide consonants. If we consonantize ꝉ and ꝉ by narrowing the mouth-opening till a buzz is produced we shall find that the resulting ɜᐱ and ɜᐯ are still quite distinct, the latter being the English **w**, the former the French sound in *oui*. So also narrow **s** may be heard in energetic hissing, wide **sh** in gentle hushing—sᐱ, ƨᐯ. Consonants seem to be generally wide in English, narrow in French.

Consonants admit of a twofold division: (1) according to *form*, (2) according to *place*.

The foundation of the consonant-symbols is a segment—c—of the open-throat symbol o. This fundamental symbol is modified to express the different forms of consonants—thus ɑ = the 'stop' **k**—and is turned in different directions to show the place of the consonant—ɑ = the 'back' **k**, ʊ = the 'point' **t**, etc.

(1) *Form*. By form there are five classes of consonants:

(*a*) *Open* consonants are those in which the passage is simply narrowed without any contact. They are expressed by the unmodified consonant-symbol or some modification of it, /sometimes by the 'open-modifier' ǁ /: c = *ch* in German and Scotch *loch*, ͻ = **f**, s = **s**. The restriction as to contact applies only to the actual friction-channel, and even then there may be slight contact, provided the current of breath is not impeded. Thus, in forming c the uvula often touches the back of the tongue, but without modifying the sound perceptibly, and even in s the tongue often comes in contact with the ridges of the gums without influencing the sound. In such a consonant as ɔ, on the other hand, the contact of the lips and teeth has the effect of forcing the breath to seek a channel elsewhere, namely through the interstices of the teeth, which form the real friction-channel. It is, however, also possible to form an **f** between the lips and the teeth without any contact.

(*b*) /*Side* or/ *divided* consonants are formed by stopping the middle of the passage, leaving it open at the sides—often only on one side, giving a 'unilateral' consonant. The commonest type of this class is the /'point-side-voice'/ ['point-divided-voice'] consonant ω **l**. These consonants are expressed by indenting the consonant-symbol, sometimes by the /'side-modifier'/ ['divided-modifier'] ʜ. The 'unilateral modifier' is ᵘ.

(*c*) *Stopped* (or shut) consonants are formed by complete closure, as in ɑ **k**, ʊ **t**. They are expressed by a bar across the consonant-symbol, or by the addition of the 'stop-modifier' ı.

(*d*) *Nasal* consonants are formed by complete closure of the mouth-passage while the nose-passage is left open. If we take any stop, such as ʊ **d**, and allow the air to pass through the nose by lowering the soft palate, we obtain the corresponding nasal, in this case ʇ **n**. The symbols of the nasals are formed from those of the corresponding stops by joining on the nasal modifier to the bar, and omitting the consonant-segment.

When an unstopped (open or divided) consonant is formed with the nose-passage open, it is said to be 'nasalized', which is denoted by the addition of the nasal modifier ʃ; thus ωʃ is a nasalized **l**.

(*e*) *Trills* (or rolled consonants) are a special variety of unstopped consonants—generally of open consonants. They result from the vibration of the flexible parts of the mouth, either against one another, as when the lips are trilled, or against some firm surface, as when the point of the tongue trills against the gums in forming the strong Scotch *r*, and the uvula against the back of the tongue in the Northumbrian burred *r*. Their common character is due to the rapid periodic interruption of the breath by the contact of the trilling body with that against which it is trilled, its elasticity—or, in the case of the uvula, its weight—causing it to resume its former non-contact, to be again driven or to fall back. Trills are therefore intermediate between open and stopped consonants. Trilling is indicated by the 'trill modifier' ʃ, thus ωʃ = Scotch *r*.

All consonants may be pronounced with *tenseness* (ʌ) or *looseness* (v), according to the degree of approximation of the organs. Thus loose ɷv is practically equivalent to the vowel ſ or ſ. Even stops may be pronounced loosely, so that, for instance, it may be difficult to distinguish between ʊ **d** and ⱱ **ð**. Tenseness and looseness are most nearly allied to the distinctions of height in the vowels, and must not be confounded with narrowness and wideness, which, in consonants as in vowels, depend on the shape of the tongue.

(2) *Place*. By place there are /five/ [six—1906 Edn.] main classes:

(*a*) *Back* (guttural), formed by the root of the tongue and the soft palate, expressed by turning the consonant-curve (representing the root of the tongue) backwards, the symbols of nasal consonants following the direction of the corresponding stop symbols. The 'back modifier' is ‹—a curtailed c. Examples are the back-stop ɑ as in *come*, the back-nasal-voice ɟ as in *king*.

(*b*) *Front* (palatal), formed by the middle part of the tongue and the hard palate, and symbolized by turning the consonant-symbol so as to be pictorial of the arched tongue, as in the front-open-voice ⋒ in *you*. The 'front modifier' is ⌃.

(*c*) *Point*, formed by the point of the tongue and the gums or teeth. This class is commonly called 'dental', but the point of the tongue is not necessarily brought against the teeth. Point consonants are symbolized by turning the points of the consonant-segment upwards in the same way as the point of the tongue is directed upwards in such a consonant as the point-open-voice ⍵ in *red*. The point modifier is ⌄.

The point-teeth consonant in *think* is symbolized by sharpening ᴜ into ᴠ so as to be pictorial of the teeth-edges.

There are two special modifications of point-consonants that require notice, *inversion* and *protrusion*. In inversion the point of the tongue is turned back—whence the 'inversion-modifier' (ᶜ)—towards the soft palate, so that the narrowing, dividing, or stopping is formed between the lower edge of the tongue-point (or blade) and the arch. ⍵ᶜ is the West-of-England inverted *r*. In protrusion the point of the tongue is extended to the lips—whence the 'protrusion-modifier' (ᵓ)—as in blowing a small object from the tip of the tongue: ʊᵓɔ.

(*d*) *Blade*, formed by the blade of the tongue. The representative blade consonant is s = **s**, whose symbol is a combination of those of front-open and point-open—ɳ and ᴜ, blade being a compromise between these two. The blade-modifier is ꞩ. *Blade-point* is blade modified by raising the point of the tongue. It is symbolized by reversing the unmodified blade symbol, and its representative is the ƨ in *she*.

[(*e*) *Fan* (spread) consonants, symbolized by the addition of the spreader ‖, are modifications of point and blade consonants, of which the Arabic 'emphatic' consonants are the best known examples, as in s‖[ꜜ>

ṣēf 'sword', ʊ꜔ǁʃɫɜ *ṭīn* 'clay' compared with *sēf* 'summer', *tīn* 'fig'. In their formation the side edges of the tongue are spread out so that the hiss of sǁ is formed not only between blade and gum, but also between the sides of the tongue and the back teeth; this lowers the pitch of the consonant, and gives it a peculiar 'guttural' effect. So also in ʊǁ the sides of the tongue are strongly pressed against the back teeth, so that when the stop is released the off-glide has the same peculiar dull sound as in sǁ. ʊ⊦ǁ, ϖ⊦ǁ may also be heard as Irish substitutes for the England *th*-sounds ᴗ and ᴗ.]

(*f*) *Lip* (labial) consonants are symbolized by turning the consonant-curve forwards, nasals following the direction of the corresponding stops, as in ɒ **p**, ꜰ **m**. The 'lip-modifier' or 'rounder' is).

Lip-teeth consonants, such as **f**, are symbolized analogously with the point-teeth consonants, by sharpening the curve of ɔ into >, which is the symbol of **f**.

Besides the simple positions, there are compound consonants formed by narrowing etc. the mouth-channel in various places at once. The most important are the front-modified consonants, formed respectively by raising the front of the tongue and narrowing the lip-opening simultaneously with some other action. These effects are symbolized by the addition of the proper modifiers. Thus ɷ\ is a combination of ɷ and ⦶ (front-modified or palatalized **l**), ɷ) is a rounded **l**. c) and ɔ(—lip-modified back-open and back-modified lip-open, the back action predominating in the former, the lip action in the latter—are for convenience made into ɕ, as in German *auch*, and ᴐ, as in *what*. The lip-back modifier is ϸ. Thus ɷϸ = **l**+**w**. There are many other combinations, expressed either by modifiers or by + between the symbols of the two elements, as in ʃᴛɑsʈɑ+ʊɷʃᴛ *exactly*. ɑ+ʊ could also be expressed by ɑ\ǀ where \ǀ = 'point-stop modifier'.

We have hitherto considered only the main 'cardinal' consonant-positions. Such a symbol as ɑ really includes an infinite variety of positions, defined more accurately by the inner and outer modifiers, [the combination ⫞⊦ being used to emphasize medium position]. The deep inner ɑ⫞⫞ is not an English sound. ɑ⫞ is the English sound before back vowels, as in *caw*, outer ɑ⊦ being the English sound before front vowels, as in *key*. The considerable difference between these varieties is clearly brought out by transposing the elements of the two words—ɑ⫞ʃ⦶, ɑ⊦ɟɫ. It will be found on trial that ɑ has a different position before each vowel, being less advanced before low front vowels, as in *can* ɑʈɜ, than before high front vowels, and so on.

The distinction between inner, medium, and outer is peculiarly important in the front consonants, where the medium position is represented by English ɷ in *you*. Outer front comes near the blade position, but is distinguished from it by absence of point-articulation, the point of the tongue being kept clear of the palate. It is still more difficult to distinguish between blade and the combination ∩⊦\—outer front+point.

The medium point position is on the gums just behind the teeth, where English **t** and **d** are formed, in which, however, the tongue is generally flattened into the blade-shape. In English and most other languages point **r** tends to the inner position—ω⊣. Hence the blade-point ꙅ in *she* is naturally more retracted than the unmodified blade-consonant S, but less so than ω. But even ω can be advanced almost to the teeth, although it ultimately merges in ⱳ. If the point is brought back to the arch-rim it practically assumes the outer inverted position—ωc⊦. Outer point implies articulation against the teeth, or with the point half on the teeth, half on the gums. When the tongue is put between the teeth, the consonant is called 'interdental', which may be indicated by ⊦⊦.

We have hitherto seemed to take for granted that the tongue always articulates against the nearest part of the palate, that, for instance, in Ω⊣ the inner front of the tongue is brought against the inner front of the palate. But it is possible to produce a compromise between ɑ and Ω in quite a different way, namely by bringing the medium front of the tongue against the outer back of the palate. The neatest way of expressing this would be to denote the palate-positions by the addition of diacritical consonants; and it is probable that as our analysis becomes more minute, some such device will be adopted. Meanwhile we will content ourselves with expressing the palate-positions by ordinary consonant-symbols in parentheses. Thus the combination we have just been considering can be written Ω⊣⊦+(ɑ⊦) or more briefly Ω(ɑ⊦).

Non-oral Consonants. The throat-consonants—the glottal stop, and the various wheezes—have been described above (pp. 46–9).

There is also a uvula-stop ʃl, but it occurs only in such combinations as **dn** in *bidden*. Here the mouth-stop is maintained from the beginning of the **d** to the end of the **n**, the sole change from the **d** to the **n** being the opening of the nose-passage required to form a nasal consonant. As this action is necessarily implied by writing ʊꞁ together, it is superfluous to indicate it further. If we devocalize the **n** of such a word as *eaten*, making it into ʃɷʊꞁ with a strongly snorted ꞁ, we can hear and feel the uvula-explosion distinctly. The action ʊꞁ is a not uncommon and very disagreeable form of sniffing.

Table of consonants and general remarks. The chief consonants are shown in the annexed table (VI, VII on pp. 104–5), with keywords.

In naming the consonants place comes first, then form, and breath, etc. last. In the stops and hisses 'breath' may be omitted. Thus ɑ **k** back-stop, ∍ **v** lip-teeth-open-voice, ɷʃ **r** point-trill-voice.

The consonants are generally easier to recognize by ear than the vowels, the chief acoustic difficulties lying in the various transitions between them and the adjacent sounds, which will be treated of under Synthesis.

But their articulation often offers great difficulties, especially in the case of the trills, which require long practice.

A Primer of Phonetics, 1890, pp. 28–37; 1906, pp. 31–40

Consonants admit of a two-fold division: (1) by *form*, (2) by *place*.

(1) *Form.* By form there are five classes:

(*a*) *Open*, in which the passage is narrowed without stoppage, such as **s**.

(*b*) *Side*, formed by stopping the middle of the passage and leaving it open at the sides, as in **l**.

(*c*) *Stopped*, formed by complete closure; the voiceless stops **k**, **t**, **p** are in English followed by a breath glide or slight puff of breath, thus *cat* almost = **khæth**.

(*d*) *Nasal* consonants are formed with complete closure of the mouth-passage, the nose-passage being left open, as in **m**. When an unstopped (open or side) consonant is formed with the nose-passage open, it is said to be *nasalized*.

(*e*) *Trills* are the result of vibration of the flexible parts of the mouth. Thus in the trilled Scotch **r** the point of the tongue vibrates against the gums, the English **r** in *red* being an open consonant without any trill.

(2) *Place.* By place there are also five classes:

(*a*) *Back*, formed by the root of the tongue, such as **k**, **ŋ** in *king* **kiŋ**. The back open consonant **x** is the sound of *ch* in the Scotch and German *loch*. The corresponding voice consonant **ʒ** is heard in German *sage*.

(*b*) *Front*, formed by the middle of the tongue, such as the open voice consonant **j** in *you*, which is really a consonantal **i**. The corresponding breath consonant **ç** is heard in German *ich* and Scotch *hue*, *Hugh* **çuu**, which in Southern English is pronounced **hjuw**.

(*c*) *Point*, formed by the tip of the tongue. In the *point-gum* consonants, such as English **t**, **d**, **n**, **l**, the point of the tongue is brought

TABLE V. CONSONANTS (*A Handbook of Phonetics*, 1877, p. 36)

Voiceless										
	1 *Throat*	2 *Back*	3 *Front*	4 *Point*	5 *Point-teeth*	6 *Blade*	7 *Blade-point*	8 *Lip*	9 *Lip-back*	10 *Lip-teeth*
Open	**ʜ, ʀh**	**kh**	**jh**	**rh**	**th**	**s**	**sh**	**ph**	**wh**	**f**
Divided	. .	**⅂h**	**ʟh**	**lh**	**ˎlh**	**(lh)**	**(ˏlh)**	**(ph)**	**(wh)**	. .
Shut	. .	**k**	**ᴛ**	**t**	**ˎt**	**(t)**	**(ˏt)**	**p**	**(p)**	**(p)**
Nasal	. .	**qh**	**ɴh**	**nh**	**ˎnh**	**(nh)**	**(ˏnh)**	**mh**	**(mh)**	**(mh)**

Voiced										
	11	12	13	14	15	16	17	18	19	20
Open	**ʀ**	**ǵh**	**j**	**r**	**dh**	**z**	**zh**	**bh**	**w**	**v**
Divided	. .	**⅂**	**ʟ**	**l**	**ˎl**	**(l)**	**(ˏl)**	**(bh)**	**(w)**	. .
Shut	**x**	**ǵ**	**ᴅ**	**d**	**ˎd**	**(d)**	**(ˏd)**	**b**	**(b)**	**(b)**
Nasal	. .	**q**	**ɴ**	**n**	**ˎn**	**(n)**	**(ˏn)**	**m**	**(m)**	**(m)**

N.B. Letters enclosed in parentheses denote varieties for which no special signs are provided.

TABLE VI. CONSONANTS (*A Primer of Phonetics*, 1890 edn., p. 38)

	VOICELESS									
	1 *Throat*	2 *Back*	3 *Front*	4 *Point*	5 *Point-teeth*	6 *Blade*	7 *Blade-point*	8 *Lip*	9 *Lip-back*	10 *Lip-teeth*
Open	ɵ **ɹ*h*** Ar. *hha*	c **x** G. a*ch*	∩ **ç** G. i*ch*	∪ **r*h*** Icel. *hr*	⋃ **þ** *th*in	s **s**	ƨ **ʃ** fi*sh*	ɔ **ɸ**	ɜ **ʍ** *wh*at	> **f**
Side	. .	ɛ **ɭ*h***	ɱ **λ*h***	ω **l*h***	ω꜔			ɜ		
Stop	χ Glot. stop	ɑ **k**	Ω **c** Hung. *ty*	ʊ **t**	ʊ꜔ F. *t*	ʊ꜕, s꜔	ƨ꜔	ɒ **p**		
Nasal	. .	⅃ **ŋ*h***	⅂ **ñ*h***	ℸ **n*h*** Icel. *hn*	ℸ꜔			ɼ **m*h***		
	VOICED									
	11	12	13	14	15	16	17	18	19	20
Open	ɵ **ɹ** Ar. *ain*	ϵ **ʒ** G. sa*g*en	ɱ **j** *y*ou	ɷ **r**	⋓ **ð** *th*en	ȣ **z**	ȝ **ʒ** rou*g*e	ɘ **β** South G. *w*	ɜ **w**	⋺ **v**
Side	. .	ȣ **ɪ** Russ. pa*l*ka	ɱ **λ** Ital. *gl.*	ω **l**	ω꜔			ȝ		
Stop	. .	ɑ **g**	Ω **ɟ** Hung. *gy*	ϖ **d**	ϖ꜔	ϖ꜕, ȣ꜔	ȝ꜔	ɒ **b**		
Nasal	. .	⅃ **ŋ** si*ng*	⅂ **ñ** Ital. *gn*	ℸ **n**	ℸ꜔			ɼ **m**		

TABLE VII. CONSONANTS (*A Primer of Phonetics*, 1906 edn., p. 41)

VOICELESS										
	1 *Throat*	2 *Back*	3 *Front*	4 *Point*	5 *Point-teeth*	6 *Blade*	7 *Blade-point*	8 *Lip*	9 *Lip-back*	10 *Lip-teeth*
Open	o˔ ɹ*h* Ar. *ḥa*	c x G. a*ch*	∩ ç G. i*ch*	∪ r*h* Icel. *hr*	∪ þ *th*in	s s	ƨ ʃ fi*sh*	ɔ ɸ	ɜ ʍ *wh*at	ɔ f
Divided	. .	ɛ ɭ*h*	ϖ ʎ*h*	ω l*h*	ωꟷ			ɜ		
Stop	χ Glot. stop	ɑ k	Ω c Hung. *ty*	Ʊ t	Ʊꟷ F. *t*	Ʊʂ, sǀ	ƨǀ	ɒ p		
Nasal	. .	ɹ ŋ*h*	Ꞁ ñ*h*	Ꞁ n*h* Icel. *hn*	Ꞁꟷ			ɼ m*h*		

VOICED										
	11	12	13	14	15	16	17	18	19	20
Open	I˔ ɹ Ar. *'ain*	є ʒ G. sagen	ɱ j *y*ou	ω r	ψ ð *th*en	ȿ z	ɛ rou*ge*	ɘ South G. *w*	ɜ w	ɔ v
Divided	. .	ɛ l Russ. pa*l*ka	ϖ ʎ Ital. *gl*	ω l	ωꟷ			ɜ		
Stop	. .	ɑ ǵ	Ω ɟ Hung. *gy*	Ʊ d	Ʊꟷ	Ʊʂ, ȿǀ	ɛǀ	ɒ b		ɔǀ Du. *w*
Nasal	. .	ɹ ŋ si*ng*	Ꞁ ñ Ital. *gn*	Ꞁ n	Ꞁꟷ			ɼ m		

against the gums just behind the teeth; in the *point-teeth* consonants, such as the point-teeth-open **þ** in *thin*, it is brought against the teeth. The voice consonant corresponding to **þ** is **ð** in *then*.

(*d*) *Blade*, formed by the blade of the tongue—that part of it which is immediately behind the point. **s**, **z** are blade consonants. In the *blade-point* consonants, such as the blade-point open **ʃ** in *she*, the blade position is modified by raising the point of the tongue. The corresponding voice consonant **ʒ** is heard in *measure* **meʒə**.

The point and blade consonants are included under the name of *forward* consonants.

(*e*) *Lip*, formed by the lips, such as **p**, **m**. The lip-open consonant **ɸ** is the sound produced in blowing out a candle; the corresponding voice consonant occurs in German in such words as *quelle* **kβelə**; **f**, **v** are *lip-teeth* consonants. **w*h***, as in *why*, and **w** are *lip-back* consonants, formed by narrowing the lip-opening and raising the back of the tongue at the same time, **w** being a consonantal **u**. In Southern English **w*h*** is often pronounced **w**.

Compound Consonants: rounding, fronting. **w*h***, **w** are really *compound* consonants, formed in two places at once. If instead of back-modifying the lip-open consonant, as in **w*h***, we lip-modify or *round* the back-open consonant **x**, we get the back-round consonant **x*w*** in German *auch*. Other consonants may be rounded in the same way, which we express by adding ***w***; thus **r*w*ed** is *red* pronounced with a rounded **r**.

When a consonant is modified by raising the front of the tongue, it is said to be *front-modified* or fronted, which we express by adding ***j***. Thus the lip-open front-modified consonant is the sound in French *huit* **β*j*it**; it is almost a consonantal **y**.

Intermediate Positions. Besides the main positions known as back, front, etc., there are an indefinite number of intermediate positions, which we distinguish roughly as *inner* or nearer the throat, and *outer*, or nearer the lips. Thus we have inner **k** before back vowels, as in *caw*, outer **k** before front vowels, as in *key*. The English **r**, as in *red*, is an inner point consonant.

The Aspirate. The aspirate **h** is partly an open throat consonant, partly a breath vowel-glide. Thus **h** in *hook* is mainly formed by unvoicing the beginning of the **u**, almost as if we were to write the word **w*h*uk**. So also the **h** in *he* resembles a weakened **ç**. **h** also occurs before the consonant **j**, as in *hue* **hjuw**.

The following is a table of the chief consonants. Those marked * do not occur in English.

BREATH

	Throat	*Back*	*Front*	*Point*	*Blade*	*Blade-point*	*Lip*	*Lip-back*	*Lip-teeth*
Open	h	*x	*ç	***r*h**, þ	s	ʃ	*ɸ	**w*h***	**f**
Side	. .			***l*h**[1]					
Stop		k	*c	t			p		
Nasal	. .	***ŋ*h**	***ñ*h**	***n*h**			***m*h**		

VOICE

Open	. .	*ȝ	j	r, ð	z	ʒ	*β	w	v
Side	. .			l					
Stop	. .	g	*q	d			b		
Nasal	. .	ŋ	*ñ	n			m		

We generally write **rh**, etc., instead of **r*h*** for the sake of convenience.

A New English Grammar, 1891, pp. 234–7

If any vocal organs are brought together so as either completely to stop the passage, as in **b**, **m**, or cause audible friction (hiss or buzz), as in **f**, **s**, a consonant is the result. All consonants go in pairs of breath and voice. Thus to the lip-teeth-breath (or voiceless) consonant **f** corresponds the lip-teeth-voice **v**. Breath consonants are sometimes expressed by adding the modifier ***h*** to the symbol of the corresponding voice consonant; thus **w*h*** in *why* is the breath consonant corresponding to the lip-back-voice consonant **w**.

Some consonants have hardly any audible friction when voiced, such as **m**, **w**, **l**. Such consonants resemble vowels, and are therefore called vowel-like (or liquid) consonants. But in their breath forms **w*h***, **l*h*** the friction is clearly audible.

Consonants admit of a twofold division by form and by place. By form we distinguish *open* consonants, such as **s**, **w**, **f**; *stopped* consonants, such as **b**, **t**, **k**; *nasal*, such as **m**, **n**; and *side* (or divided) consonants, such as **l**, formed by stopping the middle of the passage and leaving it open at the sides; and *trilled* consonants, which are the result of vibration of flexible parts of the mouth; thus in the trilled Scotch **r** the point of the tongue vibrates against the gums, the English **r** in *red* being the corresponding open consonant without any trill.

[1] Omitted presumably in error, in original, which only shows the asterisk. *Ed.*

By place we distinguish *back* (guttural) consonants, formed by the root of the tongue and the back of the mouth, such as **k**; *front*, such as **j** in *you*; *point*, such as **r**, **t**, **n**; *blade* **s**, **z**, formed by the point together with the surface of the tongue immediately behind it, from which the *blade-point* **ʃ** in *she* and **ʒ** in *rouge* are formed by raising the point of the tongue towards the **r**-position; *lip*, such as **b**, **m**; *lip-teeth* **f**, **v**; *lip-back* **wh**, **w**, formed by narrowing the lip-opening and raising the back of the tongue at the same time. There are also throat consonants: the throat-stop or glottal stop **ʼ** is the sound produced in coughing. The aspirate **h** may be regarded as a weak open throat-consonant, the peculiar Arabic consonants *ḥā* and *ʿēn* being strong open throat-consonants—**ḥ** the breath, **ʿ** the voice-consonant.

Beside the main positions back, front, etc., there are an infinite number of intermediate positions, which we distinguish roughly as *inner*, or nearer the throat, and *outer*, or nearer the lips. Thus **r** is inner point, **þ**, as in *thin*, and **ð**, as in *then*, are outer point or teeth-point, the ordinary English **t**, **d**, **n**, **l** being formed in an intermediate position.

The consonant **w** is really a compound consonant—formed in two different places at once. The German consonant **x*w*** in *auch* as compared with the simple **x** in *ach* is also a compound consonant, but in its formation the back element predominates over the lip element instead of being subordinate to it as in **w** or **wh**, so that it is a lip-modified back consonant, which we indicate by adding ***w***. So also we may use ***j*** to show front-modification. Thus the French **l** in *elle* is really **l*j***, the middle of the tongue being arched up towards the **j**-position.

. . . . .

The various open voice consonants must necessarily yield more or less distinct vowel-sounds when their positions are expanded so as to remove audible friction. Thus if we start from the back-open-voice **ɣ** in German *sage*, and increase the distance between tongue and palate, we obtain a pure vowel-sound, which will be either the mid-back-wide **a** in *father* or the mid-back-narrow **ɐ** in *come* if the **ɣ** is formed in a medium position, or the low-back-wide ***a*** of French *pâte* if we start from inner **ɣ**. Conversely, if we narrow the lip-opening of **u**, we get **w**, and the front vowels become varieties of **j** when the tongue is brought close to the palate.

The History of Language, 1900, pp. 13–15, 16

Consonants admit of a twofold division, (1) by form, (2) by place.

Thus **p**, **b** are by place lip-consonants, by form stopped consonants or stops.

Nasal consonants are formed by closing the mouth passage in different places, while the nose-passage is left open by lowering the uvula. If any stopped consonant, such as **d**, is modified in this way, it becomes the corresponding nasal, in this case **n**.

When a non-stopped (open or divided) consonant is formed with the nose-passage open, it is said to be 'nasalized'. Thus if we try to pronounce **m** with the lips a little apart we obtain the nasalized lip-open consonant **β*n***.

Open consonants are the result of narrowing instead of completely closing the passage, as in the back-open-breath **x** in Scotch and German *loch*, Spanish *hijo*. This consonant may easily be deduced from the corresponding stop in *lock* by emphasizing and isolating the 'breath-glide' after it. The back-open voice **ɣ** in Middle German *sagen* may be obtained by gabbling *gaga*.

In some open consonants there is sometimes slight contact of the organs. Thus in **þ** and **f** there is often contact of the tongue and teeth, and lips and teeth respectively. But this does not sensibly impede or otherwise modify the flow of breath, except by increasing its friction.

In *divided* (side, lingual) consonants there is central stoppage with opening at the sides of the tongue, as in the point-divided-voice **l**. When this consonant is unvoiced, the friction of the air along the sides of the tongue is both felt and heard very distinctly. The divided consonants are often formed with an opening on one side only, and are then called 'unilateral'. The voiceless Welsh *ll* is generally unilateral, the breath escaping only on the right side. Unilateral formation of voiced **l** is also not unfrequent in Welsh and other languages. Unilateral formation does not sensibly modify the quality of the sound.

Trilled (rolled) consonants are special varieties of non-stopped consonants. They are formed by the vibration of flexible parts against each other, as when the lips are trilled, or against some firm surface, as when the point of the tongue trills against the gums in the Scotch **r*r***, where ***r*** is the 'trill-modifier'. The 'burred *r*' is a uvula-trill: the uvula is lifted up by the back of the tongue, is driven upwards by the force of the outgoing air, falls by its own weight, is driven up again, and so on. In this sound—which is a frequent substitute for **r** both in individuals and in dialects—the trilling part is passive, while in **r*r*** the trilling tip of the tongue is active. In learning the latter, the tongue should be lightly thrown, as it were, against the gums; if it is held at all stiffly, trilling is impossible.

There are some more general modifications of consonants which fall under the head of form.

Thus all consonants may be formed either with *tightness* (constriction) or *looseness*, according to the degree of approximation of the organs. Thus the English **j** is much less constricted than the buzzed German consonant in *ja*—so loose, indeed, that it is almost a vowel.

Tightness and looseness must not be confounded with narrowness and wideness.

This latter distinction applies to consonants as well as vowels, although it is generally hardly noticeable in consonants, because of their harsher sound, but if the English **j** and **w** are lengthened, their wide quality becomes at once apparent. English **w** is a consonantized ***u***, while French **w** in *oui* is a consonantized **u**. This is why in French **w** the lips are pouted, while in the English **w** they are flat. English **j** is loose and wide, while English **w** is tight (constricted) and wide—that is, at the beginning of a stressed syllable. When unstressed it is loose, as in the second syllable of *wayward*. If *way* is pronounced with the loose **w** of *-ward*, the word becomes irrecognizable. This loose **w** has only the mid-rounding of ***o*** or *ö*, which latter it most nearly resembles.

By place the number of consonants, like that of the vowels, is infinite. As with the vowels, we select certain definite points of division, and distinguish intermediate positions as inner and outer. The main divisions are back, front, point, blade, fan, lip, lip-teeth.

Back (guttural) consonants are formed between the root or back of the tongue and the soft palate. In English, as in most other languages, the place of articulation varies according to the nature of the accompanying vowels. Thus in *king* **kiŋ** the front vowel draws the back stop and back nasal forward into the outer position, the contact being between the upper part of the back of the tongue and that part of the soft palate which is just behind the beginning of the hard palate. In *gong* **goŋ**, on the other hand, the low back vowel draws them back into the inner position, the contact being between the root of the tongue and the lower part of the soft palate. If we take two such words as *key* and *caw*, and transpose their consonants **k˧ii**, **k˫ɔ**, the great difference between inner and outer back becomes clearly apparent.

Front (palatal) consonants, such as the front-open-voice **j**, are formed by the middle of the tongue against the hard palate, the point of the tongue lying passively behind the lower teeth. It is easy to make **j** into the front-stop-voice **ɟ** by closing the passage. This was the sound of Old English *cg* in *hrycg* 'back' and of *g* in *sengan* 'singe', where the preceding *n* is the corresponding front-nasal-voice consonant **ñ**. The inner form of the same consonant **ñ˧** is the French *gn* in *vigne*. If **ɟ** is formed with side-openings while the central contact is maintained, it becomes the front-divided-voice **λ**, which is the sound of Old English *l* before front stops, as in *swelc* 'such', where *c* is the front-stop-breath consonant **c**, which, again, is the result of stopping the front-open-breath **ç** in German *ich* and the North English and Scotch initial consonant in such words as *hue* **çuu**, which in Southern English is generally pronounced **hjuw** with **h** followed by voice **j**.

λ and **ñ** must be carefully distinguished from the consonant-groups **lj, nj** in *million, onion*, although the **l** and **n** in these words have not exactly the same sound as the ordinary point **l** and **n** in *mill, none*; they are modified by the following **j** into a combination of point (tongue-tip) articulation with simultaneous outer front contact. If the syllables **mil** and **ɐn** in the above words are isolated, the front modification of their final consonants will be plainly heard.

Point consonants may be classified in two ways, (1) with reference to the part of the mouth they articulate against, and (2) according to the direction of the tongue. From the first point of view they are distinguished as 'inner point', formed on the arch-rim, 'medium (intermediate) point', formed on the gums just behind the teeth, and outer point or 'point-teeth' (dental), formed on the teeth. From the second point of view they are distinguished as 'flat-point', in which the tongue lies horizontal in the mouth, and 'up-point', in which it is directed upwards.

When the tongue is in the first direction, as in **þ, ð**, it naturally points to the teeth; hence these two consonants are flat-point, and at the same time point-teeth consonants. But if the flat direction is preserved, it is possible, although not natural, to form inner—or rather, innermost—**þ, ð** as far back as the arch-rim. If formed on the gums just behind the teeth, these consonants are practically indistinguishable from the normal point-teeth varieties.

When the tongue is directed upwards, as in the **r** in *red, rearing*, it naturally points towards the arch-rim; hence **r** is normally both an up-point and an inner-point consonant. And yet, if the tongue-tip is curled upwards, an **r** can be formed in the medium point position as well.

The English **r** is vowel-like in sound, being quite free from buzz, which is partly the result of its being loose, partly of diminished breath-pressure. Trilling the **r**—'rolling one's *r*'s'—is considered a defect in English, although it is not unfrequent in declamation.

In English the other point consonants, **t, d, n, l,** are formed in the medium position. In combination with **þ** and **ð** they are formed in the outer position, as in *breadth, eighth, tenth, wealth*. Outer **t, d**, etc., are the normal sounds in French, and some English dialects.

Blade consonants are formed by the 'blade' of the tongue, that is, its surface immediately behind the point. If the hand represents the tongue, then the upper blade would be roughly represented by the finger-nails. The blade of the tongue may also be regarded as its flattened point.

The blade-open consonants are in English formed against the gums just behind the teeth, in the same place as **t**, **d**, **n**, **l**. These latter are in English often formed with the tongue somewhat flattened, so that they are approximations to blade-consonants.

If **s**, **z** are modified by turning the tongue upwards and backwards, so as to bring the point more into place, they become the *point-blade* consonants **ʃ**, **ʒ** respectively. The blade-point stand to the blade consonants in the same relation as **r** stands to **ð**; **ʃ**, **ʒ** being the up-point consonants corresponding to the flat-point **s**, **z**.[1] Hence although **ʃ**, **ʒ** are naturally formed more inner than **s**, **z**, both classes can be retracted as well as advanced without being confused.

The point-blade have a deeper pitch than the blade consonants: **ʃ** is, acoustically, a dull **s**. In some languages, such as German, this dull quality of **ʃ** is exaggerated by rounding, one result of which is that the tongue-articulation tends to be neglected, so that at last nothing remains but a slight raising of the blade or outer front of the tongue. Rounding of **ʃ**, **ʒ** occurs individually in English.

When the blade-point are combined with point consonants, as in *church* **tʃəətʃ**, *judge* **dʒɐdʒ**, *singe* **sinʒ**, *Welsh* **welʃ**, they are formed with less retraction of the point, being thus intermediate between blade and blade-point consonants both in formation and sound.

Fan (spread) consonants are varieties of point and blade consonants; they are denoted by the modifier ***l***. In them the sides of the tongue are spread out, so that the hiss of such a consonant as the blade-fan-open **s*l*** is formed not only between blade and gum, but also between the sides of the tongue and the back of the teeth, which gives a peculiar deep, dull 'guttural' quality to the sound. **t*l***, **d*l*** occur in Irish English as substitutes for **þ**, **ð** respectively; in them the fan modification is supplemented by a slight raising of the back of the tongue. Fan **l** may be heard in Scotch Gaelic.

Lip consonants, such as **p**, **m**, and *lip-teeth* consonants such as **f**, offer no difficulty.

The lip-open consonant **ɸ** does not occur in English, it is the sound produced in blowing out a candle. The lip-open-voice consonant **β** can be obtained by gabbling *baba*. It is a frequent substitute for **v** in German, especially in such words as *quelle*, where another consonant precedes, and was the old-fashioned substitute for **w** in Dickens's 'Sam Veller'.

If the lip-open consonants are modified by raising the back of the tongue, they become the English *lip-back-open* consonants **wh**, **w** in

[1] The original has **ʃ** here, which is presumed to be a misprint for **z**. *Ed.*

what, *we*, which are, practically, consonantized *u*, although the back of the tongue need not necessarily be raised to the full high position. In these consonants the lip-articulation predominates.

In the *back-lip-open* **xw** of German *auch* and North Irish *wh* in *what* the back **x** is the predominant element. This was one of the sounds of *gh* in Middle English, as in *laugh*, *enough* **lauxw**, **enuuxw**.

Compound Consonants. This last is one of a large number of 'lip-modified' consonants, of which the German *sch* is, as we have seen, a further example. Lip-modified **r** is not uncommon in English as an individual peculiarity.

In a similar way consonants can be 'front-modified'. French and German **l**, as compared with the deeper-sounding English **l**, may be regarded as front-modified; in them the tongue is more convex than in English, its upper surface being arched up towards the front position of **j**. In French, **y** is often consonantized into the lip-front-open (front-modified lip-open) sound in *lui* **lβji**. Front-modified forms of **r**, **s**, **m**, and other consonants may be heard in Russian.

Shifted Consonants. In the consonants hitherto described it has been taken for granted that the tongue articulates against that part of the mouth which is opposite to it. But this is not always the case. Thus in advancing the point of articulation of a back consonant it is not necessary to stop short at the outer extremity of the soft palate—in the **k⊦** or **k⊦⊦**-position; it is possible to articulate still further forward, with the outer back of the tongue against the hard palate. In this way we get the out-back **kɔ**, which, although it is from one point of view a front consonant, is quite distinct from **c** or even **c⊣⊣**. **kɔ**, **gɔ** are the old-fashioned sounds in such words as *sky*, *garden*. To an unaccustomed ear they sound like **kj**, **gj**. In Irish Gaelic such pairs as **kɔ** and **c** are kept quite distinct: the former is heard in *ceól* **kɔool** 'music', the latter in *teacht* **ca⊦xt** 'to come'.

The out-point consonants **tɔ**, etc., are formed with the tip of the tongue against the upper lip. They do not seem to occur in articulate speech.

The in-point, in-blade, and in-blade-point consonants, generally included under the term 'inverted', occur in many languages; the in-**r** is heard in the dialects of the West of England. In their formation the tip of the tongue or its blade is turned back into the arch, so that its lower part articulates against the palate. Articulation against the arch-rise may be regarded either as outer in-point or inner point. The full in-**r** has a snarling, almost nasal effect. It can hardly be trilled. It is often formed simultaneously with—incorporated into—the preceding vowel, which then becomes an in-point-modified vowel.

The Arabic *q*, which is a **k** formed even further back than the English **k˧** in *caw*, may be regarded as an in-back consonant—**kᴄ**.

Non-oral Consonants. Some consonants are formed below the mouth.

It is, for instance, possible to produce a stopped consonant in the larynx by opening or closing the glottis on a passage of breath or voice. The opening is heard in an ordinary cough, while the convulsive closure of the glottis results in what is known as a hiccup. This 'glottal stop' **!** occurs also as an integral element of ordinary speech. In German all initial vowels in stressed syllables begin with a more or less distinct glottal stop; and this occurs also in some English dialects, and in individual pronunciation in Standard English as well. In some North English and Scotch dialects (such as that of Glasgow) the glottal stop occurs as a substitute for the ordinary mouth-stops, as in the Glasgow pronunciation of *water* **wa!ər**.

The Sounds of English, 1908, pp. 39–47

Acoustic Qualities of Consonants. The consonants are much easier to recognise by ear than the vowels, as far as their organic formation is concerned, and it is not till we come to synthetic distinctions of voice etc. that their appreciation offers any particular difficulty. The main practical difficulty with the consonants themselves is to form them with ease and certainty, many of them offering considerable difficulties to those unaccustomed to them. The trills especially require long practice.

The following table shows the pitch of the chief open consonants, according to Bell (*Fn.*: **f** and **th** I have added myself. They are omitted by Bell, who regards them as divided consonants.):

wh khw ʀh ˏkh kh f {ph / ˎkh} rh sh s ˏjh th jh ˎjh

. . . . .

Position. The various positions of the open voiced consonants must necessarily yield more or less distinct vowel-sounds when expanded enough to remove all audible friction. The relations between the consonant and vowel positions are very important, and should be carefully studied. Thus starting from the buzzed **gh**, the student should carefully increase the distance between the back of the tongue and the soft palate till all friction ceases—he will thus obtain the vowel **a**. If the movement is made very slowly, he will form the soft **r**-like **gh**, producing a combination which suggests **gra**.

The following are the more important of these relations (*Fn.*: Based on Mr Bell's tabulations with additions of my own.):

ˏ**gh** **gh** ˎ**gh** ˏ**j** **j** ˎ**j** ˏ**gh*w*** **gh*w*** ˎ**gh*w***, **w** ˏ**j*w*** **j*w*** ˎ**j*w***

correspond to

ɒ ɐ ʌ æ e i ɔ o u œ ə y

By weakening the different point and blade consonants a variety of vowels may be found, which are not included in the regular scheme of vowels.

If **r** is weakened we get a peculiar vowel-sound, which partakes of **r** itself and of the mixed vowel **æh**, the tip being raised while the rest of the tongue is nearly in the position for the low or mid mixed vowels. Most of the vowels may be modified by the tip in this way, and we thus obtain a class of point-modified vowels, represented by an *r* after the vowel-symbol. This **r**-vowel may be retracted, and we thus get another series of retracted-point vowels. In the Kentish pronunciation the retracted **r** of *sparrow*, etc. is thus incorporated into the preceding vowel, *sparrow* being pronounced **spaɪ*r*┴**.

By weakening **dh** a sound is produced which has quite the effect of a dental **r**-vowel. The Danish soft *d* is nearly this outer **r**-vowel, with the addition of front modification.

A weakened **z** gives a vowel which has the effect of a very forward **eh**, being in fact the 'blade' vowel most nearly corresponding to **eh**, and bearing the same relation to **eh** as **z** itself does to **j**.

A weakened **zh** gives the point-modified blade vowel. It has the effect of a very forward **eh** with something of an **r**-quality. All these sounds may be combined, with various degrees of facility, with the other vowels. They may all be rounded.

If **bh** is weakened, with the tongue in the neutral **eh** position, we get **eh** with lip-rounding, which is about equivalent to inner **ə**. If cheek-rounding is added, we have **oh**. (*Fn.*: The above remarks on the relations between vowels and consonants differ in some respects from those of Mr Bell, who considers the mixed vowels **ih**, **eh**, and **æh** to be related to **z**, **zh**, and **r** respectively. It is true that if we lower the tongue from the weak **r** position, we ultimately get **æh**, but the true **r** vowel is, as we have seen, something quite distinct from **æh**, which is formed without any raising of the point. Again, if I consonantize **ih** and **eh**, I get simply **j**. **ih** may, of course, be made into a weak consonant simply by devocalization, but the result bears no resemblance to **z**, but is simply a slightly gutturalized **jh**. It is in fact ˏ**jh**+ˎ**jh**, the mouth passage being narrowed in two places at once. If strengthened by raising the intermediate portion of the tongue, it passes entirely into **jh**.)

A Handbook of Phonetics, 1877, pp. 50–1, 52–4

Acoustic Qualities of Consonants. The following table shows the order of the pitches of the chief open consonants, beginning with the lowest:

ʚ ɕ c ɔ > ʊ ∨ ƨ s ∩

Observe the close analogy with the vowel-pitches, the lowest-pitched consonant ʚ being a lip-narrowed unvoiced form of the lowest-pitched vowel Ɩ, and ∩ corresponding to ſ. Within each consonant there are lesser gradations of pitch from inner to outer, thus ∩⊣, ∩⊣⊢, ∩⊢; which, again, agrees with the relations of consonants to vowels, ∩⊢ being the exact consonantal equivalent of ſ.

Relations of Consonants to Vowels. The various positions of the open voiced consonants must necessarily yield more or less distinct vowel-sounds when expanded enough to remove audible friction. The relations between the consonant and vowel positions are very important, and should be carefully studied. Thus, starting from buzzed medium є⊣⊢ the student should carefully increase the distance between the back of the tongue and soft palate till he obtains a pure vowel-sound—which will be] or]. The following are the more important of these relations:

є⊣ є є⊢ ⊕⊣ ⊕ ⊕⊢ є⊣ є є⊢, ʚ ⊕)⊣ ⊕) ⊕)⊢
ȷ] ˥ ɩ [ſ ɟ } Ɩ ɫ { f

In comparing ⊕⊣, ⊕, ⊕⊢ with ɩ, [, ſ etc., we see that the retraction of the tongue-narrowing from ⊕⊢ to ⊕⊣ corresponds exactly to a similar progression in the vowels (cp. p. 61). It would, indeed, be possible to substitute some such symbolization as ſ⊢ ſ ſ⊣ for ſ [ɩ; but this would be ambiguous and would ignore the distinctive peculiarity of vowels as opposed to consonants, namely their power of indefinitely expanding the voice-channel from which result the distinctions of height.

The point-consonant ω may be weakened into a vowel, the result being practically a low mixed point-modified vowel—ɪ\.

∨, s, and ƨ may be weakened in the same way, with similar results.

A Primer of Phonetics, 1890, pp. 37–40; 1906, pp. 40–3

Each consonant has an inherent pitch of its own. The following are the pitches of the chief open breath consonants, beginning with the lowest:

ʚ	ɕ	c	>	ɔ	ʊ	ƨ	s	∨	∩
w*h*	**x*w***	**x**	**f**	**ɸ**	**r*h***	**ʃ**	**s**	**þ**	**ç**

There is a close relation between consonants and vowels. In many open voiced consonants there is no audible friction, and such 'vowel-like' or 'liquid' consonants have quite the effect of vowels. These are ϵ **ʒ**, ɷ **j**, ɜ **w**, ω **r**, ω **l** and the nasals. But ϵ and ɷ can also be buzzed. The two closest vowels ſ **i** and ɿ **u** approximate so closely to the consonants ɷ and ɜ respectively, that it is often difficult to draw the line. When devocalized these vowels cannot be separated from ɷ and ɜ. The following are the most important of the relations between individual consonants and vowels:

ϵ⊣ ϵ ϵ⊢ ɷ⊣ ɷ ɷ⊢ ɜ⊣ ɜ ɜ⊢, ɜ ɷ)⊣ ɷ) ɷ)⊢
ɹ] ʅ ɩ [ſ ɟ } ɿ ʈ { f

ω **r** may also be weakened into a kind of vowel; in fact, the English **r** in *very* may be considered as an unsyllabic vowel.

The acoustic relations between consonants and vowels may be seen by comparing the tables of pitches. They generally agree with the organic relations. Observe that **s** and **i** are acoustically similar.

A History of English Sounds, 1888, p. 7

Sounds Formed without Expiration. All the sounds hitherto described imply expiration. It is however possible to form sounds both with inspiration, as is occasionally done in some Swiss dialects to disguise the voice (*Fn.*: See Winteler, 'Die Kerenzer Mundart', p. 5.), and without either expiration or inspiration, but solely with the help of the air in the mouth.

'Suction-stops' are formed in this way by placing the tongue or lips in the position for a stop, and then sucking out the air between the organs which form the stop; they are thus pressed strongly together by the pressure of the air in the mouth, so that when separated a distinct 'smack' is heard. These sounds are common in interjectional speech. Thus, if we denote suction by ‡ after the stop symbol, **p‡** is an ordinary kiss, **t‡** is the interjection of impatience commonly written *tut!* etc. In many of the South African languages these suctions are those essential elements of speech known as 'clicks'. (*Fn.*: This name is somewhat inappropriate: 'cluck' would describe the sounds better.) Thus in the Bushman language **p‡a** and similar combinations occur. In the Zulu language **t‡** etc. are always accompanied by some other expiratory consonant. Thus **q** and **t‡** are formed simultaneously, the **t‡** not interrupting the **q**. (*Fn.*: See Bell, *Visible Speech*, p. 125, for the Zulu clicks. Other clicks from American languages are described by Haldeman, quoted in Ellis, *Early English Pronunciation*, p. 1349.)

Other non-expiratory sounds are the implosives, where, however, the following glide is, or may be, expiratory.

A Handbook of Phonetics, 1877, pp. 54–5

All sounds hitherto described imply out-breathing or *expiration* >. It is also possible to form sounds with in-breathing or *inspiration* <. It is a common habit of speech to pronounce such words as *no* in this way, to express emphatic denial. ɔ<v is the natural symbol of drinking, and ɔ<ʌ is an ejaculation of pain.

Some sounds are produced without either out- or in-breathing, but solely with the air in the throat or mouth. The 'implosives' are formed in the former, the suction-stops or 'clicks' in the latter way. In the clicks the tongue or lips are placed in the position for a stop, and the air is sucked out from between the stop-forming organs; they are thus pressed strongly together by the air in the mouth, so that their separation produces a sharp smacking sound. This action is regarded as a kind of stopped inspiration and is accordingly expressed by adding a stop to the in-breather. Thus ɒ◃ is an ordinary kiss, ʊ̄◃ is the expression of impatience written *tut!* In many savage languages these clicks are essential elements of speech.

A Primer of Phonetics, 1890, p. 40

Consonants. These are the result of audible friction or stoppage, which may be accompanied either with breath, voice, or whisper.

Consonants admit of a two-fold division: (1) by form, and (2) by place. Thus **p**, **b** are by place lip-consonants, while by form they are stopped consonants or 'stops'.

If the mouth-stoppage is kept, and the nose-passage is opened, the stop becomes the corresponding 'nasal'; thus **b** with the soft palate lowered becomes the nasal **m**.

In 'open' consonants the sound is formed by simply narrowing the passage, as in the back-open-breath **x** in Scotch and German *loch*. In some open consonants, such as the lip-teeth **f**, there is slight contact of the organs, but without impeding the flow of breath.

In 'divided' consonants there is central stoppage with openings at the sides as in the familiar point-divided **l**. These consonants are sometimes 'unilateral'—with the opening on the side only—the character of the sound not being sensibly modified thereby.

When open and divided consonants are formed with the nose-passage open they are said to be 'nasalized'. Thus **m** with incomplete lip-closure becomes the nasalized lip-open-voice consonant.

'Trills' (or rolled consonants) are a special variety of un-stopped consonants resulting from the vibration of flexible parts against one another, as when the lips are trilled, or against some firm surface, as when the point of the tongue trills against the gums in the Scotch **r**, or the uvula against the back of the tongue, as in the Northumbrian burred **r**, and the French and German **r**, where—especially in German—the trill is often reduced to a minimum or suppressed altogether.

As regards the place of consonants, there is, as already remarked, great diversity among phoneticians, both in mapping out the palate and tongue and in the names given to these divisions. The classification and nomenclature given here is, in the main, that of Bell.

By place, then, we distinguish seven main classes of consonants: back, front, point, blade, fan, lip, and lip-teeth.

'Back' (guttural) consonants are formed between the root of the tongue and the soft palate. In most languages the positions of these consonants vary according to those of the accompanying vowels: thus the back-stop and back-nasal in *king* are more forward than in *conquer*.

'Front' (palatal) consonants are formed between the middle of the tongue and the hard palate, the point of the tongue lying passively behind the lower teeth. It is easy to make the front-open-voice **j** in *you* into the corresponding stop **ɟ** by narrowing the passage till there is complete closure, as in Hungarian *nagy* **nɔɟ** 'world'. In the same way the open breath **c** = Hungarian *ty*. **ɟ** nasalized becomes **ñ**—Italian *gn*, Spanish *ñ*, French *gn* in *vigne*. The front-divided-voice consonant is the Italian *gl* and Spanish *ll*. These are all simple sounds, distinct from the **lj**, **nj** in French and English *million* and English *onion*.

'Point' consonants when formed against the teeth are called 'point-teeth' (dental). English **þ** in *thin* is the point-teeth-open-breath consonant, **ð** in *then* the corresponding voice consonant. If **ð** is modified by turning the tip of the tongue back into the inner position—about on the arch-rim—it becomes the untrilled **r** in English *rearing*, in which position the tongue is easily trilled, the trilling becoming more and more difficult the more the tongue is approximated to the point-teeth position. In French and many other languages all the point consonants **t**, **d**, **n**, **l** etc., are formed on the teeth, except **r** which is always more retracted than the other point consonants. If the tip of the tongue is turned so far back as to articulate with its lower edge against the arch of the palate—that is, farther back than for the 'inner' position—it is said to be 'inverted'. Inverted **r** is frequent in the dialects of the south-west of England. The opposite of inversion is 'protrusion', in which the tip of the tongue articulates against the upper lip.

'Blade' consonants are formed by the blade or flattened tip of the tongue against the gums, as in English **s**, **z**, or against the teeth as in the corresponding French sounds. If these consonants are modified by turning the tongue a little back, so as to bring the point more into play, they become the 'blade-point' consonants **ʃ**, **ʒ**, as in *fish*, *measure*. **ʃ** is acoustically a dull **s**. In some languages, such as German, sounds similar to **ʃ** and **ʒ** are formed partly by rounding, which lowers the pitch of the hiss in the same way as retraction does, so that the tongue-articulation is only imperfectly carried out. When the rounding is very marked there is only a slight raising of the front of the tongue, as in some Swedish dialects; and if the tongue-articulation is progressively shifted back, and the rounding diminished in the same proportion, **ʃ** can at last develop into the pure back-open consonant **x**, as in the present pronunciation of Spanish *x* and *j*.

The English point consonants **t**, **d**, **n**, **l** are formed on the gums just behind the teeth, the point of the tongue being flattened, so that they are almost blade consonants.

'Fan' (spread) consonants—the 'emphatic' consonants of Arabic—are modifications of point and blade consonants, in which the sides of the tongue are spread out, so that the hiss of such a consonant as **s** is formed partly between the sides of the tongue and the back teeth, which gives a peculiar deep, dull quality to these sounds.

'Lip' consonants, such as **p**, **m**, and 'lip-teeth' consonants, such as **f**, **v**, offer no difficulty. The simple lip-open-breath consonant does not occur in English; it is the sound produced in blowing out a candle. The corresponding voice sound is frequent in German—especially in Middle Germany—in such words as *quelle*.

If the lip-open consonants are modified by raising the back of the tongue, they become the 'lip-back' consonants **wh**, **w** in English *what*, *we*, which may also be regarded as consonantized **u**. In them the lip articulation predominates. In the 'back-lip' consonants, as in German *auch*, the reverse is the case.

This last is one of a large number of 'lip-modified' consonants, of which the already-mentioned German *sch* is a further example.

In a similar way consonants may be 'front-modified'. **l** is peculiarly susceptible to such modifications. In French and other languages it is formed with the tongue more convex than in English, and consequently with a tendency to front-modification. Front-modified **s** and point **r** may be heard in Russian in such words as *gusĭ* 'goose', *tsarĭ* 'emperor', where the final vowels are silent.

Some consonants are formed below the mouth.

When the glottis is sharply opened or closed on a passage of breath or voice an effect is produced similar to that of a stop in the mouth, such as **k**. This 'glottal stop' is the sound produced in hiccuping; and is an independent sound in some languages, such as Arabic, where it is called 'hamza'. In German all words beginning with a stressed (accented) vowel have a more or less distinct glottal stop before the vowel.

Of the passages below the glottis, the bronchials and the windpipe are both susceptible of contraction.

Spasmodic contraction of the bronchial passages is the main factor in producing what is known as 'the asthmatic wheeze'. If this contraction is regulated and made voluntary it results in the deep hiss of the Arabic *ḥā.* If this sound is voiced, it causes a peculiar intermittent vibration of voice, which is habitual with some speakers, especially in Germany. If this effect is softened by slightly expanding the bronchial passages, an **r**-like sound is produced, which is that of the Arabic *ʿain.*

Contraction of the windpipe produces a sound similar to the Arabic *ḥā*, but weaker, which when followed by a vowel has the effect of a strong aspirate. When voiced it becomes a mere colourer of the accompanying voice-murmur, or vowel, to which it imparts a deep timbre.

Non-expiratory Sounds. All the sounds hitherto described imply out-breathing or expiration. Many of them can also be formed with in-breathing or inspiration. In English it is a not uncommon trick of speech to pronounce *no* in this manner, to express emphatic denial.

Some consonants are formed without either in- or out-breathing, but solely with the air in the throat or mouth. In forming 'suction-stops' or 'clicks' the tongue or lips are put in the position for a stop, and the air is sucked out from between the organs in contact, so that when the stop is loosened, a smacking sound is produced by the air rushing in to fill the vacuum. Thus the point-click is the interjection of impatience commonly written *tut!* In many savage languages, clicks are a part of ordinary speech.

'Phonetics', *Encyclopædia Britannica,* 11th Edn., 1911, pp. 464–5

The Arabic Throat Sounds. In addition to the ordinary back consonants and **h**, Arabic is remarkable for possessing three throat sounds. One of these is the glottal stop, found also in Danish and other European languages. Of the other two, one, the *ḥ*, is a hiss, the other, *ain*, is a voice consonant.

Czermak published in 1858 what professed to be a laryngoscopic investigation of these two sounds as pronounced by a native of Egypt, the result being to confirm an 'acute' conjecture of his friend Brücke, namely that these sounds are whisper strengthened by contraction of the larynx above the glottis. When I began the study of Arabic without a teacher about three years ago, I tried to carry out this pronunciation; but as I had the greatest difficulty in realizing its practical possibility, I was glad to have an opportunity, early in this year, of studying the pronunciation of a Scotchman born in Egypt—the Rev. H. W. Hogg. The result, as regards the *ḥ*, has been startling.

I put such implicit faith in Czermak's analysis that I was greatly disheartened to find that long after I had mastered all the other sounds, I was quite unable to pronounce the *ḥ* with even approximate correctness. All attempts to imitate it by whisper failed utterly; and I found that whenever I seemed to get near it, I was really producing an untrilled **x**˧, which is the sound usually adopted by the Greeks and Germans, and closely resembles the *ḥ*, which, acoustically speaking, stands in about the same relation to it as **ʃ** does to **s**. The *ḥ* is a remarkably strong, clear sound, bearing a close resemblance to the hiss of a goose. This clearness of sound is the result of keeping the passages above as open as possible, so as not to dull the hiss by any mixture of the **x**-sound. I had the greatest difficulty in getting rid of this tendency, even after I had found the key to the formation of the sound. When, therefore, we find Spitta in his *Grammatik des arabischen vulgärdialectes von Ægypten* directing us to form the *ḥ* by compressing the edges of the glottis, and at the same time raising the middle part of the tongue towards the palate, we can't help suspecting a combination of Czermak's analysis with his own faulty German pronunciation.

Meanwhile I was surprised to find from a subsequent article by Czermak in the same periodical that his observations were made not on the Arab, but on his own imitation of that Arab's pronunciation! Now as Spitta, who lived for years in the country, seems to have failed to master the *ḥ*, it is possible that Czermak also failed. At any rate, we can no longer regard the theory started by Brücke as scientifically certain.

I resolved therefore to start afresh. Brücke had argued that as the *ḥ* could not be formed in the glottis, it must be formed above. Failing to produce it in this way, I thought, as a desperate experiment, of trying to narrow the larynx *below* the glottis. At the first attempt I produced a sound which I had never uttered before, and which seemed to me to be the one wanted. At our next meeting my teacher admitted that I had got it nearly correct. By steady practice I strengthened the muscles of the larynx, and got rid of the mixture of the **x**-sound, till at last I was able to produce a strong, clear hiss like that of my teacher. But even then it took weeks of practice to join it on to other sounds.

My practical directions for forming the sound are therefore: (1) practice **x**˧ till you have so clear a feeling of its mechanism that you can eliminate it from your *ḥ*; (2) practice strong whisper till you know by muscular sensation where your glottis is; (3) after whisper, utter a sigh, so as to get the glottis quite open, and then try to narrow the throat below the place where you formed the whisper. To make sure that there is no **x**-sound in it, suddenly increase the force, and the presence of any **x**-sound will be betrayed by the resulting uvula trill.

The *ḥ* itself can be trilled, but this trill is quite distinct from that of the uvula, and is a sound that hardly enters into practical phonetics. The following words will serve as progressive exercises: *ḥā* (name of the letter), *rāḥ* 'went', *riḥ* 'wind', *ruḥ* 'spirit', *muḥammad* 'Mahomet' (*mm* = **m:m**), *naḥl* (*l* voiceless) 'bee', distinct from *nakhl* (**nɑxl̥**, the **x** trilled) 'palm-tree', *fatḥ* 'opening'.

If I voice *ḥ*, I get a harsh, creaking, croaking sound, in which the glottis vibrates slowly and brokenly. If I then diminish the throat-contraction, so as to allow the voice-element to become more distinct, I get the *ain*, (ʿ) as in the name *ʿabdu l-ʿaziz* 'Servant of the Mighty One'. It bears a certain resemblance to the Parisian *r*, but is, of course, a pure throat sound, without any modification by the uvula or back of the tongue. It has a remarkably clear sound, in spite of its croaking character.

It will be seen that I have incidentally given a new explanation of the formation of the *strohbass* or 'creaking voice' as due ultimately to narrowing of the lower opening of the larynx.

'The Arabic Throat Sounds', *Le Maître phonétique*, 1895, pp. 81 ff.

In my former communication on this subject [See above. *Ed.*], I arrived at the following conclusions as regards these sounds:

(1) That they are not superglottal, as was generally assumed;

(2) That they are, on the contrary, the result of narrowing the throat below the glottis.

But I did not succeed in determining the exact place of the formation.

I always felt that they were formed very low down in the throat; and if I had followed my subjective impressions more boldly, what I am writing now would have been superfluous.

Not being able to realize the possibility of throat-contraction below the larynx, I suggested an apparently impossible contraction of the lower opening of the larynx.

In the second edition of my primer of phonetics I more cautiously explain these 'deep throat sounds' as the result of narrowing the throat passages 'in a way which has not yet been explained'.

Last year one of my American pupils—Mr P. W. Carhart—surprised me by the ease with which he pronounced the throat hiss. He attributed it to his having been accustomed when a boy to imitate the asthmatic wheeze of a broken-winded horse with a similar sound. He agreed with me in locating the contraction very far down, and when I expressed doubt of the possibility of contraction in the bronchial region, he asked Why not?, and promised to investigate the question anatomically, which I hope he will do.

Meanwhile I found on reference to the medical books that they explain asthma as the result of spasmodic contraction of the muscular fibres surrounding the smaller bronchial tubes.

There is therefore no anatomical impossibility in assuming that the deep throat sounds are the result of a voluntary contraction of the same kind: that the Arabic *ḥā* is simply a bronchial hiss.

It is barely possible that Czermak did imitate these sounds correctly and that what he describes are mere secondary narrowings above the bronchial passages.

As I am obliged to give the above explanation of these sounds in my phonetic teaching, I thought it desirable to make it generally known.

'The Arabic Throat Sounds Again', *Le Maître phonétique*, 1904, pp. 36 f.

In investigating experimentally—but not instrumentally—the formation of the Arabic throat sounds [See two foregoing extracts. *Ed.*], I was surprised and somewhat disheartened by the vagueness of my subjective impressions as regards the place where I formed the sounds: sometimes the place of throat-narrowing seemed to be at or near the lower opening of the larynx, sometimes right down in the chest.

I find now that I was producing two similar, but distinct sounds; and that the strengthening of the sound after practising it was not, as I assumed, the result of any strengthening of the muscles, but simply of my definitely forming it in the bronchial region.

I was right in locating the weak throat-hiss higher up, although I was wrong in locating it in the larynx itself. It is formed in the windpipe: it is a tracheal hiss, a sound for which no symbol has yet been provided in any phonetic notation as far as I can remember. Even in Jespersen's Analphabetic Notation there is nothing between the glottis and the lungs. There can be no doubt that the windpipe is capable of contraction, for it is described as 'an elastic tube kept open by eighteen or twenty rings which do not quite meet at the back' (Behnke, *Mechanism of the Human Voice*, p. 31).

I find that when I fully contract the windpipe—for there are infinite degrees of contraction possible—I get a clear aspirate, weaker than the Arabic *ḥā*, but stronger than the ordinary glottal aspirate. I am not as yet able to say that it is the regular form of the aspirate in any language, but I believe that I have heard it from individuals of various nationalities, and have hitherto confused it with the ordinary 'strong aspirate' [See p. 49. *Ed.*].

This tracheal aspirate has a wider interest for the elocutionist and the singer.

As soon as I had fixed the sound so as to know it both by ear and feeling, I naturally went on to voice it, expecting the result to be a definite voice-consonant analogous to the Arabic *'ain*. On making the experiment I was disappointed to find that it didn't yield any definite sound at all, any more than if it had been an ordinary aspirate. Windpipe-contraction when added to a voice sound does not make a new sound of it, but only modifies its general character. When I had recognized this, and tried it with a variety of vowels, my former disappointment was amply compensated: I was delighted to find that I was at last able to clear up the mystery of the production of what the old Italian singing-masters called the 'voce coperta'—what in French is called 'timbre obscur', and in German 'gedeckter ton'. These 'covered tones' are simply the result of narrowing the windpipe. Or rather, they ought to be; for many singers confuse—and combine—the covered tone with the dull tone which is caused by narrowing the lip-passage, the high **i**'s of such singers becoming practically merged into **y**'s. It will now be quite easy for them to keep the two apart: to use windpipe-contraction for softening the shrillness of the high notes of the voice, and making their production easier, and to use lip-contraction as an independent means of voice-colouring and expression.

It has been often remarked that the wide sounds of the vowels are less distinct from the corresponding narrow sounds when sung on high notes. Some theorists have gone so far as to assert that it is impossible to pronounce an 'open' **i** or **e** on a high note without producing a harsh tone and ultimately ruining the voice. But this is quite imaginary: there is no more difficulty in combining windpipe-contraction with a wide than there is in combining it with a narrow vowel; and although the covered tone certainly makes the wideness of the vowel less distinct on a high note, it does not by any means make the wide into a narrow vowel.

Again, teachers of singing often direct their pupils to form a vowel on a high note with the covered tone, and then to sing it down the scale, preserving the covered tone as far down as possible. But I found that there is no more difficulty in narrowing the windpipe on a low than on a high note, although a vowel formed on a low note with the covered tone is unpleasant to the ear. And yet many speak habitually in this way—especially here in Oxford.

Windpipe-contraction seems to be also the key to the explanation of that much contested question: the nature and formation of the so-called 'voce mista' ('voix mixte'). This compromise between the thick and thin registers (chest-voice and falsetto) is explained by Behnke (in his book already quoted from) as the thin register combined with lowering of the larynx. But there is a general agreement now among the best authorities that the position of the larynx is always a secondary phenomenon which has no effect on sounds, and may therefore be safely ignored. And most teachers of singing agree in regarding any artificial raising or lowering of the larynx as unnatural and injurious to the voice. As far as I can make out, the voce mista is simply the thin register softened by that contraction of the windpipe which is the natural accompaniment of the higher notes of the voice.

We see then, if my theories are correct, that the function of windpipe narrowing in modifying voice-quality is exactly the opposite of that of bronchial contraction: the former facilitates the production of high, the latter that of abnormally low notes—in what Garcia calls the 'contra-bass' register.

'A New Throat Sound', *Le Maître phonétique*, 1906, pp. 56–8

E. SYNTHESIS

[The selected passages below indicate in a very general way what Sweet includes in his consideration of synthesis. The distinction he draws between analysis and synthesis has already been outlined in an earlier section (pp. 43–4). Sweet's handling of synthesis varies in detail and arrangement as between the *Handbook* and the *Primer of Phonetics*, although his general statements upon the subject remain constant. In the *Handbook* more emphasis is laid upon the distinction between 'special' and 'general' synthesis, 'the former dealing with special combinations, the latter with sound-groups generally' (*Handbook*, p. 56), and the part of the *Handbook* devoted to synthesis is arranged accordingly, in two subsections headed 'Special Synthesis' and 'General Synthesis' respectively. In the *Primer* these are abandoned in favour of a single section headed 'Synthesis', with some consequent rearrangement of the material. In the third and fourth extracts below, passages exclusive to the *Handbook* are shown between sloping lines, passages exclusive to the *Primer* in square brackets. *Ed.*]

We have now to consider the *synthesis* of sounds, that is, the different ways in which they are joined together in speech.

When sounds are joined together we have to consider their relative *quantity*, *stress*, and *intonation*.

Quantity. By quantity, sounds are distinguished as *long*, *half-long* or medium, and *short*, 'long' being often used to include half-long as well. In phonetic notation long and half-long vowels are doubled, short vowels being written single, as in **məəmə** *murmur*. The length of consonants is only occasionally marked by doubling.

Stress. There are three main degrees of stress or loudness: *strong*, *half-strong* or medium, and *weak*. Thus in *contradict* the last syllable is strong, the first half-strong, the next weak. We mark strong stress by ·, half-strong by :, these marks being put before the sound on which the stressed syllable begins, weak or unstressed syllables being left unmarked: **:kontrə·dikt.** Weak stress is marked when necessary by prefixing **-**, as in **-it reinz** *it rains*.

Sounds which occur only in unstressed syllables, such as the short **ə** in **məəmə** *murmur*, are called *weak*.

Intonation. Intonation or tone is either *level*, *rising*, or *falling*, marked respectively ¯, ´, `. The level tone is not much used in speech. The rising tone is heard in questions, such as *what*´, the falling in answers, such as *no*`. Besides these *simple* tones there are *compound* tones, formed by uniting a rising and a falling tone in one syllable. The *compound rise* or falling-rising tone (marked ᵛ) may be heard in *take care!* when used warningly; the *compound fall* or rising-falling tone (marked ^) may be heard in *oh!* when expressing sarcasm.

The level tone may be either *high* or *low* in pitch, and the other tones may begin either in a high or a low pitch. When excited, we speak in a high pitch or key: when depressed, in a low key.

The non-level tones can pass through different *intervals*. The greater the interval, the more emphatic the tone becomes. Thus *what*´ with a slight rise expresses mere enquiry, but with a long rise—rising from a very low to a very high pitch—it expresses surprise or indignation.

Glides. Glides are sounds produced during the transition from one sound to another. Thus in **kii** *key* we have the glide from the **k**-position to the **ii**-position, which does not, however, require to be written, as it is implied by the positions of **k** and **ii**.

Consonants are often joined together without any glide, not only in such combinations as **nd** in *hand*, where the **d** is formed by continuing the **n**, the nose-passage being closed at the same time, but also in such words as the English *act* **ækt**.

Syllables. A syllable is a vowel, either alone or in combination with consonants, uttered with a single impulse of stress. Every fresh impulse of stress makes a new syllable, the beginning of the syllable corresponding with the beginning of the stress. Thus **ə·tæk** *attack* has two syllables, the first syllable consisting of the vowel **ə** uttered with weak stress, the second of **tæk** uttered with a new impulse of stress beginning on the **t**. Vowel-like consonants often form syllables in the same way as vowels, as in *battle* = **bæt-l**.

Diphthongs. If two vowels are uttered with one impulse of stress, so as to form a single syllable, the combination is called a *diphthong*, such as **oi** in *oil.* Most diphthongs have the stress on the first element. If three vowels are combined in this way, we have a *triphthong*, as in **faiə** *fire.* A simple long vowel, such as **əə**, is called a *monophthong.*

A New English Grammar, 1891, pp. 227 ff.

We have hitherto considered sounds from the point of view of *analysis.* We have now to consider their *synthesis*, that is, the different ways in which they are joined together. We first have to learn to recognize the distinctions of *quantity* or length, *stress* or loudness, and *intonation* or tone.

By quantity sounds are distinguished as *long*, *half-long* or medium, and *short*, the two former being indicated by doubling.

There are also three degrees of stress: *strong* ·, half-strong or medium :, and *weak*, which is marked when necessary by prefixing -, these marks being put before the sound on which the stressed syllable begins, as in **:kontrə·dikt** *contradict*, which has exactly the same stress as the sentence **:kɐm -ət ·wɐns** *come at once!* A *syllable* is a group of sounds containing a vowel or vowel-like consonant uttered with one impulse of stress. If two vowels are uttered with one impulse of stress, they together constitute a *diphthong.*

Intonation is either *level* (-), *rising* (´), or *falling* (`). The rising tone may be heard in such questions as *what*´, the falling in answers, such as *yes*`. In intonation we must also distinguish the length of the rise or fall. Thus *what* with a short rise—beginning rather high—expresses mere inquiry, but with a long rise—beginning low—it expresses surprise or indignation. There are also compound tones formed by combining a rise and a fall in one syllable, viz. the *compound-rising* (falling-rising) tone marked ˅, and the *compound-falling* (rising-falling) tone marked ˄, as in *take care* ˅ expressing caution or warning, *oh*˄ expressing sarcasm.

Glides are sounds in which the organs of speech do not remain in any one definite position, but keep on moving, so as to form an indefinite series of different positions. We generally make glides in passing from one position to another. Thus in such a combination of sounds as **aja**, we first have the **a**-position and then the movement up towards the **j**-position, producing an indefinite number of sounds intermediate between **a** and **j**. If we stop for a moment just before we get to the **j**, we form a distinct **i**, giving **aija.**

But there are also glideless combinations, as in **hænd** *hand*, where the **d** is simply the **n** lengthened and unnasalized, so that there is no change whatever in the position of the tongue in passing from the **n** to the **d.**

The History of Language, 1900, pp. 17 ff.

We have hitherto considered sounds from a purely analytical point of view, that is, each sound has been considered by itself, as if it were a fixed, isolated element. But in language, sounds are combined together to form sentences, and many sounds occur only in certain fixed combinations. Hence the necessity for synthesis as well as analysis. Analysis regards each sound as a fixed, stationary point, synthesis as a momentary point in a stream of incessant change. Synthesis looks mainly at the beginning and end of each sound, as the points where it is linked on to other sounds, while analysis concerns itself only with the middle of the fully developed sound. /Synthesis is either special or general, the former dealing with special combinations, the latter with sound-groups generally./ [Synthesis is thus the science of *sound-joints* or 'glides'. There is also a more general kind of synthesis which deals with the *relations* of sounds to one another in sound-groups—their difference in length, loudness, pitch, etc. Synthesis, lastly, deals with the organic and acoustic *grouping* of sounds into syllables, etc., and the divisions between these groups.]

A Handbook of Phonetics, 1877, p. 56; and
A Primer of Phonetics, 1890, p. 41

The popular fourfold division of the elements of speech into letters (that is, sounds), syllables, words, and sentences, is not purely phonetic, but also partly graphical and logical. The first and most important point to see is that our ordinary word-division is a *logical* and not a *phonetic* analysis. No amount of study of the sounds only of a sentence will enable us to recognize the individual words of which it consists. We may write down every sound, every shade of synthesis, but we shall never be able to analyse the sentence into separate words till we know its meaning, and even then we shall find that word-division postulates much thought and comparison of sentences one with another. /The fixity of our conventional word-division and the mechanical way in which we learn it, blinds us to the real complexity of the questions involved in it, and to the fact that there is no word-division whatever in language itself, considered simply as an aggregate of sounds./

The only division actually made in language is that into 'breath-groups'. We are unable to utter more than a certain number of sounds in succession without renewing the stock of air in the lungs. These breath-groups correspond partially to the logical division into sentences: every sentence is necessarily a breath-group, but every breath-group need not be a complete sentence.

Within each breath-group there is no pause whatever, /and the popular idea that we make a pause after every word is quite false/

[notwithstanding the popular idea that we make a pause between every word]. Thus, in such a sentence as *put on your hat* we hear clearly the /final breath-glide or 'recoil', as it is sometimes called,/ ['recoil' or final breath-glide] which follows the final **t** of *hat*, but the **t** of *put* runs on to the following vowel without any recoil, exactly as in the single word *putting*. In *put back* there is no glide at all after the **t**.

/The other phonetic divisions of word and syllable, are clearly the result of deliberate analysis./

[The only phonetic divisions in a breath-group are those into sounds and syllables and intervening glides.]

A Handbook of Phonetics, 1877, pp. 86–7, and
A Primer of Phonetics, 1890, pp. 41–2

The most important factors of synthesis, both special and general, are force, quantity, and the theory of glides or transitional sounds.

A Handbook of Phonetics, 1877, p. 56

The most important general factors of synthesis are *quantity* and *stress*, which both modify glides and constitute relations between adjoining sounds.

A Primer of Phonetics, 1890, p. 42

Besides analysing each sound separately, phonetics has to deal with the various phenomena which accompany synthesis, that is, the succession or combination of sounds in syllables, words, and sentences. Although a sentence may consist of a single word, and that word of a single vowel, most sounds occur only in combination with others.

. . . . .

The three general factors of synthesis are quantity (length), stress (force), and intonation.

The Sounds of English, 1908, p. 49

Besides analysing each sound separately, phonetics has to deal with the phenomena which accompany synthesis or the combination of sounds. Although a sentence may consist of a single word, and that word of a single vowel, sounds mostly occur only in combination with one another. The ordinary division into sentences and words is logical, not phonetic: we cannot mark off sentences and cut them up into words until we know what they mean and are able to analyse them grammatically. But the logical division into sentences corresponds to some extent with the phonetic division into 'breath-groups', marked off by our inability to utter more than a certain number of syllables in succession without pausing to take breath. Within each of these breath-groups there is no necessary pause between the words, except when we pause for emphasis. The only necessary phonetic divisions within the breath-group are those into syllables, sounds and intervening 'glides'. But before considering these last it will be necessary to say something about the general factors of synthesis: quantity, stress, and intonation.

'Phonetics', *Encyclopædia Britannica*, 11th Edn., 1911, p. 465

1. *Force, Stress, Accent, Rhythm*

[Instructive to follow in this section is Sweet's usage with regard to such terms as 'force', 'loudness', 'stress', and 'accent', and of the relations, explicit or implicit, between them. In the second extract, the usual conventions—sloping lines for passages exclusive to the *Handbook*, square brackets for those exclusive to the *Primer of Phonetics*—are adopted, except for the Romic and Visible Speech examples, which are included without such marks. The modifications of the *Handbook* text that appear in the *Primer* are interesting. Most of them may be readily interpreted as attempts at greater clarity, precision, or accuracy, but a few are less easy to account for, as for example the substitution of French *toute* for *tête* on p. 132. *Ed.*]

Stress. This is, organically, the result of the force with which the breath is expelled from the lungs; acoustically it produces the effect of loudness, which is dependent on the size of the sound-vibrations: the bigger the waves, the louder the sound, the greater the stress.

The Sounds of English, 1908, p. 50

Force [Stress]. Force, like quantity, belongs essentially to the synthesis of sounds, for it is always relative, always implying comparison, /either of two different sounds or of different portions of the same sound, with which latter we are here concerned/ [either of two different groups of sounds or of two different portions of the same group]. Physically it is synonymous with the force with which the breath is expelled from the lungs /which is effected by upward pressure of the diaphragm/. Every impulse of force is therefore attended by a distinct muscular sensation. Acoustically it produces the effect known as 'loudness', which is dependent on the size of the vibration-waves, which produce the sensation of sound. When we say, therefore, that one sound, or group of sounds, is uttered with more force than another, as in comparing the first with the second syllable of *heavy*, we mean that in its utterance the air is expelled from the lungs with a greater muscular effort, that in consequence the size of the resulting sound-waves is greater, producing an effect of greater loudness on the ear.

/It must, of course, be understood that force has nothing to do with pitch or tone./

Force in its synthetic sense must /also/ be carefully distinguished from those variations in the friction of unstopped consonants which are due to the varying width of the configurative passage [although, of course, all articulation postulates a certain amount of force to be audible at all]. /The friction of consonants is an essential element of their organic formation, and has no special connection with synthesis. (*Fn.*: There is, however, a certain connection between the audibility of the friction and the force of the outgoing air: a certain definite position may produce audible friction under a strong impulse of breath, but not under a weak one. But the position itself is something absolute, and all articulation postulates a certain amount of force to be audible at all.)/

We have now to consider the changes of force in a single breath-impulse, as for instance in pronouncing any vowel, such as **aɪ**]ɫ. Here we have three /kinds/ [degrees] of force, (1) level, (2) increasing (crescendo), and (3) diminishing (diminuendo), which may be symbolized thus:

level	**a̿ɪ̿**	]ɫ=
increasing	**aɪ** (with < above)	]ɫ<
diminishing	**aɪ** (with > above)	]ɫ>.

In examining the force of any /stress-group/ [sound-group] it is a great help to whisper it, which gets rid of all disturbing /tone-changes/ [changes of pitch].

The general tendency of language is to pronounce with diminishing force. Thus in English the **k** of *cat* is pronounced with more force than the **t**. Hence also the end of a long is weaker than that of a short vowel, the force diminishing continuously throughout [the long vowel]. Thus the **t** of *cart* is weaker than that of *cat*. /The same phenomena may be observed in German also./ [In German the diminution of force is still more rapid than in English.] In French on the other hand the force is /more/ [nearly] equal, the final **t** of /*tête*/ [*toute*], for instance, being pronounced with almost as much force as the initial one; /but even here there is no perfectly level force/. < [Increasing force] may be heard in interjections, as, for instance, in **aɪ**]ɫ< denoting joyful surprise.

Here it is accompanied with a marked rise in pitch, but if whispered the < is unmistakeable.

A Handbook of Phonetics, 1877, pp. 57–8, and
A Primer of Phonetics, 1890, pp. 44–5

The influence of force on the actual synthesis of language is extremely important. This subject will be fully discussed under General Synthesis.[1] Here we need only remark that the sense of unity and separation is mainly due to force. As a general rule *continuity* of force gives the impression of unity, *discontinuity* that of separation. Thus $\overset{=}{\text{aɪ}}$, $\overset{<}{\text{aɪ}}$, and $\overset{>}{\text{aɪ}}$ all have the effect of single indivisible units, if prolonged ever so much. But $\overset{<<}{\text{aɪɪɪ}}$ and $\overset{>>}{\text{aɪɪɪ}}$ sound like two distinct units, even when there is not the slightest pause between them.

A Handbook of Phonetics, 1877, p. 59

The comparative force with which the syllables that make up a longer group are uttered is called 'stress'. In speaking of the stress of words in a sentence as opposed to that of syllables in a word the term 'emphasis' is commonly used, but this distinction is not admitted in phonetics, which ignores word-division, and divides sentences straight off into syllables.

There are three main degrees of stress: *strong* (·), *half-strong* or 'medium' (:), and *weak* (ᵛ). *Very strong* or 'extra strong' may be marked (;). (·) is assumed to be an abbreviation of (ᶺ), which is a modification of (ʌ). Weak stress is generally left unmarked. (ᵛ) may then be utilized to indicate a weak stress slightly stronger than another weak one. In connected texts where it is necessary to mark unstressed words, weak stress is denoted by (-). All stress-marks are put before the element on which the stress begins, so as to leave room for quantity-marks and other diacritics after it. Another advantage of this method is, that it marks the divisions into syllables. All three degrees of stress are shown in such a word as *contradict* :ɑɟɜʊɷʅ·ɷʃɑʊ. The sentence *come at once!* has exactly the same stress: :ɑ]ꟻʅʊ·ɜ]ɜs or :ɑ]ꟻ -ʅʊ ·ɜ]ɜs.

The degrees of stress are really infinite, and in a single sound-group (word or sentence) every syllable may have a different degree of stress. Thus such a word as *impenetrability* has, roughly speaking, two stresses, a strong one on the fifth, and a medium one on the first (or sometimes on the second)—:ʃꟻɒʃɜʅʊɷʅ·ɘʃɷʃ˔ʊʃ˔. But if we pronounce *-bility*

[1] The relevant passages in the *Handbook* are not included in this volume, but in substance are closely akin to the immediately succeeding extract from the *Primer of Phonetics*. *Ed.*

by itself, we shall find that all three syllables have a different stress, the third being stronger than the second and weaker than the first. In *penetra-* there is the same relation, but all the syllables are a shade weaker than the corresponding ones in *-bility*. The order of the syllables in stress is therefore as follows, 1 being the highest:

2	3	7	5	1	6	4
ʃꟻ	ɒʃ	ɿʅ	ʊωʅ	ɘʃ	ωʃ˔	ʊʃ˔
im-	pe-	ne-	tra-	bi-	li-	ty.[1]

The surest way of determining the relative force of any two syllables is to pronounce the other syllables *mentally* only, or in a whisper, pronouncing the special syllables aloud, and their relative force will then come out clearly. Thus, taking *-bility* by itself, if we utter the first syllable mentally, the other two aloud, we shall find that the second of these two has the stronger stress.

There is an important feature of stress generally which in most cases makes any minuter symbolization of stress unnecessary. This is its *rhythmic* character, or the tendency to alternate weak and strong stress. Perfect uniformity of stress is as phonetically unnatural as level force in a single syllable, but the tendency of stress is not, like that of a single force-impulse, to decrease progressively, but rather to sway to and fro. Hence in a group of three syllables, of which the first has the predominant stress, we may generally infer that the second will be weaker than the third, as in *relative*, ·ωʃωʅˇʊʃ˔ɜ. Of course, in very rapid speech these minute distinctions become unrecognizable, the two last syllables of such a word as *relative* being apparently uttered with a single, progressively diminishing force-impulse.

But stress in all languages is more or less governed by logical as well as phonetic laws, which, of course, often clash. *Level* stress is, accordingly, very common in English, as in *thirteen* when uttered by itself, while in *thirteen years* the stress on the second syllable is diminished: ·ʋɪɫ·ʊʃɱɿ, ·ʋɪɫ:ʊʃɱɿ ·ɱʃɫʅs. In French there is a general tendency to level stress, the strong syllables rising only a little above the general level.

The discrimination of degrees of stress is no easy matter in any case, because of the counter-associations of quantity, intonation, and vowel-quality, which make us apt to fancy that long, high-toned, or clear-vowelled syllables have stronger stress than they really have. A long weak-stressed vowel may be heard in the drawling pronunciation of *what a pity!* :ɔɟʊ -ʅ ·ɒʃʊʃ˔ɫ. A stressless clear vowel may be heard

[1] The orthographic gloss, which does not appear in the *Primer*, is taken from the corresponding passage in the *Handbook*. *Ed.*

in such a word as *insect* ·ʃɔsʃɑʊ compared with *edict* ·ʃɷʊʃ˗ɑʊ, whose second vowel is one that occurs only in unstressed syllables.

Difference of force in whole groups of sounds may be indicated analogously with differences of speed, thus ·o :ɑ]ꟻ ·]ɒ denotes *come up!* uttered forcibly.

A Primer of Phonetics, 1890, pp. 45–8

Force. Loudness and stress (accent) depend on the force with which the breath is expelled (generally from the lungs). In a single breath-impulse, as in the vowel ***aa***, we can have three kinds of force:

level	]ɫ=
increasing	]ɫ<
diminishing	]ɫ>

The tendency in language is to utter with diminishing force.

The influence of force on the synthesis of speech is very important, for the sense of unity and separation depends mainly on it. *Continuity* of force gives a sense of *unity*, as in]ɫ>,]ɫ<>, *discontinuity*, as in]ɫ>>, that of *separation*, the]ɫ being broken up into two syllables. Hence, every syllable (vowel-group) must be uttered with a single impulse of breath, as it would otherwise be split up into two. In language the tendency is against uttering two successive syllables with the same force.

The comparative force with which the separate syllables of a sound-group (word, clause, or sentence) are uttered is called *stress* (accent). There are three main degrees of stress: *strong* (·), *half-strong* or 'medium' (:), and *weak* (ᵛ), the last being generally left unmarked. Weak stress is also marked by (-). In practice it is often sufficient to mark the strong stress only. The stress-marks are put before the element on which the stress begins. The tendency in language is to alternate strong (or medium) and weak stress. Thus, if such a group as ***kalana*** is stressed on the first syllable, the second is generally weak, the third medium or, at any rate, slightly stronger than the second: ·ɑ]ᵛω]:ɔ]. But in rapid speech such a word might also be pronounced ·ɑ]ᵛω]ᵛɔ], with a single impulse of breath. The answer to the question, Where does the syllable begin? is, that if it has a distinct stress (strong or medium) its beginning corresponds with the beginning of the stress. If, on the other hand, the syllable is weak, it is often difficult to settle where it begins. Hence it is possible to alter the syllable division by shifting the stress from one element to another. Thus *at all* ought strictly to be pronounced ʅʊ·ɟɫω but in actual speech the second syllable begins on the ***t***: ʅ·ʊɟɫω.

The distinction between long and double consonants also depends on stress and syllabification: in ·]ɷɫ:] the consonant is long, in ·]ɷ:ɷ] or ·]ɷ(ᵛ)ɷ] it is double. Double consonants cannot occur finally or isolated.

A History of English Sounds, 1888, pp. 7 ff.

Stress is, organically, the result of the force with which the breath is expelled from the lungs; while acoustically it produces the effect of loudness, which is dependent on the size of the sound-vibrations: the bigger the waves, the louder the sound, and the greater the stress, of which we may distinguish infinite degrees. If we distinguish only three, they are called *weak*, *medium*, and *strong*. The use of stress in different languages shows the same variety as quantity. Some languages, such as French, make comparatively little use of its distinctions, uttering all the syllables of words and sentences with a more or less even degree of force. English, on the other hand, makes great use of minute distinctions of stress both to distinguish the meanings of words and to mark their relations in sentences.

'Phonetics', *Encyclopædia Britannica*, 11th Edn., 1911, p. 465

Metrical Stress. I propose now to devote a few words to the analogies of musical accentuation, which will be found both instructive and interesting. The origin of rhythm is no doubt to be sought in the natural tendency to alternate strong and weak stress—rhythm is in fact nothing but the utilization of this instinct for aesthetic purposes by making it regular and symmetrical. As in language we have sentences, words, and sounds, so in music we have phrases, bars, and notes. If we take any sound, say the vowel **a**, and repeat it several times in succession with a uniform strong stress thus **aaaaaa**, it gives no impression of rhythm whatever, except that of a succession of isolated bars or musical words, just as in such a word-group as ***b*****ig*****b*****læk*****d*****ogz**, with its equally uniform word-stress, we feel that we have a succession of isolated, independent full-words. But if we retain only the first, third, and fifth stresses, thus ***a*****a*****a*****a*****a*****a**, we feel at once that instead of six bars we have only three, beginning on each strong stress, just as in language the syllable (and often the word) begins on the strong stress. If we retain only the first and fourth stresses giving ***a*****aa*****a*****aa**, we get two bars only. It is the regular recurrence of these groups of two or three (or more) 'beats' bound together by one predominating stress which constitutes the rhythm of two, three, etc., time. It is also possible to have a rhythm of four beats, thus ***a*****aaa*****a*****aaa**. But here the principle of alternation of force comes into play, and to break up the monotony of three weak stresses in succession, a secondary accent is placed on the third note of each bar, so that the rhythm really consists of four two-beat bars ***a**a**a**a**a**a**a**a* with two predominating stresses on the beginning of the first and third bars.

It is important to observe that the principles of metrical stress apply not only to music and poetry, but also, to a certain extent, to ordinary speech as well. Besides the purely logical stress which indicates the various relations of full-words, half-words, etc., there is a purely metrical stress, which often runs counter to the other. Thus in the sentence **itizsou** the first two syllables are half-words, the second being simply a sign of predication, and therefore hardly a word at all, and the only full-word in the group is the adverb **sou**. The logical accentuation can therefore only be **itiz*s*ou**. But as a matter of fact the usual accentuation is **it*i*zsou**, the full stress falling on the most insignificant syllable in the sentence! The explanation is a purely metrical one: the ear prefers to hear the alternation of weak, strong, weak, to hearing two weaks together followed by a strong. Similarly we often accent ***k*ænyu*t*elmiydhə*w*eitu** . . . instead of the logical **kənyu*t*elmiy** . . . And it is probable that certain collocations are preferred to others on purely metrical grounds.

In the ordinary musical notation the bars are divided by vertical lines or bars. The same method is adopted in the tonic sol-fa notation, and the beats are divided by :, thus

| a:a | a:a | a:a ||, | a:a:a | a:a:a ||.

Although regular and consistent, this method is extremely cumbrous, and my own practice has been for some time to discard the lines, etc., entirely, and write each bar simply as a word with nothing but a space between each group, thus **aa aa aa, aaa aaa**. With the help of a few simple signs for pauses and for holding or continuing a note, and a few diacritics to indicate fractions of notes (which often need not be expressed at all), music can thus be written almost as quickly as ordinary writing.

'Words, Logic, and Grammar', *TPS* 1875–6; in *Collected Papers of Henry Sweet*, 1913, pp. 11–12

2. *Quantity*

We may distinguish five degrees of quantity or length:

very long
long
half long or medium
short
very short

but for practical purposes the three distinctions of long, half long, and short are enough. Long is denoted by **ıı**, half-long by **ı** after the sound symbol, and short is left unmarked. If only two degrees are marked, **ı** is used for long, short being unmarked.

The quantity of any one sound is apt to vary according to its circumstances. Thus in English final long vowels, as in *see*, and before voice consonants, as in *seize*, are really long, while before breath consonants they are shortened to half-longs, as in *cease*. But in German full length is preserved before voiceless consonants as well as voice ones, so that the **o** in *noth* is as long as the English *node*, not half-long as in *note*.

In many Scotch dialects there are no full long vowels at all, all long vowels being shortened to half-longs.

In some languages, such as French, the distinctions of long and short are not clearly marked. In French most vowels are half-long, and are only occasionally lengthened or shortened into full longs and shorts. In French, distinctly short accented vowels are generally final, as in *oui*, which is directly opposed to English usage.

The distinctions of quantity apply to consonants as well as vowels. Thus in English consonants are long after short, short after long vowels, as in **hilı**, **hiıl** = *hill*, *heel*. **l** and the nasals are long before voice, short before voiceless consonants, as in **bilıd**, **bilt** = *build*, *built*. Even stops are lengthened finally after short vowels, as in **bædı** = *bad*. The English student should practise lengthening and shortening consonants under all circumstances. The short final consonants after short vowels will be found difficult. They may be heard in German pronunciation, as in *mann*, *hat*, and still more clearly in Danish, as in *ven*, *hat*, which have a very abrupt sound to English ears.

A Handbook of Phonetics, 1877, pp. 59 f.

We may distinguish five degrees of quantity or length:

very long	]♦♦
long	]♦
half long or medium	]▴
short	]▾
very short	]▾▾

but for practical purposes the threefold distinction of long, half long, and short is generally enough. Often, indeed, it is not advisable to do more than denote the distinction of long and short, assigning ♦ to long, and leaving short unmarked.

Full length may be heard in English stressed vowels when final, as in *sea*, and before voiced consonants, as in *seize*, half-length in stressed vowels before breath consonants, as in *cease*. Short final stressed vowels, as in French *si*, are difficult to English speakers.

The distinctions of quantity apply to consonants as well as vowels. In English consonants are long after a stressed short vowel, as in *hill*, short after a stressed long vowel, as in *heel*. But in such cases the length is often distributed equally over vowel and consonant. It may also be observed that length in the case of a breath stop like **t** means length of pause or cessation of sound. Short consonants after short stressed vowels offer great difficulties to English speakers; they may be heard in German words such as *mann*.

We can also distinguish degrees of *rapidity* of speech in different breath-groups or longer periods. Such differences of 'tempo' may be indicated by prefixing the quantity-marks + the symbol of breath: oǂ :ɑ]ꟻ ˙]ɒ = *come up* uttered slowly.

A Primer of Phonetics, 1890, pp. 43 f.

Quantity. Although in the broad phonetic notation of English it is necessary to mark only two degrees of vowel-quantity, it is easy to distinguish at least five: over-long ǂǂ, long ǂ, half-long or medium ˑ, short ˌ, and very short or abrupt ˌˌ. ǂ is written as a notched stroke.

The distinction between long and medium is well marked in English, although it does not generally require to be indicated in writing, as it is regularly dependent on the nature of the following consonant. The rule is that strong-stressed vowels when final or before a voice consonant are long, while before a voiceless consonant they are only half-long, as in *see* **siǂ**, *seize*, *broad* compared with *cease* **siˑs**, *eat*, *brought*. The difference is equally marked in the diphthongs, as in *no*, *ride*, *oil*, compared with *right*, *voice*. In other languages full length is preserved before voiceless as well as voiced sounds, as may be heard in the German pronunciation of *all right!*

The distinctions of quantity apply to consonants as well as vowels. In English there is a tendency to lengthen final consonants after strong short vowels, as in *man* compared with German *mann*, where the final consonant is quite short. There is also a tendency in English to lengthen soft consonants before voice consonants, and shorten them before voiceless consonants, as in *build* **bilǂd**, compared with *built* **bilt**.

The Sounds of English, 1908, pp. 49 f.

As regards quantity, it is enough for ordinary purposes to distinguish three degrees: long, half-long or medium, and short. In English what are called long vowels keep their full length when stressed and before final voice consonants, as in *see*, *broad*; and become half-long before voiceless consonants, as in *cease*, *brought*. In most other languages full length is preserved alike before all classes of consonants. The Romance languages have short final stressed vowels, as in French *si*. Unstressed vowels tend to become short in most languages. The distinctions of quantity apply to consonants as well as vowels. Thus English tends to lengthen final consonants after short stressed vowels, as in *man* compared with German *mann*, where the final consonant is quite short. Consonants, like vowels, tend to become short when unstressed. But in some languages, such as Finnish and Hungarian, stress has no effect on quantity, so that in these languages long vowels and double consonants occur as frequently in unstressed as in stressed syllables. Even in English we often lengthen final unstressed vowels in exclamations, as in *what a pity!* Some languages, such as the Romance languages and Russian, tend to level the distinctions of vowel-quantity: most of their vowels are half-long.

'Phonetics', *Encyclopædia Britannica,* 11th Edn., 1911, p. 465

3. *Syllables, Syllable Division, Syllabification*

[The fairly extensive textual differences between the *Handbook* and the *Primer of Phonetics* in the sections of these works that deal specifically with the topic of syllable division make it necessary to present them separately. The textual differences themselves derive, in part at least, from the absence in the part of the *Primer* headed 'Synthesis' of separate subdivisions for 'Special Synthesis' and 'General Synthesis' and from the rearrangement of the material that this entails (see p. 126), and in particular from the fact that in the *Primer* the section on 'Syllable Division' follows that on 'Force (Stress)', whereas in the *Handbook* it precedes it. *Ed.*]

A sound which can form a syllable by itself is called *syllabic*. Syllabicness implies an appreciable duration and force. The distinction between syllabic and non-syllabic is generally parallel to that between vowel and consonant. But those 'vowel-like' or 'liquid' voiced consonants which are unaccompanied by buzz are often also syllabic. These are ω **r**, ω **l**, and the nasals. Even voiceless consonants can be syllabic as in ɒsɫʊ *pst*, where the **s** is syllabically equivalent to a vowel by virtue of its length and stress, the unsyllabic ɒ and ʊ being comparatively momentary and stressless. A syllabic consonant is denoted by]: ɘʅʊω] = '*battle*'.

A vowel, on the other hand, can lose its syllabicness, especially in combination with another vowel, with which it then forms a *diphthong*. These diphthongic or 'glide-' vowels are written consonant size in Visible Speech, being, from a syllabic point of view, consonantal vowels, as in Jɾ **ai**, where the group is uttered with one impulse of diminishing force, ɾJ **ia**, which implies increasing force, the latter diphthong being almost equivalent to ɷJ **ja**. Jɾ is called a 'falling', ɾJ a 'rising' diphthong. Jɾ· with the second element lengthened ought to be considered a dissyllable, but it has the effect of a diphthong if the ɾ· is kept stressless.

A History of English Sounds, 1888, p. 9

A syllable is a vowel, either alone or in combination with consonants, uttered with a single impulse of stress. Every fresh impulse of stress makes a new syllable, the beginning of the syllable corresponding with the beginning of the stress. Thus **ə·tæk** *attack* has two syllables, the first syllable consisting of the vowel **ə** uttered with weak stress, the second of **tæk** uttered with a new impulse of stress beginning on the **t**. Vowel-like consonants often form syllables in the same way as vowels, as in *battle* = **bæt-l**.

A New English Grammar, 1891, p. 229

We may now turn to the important question of syllabification. The definition of a syllable is easy enough; it is a group of sounds containing a vowel, or, in some cases, a vowel-like consonant. To determine the number of syllables in a word, we have simply to count the number of vowels. The difficulty is to tell where the syllable begins. Here I am compelled to differ both from Mr Bell and Mr Ellis. Mr Bell considers that the division into syllables is determined by the nature of the sounds which constitute the syllable, whereas I hold that syllabification has nothing to do with the sounds themselves, but depends entirely on the force with which we pronounce them. (It must be understood that I speak of the natural syllabification of spoken language, not of the artificial syllabification of the spelling-books.) Let us consider the syllabification of a natural, simple sentence, such as ***t*eikəpdhə*t*iykəp**. Here we at once feel that the first **k** belongs to the preceding syllable, that the syllabification is clearly **teik-əp**, while the second **k** belongs to the following syllable, the division being **tiy-kəp**, the consonant being the same in both cases. The difference is simply one of stress, the first **k** being pronounced with weak, the second with strong force. (We may for the present disregard the fact that the stress is in both cases secondary.) The influence of the syllable-stress in determining the meaning of words is so important that if we reverse that of **teikəp** by beginning the secondary stress not on the vowel, but on the preceding **k**, the word becomes quite unintelligible, or rather, sounds like an Irish pronunciation of 'teacup'. Other examples of varying syllabification are **notət*a*ol** (*Fn.*: Generally, however, pronounced **notə*t*aol,** just as **ət*h*oum** becomes **ə*t*oum.**) and **ə*t*aol*m*æn**, **ə*t*æk** = 'attack' and **ət*æ*k** = 'at Ack' (name of place). We see, in short, that a syllable is a vowel-group beginning with a certain degree of force, which decreases up to the end of the syllable, till a new stress marks the beginning of another syllable. This decrease of force is observable in monosyllables also: in **kæt**, for instance, the **k** is much stronger than the **t**—we do not pronounce **kæ*t*** or even ***k*æ*t***, but only ***k*æt**. Indeed, it may be stated as a general law that perfect uniformity of force is something exceptional: force is followed by weakness of stress, and uniform weakness, again, cannot be sustained, but requires force to relieve it. These principles are clearly shown in the accentuation of polysyllable words. If we carefully measure the degrees of force with which the different syllables of a word like **impenətrə*b*ilitI** are pronounced, we shall find that every syllable has a different degree of force. Simple sentences, which are phonetically identical with polysyllabic words (or even in some cases with monosyllable ones), follow the same laws. They always have one predominant stress which dominates over the simple word-stress. The great distinction between words and sentences is that in the former the predominant stress is fixed and invariable, while in the latter it varies according to the principle of emphasis, which gives the strongest stress to the most important word.

Before leaving the subject of syllabification, I have only to warn against the error of imagining that the division into the syllables is ever made by any kind of pause—the truth is that there is no more break in **ət*a*ol** than there is in **ə*t*aol*m*æn**, and the idea that we pause between **ət** and **aol** is simply due to the association of the graphic separation in 'at all'. Mr Ellis considers that there is often a distinction made by omitting the 'glide' from vowel to consonant, or vice versa, but it seems to me that he is confusing *absence* of glide with mere *weakness* of glide. When we pronounce a stopped consonant wth stress, the air naturally escapes with greater force, which of course makes the glide more audible; but the glide is always there, however weakly it may be pronounced.

'Words, Logic, and Grammar', *TPS* 1875–6; in *Collected Papers of Henry Sweet*, 1913, pp. 9–11

Syllable Division. The audibility of language depends mainly on its vowels. It would be easy enough to construct a language composed entirely of consonants, but such a language would be inaudible except at very short distances. Acoustically speaking, consonants are mere modifiers of the vowels, and the ideal of distinctness would be reached by a language in which each consonant was separated from the next by a vowel.

Hence the ear soon learns to divide the sentences (breath-groups) of language into groups of vowels, each vowel being flanked by subordinate consonants. The analysis into separate consonants is a later one, as proved by the universal priority of syllabic over single-letter alphabets.

It often happens that a vowel-like consonant takes the place of a vowel, or rather of a vowel and a consonant. Thus in English **l*i*tl** = 'little' suggests **l**+the neutral vowel **l*i*t*e*hl.** In such a word as the Bohemian **kĝh*r*k** there is no vowel at all.

Some of the breath-sibilants are audible enough in themselves, and there are several interjectional words in which they have a distinctly vowel-effect. Thus **shı** by itself is used, and in combination with stops **sıt** and **psıt**, etc. The want of vocality, however, makes the ear somewhat unwilling to recognize the syllabic value of these consonants. The influence of voice in giving syllabic effect is strikingly shown in the stops with final voice glide. (See p. 161.)

If often happens that when two vowel-like consonants come together, one is regarded as a vowel (with a consonant), the other as a consonant. As a general rule the one that has the greater force (stress) and is the longest is felt to contain the vowel. Thus **mn·** (*Fn.*: The · indicates stress, beginning on the preceding sound.) suggest **m-*e*hn**, and **m·n** ***e*hm-n.**

We see, then, that the conception of a syllable is necessarily a somewhat vague one, which may vary in different languages, and may also be partly dependent on the associations of the written languages.

The question now arises, where does each syllable begin?

As we have seen, the sense of unity is mainly due to continuity of force. If sentences were uttered with level force throughout, the question of syllable-division could not be raised at all; we should be able to count the number of vowels, and thus determine the number of syllables, but we should never be able to settle where one syllable left off and another began, unless we adopted purely arbitrary criteria.

We find, however, that the different syllables of which any sound-group is composed are uttered with various degrees of force. This relative force of syllables is called 'stress' or 'accent'. For the present it is enough to distinguish between weak and strong accent, marking the latter by a · after the sound on which the stress begins. We have already seen that the strength of each separate force-impulse, such as we give to the separate syllables of any sound-group, tends to diminish progressively, until a new impulse begins, which in its turn diminishes progressively. The beginning of each of these force-impulses marks the beginning of the syllable. Thus the two sound groups **ʌn·eɪ*i*hm** and **ʌne·ɪ*i*hm** differ solely in the place where the stress begins, but their meaning is totally distinct, the first signifying 'a name', the second 'an aim'. In the first the stress, and consequently the syllable, begins on the **n**, in the second on the vowel. Similarly **ʌt·reh*i*h** = 'a try', **ʌtr·*e*h*i*h** = 'at Rye', **ʌtɔɪ·lt·*e*h*i*hmz** = 'at all times', **ʌt·ɔɪlm·æn** = 'a tall man'.

We see from these examples that the beginning of syllables is partly indicated by the ordinary word-division, that is, in all cases where a word happens to begin on a syllable with a strong stress. If a word begins on a weak-stressed syllable the beginning of its strong syllable is not indicated, thus 'attack' might be either **ʌt·æk**, which is the actual pronunciation, or **ʌtæ·k**, which would suggest 'at Ack'. Similarly, if we were to write 'atall' in one word, it might be pronounced either **ʌt·ɔɪl** or **ʌtɔ·ɪl**. In 'at all', when used as an adverb, as in 'not at all' (and 'at home', as generally pronounced), the word-division does not indicate the true syllabification, which is **ʌt·ɔɪl** in ordinary speech.

The only phonetic function of word-division is, therefore, to indicate occasionally the syllable-divisions in sentences.

It must be noted that syllabification depends not on mere force, but on discontinuity of force. Thus in 'ticket' and 'take it' the syllabification is exactly the same, the **k** belonging to the first syllable in both groups, and although the **k** is pronounced stronger in 'ticket' than in 'take it', it does not therefore begin a new syllable. In both cases the **k** is uttered with part of the same force-impulse as the preceding vowel, and the difference in force of the two **k**s is simply due to the different lengths of the two vowels. To make **k** in 'ticket' the beginning of the second syllable, it would be necessary to diminish the force of the **t*i*** very rapidly, so as to be able to begin a fresh impulse of force on the **k**; nor need this impulse be strong—only just enough to break the continuity of the force decrease. If the **k** and the following vowel are pronounced with a stronger force-impulse than the **t*i***, the syllabification and the stress are both changed, **t·*i*k-*i*t** becoming **t*i*-k·*i*t**.

The distinction between long and double consonants is purely syllabic. In **a·tɪa, a·lɪa**, the consonant positions are simply held with uniformly diminishing force until the **a** is reached, on which a new impulse begins. In **atta, alla** the consonants are held as long as in the former cases, but the new force-impulse begins in the second half of the held consonants, without waiting till the vowel is reached, which, of course, breaks the sense of continuity.

The distinction between 'cut short' **kɐtsh·ɔɪt** and 'achieve' **ʌt·shiɪv**, 'outside' **æhohts·ehihd** and the German 'geziemen' **ġeht·siɪmehn**, is exactly analogous.

A Handbook of Phonetics, 1877, pp. 87–91

Sounds differ much in *sonority*—the force with which they strike the sense of hearing. The most sonorous sounds are those formed with voice, and the less the voice is impeded, the more sonorous the sound. The two extremes are the opener vowels, such as], ɟ, and the stops, the high vowels, such as ſ, being about on a level with the vowel-like consonants, of which the nasals are the most sonorous. Of the voiceless consonants the high-pitched hisses are the most distinct.

The audibility of language depends then, roughly speaking, on its vowels. Acoustically consonants are mere modifiers of the vowels, and the ideal of distinctness would be reached by a language in which each consonant was separated from the next by a vowel.

Hence the ear learns to divide a breath-group into groups of vowels (or vowel-equivalents), each flanked by consonants (or consonant-equivalents)—or, in other words, into syllable-formers or *syllabics*, and *non-syllabics*, each of these groups constituting a *syllable*. Syllabics are marked], non-syllabics), when necessary.

The relation between syllabic and non-syllabic is evidently a purely relative one. In such a group as *clay* the sonority of the vowel completely overpowers that of the **l** and makes it non-syllabic, but the **l** in *cattle* ɑʅʊω = ɑʅʊω] is so much more sonorous than the ʊ that the whole group is disyllabic to the ear, as if the **l** were accompanied by a vowel. Even a voiceless hiss may be syllabic in such a combination as ɒsɪʊ or even ɒsʊ.

The same sound varies in audibility according to the length and force with which it is uttered. When two vowel-like consonants come together, the one that has the greater length and force is regarded as the vowel. Thus ꜰ·ʒɪ = ꜰ)ʒ] suggests ꜰ]ʒ, while ·ꜰʒ = ꜰ]ʒ suggests]ꜰʒ or rather ·]ꜰ1ʒ.

So also a vowel can lose its syllabicness in combination with another vowel, with which it then forms a *diphthong*. These diphthongic or glide vowels are written consonant size, being from a syllabic point of view consonantal vowels, as in]ɾ **ai**, where the group is uttered with one impulse of diminishing force, and ɾ] **ia**, which implies increasing force, the latter diphthong being equivalent to ɷv]. Want of stress is more essential than gliding quality, for]ɾɪ with the diphthongal vowel lengthened is still mainly diphthongal to the ear if the ɾɪ is kept stressless.

The unsyllabic element of a diphthong is generally a closer vowel than that which constitutes the syllabic element. The most perfect types of diphthongs are, therefore, **ai** and **au**, which are also the commonest. When clearly formed—ɾ ſ, ɾ ɪ—the second elements are almost consonantal in character—suggesting **aj**, **aw** to an English ear—because English and most other languages content themselves with making the second element a mere approximation to the high position; thus in English the nearest equivalents of the above diphthongs are]ɾ [ɾ—1906 Edn.] and ɾɪ, the second elements being still more obscured in Cockney pronunciation.

Such combinations as ʊɜ may be regarded as consonantal diphthongs.

The answer to the question, Where does the syllable begin? is, that if it has a distinct stress (strong or medium) its beginning corresponds with the beginning of the stress, as we see in comparing such pairs as]ʊ·ɟɷ:ʊ]ɾɛ and]·ʊɟɷ·ɾʅ,]ʊ·ɾɑʊ] and]·ʊɾɑ = *at all times, a tall man*; *at Acton, attack.*

The difference between long and double consonants is a syllabic one. In]ʊ] the consonant positions are simply held with uniformly diminishing force till the] is reached, when a new impulse may begin. In]ʊʊ] the consonant is held as long as in the preceding case, but the new force-impulse begins in the second half of the held consonant, which, of course, breaks the sense of continuity. This break is very distinct in such a group as *bookcase* ·ɒɪɑ:ɑ[ɾs, because of the medium stress on the second syllable.

The distinction between ·ɑ]ʊ·ɜɟʊ and]·ʊɜſɷ> *cut short* and *achieve*, ·ɪʊ·s]ɾʊ *outside* and the German ɐ]·ʊsſɾ *geziemen* is exactly analogous.

The distinction between *close* and *open* stress is also syllabic. In the close stress of English and generally North German in such words as *better*, *vetter*, the ʊ is uttered with the same force-impulse as the preceding vowel—although this force-impulse has diminished by the time it reaches the ʊ (more so in German than in English)—any new impulse beginning on the following vowel: ·ɒ[ʊ], ·>[ʊ]ɛ. In the open stress of South German, and the South European languages generally, the fresh impulse of force begins on the ʊ in such a word as *vetter*—·>[ʊ]ɷ. Open stress—which is also heard in Welsh—sounds less abrupt than close stress, and to the unaccustomed ear suggests doubling of the consonant. The otherwise superfluous ^ may be used to indicate open stress, as in the South German ^>[ʊ]ɷ, Welsh ^ɑ]ʊɪ *cadw.*

When several syllables are uttered with one impulse of force, it is, of course, impossible to mark off the boundaries of the syllables by stress, and syllable-division becomes a subjective problem. It is, for instance, difficult to hear much syllable-division in such a word as *necessary*, when uttered rapidly. Syllable-division is most clearly marked when it turns on stopped consonants, because of their greater force and abruptness. It is less clear when it turns on other consonants. Thus the difference between *an aim* and *a name*, between *alla* with long and with double **l** is not very marked.

A Primer of Phonetics, 1890, pp. 60–4

On stress depends *syllable*-division. A syllable consists of a 'syllabic' (syllable-former), either alone or accompanied by non-syllabics. The distinction between the two depends on sonority: the more sonorous a sound is, the more easily it assumes the function of a syllabic. The most sonorous sounds are the voiced ones, among which the most open are the most sonorous, the most sonorous of all sounds being the clear, open **a**. But the difference is only a relative one. When a vowel and a consonant come together, the syllabicness of the vowel overpowers that of the consonant; but in such a word as *little* **litl** the second **l** is so much more syllabic than the preceding voiceless stop that it assumes syllabic function, and the word is felt to be disyllabic, although it only contains one vowel. The syllabic quality of the final consonant in *little*, *reason* **riizn**, *open*, etc., does not require to be marked, because as long as these final consonants are voiced they are necessarily syllabic. If it is necessary to indicate syllabicness of a consonant in the interior of a word, this can be done by putting **-**, or whatever stress-mark is required, after it, as in **bɐtn-iŋ** *buttoning*, **botl-ə** *bottler* compared with *butler*.

The beginning of a syllable corresponds to the beginning of the stress with which it is uttered. Thus in *atone* the strong stress and the second syllable begin on the **t**, and in *bookcase* **buk:keis** on the second **k**, the first **k** belonging to the first syllable so that the **kk** is here really double —that is to say, there are two of them—not merely long, as in *book* **buk˖** by itself.

Two vowels in succession uttered with one impulse of stress, so as to form only one syllable, constitute a *diphthong*. The English diphthongs ***ai***, ***oi***, ***au*** are 'falling' diphthongs, having the stress on the first element, so that it is the second element which is non-syllabic. The *u* and *eu* in such words as *union*, *euphony*, was also a falling diphthong ***iu*** in the Early Modern English of the sixteenth century. In the beginning of the eighteenth century the stress in this diphthong was shifted on to the second element, so that it became the 'rising' diphthong **i·u**, **i·uu**. As the unsyllabic vowel in such a diphthong is practically indistinguishable from a loose **j**, it is best to write it accordingly, **ju**, **juu**, keeping the notation **iu** for the falling diphthong. In English the falling diphthongs weaken their second elements, so that they are no longer full **i**, **u**, as in some languages and even in some English dialects; thus **au** in Scotch is full [**au**], that is, **ɐ** followed by a high narrow **u**, so that it might also be written **aw.**

It is not always easy to draw the line between diphthongic and disyllabic pronunciation, as in the English murmur-diphthongs such as **iə**, which when uttered slowly have more or less of a disyllabic effect. This is still more the case with triphthongs such as **aiə.**

Conversely, in very rapid and careless speech even such vowel-sequences as those in *poetical, coerce, Æolic,* **pou·etikl, kou·əəs, ii·olik** often become shorter by a syllable, so that they might be roughly symbolized by **pwetikl, kwəəs, jolik.**

The Sounds of English, 1908, pp. 50–2

With stress is closely connected the question of *syllable-division.* A syllable is a group of sounds containing a 'syllabic' or syllable-former which is, of course, able to constitute a syllable by itself. The distinction between syllabics and non-syllabics depends on sonority, the more sonorous sounds being the voiced ones, while of these again, the most open are the most sonorous, the most sonorous of all being the vowels, among which, again, the openest are the most sonorous. But these differences are only relative. When a vowel and a consonant come together the sonorousness of the vowel always overpowers that of the consonant, so that the two together only constitute one syllable. But in such a word as *little* the second **l** is so much more sonorous than the accompanying voiceless stop that it assumes syllabic function, and the whole group becomes dissyllabic to the ear. The beginning of a syllable corresponds with the beginning of the stress-impulse with which it is uttered. Thus in *atone* the strong stress and the second syllable begin on the **t**, and in *bookcase* on the second **k**, the first **k** belonging to the first syllable so that the **kk** is here double, not merely long, as in *book* **bukk** by itself.

'Phonetics', *Encyclopædia Britannica,* 11th Edn., 1911, p. 465

4. *Glides*

[Sweet's insistence upon the importance of glides and his detailed descriptions of them are in marked contrast to the perfunctory attention they have received from most of his successors. It is perhaps for this reason that Sweet's writings on the subject of glides seems to be particularly rich in the insights they have to offer the modern reader, and the feeling for the dynamic nature of spoken language that pervades them is an excellent corrective to those whose training has tended to overemphasize its supposedly static aspects. Of his own use of the term 'glide' Sweet himself wrote in a footnote to the *Handbook*: 'This term was first used by Mr Ellis. Mr Bell also adopted it, but limited its application to glide-vowels. I use it here in the same sense as Mr Ellis.' *Ed.*]

Glides are sounds produced during the transition from one sound to another. Thus in **kii** *key* we have the glide from the **k**-position to the **ii**-position, which does not, however, require to be written, as it is implied by the positions of **k** and **ii.**

Consonants are often joined together without any glide, not only in such combinations as **nd** in *hand*, where the **d** is formed by continuing the **n**, the nose-passage being closed at the same time, but also in such words as the English *act* **ækt.**

A New English Grammar, 1891, p. 229

Glides. In pronouncing any sound-combination, such as ɑſ **ki**, we not only have the two sounds ɑ and ſ, but also the 'glide' or sound produced in passing from the one position to the other, which is implied by the juxtaposition of the symbols. The glide is called the 'off-glide' of ɑ, the 'on-glide' of ſ. If the transition is made slowly, the glide becomes so distinct that it becomes necessary to write it separately. Thus]ɱ] **aja** may be developed into full]ɾɱ] **aija.** Glideness and nonsyllabicness generally go together, but it is often difficult to draw the line between gliding and fixed configuration, especially in the consonants. Gliding quality is marked), when necessary, as in ʊʋ)ɷ˥ɾ˗ = 'try', where ʋ and ɷ together have the same length as the single ɷ in ʊɷ˥ɾ˗ = 'dry'.

Initial and Final Vowel-glides. Vowels may be begun and finished in various ways:

(*a*) The glottis is gradually narrowed, passing through the various positions for breath and whisper till voice is produced. This gives the 'gradual' beginning ◦]ɫ.

(*b*) The breath is kept back till the glottis is closed for voice, which begins at once without any introductory breath. This is the 'clear' beginning ˈ]ɫ.

In both these cases the stress begins on the vowel. If it is thrown on to the preceding glides, they are at once recognized as independant elements, ◦]ɫ becoming o]ɫ **haa,** with the ordinary 'aspirate', while ˈ]ɫ becomes x]ɫ, with the glottal stop. o is generally modified by the following vowel, whose configuration it partly anticipates. It is, therefore, the voiceless glide vowel corresponding to the vowel which follows, and is then written ϱ. ϱſ, ϱɫ **hi, hu** are, in fact, equivalent to ɾ꞉ſ, ɫ꞉ɫ, being almost equivalent to weaker forms of ∩ſ, ɔɫ **jhi, whu.**

Vowels are finished analogously:

(*a*) by a gradual opening of the glottis, the final glide passing through whisper to breath, giving the 'gradual' ending ſ°.

(*b*) by a cessation of expiration while the glottis is still closed for voice, giving the 'clear' ending ſ'. If uttered with stress these endings become respectively ſ○ or ſϱ and ſχ.

Consonant-glides. All consonants consist of three elements, (1) the consonant itself, (2) the on-glide, and (3) the off-glide. Each of these elements may be either breathed or voiced, and may be modified in various ways. The off-glides of stops are the most important.

The following are the combinations, as regards breath and voice:

Initial	*Medial*	*Final*
ɑ°ʃ	ʃɑ°ʃ	ʃɑ°
ɑ'ʃ	ʃɑ'ʃ	ʃɑ'
ɘ°ʃ	ʃɘ°ʃ	ʃɘ°
ɘ'ʃ	ʃɘ'ʃ	ʃɘ'

ɑ° is the E. **k** in all positions, ɘ° the E. final **g**, as in *egg*, and ɘ' the E. medial **g**, as in *eager*. ɑ' is the Middle and South German **k**. E. initial **g**, as in *go*, is often nearly ɑ', but there seems to be a trace of vocality in the stop itself. On-glides after vowels are generally voiced, but are breathed in some languages, as in Icelandic: ʃ'ɑ°, ʃ°ɑ°.

All stops, especially when voiceless, postulate a certain compression of the breath behind the stop, so as to produce an audible explosion when the stop is removed. However strong this explosion of a breath-glide, it is not felt as an independent element, unless the initial force is maintained during the formation of the glide itself. In this latter way are formed the Danish *aspirates* ɑ○, etc., as in *komme*.

The glides of unstopped consonants are less marked, but the vocality of the consonants themselves is, on the other hand, more distinct than in the case of the stops. **s z**, etc., admit of 'gradual' and 'clear' beginnings and endings, analogous to those of the vowels; final **z** in E. has the gradual ending ѕѕɒ°. After another buzz or voiced stop it is completely whispered in English, as in ϱ[ɷѕɒ *heads*.

Consonant-glides may be variously modified by rounding, etc. Thus English *cool* is really ɑ°ɒɫɜɷ. We can also have such a combination as ɑ°ɒʃ, distinct from ɑɔʃ **kʌa**, which is equivalent to ɑ○ɒʃ. In such cases the rounding is generally begun before the stop is loosened.

Glideless Combinations. In speech the general principle is to take the shortest way between two sounds. This often results in combinations which are effected without any glide at all. This is regularly the case in sequences of consonants having the same place and differing only in form. Thus in passing from ℸ **n** to ℧ **d** in ℸ℧ all that is done is to close the nasal passage. Similarly in ℧ω **dl** the transition is made by simply opening the side apertures, the tip of the tongue retaining its position. Combinations in which a stop is followed by open consonants formed in the same, or nearly the same, place are effected either with no glide at all, as in ɒɔ **pɸ**, or with a very slight one, as in ɒ> **pf.** In such combinations as **tʃ**, **tf** the places of the two consonants are generally approximated as much as possible, so as to get rid of the glide, thus English **ts** is really ℧ʂs or sɪs, English **ch** ℧ƨ⊦. Even when consonants formed in different places come together, it is possible to combine them without any glide, although in these cases the gliding must be regarded as the normal form. Absence of glide is marked ∘. Thus English *act* is ɽɑ∘℧, the tip of the tongue being brought into position before the ɑ-contact is loosened, while in French and other languages there would be a breath-glide between the two consonants.

Glide-consonants in the special sense of the word are consonants formed without any fixed configuration, however much the transition may be prolonged. The most distinct glide-consonants are the *flaps*, of which the Norwegian 'thick' *l* is an example: an inverted **r** finished off with a momentary contact of the tongue-tip with the inside of the palatal arch, the tongue moving forward all the time.

A History of English Sounds, 1888, pp. 9–12

[The reader is reminded that in the long extract that follows square brackets are used in conformity with Sweet's own practice in the *Handbook*, namely, to indicate glides.

In addition to footnotes, the *Handbook* contains a number of 'additional notes' at the end of the book. These are included in the extracts at the relevant places in the text. Like the footnotes, they are enclosed in parentheses, but to distinguish them from footnotes they are entitled 'Additional notes' and a reference to the page of the *Handbook* on which they appear is given. *Ed.*]

Synthesis introduces us to a special class of elements called 'glides', or transitional sounds, produced during the transition from one sound to the other. Thus, in pronouncing any combination, such as **ki**, we have not only the two sounds **k** and **i**, but also the sound produced in passing from one position to the other. This 'glide' differs from the two extremes **k** and **i** in having no fixed configuration, it is, in fact, composed of all the intermediate positions between **k** and **i**, through which it passes without dwelling on any of them. If the tongue were arrested at any one intermediate point, a single definite sound would be produced, and instead of one uninterrupted glide from **k** to **i**, we shall have two, one from the **k** to the intermediate point, another from there to the **i**.

It would clearly be impossible to symbolize all the infinitesimal intermediate positions of which a glide is made up; nor is it ever necessary, the general principle being that in all cases of transition from one fixed position to another the shortest way is taken: given, therefore, the symbols of the fixed positions, the character of the glide follows as a matter of course. Glides are implied simply by the juxtaposition of the symbols of the fixed positions between which they lie, as in the case of **ki**.

Besides these essential, implied glides, there is another class of 'unessential' glides, which require to be written separately. Thus, instead of passing direct from **k** to **i**, the organs can move up to the **u** position, and without stopping there pass on to **i**. Here there is a continuous glide from **k** to **i**, but it is a roundabout glide, and not implied by the positions of the **k** and **i**. These 'glide-sounds' (glide-vowel in the present case) have a definite, though not a fixed configuration. Thus, in the present case, there is an essential glide implied from the **k** to the **u** position, and from there to the **i** position, and the **u** position is therefore the distinct *limit* of the glide-vowel, but it is itself no more a fixed configuration than any one of the intermediate positions between it and the **k** or **i** positions—like them it is simply one of a series. These glide-sounds are symbolized by being enclosed in brackets, thus **k[u]i**, distinct from **kui**, in which the **u** position is maintained unchanged for an appreciable period. The brackets are omitted whenever it can be done without causing ambiguity.

Glides are distinguished according as they precede or follow the sounds as 'on'- and 'off'-glides. (*Fn.*: The names were first suggested by Mr. Ellis.) Thus the glide in **ki** is the off-glide of **k**, the on-glide of **i**. Initial glides, such as the on-glide of **k** in **ki**, which are only preceded by a silence, are generally inaudible. Final, or 'on-silence' glides, such as the off-glide of **k** in **ik** are generally audible. (*Additional note* on p. 213: I learn from Mr Ellis that there is a very interesting distinction made between aspirated and unaspirated final breath-stops in some of the modern Indian languages, *akh* being pronounced like final **k** in English = **ak**[H], while in *ak* the off-glide is made inaudible by cessation of outgoing breath.)

The acoustic effect of glides varies according to the force and the rapidity with which they are pronounced. If the transition from one position to another is made very rapidly and with slight force the glide is hardly heard at all, although any break, however slight, would at once be heard. On the other hand, even an essential glide, if formed slowly and with certain force, is often heard as a separate element. Thus in such a combination as **aja** there is always an essential glide from the first **a** to the **j**, but if the **a** is pronounced with rapidly diminishing force, and a second force-impulse follows on the **j**, thus **ȧjȧ**, the glide is not noticed at all; whereas, if the transition is made slowly and with only a gradual alteration of force, the glide from the **a** to the high-front position is distinctly heard, and the effect is **a[i]ja**. (*Fn.*: What Mr Ellis describes as *absence* of glide is rather *weakness* of glide.)

The distinction between glide and fixed configuration is not so clearly marked in the consonants as in the vowels, and it is often doubtful whether a consonant is not to be considered rather as a glide than a fixed element. This applies especially to initial consonants, such as **s** and **l** in **sa** and **la**, where the position is only momentary, and most of all to the aspirate **H**, which seems to vary indefinitely between glide and fixed configuration. The breath stops are pure glides acoustically. These fluctuations make it impossible to apply the sign [ ] with perfect uniformity.

Initial and Final Vowel-glides. Vowels may be begun and finished in various ways:

(1) The glottis is gradually narrowed, passing through the various positions for breath and whisper till voice is produced. This gives the 'gradual' beginning **[H]a**, which is the ordinary way of beginning a vowel.

(2) The breath is kept back till the glottis is closed for voice, which begins at once without any introductory breath. This is the 'clear' beginning **[ʌ]a**, well known to singers, who are always taught to avoid the 'breathy' gradual beginning.

In both cases the stress, or force-impulse, of the syllable begins on the vowel. If the stress begins on the glides they are at once recognized as independent elements, **[H]** giving **H** the ordinary 'aspirate', or letter *h*, while **[ʌ]** develops into **x**, the glottal catch, which is practically a stopped consonant, just as **H** is an open consonant, or consonant-glide. (*Fn.*: The distinction between the gradual vowel-beginning and **H** is a very instructive instance of the importance of force in determining the synthesis of sounds. The mere force with which the breath is driven through the narrowed glottis is of secondary importance—the real distinction lies in where the force begins. In **Ha** we may pronounce the **H** with as much force as possible, but if a fresh impulse, however slight, begins on the **a**, we hear simply **a** with the gradual beginning, whereas the gentlest stress, if it only begins on the **H**, and is carried on to the **a** without discontinuity, gives the effect of **Ha**.)

It is important to observe that mere 'breath' (the open glottis) is sometimes distinct from aspiration. The feeble friction of breath passing through the open glottis is heard equally in all the passages above the glottis, while that of **H** is distinctly localized in the narrowed glottis.

Although **H** is essentially a transition sound between breath and voice, it is not therefore necessarily a glide, and indeed it often happens that some definite narrowing of the glottis is held a moment before voice is formed. (*Fn.*: According to Czermak this is usually the case.) **H** is, however, liable to have its character modified by the configuration of the mouth; and the position for the vowel which follows the **H** being generally assumed, or at least prepared, while the **H** is being formed, the **H** naturally assumes the character of that vowel. It is in fact the voiceless (or whispered) glide-vowel corresponding to the vowel it precedes, (*Fn.*: It may also precede consonants, such as **l**, etc.) and it is easy to tell by the sound of the **H** what vowel is to follow. (*Fn.*: This was noticed by Mr Bell, who communicated it orally to me many years ago.) **H** is therefore in the glottis a consonant, in the mouth a voiceless glide-vowel. (*Fn.*: Mr Ellis regards the normal **H** as simply a 'jerk of the voice', without any breath. Mr Ellis's own pronunciation does not appear to me to differ essentially from my own. He simply reduces the breath effect to a minimum by contracting the glottis and giving a short impulse of force, passing on at once to the vowel, which, of course, gets rid of the 'breathiness' which so often accompanies the **H**. Mr Ellis's **Ha** is in fact almost **'ʌa**. The only 'jerk of the voice' I can produce is **xa**.) **H** before **a** has a back, before **i** a front quality, and if exaggerated **Ha** and **Hi** develop into weak **kha** and **jhi**. In Japanese the aspirate varies in this way before different vowels. Before high vowels it has a distinctly consonantal effect **jhiɪ**, **ph*u*hɪ**, while before mid-vowels it seems to be merely a strong aspirate **Haɪ**, **H*e*ɪ**, **H*o*ɪ**. (*Fn.*: I find, on referring to my notes on the pronunciation of the same Japanese gentleman who dictated the sounds to Mr Ellis, that I wrote **khaɪ**, **kh*o*ɪ**, and **H*e*ɪ**, the last only agreeing with Mr Ellis's appreciation. This will show how difficult the distinction is.)

Vowels are finished in different ways analogous to those in which they are begun.

(1) By a gradual opening of the glottis, the final glide passing through whisper to breath, which gives the 'gradual' ending.

(2) By a cessation of expiration while the glottis is still closed for voice, giving the 'clear' ending.

If uttered with stress, after the vowel **a** for example, (1) becomes **aH**, which is still the Sanskrit visarga, and (2) becomes **ax**, the Danish 'stödtone'.

Final **H** has a consonantal character when pronounced forcibly, especially after the high vowels. If the high position is relaxed slowly the consonantal hiss becomes very marked, even if there is but little force on the glide. The Icelandic final **i** and **u** are pronounced in this way, as in *í* and *nú* **iɪH**, **nuɪH**, almost = **iɪjh**, **nuɪwh**. So also in Danish, often also in Dutch.

Glide-vowels and Diphthongs. Glide-vowels generally occur in combination with full vowels (vowels formed by a fixed configuration), forming 'diphthongs', to which we will return immediately. Undiphthongic glide-vowels occur however also, the commonest of which is the 'voice-glide' ʌ, produced by emitting voice during the passage to or from a consonant. It has no definite relation to any one vowel, although it approaches most nearly to the neutral vowel **eh** or **æh.** The voice-glide is an essential element of many combinations, and often occurs as an essential element in such words as *against* [ʌ]**gænst**, *bigger* **big**[ʌ], *together* **t**[ʌ]**gædh**[ʌ], etc. It may be rounded, and this [ʌ*w*] may be heard in a rapid pronunciation of such words as *follow*.

A diphthong is the combination of a full vowel with a glide-vowel before or after it. Thus, if we place the vocal organs in the position for **i**, and then allow voice to sound while passing from the **i** to the **a** position, and hold the **a** long enough to give it a fixed character, we have the diphthong [**i**]**a**. If we begin with a full **a** and then pass to the **i** position, letting the voice cease as soon as the **i** position is reached, we have **a**[**i**].

These are the *essential* elements and conditions of every diphthong. The glide-vowels can, however, be held or lengthened into true vowels without destroying the diphthongic character of the whole combination, provided the continuity of stress be observed. Thus $\overline{\text{a[i]i}}$**ɪ** . . . may be prolonged to any extent, and the whole group will still be felt to be one diphthong.

In the quantity of diphthongs we must distinguish between the quantity of the vowel and of the glide, which, if we allow only long and short quantity, gives four varieties:

(1) **a**[**i**]
(2) **aɪ**[**i**]
(3) **a**[**iɪ**]
(4) **aɪ**[**iɪ**]

(2) is heard in the English *say*, and (3) is the quantity of English *eye*. The lengthening of the glide in *eye* is to compensate for the shortness of the vowel: if both vowel and glide were short, we should have a short monosyllable, which is contrary to the general character of English.

In English the older diphthongs of the **ai**, **au**, and **oi** type have short vowels and long glides, while the later diphthongized **eɪ** and **oɪ** have the vowel long and the glide short.

The length of diphthongs before consonants in English varies according to the consonant. Before voice consonants they have the same length as when final, as in *rise*, *ride* = (3), *save*, *raid* = (2), but before voiceless consonants both vowel and glide are shortened, the final consonant being lengthened by way of compensation, as in *rice*, *write*; *race*, *rate*. If the diphthongs in these words are isolated by suppressing the final consonants, it will be found that they have an abrupt effect, quite different from that of final *eye*, etc.

The popular conception of a diphthong is, to a great extent, dependent on the associations of written language. Diphthongs in which the glide precedes the vowel, 'fore-glide diphthongs', are generally denoted in written language by a consonant, and hence the glide is generally assumed to be a consonant, or else these diphthongs are called 'spurious', it being supposed that the connection between their elements is less intimate than in the case of other diphthongs.

Of the diphthongs in which the glide follows the vowel, 'after-glide diphthongs', the most frequent are varieties of what may be called the **ai** and **au** types, as in *high* and *how*. It has accordingly been laid down as a general law that in all diphthongs the movement must, as in these diphthongs, be in the direction of narrowing, and that 'none others are genuine'.

Again, it has been assumed from the spelling *ai* and *au* that the second element of these typical diphthongs must necessarily be **i** and **u**, whereas the fact is that they usually stop at some lower position.

Until these prejudices are got rid of, no one can attempt the very difficult task of analysing diphthongs into their elements. (*Fn.*: Mr Bell's 'glides' are, as Mr Ellis has remarked, 'mere evasions of the difficulty'.)

The peculiarity of diphthongs is that their elements may vary almost indefinitely, if only the *general relations* of glide and vowel are preserved. The following general laws may be laid down:

(1) Glides (that is, glide-vowels) before a vowel have the effect of consonants.

(2) Back-glides before and after vowels have the effect of **r**. Examples: [*a*]**i**, [**u**]æ, **i**[ɔ], e[*a*].

(3) Front-glides before a vowel have the effect of [**j**]: [*i*]a, [**i**]æ, [æ]**u**.

(4) Glides after front vowels which have an upward movement, and glides after back vowels which have a forward and upward, or simply forward movement, have the effect of [i], as **ai**, **e**[**i**], **œ**[**e**], ***a***[**æ**], ***a***[**eh**].

(5) Round-glides which move upwards (not forwards as well) after back, or upwards and backwards after front vowels, have the effect of [**u**] as in **au**, (if the movement is downwards the effect is that of **r*w***: **a**[***o***], **o**[**u**], **æ**[**u**]).

The glides may be rounded without disturbing these general relations.

Mixed-glides have a somewhat doubtful character. The high-mixed has quite a front character in diphthongs, whereas the low-mixed has more of the back quality, the mid-mixed being either front or back in its character according to the direction of movement.

A few actual examples may now be given of each category.

(2) [***u***] frequently occurs as a substitute for **r**, as in [***u***]**æd** = *red*. Before another ***u***, as in [***u***]***u*k** = *rook*, it is not very distinct, but is still distinctly audible. Here there is no change of position whatever, and the distinction between glide and vowel is simply one of force, the beginning of the [***u***]***u*** = ***u*ɪ** being pronounced with weak stress, which suddenly becomes stronger, and is held a moment at its greatest degree. If the ***u*ɪ** is pronounced with gradually increasing force the vowel is heard simply as a long ***u***. It must, however, be understood that there is nothing in the sound of [***u***]***u*k** that *necessarily* suggests a glide. It is only the frequent hearing [***u***] for **r** in such words as *red*, where it is distinctly audible, that prepares the ear to expect it in other familiar combinations.

[**æh**] or [**æh**], or the simple voice-glide [**ʌ**], is the regular English substitute for **r** wherever the **r** is not followed by a vowel, as in *here* **h*i*ɪ**[**æh**], *there* **dhæɪ**[**æh**], *ore* **ɔɪ**[**æh**]. In 'affected' pronunciation there is a further retraction of the glide to the ***a*** position.

All these substitutes for **r** are closely allied to weak **gh**, and it is not always easy to determine whether the sound is a consonant or a glide-vowel.

(3) The English *y* is often weakened into glide-***i*h**, as in *you*, *young*, or perhaps also into raised ***e***. All the front-glides may have the effect of a **j** before other vowels, the effect being of course most marked when the glide is closer than the vowel. In fact [**æ**]**i** would hardly suggest **ji** at all, but rather **æ**[**i**], according to the next class.

(4) These diphthongs, as far as the unrounded ones are concerned, fall into two main groups, the **ai** and the **ei** type, according as the first element has a back or a front character. When the vowel is **e** or ***e***, there can, of course, be no doubt as to the character of the diphthong, any more than when the vowel is a back one. But when it is **æ** or ***æ*** the

combination has almost the effect of a very forward diphthong of the **ai** type. Thus the first element of 'long *a*' in English, as in *take*, is generally **e** or ***e***, but in broad Cockney pronunciation it is **æ**, and the resulting diphthong is not only heard as belonging to the **ai** type, but actually passes over to it, the first element becoming the mid-mixed **eh**, as in the ordinary pronunciation of *eye*. (*Fn.*: I believe, however, that those who thus broaden the diphthong in *take*, generally keep it distinct from that of *eye*, by making the first element of the latter **a** or ***a***.)

As already remarked, the second element of these diphthongs is not necessarily **i**, but may be some lower vowel. Pure [**i**] or [***i***] may be heard in the Icelandic diphthongs, as in *nei* **neiH**, *sæ* **saiH** (*Fn.*: I am not certain of the narrowness of the [**i**]; Mr Ellis writes [***i***].), also in the common Dutch diphthongized *ee*, as in *been* **beɪin**. In English the glide is always wide, and never seems to reach ***i***. Its precise nature is difficult to determine, but it seems to be generally ***i*h**. (*Fn.*: I have sometimes thought it was raised ***e***; possibly both occur, as ***e***[1] might easily pass into ***i*h**.)

Sievers makes out the glide in the German *ai* to be **e**, by which he may however mean [***e***[1]]. (*Fn.*: Sievers' ingenious proof, which consists in introducing two fingers into the mouth so as to form an artificial palate, can also be applied to English; it will be found that perfectly good **ai**-diphthongs can be formed under these circumstances, but no **i**.) The broad London ***a*ɪ*i*h** frequently shortens the distance between glide and vowel by substituting the neutral **eh** for ***i*h**, giving ***a*ɪeh**, which makes 'pie' sound like 'pa'. This **eh**-glide may also be heard in Scotch pronunciation.

If the vowel is a rounded one, we get various diphthongs of the **oi** and **əi** type, according as the vowel is a back or front one, such as the English diphthong in 'boy' **boeh**, and the Icelandic *au*, as in 'launa' **ləina.**

Rounding of the glide does not alter the character of these diphthongs. The German *eu* in some of its varieties is an example, *neu* being pronounced **naə** and **n*o*ə**, in North German **n*oi*** or rather **no**[***e***[1]].

(5) These diphthongs are closely analogous to those just described. Like them, they fall into two classes, the **ou** and the **au** type, according as the first element is regarded as a rounded or an unrounded vowel. Just as there is a broad **ai**-like form of **eɪ*i*h**, so the regular **oɪ*u*** varies as ***o*ɪ*u*** and **ɔɪ*u***, which last has very much the effect of **au**, so that **nɔɪ*u*** = *no* seems really to pass into **naɪ*u***. (*Fn.*: In the pronunciation of those who seem to make *no* into *now* the first element of *ow* becomes distinctly *æ*, so that the two diphthongs are kept perfectly distinct.)

It is, however, difficult to distinguish between **ɔɪ** with its rounding reduced to a minimum and ***a*ɪ** pronounced, as it often is in English, with half-closed mouth.

The first element of the **au** type is often represented by a mixed vowel, as in the E. *how* **hæhoh**.

It will be noticed that the glide-vowel of the **au** type is simply the neutral vowel rounded, just as that of the English **oi**-diphthong is the unrounded **eh**. The German *au* in *haus*, has, according to Sievers, **o** for its glide—**haos** or **h*a*os**. (*Fn.*: Perhaps rather **ha*o*s**?) In **oɪ*u*** there is generally no change at all in the tongue position, the lips being simply narrowed as for ***u***. The second element is then the wide form of the Scandinavian **o**. There may, however, occasionally be also a slight raising of the tongue as well.

Of diphthongs of the **iu** type, whose first element is a front-vowel, there are no certain examples. The nearest approach is the American diphthong in *new*, which Mr Bell writes **n*iy***. These diphthongs, in which the glide is simply the vowel rounded, of which the G. **a*o*** = *au* is also an example, form, strictly speaking, a class by themselves.

Consonantal Diphthongs. The mid-vowels **eɪ** and **oɪ** are diphthongized by raising the tongue towards **i** and **u**. If we attempt to diphthongize **iɪ** and **uɪ** in the same way, they necessarily develop into consonants **iɪj**, **uɪw**. If the consonants are simply squeezed, not buzzed, the combination has quite a diphthongic character, as in the usual English pronunciation of *he* and *who*. There are several intermediate stages possible. Thus, if the vowel position is slightly lowered, a diphthong may be produced simply by moving the tongue up to a closer, but still a vowel position. This seems to be often the case with the English **iɪ**. In *who* there can be no doubt as to the final consonant.

In English the vowels themselves are generally half wide, half narrow, though they may also be quite wide.

Consonants. All consonants consist of three elements, (1) the consonant itself, (2) the on-glide, and (3) the off-glide. Each of these elements may be either voiceless or voiced, and may be modified in various other ways. Consonant synthesis is most clearly seen in the stops, whose synthesis is at the same time the most important.

Stops. The great peculiarity of voiceless stops is that in themselves they have no sound whatever, they are, acoustically speaking, pure glide-sounds, which are only audible in the moment of transition from or to some other sound. Voice stops, on the other hand, can have a distinct sound of their own in addition to that of their glides, but as stops can only be voiced by driving voiced breath into an air-tight chamber (*Fn.*: Forming what German phoneticians call a 'Blählaut'.), they cannot be continued for any length of time.

Confining our attention for the present to the off-glide, we may distinguish four chief kinds of voiceless and voice stops: (1) voiceless stop and breath glide **k[H]a**; (2) voiceless stop and voice glide **k[ʌ]a**; (3) voice stop and breath glide **ġ[H]a**; and (4) voice stop and voice glide **ġ[ʌ]a**. These sounds may be heard in initial **k**, initial **ġ**, final **ġ**, and **ġ** between vowels respectively.

(1) In **k[H]a**, as in **ka-**, the glottis is left open while the stop is being formed, and the chords are not brought into the voice position till the moment of loosening the stop, so that before the glottis has time to form voice there is a slight escape of breath between the stop and the vowel—the glide from the stop to the vowel is breathed.

(2) In **k[ʌ]a**, as in **ġa-**, the glottis is in the position for voice during the stop, but without any air being forced through it, and consequently the stop is as inaudible as in the case of **k**, but voice begins the moment the stop is loosened, and the glide is therefore voiced.

(3) In **ġ[H]**, as in **-aġ**, the voice runs on from the vowel to the stop without break, but the glottis is opened simultaneously with the loosening of the stop, which causes a puff of breath, just as in final **-ak**.

(4) In **ġ[ʌ]**, as in **aġa**, the voice runs on from vowel to vowel without intermission, both stop and on- and off-glide being voiced.

Consonants with voiceless stop and breath off-glide are called 'breath' or 'voiceless' stops; consonants with voiced stop are called 'voiced' stops; and those with voiceless stop and voice glide (**ġa-**) may be called 'half-voiced' stops.

It appears, then, that initial, medial, and final **ġ** are really three distinct sounds. Initial **ġ** is **k[ʌ]**, medial **ġ[ʌ]**, and final **ġ[H]**. **k**, on the other hand, is always the same—**k[H]**. (*Fn.*: The above details differ considerably from those of Mr Ellis's latest views, as given in *Early English Pronunciation*, pp. 1097, 1111, etc. Mr Ellis considers initial **ġ** to be always voiced, and that there is no necessary breath-glide after **k**. He therefore identifies initial **ġ** with **ġ[ʌ]**, and initial and medial **k** with **k[ʌ]**, my initial **ġ**.)

The following table gives all the possible combinations, initial, medial, and final:

Initial	Medial	Final
***k[H]a**	***ak[H]a**	***ak[H]**
***k[ʌ]a**	**ak[ʌ]a**	**ak[ʌ]**
ġ[H]a	**aġ[H]a**	***aġ[H]**
ġ[ʌ]a	***aġ[ʌ]a**	**aġ[ʌ]**

Of these combinations those marked * occur in E. The others require careful practice till they are familiar.

g[ʌ]a is easily obtained by pronouncing **aga**, dwelling on the **g**, and then dropping the initial **a**. These 'full' initial voice-stops suggest the corresponding nasals to an unaccustomed ear, **d[ʌ]a**, for instance, sounding like **na**.

In forming **g[H]a** and **ag[H]a** be careful not to exaggerate the breath-glide, and in the latter not to separate it from the **g**. **ag[H]a**, and thence **g[H]a**, may easily be obtained from the familiar **ag[H]** by joining on an **a**.

ak[ʌ]a is difficult for English students. It can be formed by prefixing **a** to initial **ga-**, although it is difficult to do so without making the stop voiced; or by trying to sound **aka** without any breath after the stop. These half-voice stops are the regular sounds of double *k*, *t*, *p*, between vowels in Danish, as in **ik[ʌ]eh** = *ikke*, **sæt[ʌ]eh** = *sætte*, **dyp[ʌ]eh** = *dyppe*. (*Fn.*: It appears now (Sievers, *Grundzüge der Lautphysiologie*, p. 64 foll.) that the South German 'mediae', which were formerly assumed, on the authority of Brücke, to be 'whispered' consonants, are really these half-voiced stops. My own analysis of the Danish *kk*, etc. was made some years ago, at a time when I still believed in the South German whispered stops.)

There still remain final **ak[ʌ]** and **ag[ʌ]**. The latter is easily formed, and is, in fact, sometimes heard in English in such words as 'bigger' **big[ʌ]**, when pronounced very rapidly. It is simply the influence of the spelling that makes us hear the final voice murmur as a separate syllable, even when it is reduced to its minimum. We also hear **big[ʌ]** as a dissyllable partly because the **g** is short, whereas the regular final **g** in 'big' is long, so that the 'dissyllable' **big[ʌ]** is actually shorter than the monosyllable **bigɪ[H]**. If we lengthen the **g** of **big[ʌ]**, making it into **bigɪ[ʌ]**, it has much more of a monosyllabic effect.

On-glides. The on-glide after a vowel is voiced in most languages: **a[ʌ]k[H]a, a[ʌ]g[ʌ]a.**

Voiceless on-glides occur in Icelandic regularly before double voiceless stops, as in **sæ[H]tta** = *setta*, **flo[H]kka** = *flokka*. They may also be heard in Scotch, in such words as *what* **who[H]t.**

Initial on-glides are, of course, inaudible when breathed. They may sometimes be heard voiced in such English words as *attempt* **[ʌ]tæmt**, *ago*, etc.

Stress-glides (Aspirated stops). All stops, especially when voiceless, postulate a certain compression of the breath behind the stop, so as to produce an audible explosion when the stop is removed. On the force of this compression, which is caused by upward pressure of the diaphragm, the force of the glide and consequently the audibility of the stop mainly depend. The English **k** etc., is generally pronounced with but little force, but in the German **k**, as in *kann*, there is a strong puff of breath, which may, however, be heard in English as well in emphatic pronunciation.

But even in German the force of the breath-glide is something secondary, due only to the compression with which the stop is formed. If, however, a *separate* impulse is communicated to the glide, the glide is felt as an independent element. In this way the Irish and Danish 'aspirates' are formed, which are identical in sound, and entirely distinct from the German **k** in *kann*. Examples are the Irish *tell* **tHæljɪ**, *paper*; in Danish *tale* **tHaɪleh**, *penge* **pHæqeh**, *komme* **kHɔmeh**. These sounds have nothing harsh about them, their characteristic feature being the distinctness of their glide, which has something of the character of the preceding stop, so that **kHa**, for instance, sounds like a weak **kkha**, etc. The analogies with the different vowel-beginnings are obvious. (*Additional note* on p. 213: As **ta** develops into **tHa** by throwing an independent stress on to the glide, so **da** becomes **dʌa** by emphasising the voice-glide. I have lately convinced myself by personal audition of the correctness of this (Mr Ellis's) analysis of the Indian *dh* etc. in *dhanu*. Initially, of course, **t[ʌ]a** = *da* develops into **tʌa**.)

It is also possible to substitute for the breath-glide an emission of breath through the fully opened glottis, with a separate impulse of breath, followed by a glide on to the vowel **kHh[H]a**. This may be the one form of aspiration in the modern Indian languages, which has been described as making one imagine the speakers were out of breath. (*Fn.*: Quoted somewhere by Rumpelt, *Natürliches System der Sprachlaute.*)

Implosive Stops. These Saxon German sounds were first described by Merkel (*Physiologie der Sprache*, p. 149). In Saxon German there is no distinction between *t* and *d* etc., both being half-voiced **t[ʌ]**, with the stop formed implosively. The implosion consists in closing the glottis simultaneously with the stop position, and then compressing the air between the glottis stoppage and the mouth one, by raising the glottis like a plug by the action of its muscles and by upward pressure of the diaphragm, as in force generally. This action produces no sound while the stop is being formed, but modifies the off-glide in a very peculiar manner, giving it a 'choky' effect.

Sievers' description of the Tiflis Armenian and Georgian implosives is very similar. He states that the raising of the glottis is very energetic, amounting to fully a half- to three-quarters of an inch. (*Fn.*: The above details have been gathered partly from Merkel's description, partly from Professor Sievers' pronunciation, who is familiar with both the Saxon and the Armenian sounds. Sievers, however, asserts that the Saxon implosives are not formed in the same way as the Armenian, although he admits a certain similarity. He thinks it possible that the Saxon implosives are formed by first compressing the air in the mouth by the usual action of the diaphragm, and *then* closing the glottis.)

Unstopped Consonants. With unstopped consonants there is no difficulty in voicing the stop itself, and there are many consonants, especially the 'vowel-like' ones, which are only occasionally devocalized. The glides of these consonants are always voiced as well.

In the breath unstopped consonants both the consonant itself and the off-glide are breathed, as in the corresponding stops: **s**[H]**a**, **as**[H]**a**, **as**[H]. But the breath-glide of the unstopped consonants is always weaker than that of the stops, because the explosive effect of the latter is wanting.

Hence also the aspirates of these consonants are weaker and less marked than those of the stops, but they may be heard in the Irish *sir*, and the Icelandic *það* **thHaɪdh.**

The voiced buzzes admit of more variety than the voiced stops, because with them the different stages of glottis-narrowing that may precede voice are distinctly audible, whereas in the voiced stop there is nothing between full vocality and absolute silence.

In medial **z**, as in **aza**, there can be no doubt of the vocality of the consonant, but initial and final **z** admit of various degrees of vocality.

(1) The glottis only begins to put itself in the position for voice when the **s** position is assumed, and consequently all the intermediate stages between full breath and full voice are heard in succession while the **s** position is being maintained. This is the 'gradual' initial **z**, etc.

(2) The **z** is fully vocal throughout—that is, the glottis is closed for voice simultaneously with the beginning of the **z**. This is the 'clear' initial **z**.

It will be observed that these varieties of initial buzzes are exactly analogous to the two ways of beginning vowels.

(3) The glottis is open during the formation of the consonant, and is only brought together at the moment when the off-glide begins. This is the 'half-voice' **z** = **s**[ʌ], corresponding to initial **g̊a-**. As it is not easy to make the beginning of the voice correspond exactly with the beginning of the glide, this last variety is often modified into a compromise

between (1) and (3), formed by beginning to narrow the glottis during the end of the consonant itself, so that the transition from breath to voice is completed just *before* beginning the glide.

If we compare these three varieties we find that they all agree in having voiced glides, and that in (2) the consonant itself is fully voiced, in (1) gradually voiced, and in (3) breathed.

The English **z** in *zeal* may be fully voiced, but is generally only gradually voiced. The half-voiced **z** seems to be the North German and Dutch initial **s**, as in *so*, *zoo*. To an English ear it sounds like **sz**.

Final **z** may also be either fully vocalized throughout, or else gradually devocalized, passing from voice to whisper while the consonant position is still being maintained.

Both may be heard (but generally the latter) in the English *is*, etc. In final buzzes after other voice consonants the gradual devocalization is very clearly marked in English. Thus in the final buzz in *bills*, *thieves*, *adze*, etc. the vocality is of so short duration that the final **z** is almost a purely whispered consonant.

In this last case the glottis is not fully opened till the consonant is finished, which therefore consists of voice passing into whisper, followed by a breath-glide. If the transition from voice to breath is completed during the beginning of the consonant itself, we have the Icelandic final **s**, *ís*, *las*, etc., which sounds like **zs**.

The vowel-like consonants when final occasionally end in a breath-glide. Thus, in pronouncing final **l** in Icelandic, the glottis opens just as the tongue is removed from the palate, making the resulting flap voiceless, as in *vel* **veɪl**[H], which sounds like **veɪl-lh**. In French final **j** is pronounced in the same way, as in *fille* **fij**[H].

It is possible that in both these instances the glottis may be opened just *before* relaxing the consonant position.

Whispered Consonants. Whisper, being an intermediate stage between breath and voice, is often generated as a secondary effect in the transition from one to the other. Thus the English *s* in *heads* is distinctly whispered, although the beginning of it is voiced, together with the preceding **d**. It seems, however, that the **z** may also be pronounced uniformly whispered throughout, in which case it must be regarded as a true whispered consonant **hed'z**, in which the whisper is not merely something secondary.

In the case of stops the whisper is inaudible in the stop itself, and is only heard in the glide. In most cases a whispered glide would be felt as a transition to or from voice, and would therefore have simply the effect of a weak breath-glide. Indeed, it is very probable that the breath-glide in **k[H]a** and **aĝ[H]** may often be really **k[ʻʌ]a** and **aĝ[ʻʌ]**, or rather consist of both, the one gliding insensibly into the other.

ak[ʻʌ], on the other hand, is distinguishable from **ak[H]**, and this seems to be the pronunciation of final *gg, dd, bb* in Icelandic, as in *egg* **æʻgɪ.**

Other Modifications of Consonant-glides. We have hitherto considered consonant glides as modified mainly by voice, breath, and force. But they are capable of other modifications. Thus, if during the formation of a **k**-stop the lips are brought into the **ph** or **wh** position, the off-glide will assume a distinctly labial or labio-guttural character **k[H*w*]a**, which, although not very marked, is distinctly audible. If this **k[H*w*]a** is made into an aspirate we obtain **kH*w*a**. The former occurs in the English *cool*, the latter in the Danish *kunde* **kH*w*o¹neh**, in both cases with cheek-narrowing as well, the rounding of the glide being nothing but an anticipation of the position of the following vowel.

In the same way the off-glide in **ta** may be gutturalized or palatalized and modified in various other ways.

These effects are mostly due to assimilation, and therefore of a secondary character.

Glideless Combinations. The consistent application of the principle already enunciated, namely that in passing from one sound to another the shortest way is taken, occasionally results in combinations which are effected without any glide at all. Such combinations are impossible in the case of vowels, but are frequent in that of a sequence of consonants formed in the same place and differing only in form. Thus, if a nasal is followed by the corresponding voice stop, as in **nd**, all that is required to pass from one to the other is simply to close the nasal passage. Similarly, in the combination **dl** the transition is made by simply opening the side apertures, the tip of the tongue retaining its position. In such cases the absence of glides, the 'glideless transition', is implied by the juxtaposition of the elements of the combination, just as a glide is necessarily implied by the juxtaposition of two vowels. (*Additional note* on p. 213: In some cases there is not only no glide, but the consonants are even formed simultaneously. Thus *open*, in my pronunciation, ends with an **m** and an **n** formed simultaneously, the lip-closure of the **p** being continued during the formation of the **n—oo¹pn*m**.)

Combinations such as **ts**, **tsh**, **pph**, **pf**, etc., in which a stop is followed by open consonants formed in the same, or nearly the same, place, are either absolutely glideless, as in the case of **pph** or **ts** when the **t** is a blade-stop, or the glide is so insignificant as to be practically non-existent, as in the case of **tsh**. These combinations are very similar in sound to the simple aspirates **tH**, **pH**, etc., and the open consonants may almost be regarded as substitutes for the breath-glide—we might, in short, define **ppha** as **p** gliding on to **a** through the **ph** position, were it not that the **ph** has a definite configuration, which, although extremely short, is held for a moment.

Even when consonants formed in different places come together it is possible to combine them without any glide, although in this case the gliding combination must be regarded as the normal form. Thus the transition from **k** to **t** in **akta** is effected by removing the back of the tongue from the **k** position and then forming the **t** position with the point, so that there is an audible breath-glide **ak[H]ta**. The Swedish **akta** is pronounced in this way, and the same pronunciation is the regular one in French. In English, on the other hand, there is no glide whatever, the tip of the tongue being brought into position before the **k** contact is loosened, so that the stoppage of the mouth passage is maintained from the beginning of the **k** to the end of the **t**: all that is heard, therefore, is the on-glide of the **k** and the off-glide of the **t**. All combinations of consonants are effected in this way in English and many other languages—probably in most, the glide being either entirely omitted, or else reduced to practical inaudibility. Thus **k** and **l** are joined together in English in exactly the same way as **k** and **t**, while in **lk** the **k** position is assumed so immediately after the **l** that the glide is reduced to practically nothing at all. The difference between **kl** and **lk** is that in **kl** the **l** can assume its position simultaneously with the **k** without modifying its sound, whereas the stop **k** would at once destroy the sound of **l**. (*Additional note* on pp. 213–14: In such glideless combinations as **kl** in English, the off-glide of the **k** is often heard as a devocalization of the beginning of the **l**, which might be expressed by writing **k[lh]l**. This makes it difficult to distinguish between **tsh** and **t[jh]j** in such words as *nature*.)

There are, however, many fine distinctions to be observed in language. Thus in the Dutch *volk* there is a distinct voice-glide from the **l** to the **k**, which gives the word something of a dissyllabic effect. Initial **kn** in German, as in *knie*, is often **k[H]n**, with a distinct breath-glide, while in Danish there is no glide; and as initial voiceless stops are aspirated in Danish **kHn** becomes **knh**, as in **knheex** = *knæ*, **nh** being substituted for the simple breath-glide.

Glide Consonants. A glide consonant is one which is only heard in its transition to or from another element, the consonant itself being either not formed at all, or made inaudible by want of breath.

Thus the peculiar Japanese **r** seems to be formed by first bringing the tip of the tongue against the gums without any emission of breath, and then passing on to an untrilled **r**, allowing voiced breath to pass at the moment of removing the tongue. As Mr Ellis remarks, the Japanese 'seem unable to pronounce **r** without striking the palate first'. This **r** may be represented by [**d**]**r** or [**l**]**r**. An unaccustomed ear hears it as something between **r**, **l**, and **d**. The Japanese pronounce all foreign **l**'s and **r**'s as this sound, so that when a Japanese says *a little man*, it sounds to an English ear like *a literal man*. (*Additional note* on p. 214: I have now, by the help of Professor Storm's directions, acquired the 'thick' Norwegian *l*. It is **r**⫰ finished off with momentary contact of the tongue-tip and the inside of the arch, the tongue moving forwards all the while, and seems, therefore, to be a sort of inversion of the Japanese **r**. The second element is quite instantaneous in its formation, almost like a single strong trill. I would write this sound **r**⫰[**l**⫰] rather than **r**⫰[**d**⫰], there being no stoppage of the mouth passage, but only contact of the tongue-tip. The effect is mainly that of **r** with a slight **l** quality.)

In English, when a stop follows a vowel, the breath impulse is often so feeble that nothing is heard but part of the glide on to the consonant, the actual closure being formed without any breath at all. Thus **b*i*ġɪ** becomes **b*i*[ġ]**. With nasals **mænɪ** becomes **mæ[ʌ*n*]**, only a nasal glide being audible.

A Handbook of Phonetics, 1877, pp. 60–85

[The text of the extract below is the same for all editions of the *Primer of Phonetics* except for the short interpolation shown in square brackets on p. 168 which was added in the 1906 edition. *Ed.*]

Vowel-glides are expressed in the same way as an 'unsyllabic' vowel, namely by writing the vowel symbol consonant size, thus ɾ = glide-ſ. Consonant-glides are expressed by adding), thus ෆ) = glide ෆ.

Glides are distinguished, according as they precede or follow a sound, as 'on-glides' and 'off-glides'. Thus in]ɑſ (or English *echo*) the on-glide of ɑ is that from the], and the off-glide of ɑ is that which joins it to ſ. Initial glides, such as the on-glide of the ɑ in ɑſ, being only preceded by a silence, are generally inaudible.

Although the *direction* of a glide is implied by the position of the two fixed points between which it lies, its *character* may be varied.

The acoustic effect of glides varies according to the force and rapidity with which they are uttered. If in such a group as]ෆ] the transition from the] to the ෆ is made rapidly and with slight force the glide is not noticed at all, although any break, however slight, would be at once heard. But if the transition is made slowly and with only a gradual diminution of force, we hear the glide from the ʃ up to the front position of the ɷ as the second element of a diphthong, giving the effect of **aija**. In such combinations as ɷʃ, as in Spanish *llano*, it is often difficult to know whether to write the glide or not, whether to write ɷʃɿɟ or ɷɾʃɿɟ, (ɷɷ)ʃɿɟ). The former is however the correct notation.

Vowel-glides. Vowels may be begun and finished in various ways:

(*a*) The glottis is gradually narrowed, passing through the various positions from breath and whisper till voice is produced. This gives the 'gradual' beginning °ʃɨ, which is the usual one in English, and in most other languages.

(*b*) The breath is kept back till the glottis is closed for voice, which begins at once without any introductory breath. This is the 'clear' beginning ˈʃɨ, well known to singers, who are taught to avoid the 'breathy' °ʃɨ. It is the usual way of beginning a vowel in German.

In both these cases the stress begins on the vowel. If it is thrown on to the preceding glides, they are at once recognized as independent elements, °ʃɨ **aa** becoming oʃɨ **haa** with the 'aspirate', while ˈʃɨ becomes xʃɨ with the glottal stop. o, [which is simply a glide-o,] is generally modified by the following vowel, whose mouth-configuration it partly anticipates. It is then partly a weak throat-consonant, partly the voiceless glide-vowel corresponding to the vowel which follows, and is then placed on a shortened vowel-stem, being written ǫ. ǫſ, ǫɬ are thus almost equivalent to ɾːſ, ɨːɬ or ᴖᐯſ, ɔᐯɬ.

Vowels are finished analogously:

(*a*) By a gradual opening of the glottis, the final glide passing through whisper to breath, giving the 'gradual' ending ʃ°.

(*b*) By a cessation of expiration while the glottis is still closed for voice, giving the clear ending ʃˈ, which is the usual ending in English.

If uttered with stress these endings become respectively ʃo or ʃǫ, which is still the Sanskrit visarga, as in *manaḥ*, and ʃx, the Danish 'stöd-tone'. If a high vowel-position is relaxed slowly before o or ǫ, the off-glide has a strongly consonantal character, even if there is very little stress, giving ſᴖᐯ, ɬɔᐯ, etc., which is frequent in the Scandinavian languages.

Consonant-glides. Stops: *Off-glides*. All consonants consist acoustically of three elements, the consonant itself, and its on- and off-glide. Each of these three elements may be breathed or voiced, and modified in other ways as well.

The glides of stops are peculiarly important. Voiceless stops, indeed, are acoustically speaking pure glide-sounds, only audible at the moment of transition from or to some other sound. Voiced stops, on the other hand, can have a distinct sound of their own in addition to that of their glides, but as they can only be voiced by driving voiced breath into an air-tight chamber—forming the celebrated 'blählaut' of the German phoneticians—they cannot be maintained for any length of time.

Confining our attention for the present to the off-glides, we may distinguish four chief kinds of breath—or rather voiceless—and voice stops: (*a*) voiceless stop and breath glide ɑ°ʆ, as in *come*; (*b*) voiceless stop and voice glide ɑ'ʆ, nearly as in *go* when no vowel precedes; (*c*) voice-stop and breath-glide ɑ̵°, as in *egg*; and (*d*) voice-stop and voice-glide ɑ̵', as in *eager*.

The following table gives all the combinations—initial, medial, and final—those that occur in English being marked *:

Initial	Medial	Final
*ɑ°ʆ	*ʆɑ°ʆ	*ʆɑ°
*ɑ'ʆ	ʆɑ'ʆ	ʆɑ'
ɑ̵°ʆ	ʆɑ̵°ʆ	*ʆɑ̵°
ɑ̵'ʆ	*ʆɑ̵'ʆ	ʆɑ̵'

(*a*) In ɑ°ʆ the glottis is left open while the stop is being formed, and the chords are not brought into the voice-position till the moment of loosening the stop, so that before the glottis has time to form voice there is a slight escape of breath between the stop and the vowel—the glide from the stop to the vowel, or from the stop to silence, is breathed. In English the puff of breath varies in force according to emphasis, etc., and is always weaker medially than initially or finally, as may be seen by comparing the second ɑ in *cooking* with the two ɑs in *cook*, where, again, the initial ɑ has the stronger glide of the two, because of the progressive diminution of stress, whence also the force of the breath glide is still more diminished after a long vowel, as in *eating*.

(*b*) ɑ' seems to be formed in two ways. In initial English *go* at the beginning of a sentence the glottis is in the position for voice during the stop, but no air is driven in, and so the stop is inaudible as in **k**, but voice begins the moment the stop is loosened, and the off-glide is therefore voiced. In this kind of stop the voice is apt to break out a little before the end of the stop or at any rate to whisper part of the stop—ɑɒ'ʆ. Pure ɑ' is formed by sounding voice simultaneously with the loosening of the stop, so as to prevent any escape of breath. The French and South-German (South European generally) **k, t, p** are formed in this way, which makes them sound like **g̊, d, b** to an unaccustomed ear.

These sounds offer great difficulties to English speakers, who, however, will find initial **g̊** in *go* a convenient stepping-stone. But they must be practised carefully, for the breathy stops in English *come*, etc. are very offensive to a South European ear. The student must not be satisfied till he can explode a vowel loudly from the ɑ, ʊ or ɒ position without the slightest escape of breath or voicing or whispering of the stop.

(*c*)]ɑ°], and thence ɑ°], may be easily obtained from the familiar]ɑ° by joining on a].

(*d*) ɑ']] is obtained by pronouncing the familiar]ɑ'], dwelling on the consonant, and then dropping the initial]. These 'full' initial voice-stops, which are common in the South European languages, suggest the corresponding nasals to an unaccustomed ear when sounded very fully. Final ɑ' may be obtained by shortening such a word as *bigger*. The French final ǵ, as in ɒ]ɫɑ' *bague*, often has this sound.

Stops: *On-glides*. The on-glide after a vowel is generally voiced:]'ɑ°,]'ɑ°. Breath on-glides before voiceless stops occur in Icelandic and occasionally in Scotch, as in ɔ]°ʊ° *what*.

. . . . .

A final buzz preceded by a buzz or a voiced stop is completely whispered in English, as in *thieves, rage* ʊſɷ>sɒ, ɷ[ɾ-ʊƨɒ.

In this last case the glottis is not fully opened till the consonant is finished, which therefore consists of voice passing into whisper, followed by a breath off-glide. If the transition from voice to breath is completed during the beginning of the consonant itself, we have the 'half-breath' final z—]sː.

The vowel-like consonants when final occasionally end in a breath-glide. Thus in French *fille* = >ſɷː, in Icelandic *vel* = >[ɫɷː.

. . . . .

Glide-consonants. Most consonants, as compared with vowels, have more or less the character of glides. Breath stops are acoustically pure glides. In such combinations as ʊƨ in *chill*, ʊs in German ʊs[ɾ-ʊ *zeit*, the hiss is acoustically a mere modification of the breath-glide in *till*: we may almost say that the ƨ or s is the glide between the ʊ and the next vowel.

In slovenly speech, when a stop follows a vowel, the breath impulse is often so feeble that nothing is heard but part of the glide on to the consonant, the actual closure being formed without any breath at all: ɒſɑ) *big*. With nasals *man* becomes ꟻ[ɪ), only a nasal glide being audible. Other consonants are weakened in a similar way.

But there is a class of *Flap-consonants* which are pure glides, organically as well as acoustically, there being absolutely no fixed point in their formation. The East-Norwegian and Swedish 'thick *l*' is such a sound. It is an inverted **r** finished off with momentary contact of the tongue-tip against the inside of the arch-rim, the tongue moving forwards all the while from the moment of its being turned back to the single strong trill which finishes it. This sound can be roughly symbolized by ωc\, as in Norwegian ˋ}ɵ)¯ωc\] [*Ola*] = *Olaf*.

A Primer of Phonetics, 1890, pp. 49–60 *pass.*, and 1906, pp. 52–64 *pass.*

[The texts of *The Sounds of English* and the article on 'Phonetics' in the 11th Edition of the *Encyclopædia Britannica* are collated below by showing passages exclusive to the former in sloping lines, passages exclusive to the latter in square brackets. In general, the textual changes in the *Encyclopædia* article appear to be dictated by the need for the optimum conciseness and clarity, but readers will note, by way of contrast, the addition of passages on certain modifications of consonant-glides (p. 173) and upon the especial importance of glides 'from an acoustic point of view' (p. 172). *Ed.*]

Consonant-glides. Such a word as *cat* consists not only of the vowel and the two consonants of which it is made up, but also of glides or /positions/ [transitions] between these sounds The glide from the initial consonant to the vowel consists of all the intermediate positions through which the tongue passes on its way from the **k**-position to that of **æ**. The number of these positions is infinite; but they are all implied by the mere juxtaposition of the symbols of the fixed sounds, it being assumed that in all transitions from one position to another the shortest way is taken.

Although the direction of a glide is thus dependent on the positions of the two fixed points between which it lies, its character may be varied both by the shape of the /throat-and mouth-passages/ [configurative passages]—especially the glottis—and by stress and quantity.

In the word given above the two 'off-glides' from the consonants are both breath-glides, the glottis being kept open during the transition /from the **k** to the **æ**, and also during the loosening of the stop of the final consonant—that is to say, during the transition from the **t** to silence/ [from the voiceless consonant to the following vowel, or, as in the case of the final consonant, to silence.] The 'on-glide' from the vowel to the **t** is, on the other hand, a voice-glide, /the vibration of the chords/ [the closure of the glottis] being maintained till the stop is made.

In French and most of the languages of the South of Europe voiceless consonants are generally followed by voice-glides. Thus in French *qui* there is no escape of breath [after the **k**,] as [there is] in the English *key*. /Nearly the same pronunciation may be heard in Scotch./

/Some of the languages of the North of Europe/ [Other languages again] have breath on-glides before voiceless stops, /as if **t**, **k**, etc. were preceded by a **h**/.

/If an independent strong stress is put on the breath-glides after the consonants in such words as *two*, *key*, they are heard almost as full consonants—as weak **þ** and **x** respectively. Such consonants are said to be 'aspirated'. Initial voiceless stops are regularly aspirated in Irish-English and in Danish. Sanskrit and Old Greek *kh*, *th*, *ph* were no doubt pronounced in the same way—as, indeed, they still are in India.

/The voice-glide after the voice-stops **ğ**, **d**, etc. may be emphasized in the same way, giving the 'sonant aspirates' *gh*, *bh*, etc., of Sanskrit.

/Voice consonants between vowels in English, as in other languages, have both their on- and off-glides voiced, as in *ago*, where the chords vibrate continously throughout the whole word. But if a voice stop in English is not preceded by a vowel or other voiced sound, as when *go!* is uttered by itself, it is not voiced throughout, the chords being only gradually brought together, so that full voice is not heard till just before the transition to the vowel. So also with buzzes (voiced hiss consonants) as in *zeal*. When these latter consonants come at the end of a word and are not followed by voiced sounds, they have full vocality only at the beginning, so that they end with something between voice and whisper, as in *ease* compared with *easy*. In French and many other languages such consonants preserve their full vocality in all positions./

[If an independent strong-stress is put on the breath-glide of English *key*, it is heard almost as a full independent consonant, and becomes an 'aspirate'. Aspirated stops may be heard in the Irish-English pronunciation of such words as *tell*, and also in Danish, and in Sanskrit as pronounced in India. If the voice-glide after a voice stop is emphasized in a similar way the 'sonant-aspirates' of Sanskrit and its modern descendants are produced, as in Sanskrit *dhanu*.

[Glides are especially important from an acoustic point of view. Acoustically speaking, indeed, voiceless stops are pure glide-sounds, the stop itself being inaudible. In voice-stops, on the other hand, the stop itself can be made audible as well as the intervening glides. In English these latter are fully voiced when they come between voice sounds, as in *ago*; but when preceded by voiceless sounds or by a pause, as in *go!*, they are formed with imperfect vocality, full voice being heard only just before the stop is loosened. So also initial English **z** as in *zeal* is formed with imperfect vocality under the same conditions, so that it sounds like **sz**. In French and other languages which have voice-glides after voiceless consonants initial **ğ**, **z**, etc., are fully voiced.

[Consonant-glides may be further modified in various ways. In the formation of 'implosive' stops, such as occur in Saxon German, Armenian and other languages, voiceless stops followed by voice-glides are modified by simultaneous closure of the glottis, the larynx being raised by means of its muscles, so that it acts like a plug, compressing the air between the closed glottis and the mouth-stop, so that when the latter is released a peculiar choky effect is given to the off-glide.

[Rounded glides may be heard in Russian in such words as *komnata*, where the rounding of the **o** is anticipated in the preceding consonant, being heard, of course, only in the off-glide of the consonant. The acoustic effect is between that of **kwo** and ordinary **ko**.]

Glideless [consonant-] combinations remain to be considered. The [general articulative] principle of taking the shortest cut between sounds in juxtaposition necessarily results in certain transitions being effected without any glide at all. This is regularly the case when the two sounds are consonants having the same place, and differing only in form /as in *and*, *halt*, where the point of the tongue remains unmoved throughout the two consonants, the transition from the **n** to the **d** being effected simply by opening the passage into the nose, and that from **l** to **t** by opening the passages at the sides of the tongue, and opening the glottis at the same time/ [as in **nd**, **dlt**, where the point of the tongue remains unmoved through the whole sound-group]. In such combinations as **mf** the slight glide between the two consonants is in most languages got rid of by assimilating the place of the first consonant to that of the second: /thus in English *nymph* the **m** is a lip-teeth instead of a pure lip-nasal/ [so that the **m** becomes a lip teeth consonant, as in English *nymph*].

Even when consonants are formed in /quite different places/ [different parts of the mouth], it is often possible to join them without any glide. /In English, stop-combinations are glideless, as in *active*, *apt*, *robbed*, *headpiece*, the second stop being formed before the preceding one is loosened. In French and most other languages such combinations are separated by a breath or voice glide./ [In English such combinations as **kt**, **pt**, are glideless, the point of the tongue being brought into position before the preceding stop is loosened. In French, and most other languages, such consonants are separated by a breath-glide.]

Combinations of /soft consonants with other consonants, whether hard or soft/ [stops and vowel-like consonants **tr**, **gl**, **kw**] are glideless in [English and] most [other] languages, /as in English *try*, *quite*, *glow*, *bulb*. In English the breath-glide after a stop in such a word as *try* unvoices the first half of the following soft consonant, so that *try* might almost be written **trh-rai**/ [In English the breath-glide after a voiceless stop unvoices the beginning of the following vowel-like consonant; thus *try* is almost **trh-rai**].

Vowel-glides. Vowels are begun and ended in various ways. In the 'gradual beginning', which is the usual one in French and English, the glottis is gradually narrowed while breath is being emitted. /Thus in pronouncing **aa** with gradual beginning the glottis begins to close at the same moment that the tongue begins to move from the neutral mixed position into the mid-back one. In the 'clear' beginning the breath is kept back till the chords are in the position for voice and the tongue is in the position for the vowel, so that the vowel begins at once without any of the preparatory 'breathiness' of the gradual beginning. In German the clear beginning is generally exaggerated into a glottal stop./ [In the 'clear' beginning the breath is kept back till the glottis is closed for voice, which begins without any 'breathiness'. German favours the clear beginning, generally exaggerating it into a glottal stop.]

In the gradual as well as the clear beginning the stress begins on the vowel itself. If in the former /the stress begins on the breath glide/ [it is thrown back on to the breath-glide], this glide is felt as an independent element, /just as in the aspiration of consonants,/ and becomes the 'aspirate' **h**, /which in its ordinary English form is a glide both in the throat and in the mouth/ [which in English and most other languages is a glide not only in the throat but in the mouth as well, the tongue and lips gradually moving up into the position for the following vowel while the glottis is being closed].

/Some languages have a 'strong aspirate', in which the full position for the following vowel is assumed at the moment when breath begins to be emitted, the aspirate in this case being simply a voiceless vowel, so that, for instance, **hii** with the strong aspirate sounds almost like **çii** and **haa** like **xaa**. The strong **h** may be heard in American English./

[There is also a 'strong' aspirate, which occurs in Finnish and other languages, in the formation of which the full vowel position is assumed from the beginning of the aspiration, which is therefore a voiceless vowel.]

In most languages, when an aspirate comes between voiced sounds, it is formed with /'half-voice' or/ imperfect vocality, [the contrast of which with the full vocality of the other sounds is enough to produce the effect of breath]. /Thus in English *behold!* compared with *hold!* the chords vibrate throughout the whole word, but their vibration is so feeble during the **h** that the contrast of this weak vocality with the full vocality of the other sounds is enough to produce the effect of aspiration. In the emphatic *aha!*, on the contrary, the glottis is opened enough to let out a distinct puff of air, instead of merely relaxing its closure, as in half-voice./ [Thus in English *behold* the voice runs on without any actual break, the glottal closure being simply relaxed, not fully opened for breath, as in the emphatic *aha!* In some languages, such as Bohemian, this 'voice-aspirate' is used everywhere, initially as well as medially.]

The Sounds of English, 1908, pp. 53–6; and 'Phonetics', *Encyclopædia Britannica*, 11th Edn., 1911, pp. 465–6

5. *Pitch, Tone, Intonation*

[In Sweet's varying use in these extracts of such terms as 'pitch', 'tone', 'tones', 'intonation', one recognizes the same groping after an acceptable expositive language as in Section E 1 on pp. 131–7. 'Pitch' is seemingly equated sometimes with 'tone' (pp. 175, 178), sometimes with 'key' (pp. 177, 179), while 'tone' is sometimes also equated with 'intonation' (p. 178).

The short extract on p. 179 from Sweet's early paper on 'Danish Intonation' should be followed up by a reading of the whole of the first part of this paper for the light that it sheds upon what Sweet meant by 'tone'. *Ed.*]

It need hardly be said that many of the statements in this book—whether the result of my predecessors' or my own researches—will require careful examination by others before they can be either fully received or rejected. The whole subject of intonation, especially, requires to be thoroughly investigated by a thoroughly competent observer, which I am very far from being, my natural aptitude and my training being equally defective. It is in this branch, in the study of voice-timbre and of synthesis generally, that the work of future phoneticians must be concentrated.

Preface to *A Handbook of Phonetics*, 1877, p. x

[In the conflated extract below, passages found only in the *Handbook* are enclosed in sloping lines, passages found only in the *Primer of Phonetics* in square brackets.]

Tones and Pitch. /Variations of pitch (or tone)/ [Intonation, or variations of tone (pitch)] depend . . . on the rapidity of the sound-vibrations, which again depend on the length of the vocal chords.

Changes of tone/s/ may proceed either by leaps or glides. In singing the voice dwells without change of pitch on each note, and leaps upwards or downwards to the next note as quickly as possible, so that although there is no break, the intermediate /'glide-tone'/ [glide] is not noticed. In speech the voice only occasionally dwells on one note, but is constantly moving upwards or downwards from one note to the other, so that the different notes are simply points between which the voice is constantly gliding. [An absolutely level tone hardly ever occurs in speech, whose level tones are only relatively level, generally ending in a slight rise. There is often in speech a marked difference between a rapid rise or fall in which the ear is mainly impressed by the beginning and end of the voice-inflexion, and a slow glide which allows the intermediate tones to come out. We may distinguish these as *voice-leaps* and *voice-glides*, remembering that the distinction is only a relative one, which cannot always be made with certainty. The difference between voice-leap and voice-glide is analogous to that between]ɷ] and]ɾɷ].]

There are/, therefore,/ three primary 'forms' or 'inflections' of /tones/ [intonation]:

level –
rising ˏ [⌐]
falling ˎ [⌐].

[ˏ and ˎ are, strictly speaking, symbols of voice-glides only, though in practice they are used to denote voice-leaps also, whose proper symbols are ⌐ and ⌐.]

The level tone [—or an approach to it—] may be heard in *well* as an expression of musing or meditation; the rising in questions or doubtful [hesitating] statements [as *are you ready?*]; the falling in answers, commands, or dogmatic assertions [as in *yes, I am*].

/It is also possible to have level tones connected by intermediate glide-tones, as in the 'portamento' in singing./ Besides the simple /rise and fall,/ [tones,] there are compound tones, formed by uniting both in one syllable:

the compound rising ∨[ˇ]
the compound falling ∧[ˆ]

[The compound rise ˇ]∨ may be heard in such a sentence as *take care!* when uttered warningly; [the compound fall ˆ]∧ in *oh! oh really!*, when implying sarcasm. /These tones, are, however, best learnt by combining their elements./

It is possible to combine three tones in one /syllable/ [inflection].

Thus we can have ^ /followed by /´, which has the effect of ˇ, only somewhat more emphatic.

All these tones can be varied indefinitely according to the interval through which they pass. As a general rule, the greater the interval the more marked the character of the tone. /Thus, a rise through a small interval (a second for instance) denotes mere enquiry, through a large one (such as a sixth) surprise. Again, the semitone (minor) interval has a plaintive effect, but here the less the interval the more marked its minor character, most of all therefore in the simple semitone or half-tone. The reason of this is that sadness, like all un-energetic emotions, naturally expresses itself in inflections of narrow range./ [For ordinary purposes it is enough to distinguish between a high rise ´ and a low rise ˏ, the former passing through a less interval than the latter. Conversely a high fall ` passes through a greater interval than a low fall ˎ. A high rise may be heard in *what?* as an expression of mere inquiry ´ɔɟʊ, a low rise in ˏɔɟʊ as an expression of surprise. In music semitones have a plaintive effect, and this is to some extent the case in speech also, where, however, plaintiveness is also expressed by modifications of the quality of the voice.]

/The whole relation of tone to language has as yet been only imperfectly studied, and all that can be expected from the student in our present state of knowledge is the power of discriminating the four inflections ´, `, ˇ, and ^.

/The use of tones varies greatly in different languages. In English the tones express various logical and emotional modifications, such as surprise, uncertainty, etc. In some languages there is a tendency to employ one predominant tone without much regard to its meaning. Thus in Scotch the rising tone is often employed monotonously, not only in questions but also in answers and statements of facts. In Glasgow Scotch the falling tone predominates. In American English the compound rise is the characteristic tone.

/In all these cases the tones are functionally 'sentence-tones', that is, they modify the general meaning of the whole sentence. In some languages, however, such as Swedish, Lithuanian, Chinese, Siamese, and the Indo-Chinese family generally, each word has its own special tone (rising, falling, etc.), which is as much an integral part of it as the sounds of which it is composed, and does not, therefore, vary with the general sense of the sentence. This tone may be called 'word-tone'./

Besides the separate inflections of which it is composed, each sentence, or sentence-group, has a general pitch, or 'key' of its own. [Key is marked by prefixing the voice-leap symbols in the same way as with the other group-modifiers, thus ⌐o :ɑ]ꟻ·]ɒ = *come up!* in a high key.]

For ordinary purposes it is enough to distinguish three /representative/ keys—

high ┌
middle ┌┘
low ┘

[the middle key being generally left unmarked]. /The middle key may also be left unmarked./ The high key is /natural in all strong/ [the natural expression of energetic] and joyful emotions, the low /in/ [of] sadness and solemnity.

Change of key has /often/ [also] a purely logical significance. Thus questions are naturally uttered in a higher key than answers, and parenthetic clauses in a lower key than those which state the main facts. In all natural speech there is incessant change of key.

Changes of key may proceed either by leaps or progressively. Progressive change of key /is indicated by prefixing ˊ or ˋ to the signs of key-change/ [may be expressed by using ˊ, etc., as group-modifiers]. Thus ˊ┌ [ˊo] is heard in all cases of passion /increasing/ [rising] to a climax.

A Handbook of Phonetics, 1877, pp. 93–6,
and *A Primer of Phonetics*, 1890, pp. 64–7

Intonation. Changes of pitch or tone may proceed either by leaps or glides. There are three primary intonations: (1) the *level* –, (2) the *rising* ˊ, and (3) the *falling* ˋ. There are also compound tones, formed by uniting a rise and fall in one syllable: (1) the *compound-rising* ˇ, (2) the *compound-falling* ˆ.

A level tone can be of any *height*, but it is enough to distinguish high-level ¯ and low-level _. The gliding tones can also begin at any height—low-rising ˏ, high-rising ˊ, etc. They can also be varied indefinitely according to the *interval* through which they pass.

Besides the separate intonations of which it is composed, each sentence, or sentence-group, has a general pitch or *key* of its own, which may be high or low. Changes of key may proceed either by leaps or by glides.

A History of English Sounds, 1888, p. 12

Intonation or tone is either *level*, *rising*, or *falling*, marked respectively –, ˊ, ˋ. The level tone is not much used in speech. The rising tone is heard in questions, such as *what*ˊ, the falling in answers, such as *no*ˋ. Besides these *simple* tones, there are *compound* tones, formed by uniting a rising and a falling tone in one syllable. The *compound rise* or falling-rising tone (marked ˇ) may be heard in *take care!* when used warningly;

the *compound fall* or rising-falling tone (marked ^) may be heard in *oh!* when expressing sarcasm.

The level tone may be either *high* or *low* in pitch, and the other tones may begin either in a high or a low pitch. When excited, we speak in a high pitch or key; when depressed, in a low key.

The non-level tones can pass through different *intervals*. The greater the interval, the more emphatic the tone becomes. Thus *what*ˊ with a slight rise expresses mere enquiry, but with a long rise—rising from a very low to a very high pitch—it expresses surprise or indignation.

A New English Grammar, 1891, pp. 228–9

The influence of tone on the general synthesis of language is very important. In such a language as English each tone has a general signification, and may be applied to any word indifferently. Thus by a simple inflexion of the voice a single word will often express what in other languages could only be adequately stated in a complete sentence. We may therefore call this kind of tone *sentence-tone*. The Greek tones on the other hand are strictly *word-tones*: each word has but one tone, which is absolutely inherent in it, being as much an essential part of it as its consonantal or vowel structure.

The interesting question now arises, how do such languages express these general ideas (interrogation, affirmation, etc.), which it is the function of the English tones to express? As regards Norwegian, I find that there is generally no difference of inflexion in assertive and interrogative sentences, and that when the interrogation is very emphatic, all that is done is simply to increase the range of the tone.

'On Danish Pronunciation', *T.P.S.* 1873–4; in *Collected Papers of Henry Sweet*, 1913, p. 349

[In the following extract, passages exclusive to *The Sounds of English* are shown in sloping lines, those exclusive to the *Encyclopædia Britannica* article in square brackets.]

Intonation. /This depends on the rapidity of the sound-vibrations: the quicker the vibrations, the higher the pitch, the sharper and shriller the tone. Voiced sounds are the only ones capable of variation of pitch, which in speech and song depends on the tension of the vocal chords and the length of their vibrating portion: the tighter and shorter a string or similar vibrating body, the higher the pitch./ [Intonation or variation of tone (pitch) depends on the rapidity of the sound-vibrations: the more rapid the vibrations, the higher the pitch. Intonation is heard only in voiced sounds, as being the only ones capable of variations of pitch].

In singing, the voice generally dwells on each note without change of pitch, and then leaps up or down to the next note as /smoothly and/ quickly as possible, so that the intervening /pitch-glide/ ['glide'] is not noticed, except in what is called 'portamento'. In speech, on the other hand, the voice hardly ever dwells on any one note, but is constantly /moving/ [gliding] upwards /and/ [or] downwards, /sometimes by leaps, but more generally by glides, in which all the intermediate notes are heard in more or less rapid succession, as in portamento/ [so that an absolutely level tone hardly ever occurs in speech. But in the rising and falling inflections of speech we can distinguish between 'voice-glides' (portamentos or slurs) and 'voice-leaps', although the distinction is not so definite as in singing].

/The different tones—rising, falling, etc.—vary in character according to the interval through which they pass. The greater the interval, the more emphatic the tone. Thus a high rise, which begins high, and consequently can only rise a little higher, expresses simple question; while the same word, if uttered with a low rise extending over an interval of an octave or even more, expresses surprise or indignation, as in *what!* compared with the simply interrogative *what?*/

[Of the three primary forms of intonation the level tone - can be approximately heard in *well* as an expression of musing—although it really ends with a slight rise; the rising ˊ in the question *well?*; the falling ˋ in the answer *yes*. There are besides compound tones formed by uniting the two last in one syllable. The compound rising tone may be heard in *take care!* the compound falling tone in the sarcastic *oh!* All these tones may be varied according to the intervals through which they pass. The greater the interval, the more emphatic the tone. Thus a high rise, which begins high, and consequently can only rise a little higher, expresses simple question, while the same word, if uttered with a low rise extending over an interval of between a fifth and an octave—or even more—expresses various degrees of surprise or indignation, as in the emphatic *what!* compared with the simple interrogative *what?*

[In English and most European languages, intonation serves to modify the general meaning and character of sentences. This is *sentence-intonation*. But some languages, such as Swedish and Norwegian, and Chinese, have *word-intonation*, by which words, which would otherwise be identical in sound, are distinguished. The distinction between Greek *oíkoi* and *oîkoi* was no doubt one of intonation.]

The Sounds of English, 1908, pp. 52–3, and 'Phonetics', *Encyclopædia Britannica*, 11th Edn., 1911, p. 465

6. *Connection between Force, Quantity, and Pitch*

[In the first extract below passages exclusive to the *Handbook* and the *Primer of Phonetics* are indicated in the usual way by sloping lines and square brackets respectively. *Ed.*]

There is a natural connection between force, length, and high pitch, and conversely between weak force, shortness, and low pitch.

The connection between force and pitch is especially intimate. All energetic emotions naturally express themselves in high tones and forcible utterance, and increased vehemence of emotion is always accompanied by a rise in force and pitch.

The association of force and quantity is less intimate. There is, however, a natural tendency to pass over the less important unaccented elements of speech, /and to dwell on the prominent stress-syllables, whence that shortening of unaccented long, and lengthening of accented short syllables which is so common in modern languages/ [and to dwell on and lengthen the more prominent ones].

It is, however, a(n) /entire/ mistake to suppose that these natural tendencies represent necessities, and that high tone and strong stress can be regarded as convertible terms. Just as on the piano the lowest note in the bass can be struck with the same force as the highest one in the treble, so in language if often happens that strong stress is combined with low pitch, and vice-versa. Still less can /quantity/ [length] be identified with stress.

A Handbook of Phonetics, 1877, pp. 96–7, and *A Primer of Phonetics*, 1890, p. 67

A knowledge of sentence stress and intonation is not only an essential part of elocution and correct pronunciation, but is also an integral part of the syntax of many languages.

The Practical Study of Languages, 1899, p. 49; L.A.L.L. Edn., p. 48

There are five ways of indicating the relations between words in word-groups and sentences: (*a*) word-order, or position, (*b*) stress, (*c*) intonation, (*d*) the use of form-words, and (*e*) inflection.

The simplest and most abstract way of showing the relations between words is by their *order*. We see how the meaning of a sentence may depend on the order of its words by comparing *the man helped the boy* with *the boy helped the man*, where the distinction between subject and adjunct to the predicate depends entirely on the word-order.

We can see how *stress* alters the meaning of a sentence by comparing *that is -my book* with *that is ·my book*; the latter really means 'it is my book and not someone else's'.

We can see how *intonation* shows the relation between words by comparing a sentence such as *you are ready?*´, uttered with a rising tone, with the same sentence uttered with the falling tone of such a sentence as *I am ready*`. While the falling tone expresses statement, the rising tone expresses question, so that the rising tone in *you are ready*´ has the same meaning as the change of word-order in *are you ready?*

The above are examples of *sentence-stress* and *sentence-intonation* as distinguished from *word-stress* and *word-intonation*. English uses both sentence-stress and word-stress to express differences of meaning (the latter in such pairs as ·*abstract* and to *ab*·*stract*), while intonation is used in English only to modify the meaning of sentences. Word-intonation occurs in many foreign languages, such as Old Greek and Chinese (the 'Chinese tones'), where it is used to distinguish the meanings of separate words. Thus in Old Greek *oíkoi* 'at home' and *oîkoi* 'houses' were distinguished solely by their intonation, both words having the same sounds and the same strong stress on the first syllable.

Stress and intonation, however, have not much influence on the grammatical structure of sentences, sentence-stress being used mostly for emphasis, and intonation to express shades of feeling, such as curiosity, dogmatism, contempt, though, as we have seen, it is also used to express purely logical meanings such as question. Variations of stress and intonation are also limited in number. The distinctions that can be made by word-order are still more limited, so that if a language depended entirely on word-order to show grammatical relations, it would have to use the same word-order to express a great variety of different meanings. Hence no language can rely exclusively on these three, but requires the help either of form-words or inflections, which afford as many grammatical distinctions as are necessary.

A New English Grammar, Pt. I, 1891, pp. 30–2

7. *Voice Quality, Timbre, Organic Basis*

[The text of Sweet's contributions to these much neglected aspects of phonetics differs sufficiently in the *Handbook* and the *Primer of Phonetics* to warrant their separate presentation here. The slight difference in the texts of the earlier and later editions of the *Primer* (here indicated as usual in the conflated extract by using sloping lines for the passages occurring only in the 1892 edition, square brackets for the 1906 edition) is doubtless to be ascribed to Sweet's research into the Arabic throat sounds, as described on pp. 121–6. *Ed.*]

Voice Quality (*Timbre*). Besides the various modifications of stress, tone, etc., the quality of the voice may be modified through whole sentences by various glottal, pharyngal, and oral influences.

The most important are those known as the 'clear' and the 'dull' qualities of the voice. The latter is due to lateral compression, the former to its absence. There are, of course, various intermediate degrees, and the dull quality may be exaggerated by cheek and lip rounding, as we hear in the pronunciation of those badly-trained singers who make **a** nearly into ***o*** on a high note. This exaggerated dulling of the voice may also be heard as an individual peculiarity, giving what is commonly called a 'sepulchral' tone. The dull quality is the natural expression of sadness, solemnity, or tenderness, and is so employed instinctively in natural speech and in singing.

Among the many other varieties of voice quality, which are mostly individual or national peculiarities, the following may be noticed:

Narrowing of the upper glottis (**R**) gives an effect of strangulation. It is common among Scotchmen, and combined with high key gives the pronunciation of the Saxon Germans its peculiarly harsh character.

Partial closure of the mouth is a common English peculiarity. It has a tendency to labialize back vowels, and even where there is not actual labialization it gives the vowels generally a muffled sound, so that ***a***, for instance, is not easily distinguished from **ɔ**. It also tends to make the general speech nasal, for the breath being impeded in its passage through the mouth, naturally seeks another through the nose. Germans sometimes say of the English, with humorous exaggeration, that they speak, not with their mouth like other people, but with their nose and throat.

Lip-influence is very important. General lip contraction is a natural accompaniment of partial mouth closure and nasality, also of the dull quality of the voice. Conversely, the clear quality may be made more decided by spreading out the corners of the mouth, as in the pronunciation of **i**. This is frequently employed by singers to give a laughing effect. In many languages, such as French and many Scotch dialects, the lips are often protruded in forming rounded sounds, while in others, such as English, the lips are not employed more than is necessary, inner rounding being chiefly relied on.

These modifications must be carefully distinguished from those which are due to peculiarities in the organs of speech themselves. Thus defects in the palate may cause permanent nasality (together with a peculiar hollowness of sound), an abnormally large tongue, gutturality, etc. All of these peculiarities are inseparable from the individual.

A Handbook of Phonetics, 1877, pp. 97–9

Voice-quality. Besides the various modifications of stress, etc., the quality of the voice may be modified through whole sentences by various glottal, pharyngal, and oral influences.

The influence of the lips is seen in the two qualities of the voice known as 'clear' and 'dull'. The clear quality is the result of opening the mouth widely and spreading out its corners. When exaggerated it gives a harsh, screaming character to the voice.

The dull quality of the voice is the result of slight separation of the jaws and neutral lip-position. English speech generally tends to the dull quality. When exaggerated it gives a 'muffled' character to the voice, which, when accompanied by low pitch, results in what is called the 'sepulchral' tone.

The dull quality of the voice naturally leads to nasality, for the breath, being impeded in its passage through the mouth, seeks another passage through the nose. Slight nasality is almost universal in English speech. Its presence is at once made manifest in singing.

Narrowing of the /upper glottis/ [bronchial passages] gives a wheezy character to the voice, sometimes approaching to strangulation. This effect is familiarly known as 'the pig's whistle'. It may be heard from Scotchmen, and combined with high key gives the pronunciation of the Saxon Germans its peculiarly harsh character.

These modifications—which are the result of controllable organic positions—must be carefully distinguished from those which are due to peculiarities of the organs of speech themselves. Thus defects in the palate may cause permanent nasality (together with a peculiar hollowness of sound), an abnormally large tongue gutturality, etc. All these peculiarities are inseparable from the individual, while those first described may—and often do—characterize the speech of whole communities.

Voice-quality may be readily symbolized by prefixing modifiers:

oV|| = clear quality
oΛ) = dull quality
oʃ = nasality
/oDΛ/[oo⊤] = wheeziness
o(= gutturality

Organic basis. Every language has certain general tendencies which control its organic movements and positions, constituting its organic basis or basis of articulation. A knowledge of the organic basis is a great help in acquiring the pronunciation of a language.

In English we flatten and lower the tongue, hollow the front of it, and draw it back from the teeth, keeping the lips as much as possible in a neutral position. The flattening of the tongue widens our vowels, its lowering makes the second elements of our diphthongs indistinct, front-hollowing gives a dull resonance which is particularly noticeable in our **l**, its retraction is unfavourable to the formation of teeth-sounds, and favours the development of mixed vowels, while the neutrality of the lips eliminates front-round vowels. Our neutral tongue-position is the low-mixed or mid-mixed one of the vowels in *further* >ɪ̱ꜜᴜ˥̡.

In French everything is reversed. The tongue is arched and raised and advanced as much as possible, and the lips articulate with energy. French therefore favours narrowness both in vowels and consonants, its point-consonants tend to dentality, and, compared with the English ones, have a front-modified character, which is most noticeable in the **l**, while the rounded vowels are very distinct.

The German basis is a compromise between the English and French, standard North German approaching more to the French.

No language, however, carries out the tendencies of its basis with perfect consistency.

Thus in English we have the point-teeth ᴜ; and mixed vowels occur in French and German, etc.

A Primer of Phonetics, 1890, pp. 67–80; 1906, pp. 72–5

The general character of English speech depends on the following peculiarities of its organic basis:

The tongue is broadened and flattened, and drawn back from the teeth (which it scarcely ever touches), and the fore part of it is hollowed out, which gives a dull sound, especially noticeable in **l**.

Rounded (labial) sounds, such as **w**, **uw** in 'who' are formed without any pouting of the lips.

In unrounded vowels, such as **aa**, **i**, the lips have a passive, neutral position. In the formation of front vowels such as **i**, **e**, there is no 'chinking' or spreading out of the corners of the mouth, by which in other languages their sound is made clearer.

A Primer of Spoken English, 1890, p. 4

Each national sound-system shows certain general tendencies which control the formation of its sounds, constituting its *organic basis* (basis of articulation). The general tendencies of present English are to flatten and lower the tongue, and draw it back from the teeth, the lips being kept as much as possible in a neutral position. The flattening of the tongue makes our vowels wide, and favours the development of mixed vowels. It also gives a dull character to our sounds, which is especially noticeable in the **l**. The retraction of the tongue gets rid of point-teeth consonants. The neutrality of the lips has eliminated the front-round vowels.

But these tendencies are not carried out uniformly. Thus the desire of distinctness has preserved the point-teeth consonants **þ, ð**.

The Sounds of English, 1908, pp. 57–8

Phonetics in a wider sense is something more than the science of speech-sounds and the art of pronunciation. It includes also voice-production; which, again, is the foundation of elocution and singing. These two latter subjects are, however, only partially comprised under the science of speech-sounds—even in its widest meaning: they stand to it much in the same relation as the practical study of languages does. And although voice-production is really a part of the science of speech-sounds, it is most convenient to separate it from phonetics, and make a special study of it in conjunction with the other two, of which it is the foundation.

The essential difference between phonetics in the narrower sense of the word and voice-production is that the former aims only at correctness of pronunciation, while the latter is concerned mainly with the quality of the voice. Two natives may speak their own language with an equally correct pronunciation, but the voice-production and elocution of the one may be better than that of the other; and a foreigner or provincial speaker who is unable to pronounce correctly may be a still better elocutionist: his voice may carry further and with less effort, its tone may be clearer, and more resonant and harmonious.

These qualities of the voice—which are even more important in song than in speech—depend mainly on the way in which the vocal chords are made to vibrate. This again depends on the voice-register which is employed: in the lower of these, the 'thick' or chest register, there is more vibration than in the higher, the 'thin' or head register, which in men's voices is called 'falsetto'. The voice-trainer, whether in speech or song, has further to take into account the natural differences between the voices of men on the one hand, and the higher-pitched voices of women and children on the other, together with the classification of the different voices according to their natural height and compass as bass (contralto), baritone (mezzo-soprano), tenor (soprano), and the subdivisions of these. All this does not directly concern the phonetician: to him a given vowel remains the same whether it is uttered by a man or a woman, whether it is produced with good or bad tone.

In one respect, however, phonetics really works hand in hand with elocution, and that is in developing distinctness of articulation. It is not necessary that the teacher of phonetics should insist specially on this point: the knowledge of the organic movements and the conscious practice of them naturally tends to give them greater strength and decision.

The Sounds of English, 1908, pp. 76–7

Organic Basis. Every language has certain general tendencies which control the formation of its sounds, constituting its *organic basis* or the basis of articulation. The tendency of the present English is to flatten and lower the tongue and draw it back from the teeth, while the lips are kept as much as possible in a neutral position. The flattening of the tongue makes our vowels wide and favours the development of mixed vowels, and gives the dull quality which is especially noticeable in our **l**; and its retraction is unfavourable to the development of teeth sounds; while the neutrality of the lips eliminates front-round vowels. In such a language as French everything is reversed. The tongue is arched, and raised, and advanced, and the lips articulate with energy. Hence French sounds tend to narrowness, dentality, and distinct rounding.

'Phonetics', *Encyclopædia Britannica*, 11th Edn., 1911, p. 466

IV. Writing, Spelling, Phonetic Notation

A. WRITING

Origin of Writing. Wherever we can trace the history of sound-writing, or writing proper—the art of representing speech-sounds by graphic symbols—we shall find that it was never the result of immediate invention, but was evolved by slow degrees from the more primitive art of picture-writing with hieroglyphs, whose form more or less directly suggests the idea to be expressed without reference to its sound, as when the sun is represented by a circle. The first step towards sound-writing would be—supposing the language to be written were English—to use the circle as the symbol not only of **san** = 'sol' but also of **san** = 'filius', and then of the syllable **san** or **sa**, until finally it came to denote the single sound **s**, or **s** followed by any vowel.

Such is the origin of the Latin alphabet. It was originally an adaptation of one of the Greek alphabets, which in their turn were an adaptation of the Phenician alphabet. The Phenician alphabet itself was a selection from the numerous symbols of the Hieratic writing of the Egyptians, which was a compromise between sound-writing and picture-writing, evolved by the exigencies of practical life out of the older purely hieroglyphic system.

Laws of Form-change. The laws of form-change in writing—whether hieroglyphic or phonetic—bear a striking analogy to those of sound-change: change is always going on, it is gradual, and it follows definite laws.

Form-change is always going on, because it is impossible for the human hand to repeat indefinitely the same movement without altering its direction and length. Handwriting varies not only from generation to generation, and between individuals of the same generation, but also in the individual himself according to speed and care of writing, etc.

Form changes are partly determined by the nature of the material written on and the instrument written with. Thus letters cut on stone or wood will be angular and detached, while writing with a pen will tend to roundness and joining—in short to cursiveness,—writing with a style on wax tablets will have a different character from writing with a nibbed pen on vellum or paper, and so on.

The most elementary change is one which we make unconsciously whenever we write; a variation in the relative lengths either of the strokes of which a letter is composed, or of the letters themselves. We see the former change in the development of h out of H, the latter in that of j out of I, and both together in l out of L.

In all cursive writing there is a tendency to round off angles, in order to avoid the sudden check and consequent waste of force and time caused by an angle, as we see in comparing E with e. In a stronger form this tendency leads to slurring or degradation, which is generally accompanied with shortening, as in the second element of r compared with R. The tendency of degradation is, of course, to reduce originally distinct letters to one form, as we see in the confusion of þ and y in y^{e}, etc. Of course, if any element of a letter is superfluous for purposes of distinction, there is a tendency to drop it altogether, as in b from B, where the upper loop of the latter has been discarded. The opposite phenomenon of exaggeration of an originally subordinate element of a letter, which is at the same time lengthened, is seen in the development of the side-stroke of G and Q into the lower circle of g and the upright stem of q respectively, and very strikingly in the development of the Black Letter or Gothic alphabet, in which originally merely accidental and ornamental tags have been exaggerated so as to obscure the original elements of the letters. These changes are, of course, due partly to the organic tendency to variation, but also to the striving after distinctness. While there is a general tendency to round off angles, as in C from ⟨, there is a tendency not only to keep acute angles, as in our W compared with U, but also to turn sharp curves into angles, as in the development of ſ out of s.

In writing with a nibbed pen the down strokes are thick, the upstrokes are thin—a peculiarity which still attests the origin of our printing letters from quill- or reed-written ones. Hence the tendency to employ the thicker and distincter down-stroke when it is more or less perpendicular, and as variations of slope are inconvenient in many other ways, all but perpendicular down-strokes are eliminated as much as possible, or oblique strokes are made upright, as in q from Q. Oblique strokes are often got rid of even at the cost of an angle or break, as in d from ð. In y, x, and some others, the slopes were kept for the sake of symmetry of form, and distinctiveness.

The above are isolative changes. But there are also combinative ones. In writing, the instinct which rebels against angles tends also to eliminate breaks as much as possible: in all swift and easy writing the letters of a word are not only formed individually without breaks, but the whole word is written, as far as possible, without lifting up the pen. It may happen, as in the case of our script x, that a letter may have a break in it, and yet be joined without a break to the preceding and following letter. This peculiarity was strongly developed in the Old Roman cursive hands, as is seen in the Ravenna papyri, the result being that the shapes of individual letters varied according to their position and combinations. We see the results of this system in the Arabic alphabet, where many letters have three different forms—initial, medial, and final. Even in the modern Latin alphabet we have—or had, till lately—the distinction of initial and final s and medial ſ.

The final result of unchecked organic changes would be to make writing unintelligible. This actually happened in the case of the Arabic script. The difficulty was met by the adoption of diacritics: the letters which had run together were differentiated by the addition of dots, as many as three being sometimes placed on one letter. So also in the Middle-Age Latin alphabet *ni* had become confused with *m* and so on, so that the *i* had to be marked with a diacritic—a clumsy device which we are still forced to keep up.

But the logical reaction generally begins long before cursive writing has reached the Arabic stage. The first step is to detach the letters, selecting from the various cursive forms those which are the simplest and most compact—involving fewest breaks—and the most distinctive. A good specimen of such a detached cursive is afforded by the imperial Chancery hand of the Romans. The reaction against slurring leads to detaching the strokes even of separate letters. Thus we find the top stroke of ʒ from G, which was originally an exaggerated flattening of the top curve, completely detached in the oldest Roman cursive writing, and so with many other letters. One of the most effective means of securing simplicity and distinctiveness, is by utilizing projection above and below the line, which developed itself spontaneously in the Roman capital writing, and after much fluctuation settled down into the usage of our present minuscule or lower-case alphabet, in which, for instance, i j l represent distinctions that were once almost entirely dependent on projection.

A History of English Sounds, 1888, pp. 59–63

Word-division in Writing. We may now turn to the practical question of word-division in writing. If we are to be guided consistently by logic, we must either write all half-words, derivative syllables and inflexions as separate words, or else incorporate them into the full words. The difficulty is that, although word-division is mainly logical, the purely formal side of the question must also be considered. Thus, although it would be as easy to write the plural of **fish** in two words **fish iz**, as it would be if the **iz** were the verb substantive, it would be impossible with the plural of *foot* **fut**, unless indeed we were boldly to write **ft iy**, although even this spelling would ignore the fact that the **iy** is as much part of the word itself as a sign of the plural. Cases in which unpronounceable letter-combinations would have to be written separately have also to be considered. The isolating system is thus found to be impracticable if carried out consistently, and nothing remains but that of joining the half-words on to the full-words. This method, while offering considerable difficulties of detail, is practicable, although it has not been carried out consistently in any language I know. Our present word-division is a compromise between the two extremes of isolation and agglutination. As a general rule we agglutinate inflexions and derivatives, and isolate half-words whose connexion with the whole-word to which they belong is less intimate than in the case of inflexions and derivatives. Inflexions are only acknowledged when sanctioned by Latin Grammar. Such purely modern inflexions as the negative **ai*k*aant** from **ai*k*æn** where the **nt** = **not**, although conventionally only a half-word not a true inflexion, could not be written as an isolated word, are shirked by that convenient compromise the apostrophe ': by writing 'can't', we keep up the fiction of the divisibility of a monosyllable into two separate words.

All these considerations show the hopeless confusion into which orthography falls when it attempts to overstep its legitimate function—that of giving a faithful graphic representation of the sounds of the spoken language. The attempt to indicate simultaneously the formal and the logical side of language by the same alphabet—an alphabet, it may be remarked, which is barely capable of fulfilling its purely phonetic duties alone—is about as successful as most compromises, that is, instead of doing one thing properly, it does two things badly. If, for instance, it is convenient to denote a substantive by a capital letter in German, why should we not do so in English, and why should not the same principle be extended to the other parts of speech? Adjectives, for instance, might be written with a turned capital, verbs with an italic, adverbs with a turned italic. Again, in Latin it would be very convenient to have a series of marks to indicate the different cases, independently of their form, and would much facilitate the understanding of Latin. Others, again, think that the spelling of every word ought to give a brief epitome of its etymology and history. If carried out consistently, all this would postulate an entirely independent set of signs, which, for special purposes, would be written between the lines of ordinary phonetic writing, forming a sort of short-hand logical, grammatical, or historical commentary, as the case might be. In the same way I should consider word-division simply as a logical commentary on the phonetic text: in short, I would abolish the ordinary word-division altogether.

But the abandonment of conventional word-division by no means postulates a return to the old system of writing each sentence without a break. On the contrary, it is clear that the great assistance afforded to the reader by presenting the letters in groups of moderate length was the one great reason for abandoning the original system of non-division. As we have seen, the most important element in the synthesis of speech-sounds is stress. I propose, therefore, to follow the analogy of musical notation, and divide our sentences into bars, making the beginning of each group of letters coincide with a full-stress. The accent-mark otherwise required to make the full-stress would be available for the secondary stress, and the same mark, when placed before a letter-group or 'stress group', as we may call it, would indicate the emphatic sentence-stress. Thus with a single mark we should be able to indicate no less than four degrees of stress. We should, however, also require a mark to indicate absence of stress at the beginning of a sentence. If we added a sign for breath-taking and two accents to indicate the rising and falling tones, we should be able to dispense entirely with the present unsatisfactory system of punctuation, etc., and to express clearly and precisely what they indicate only imperfectly and vaguely.

'Words, Logic and Grammar', *T.P.S.* 1875–6; in *Collected Papers of Henry Sweet*, 1913, pp. 12–14

The difficulties caused by the written form of the language, such as the complexity of its alphabet—which, again, may be the result of the writing being partly hieroglyphic—the ambiguity or unphonetic character of its orthography, are all purely external: Arabic is still Arabic when transcribed into Roman letters, nor is Japanese any more Japanese for being written in a mixture of disguised hieroglyphs and syllabic alphabetic writing, both borrowed from China. No existing system of writing is anything but an external disguise borrowed from some other language: Arabic is disguised Syriac writing, and the Russian alphabet is Byzantine Greek.

The Practical Study of Languages, 1899, p. 54; L.A.L.L. Edn., p. 53

Alphabets. The angular and detached letters of the Roman lapidary alphabet were, however, modified differently for different purposes. The old alphabet was used for writing books long after a fully developed cursive had come into use for the ordinary purposes of life, this cursive itself being nothing but a degradation of the book alphabet. In the 'uncial' alphabet A, D, E, M are rounded off in the direction of a, ꝺ, e, m, and certain letters project above and below the line. The cursive writing itself split up into a variety of forms, as in the alphabet of the wax tablets, the Ravenna papyri, and the detached 'half-cursive' Chancery hand. About the fourth century all these alphabets existed side by side —as they still do in such forms as A a *a*—and modified each other in various ways. A special development of a very old Roman cursive—or rather of a degraded capital writing—artificially modified and systematized, was the Roman shorthand—the 'Tironian Notes'. The chief influence of the Tironian notes was on the Middle-Age system of contractions, which, again, has in some cases permanently influenced the alphabets of modern Europe, the Spanish tilde in *año*, for instance, being nothing but the old *m*-contraction (¯), itself probably a degraded M written over the line. But the history of the later alphabets is, in the main, one of an incessant action and reaction of the detached and formal book hands and the cursives on one another, which latter were only exceptionally employed in writing books.

When the Roman empire broke up, separate national hand-writings sprang up in the different provinces in the same way as Latin is split up into separate languages. A very marked variety of minuscule was developed among the christianized Celts of Britain, being mainly a compromise between uncial and cursive. This alphabet, which is still preserved almost unchanged in Ireland, was adopted by the Anglo-Saxons, who afterwards adopted þ and ƿ **w** from their own Runic alphabet—at first in their original angular forms—instead of *th* and *u*(*u*). They also modified ꝺ into ð to express the sound ʋ, which was probably suggested by the use of crossed *d* (as of other crossed letters) in contractions.

By the time of Alfred the English hand had developed a character of its own, the uncial writing having been abandoned in favour of the minuscule, from which—at least in its book form—many of the older cursive elements were eliminated.

The chief subsequent changes were in the tags with which the strokes were generally finished off in British writing. After about 950 there is a general tendency to curve inwards the lower ends of upright strokes in such letters as *i*, *n*, *m*, *h*. About 1050 the ends of low stems are curved outwards in such letters as ꞃ, ꞅ, þ, while *p* retains its older straight stem. Sometimes these low stems were finished off with a cross-stroke or 'serif', as in our printing letters. Earlier in the century they began to wave and lengthen the top tags of *i*, *n*, *h*, etc. *y* occurs dotted in the very oldest writings, but the dot was afterwards generally dropped, and not restored till about 1000. This, and other changes, were partly due to the influence of the French hand, which towards 1000 began to be generally used in writing Latin. In the earlier charters the Latin and English portions are all in the British hand, but after 1000 the Latin is in the French, the English portions (boundaries, etc.) in the national hand.

This French hand—the 'Caroline minuscule'—was developed in France at the beginning of the ninth century by a reform of the earlier Merovingian cursive. It is practically almost identical with our present Roman lower-case printing letters, which were modelled on it. It dots the *y* leaving the *i* undotted, and prefers ſ to *s*. The stems of the letters are only slightly tagged. Its characteristic letters, as compared with the English hand, are *r*, *f*, *g*. The upright *d* and the high ſ occur in the older English handwriting, but in Alfred's time they had been generally supplanted by ꝺ and ꞅ, so that their reappearance in Latin writings of this period must be ascribed to French influence.

In the first hand of the Peterborough Chronicle, which ends at 1124, *s* and *d* still retain their English forms, though the French *d* is occasionally used. The high ſ appears beside ꞅ not only in this Chronicle, but also in other English mss even of the first half of the 11th century. After 1124, the Peterborough Chronicle is written in a variety of hands down to 1154, and in this portion the French forms of *f*, *g* etc. appear for the first time in English words, side by side with the British forms. Here also occurs the French *w*, formed by interlacing two *v*'s, but only in French names.

Henceforth writing in England follows the general European development. Exaggeration of the tags and stem-bending increase, and in the course of the 14th century the letters become more and more angular, resulting in the crabbed and interlaced forms of the Gothic or Black Letter and German alphabets. Then the Humanists restored the minuscule of the 12th century. Both types of writing—the Latin and Gothic—were finally fixed by the invention of printing. The influence of the Middle-Age cursives is shown in our Italic alphabet. We still keep the old Roman capitals unchanged, but only for special purposes of ornament and distinction.

New Letters. Every alphabet is liable to the demand for new symbols either through sound-change in the language which is written in it, or through its application to some other language. If the change of any sound is carried out regularly in a language, the symbol is generally kept also, however much the sound may have altered, as we see in French *u* = f, Italian *g* before *e* = ϖε etc. If, however, a sound splits up into two different ones with a corresponding difference of meaning, as in German *gute*, *güte* = older *guoto*, *guotī*, the want of a new symbol makes itself felt. Again, in adapting such an alphabet as the Roman to a new language, the letters will be assigned to their nearest equivalents, minute differences being disregarded, as when Latin *f* was used to denote ɜ in Old Irish. Often, however, new distinctions have to be made, as between *l* and ω in Welsh, or totally new sounds have to be symbolized. This is effected in various ways:

(*a*) By assigning *new values* to superfluous letters, as when the Greeks made the Phenician o into a vowel-symbol, there being no Greek sound answering to the throat-consonant ɵ it stood for in Phenician. In this case the change of value, though considerable, is by no means arbitrary. Even the change by which E, originally the aspirate *he*, was made into a front vowel, and the later one by which H, originally the throat *h'eth* ɵƒ, came to represent first *h* and then *ē*, can be explained by the names of these letters, both of which begin with *e* modified by a mere breath-glide, or what would easily be weakened into it. No doubt there may be cases of arbitrary assignments of values, but they are certainly rare.

(*b*) By utilizing originally unmeaning *variations*. Thus, up to the 16th century *v* was simply another way of writing *u*, and *j* of *i*: in the 15th century *v* and *j* were ornamental varieties which were especially used at the beginning of words, and so naturally came to be regarded as consonant symbols. So also the French *ç* is only a variety of a descending *z*. In Old Icelandic consonant capitals were utilized as double letters, as in *maNa* = *manna*.

(*c*) By *digraphs*, such as *th*, *ps* with which the Romans transcribed the Greek *θ*, *ψ*. Both of these, however, were compound sounds ʊ°, ɒs, so that digraphs are really expansions of contractions. But when the Romans expressed Greek initial *r* by *rh* in *rhetor*, etc., they were using two letters to express one simple sound, the *h* being here a breath-modifier, as if we were to express ʋ by ωː in Visible Speech. Of course, when *th* and *ph* in Latin became simple ᴜ and ɔ, *h* came to be regarded as an open-modifier. *h* afterwards came to be a general, almost arbitrary, modifier, to show not only opening and unvoicing, but also fronting, as in Provençal and Portuguese *lh* = ꝏ, vowel-length, as in German *ohne* and English *ah*—a usage which was already developed in Umbrian and Oscan—while in Italian *gh* it was added to show that *g* kept its original back articulation. *Doublings* are a special form of digraphs. In vowels it is a common method of indicating length, as also with consonants. Some languages which have no double consonants use consonant-doubling as a 'strengthener' or arbitrary modifier. Thus in Spanish *ll* = ꝏ, in Welsh = ɷ, where also *dd* = ʋ, *ff* = >, *f* keeping its old British value of ≯. Greek *gg* = ɘɑ is an example of what may be called a compound doubling. *Trigraphs* also occur, as in German *sch*, Swedish *skj* = English *sh*.

(*d*) By *ligatures*, such as *æ* and *œ* = *ae, oe*, which in Latin were originally diphthongs ʃɾ˔, ʄɾ˔, but were afterwards simplified to ɭ̇ and ʄ̇ respectively. Our *w* is a consonant-ligature, which preserves an extinct form of the vowel *u*.

(*e*) By *diacritics*. One way in which diacritics may be developed is by writing one letter above another, which was a natural device to save space, especially at the end of a line, and would easily be utilized phonetically, as in the German *ü*, originally *uͤ*, where the *e* is a front-modifier. So also in Swedish *å* = ɟ̇) the *o* is a rounder. As we see, such an overwritten letter soon gets degraded into mere dots or strokes. Special contraction-marks were also utilized as diacritics, as we see in the Spanish *ñ* and OE ð. Another way in which diacritics develop is by degradation of a ligature-letter, as in *ę* from *æ*, where the tail is a degraded *a*.

Correspondence of Sound and Symbol. All writing which has once emerged from the hieroglyphic stage is at first purely phonetic, as far as its defective means will allow. But as the association between sound and symbol is almost entirely arbitrary, there is always a tendency for the symbol to lag behind the changes of the sound.

One result of this is the retention of *superfluous* symbols as when we write *q* instead of *c* or *k* in the combination *qu*, this *q* having originally represented the Semitic inner ɑ˧. The worst form of superfluity is writing 'silent' letters, as in the English *know*.

The opposite of superfluity is *ambiguity*, by which one symbol has to represent more than one sound. To some extent, this defect is inherent in all sound-notation: even in Visible Speech we often omit the minuter glide-symbols, etc., and in speaking of a practical alphabet we should hardly characterize it as unphonetic because it neglected—as most of them do—to mark even such necessary elements as vowel-quantity and stress. If an orthography makes a consistently phonetic use of the materials it has: if it restricts every individual symbol to one distinctive sound (which may include slight varieties, such as ɾ, ɾ˔ in English *pity*), and does not continue to write silent letters, we call it 'phonetic'. If, for instance, in English the vowels in *it, see, set, say*, were invariably expressed by *i, ii, e, ee* we should say that English spelling was, so far, phonetic, even if we admitted that the long vowels were really diphthongs. If we found these vowels written respectively *i*, *ee*, *e*, *ai* as invariably as on the other system, we should say that English was 'half-phonetic', or phonetic on an unphonetic basis, for it is evidently unphonetic and irrational to make *ee* the long of *i*. But when we find such a vowel as that in *see* expressed also by *e*, *ea*, *i*, we must call English spelling simply unphonetic. It would be a rhetorical exaggeration to call it wholly unphonetic as long as such a symbol as *ee*, together with many of the consonants, retains its present uniform value.

We see, then, that unphoneticness is mainly the result of the retention of originally phonetic spellings after they have become unphonetic through sound-change. It is, therefore, the result of tradition. Where there is no traditional spelling handed down, as when such a language as Old English was first written in Latin letters, spelling can hardly help being phonetic; where, on the other hand, there is a large literature, and, perhaps, a class of professional scribes, the influence of the traditional orthography becomes stronger and stronger, till, at last, the invention of printing and the growth of the newspaper press made changes of spelling as inconvenient as they were formerly easy. The ideal of a printer's orthography is one which is absolutely uniform over the whole territory of the language, and absolutely unchangeable. Such an orthography as that of the present English is, consequently, one in which there is no longer any living correspondence between sound and symbol—it is, in intention at least, wholly unphonetic: it is preserved by graphic, not phonetic, tradition.

But unphoneticness has its practical limits. A purely hieroglyphic writing, though cumbrous, would not overtax the average intelligence, but an absolutely unphonetic degradation of an originally phonetic system—one in which the separate letters had become phonetically unmeaning—could not be mastered even by the most retentive memory. Hence a phonetic reaction becomes inevitable sooner or later. In the early Middle Ages, when the multiplicity of dialects and the fewness of books made a uniform and fixed orthography impossible, the spelling periodically readjusted in accordance with the changes of pronunciation. Thus, when in German *hūs* had developed into the fully diphthongic **haus** they wrote it *haus*. This was easy enough as long as the phonetic tradition of the values of the Roman letters was kept up, and as long as the alphabet itself was preserved in its integrity; but, when such a ligature as *æ* had been degraded into ę and then by the carelessness and haste of scribes had been levelled under *e* together with *œ*, and Latin *c* and *g* had come to represent two different sounds each—all this happening in Old French orthography—the phonetic tradition was broken, and spelling could only be half phonetic.

The influence of Latin spelling in the Romance languages—due, of course, to the continuity of the languages themselves—is shown not only in the retention of 'soft' *c* and *g*, but also in the later French 'etymological' spellings by which *dette* was made into *debte* with a 'silent' *b*, after Latin *debitum*. It is, however, doubtful whether this was done with any etymological intention—at least at first. Scribes who were continually copying texts written in an endless mixture of dialects would naturally seek refuge in the comparative uniformity of the Latin spelling they were taught to reverence, and so would half unconsciously modify their unsettled French in the direction of the fixed Latin spelling. No doubt the pedants of the Renaissance did attempt to 'reform' spelling on etymological grounds, and occasionally with success, but nearly all the modifications of spelling that have been made in Europe since the introduction of printing have been phonetic, such as the dropping of silent *e*, the distinction between *oa* and *oo* in English. The reason why comparatively so few of the ceaseless attempts at similar reforms have succeeded, is that the early spelling reformers had not enough scientific knowledge and experience to grapple with the great changes in pronunciation and the corruption of the Roman alphabet.

A History of English Sounds, 1888, pp. 63–70

B. SPELLING AND SPELLING REFORM

[Not all phoneticians nowadays share Sweet's belief in the 'absolute necessity' for spelling reform, but the wisdom, experience, and linguistic insight that he packed into his writings on the subject are still highly relevant to all practitioners and students of phonetics and linguistics. No apology is needed, therefore, for the inclusion in this section of the whole of Sweet's treatise on Spelling Reform[1] which appeared as an Appendix to the *Handbook of Phonetics*. As the author himself said of it, in the Preface to the *Handbook*:[2] 'The Appendix on Spelling Reform will I trust be not unacceptable to those who wish to acquire a general knowledge of the main facts and principles involved in the question, without being obliged to go into the minutiae of phonetic science. It may also prove useful to travellers, missionaries and others, who wish for some aid in writing the sounds of unwritten dialects or savage languages.'

The treatise is also useful for its detailed and critical comparison of Ellis's Glossic and the author's Romic, and there is on p. 205 an admirable simple introduction to Visible Speech, a detailed account of which

[1] With the exception of the two pages of Specimens.

[2] p. xii.

is given in a later section. As a point of minor interest, those who may have wondered at Sweet's idiosyncratic refusal to use capital letters in German will find reasons given for his objection to them on p. 208. Those who seek to find in Sweet passages that appear to foreshadow later phonemic theories will attach special importance to the remarks about 'distinctive differences' on p. 212. *Ed.*]

When we contrast the regularity of modern spelling with the irregularity of that of the Middle Ages, in which the same word may be spelt in half-a-dozen different ways on the same page, we are apt to assume that the older usage reflects the freedom of nature, the modern regularity being purely artificial. But we soon find that such varieties as ME. *cume*, *kume*, *come* all mean exactly the same thing, and that where there are real underlying distinctions of sound, they are due to mixture of dialect—a mixture which, however, is often only apparent: the result of a scribe copying a ms written in another dialect which he only partially transliterates into his own. Another source of confusion is copying an older ms in an archaic spelling, which spelling, as a general rule, is neither retained nor discarded consistently, the result being more or less of an anachronism.

The remedy for this confusion is *normalizing*, which takes one definite dialect, and selects one definite spelling for each sound, the result being a more or less absolutely uniform orthography, of which the ME. Ormulum is one remarkable example, classical Sanskrit another. Normalizing has nothing to do with fixity of orthography. As we see, Sanskrit orthography was stereotyped together with the language itself, while Orm's spellings perished with their author. The present English spelling, again, though fixed, is not perfectly normalized. Thus we denote the **ou** from OE. *ā* by *o*+*e* in *stone*, but by *oa* in *moan*, although these two words have always had the same vowel from the beginning, and so on.

A normalized spelling on a rigorously phonetic basis will, of course, ignore such non-phonetic considerations as word-division, and will reproduce all the modifications which words undergo in different surroundings, as in the Sanskrit sandhi. It ought also to preserve the distinction between such doublets as **ðæt** and **ðət**. But in practice this is seldom done, it being found more convenient to write the emphatic form everywhere. The scribe, too, in writing has to pronounce each word to himself detached, and therefore in its emphatic form and free from such influences as sandhi and consonant-mutation. Of course, where variations in the form of a word are associated with marked divergencies of meaning, as in the Celtic mutations and such pairs as English *one*, *a*(*n*), *off*, *of*, they are recognized in writing.

This leads also to a general disregard of synthesis. Sanskrit denotes vowel-quantity everywhere, Greek only in some of the vowels which have distinct signs for the longs. In Latin the quantity is marked only by a diacritic which is generally omitted. Intonation is marked in Vedic Sanskrit and in some of the pre-classical Brahmanas. It was not marked in Greek till the Alexandrian philologists devised a scheme of accentuation for the benefit of foreigners. In modern languages quantity is often marked by doubling, as in Dutch, and less regularly in German and English, and stress by an acute accent, as in Spanish; this acute being primarily a mark of high or rising intonation, which was however—in Greek at least—combined with stress. Our punctuation-marks seem to have been originally modulative, and a comma is still more or less equivalent to ˊ, though punctuation is now mainly logical.

Word-division is disregarded in Sanskrit, though not in most Eastern languages. It was generally disregarded in Greek and Latin, the division between words being marked—whenever it was marked—not by spaces, but by a point. In the early Middle Ages subordinate words—especially prepositions—were generally run on to the following noun, etc., to which they belonged. The grouping of subordinate words round their centre was carried to a great extent in Old Irish, where, for instance, *indfhirsin* was written for *ind fhir sin* 'of-the man this', 'of this man'.

A History of English Sounds, 1888, pp. 70–2

Normalized Phonetic Spelling. Phonetic spellings may be criticized from two distinct points of view. We may ask, first, Does this text afford a faithful representation of the pronunciation of its writer? Secondly, we may ask, Is it easy to read? These two points of view are not only distinct, but they are, if carried to an extreme each way, absolutely antagonistic. If it were possible to give an exhaustively, minutely accurate representation of the pronunciation of any one speaker by means of alphabetic signs, such a transcription would not be legible in the practical sense of the word: it would only be, at the best, decipherable.

But phonetic texts are not written solely as specimens of pronunciation; they may be written simply to convey information. Most of the texts in the *Maître Phonétique* are of this character—even when they deal with purely phonetic questions. And when we are reading about a subject in which we are interested, we naturally prefer to have the exposition written in that spelling which enables us most easily and rapidly to recognize the words of which it is composed.

Rapidity of recognition depends on uniformity: the more the spelling of the new text differs from that to which we have hitherto been accustomed, the more difficulty we have in reading it. Thus, if we have been used to **mai litl haus,** we are apt to stumble over **məĕ lɪtl̩ hæŏs**; and if we have once accustomed ourselves to such German spellings as **vi:r baidə** and **ve:gən dər ainfaxhait unt le:zbarkait,** we can hardly be blamed for hesitating over **viă paĭdə** and **ve:ŋ dɑ ãĭnfɑx-haĭt ŭnt le:spɑʀkhaĭt** (*Maître phonétique* '95. 1, p. 116).

I object to such spellings as **maɪ, maĕ, məɪ˞** etc., because they are not only practically inconvenient and a source of confusion, but because they are superfluous, and therefore to some extent even misleading. When a foreigner compares **ai** with the other spellings, he is apt to assume a difference of pronunciation which perhaps does not exist.

My objection to the last transcription quoted above is not the result of any dislike of the Vienna dialect. And even if it were, I should still have to admit that for the writer to transliterate his natural pronunciation into that of North Germany would be a violation of phonetic principles.

But the acceptation of the general principle that each is to write his own pronunciation still leaves open the question, How far is he to go in reproducing its niceties?

The main objection from this point of view to such a spelling as **lɪtl̩** compared with **litl** is that the special information it conveys is worthless: everyone knows that the English **i** is wide; and the mark under the **l** would be superfluous even in a minutely scientific notation, for the **l** under the circumstances cannot be anything else than syllabic.

So also there is little gained by marking the nasality in German **ũnt**: we all know that German vowels tend to become nasal before nasal consonants.

Then as regards the diphthongs, we all know that their second elements both in English and German are not pure **i** and **u**, and that their first elements vary almost from mouth to mouth even in the same dialect, and that it is almost impossible to express these minute distinctions adequately, so that it is not only more practical but also less misleading to write **mai haus** in all cases where these spellings are not absolutely unphonetic. Of course, when the first element of **ai** is distinctly rounded, we must then write **moi.**

So also I think it is a mistake in a practical alphabet to try to distinguish the different **r**-sounds, and that it is better to write simply **r** alike in English, French and German. When I find **ʀ** instead of **r** in a French text, it simply irritates me without conveying any information; for I know already that the ordinary French *r* is not a point consonant. So also in German.

In short, when I am trying to get at a writer's meaning I am not at all interested to know where he forms his **r**, or whether or not he nasalizes his vowels before nasal consonants. If he wishes to call my attention to peculiarities of his pronunciation, let him do so in an initial note—'vowels nasalized before nasal consonants, *r* = **R**' etc. Or let him give a few sentences in a minutely accurate notation, and then leave me to weigh his arguments without having my attention distracted by unnecessarily uncouth eccentricities of spelling.

What I suggest therefore is that the Association Phonétique should set up a standard of practical phonetic spelling for each language on the lines indicated, from which such deviations only would be allowed which are necessary to preserve the phonetic principle.

This could not, of course, be carried out with equal certainty in all details: some points would have to be left open; for the phonetic principle itself allows of some latitude.

But even a limited uniformity would be better than the present chaos. And it would certainly tend to make phonetic texts easier to write, print, and read, and to make phonetic spelling less repellent to the general public.

'Normalized phonetic spelling', *Le Maître phonétique*, 1906, pp. 71–3

Simplified Phonetic Spelling. In attempting to popularize phonetic spelling we are apt to forget that the general public will always prefer that system of writing which is most convenient. No amount of propaganda will get over this. Even enthusiasts when writing in a hurry will insensibly slip back into the traditional orthography if the latter is easier to write on the whole.

The traditional orthographies have three points in their favour: (1) they are familiar, (2) they are uniform, and (3) they are comparatively easy to write. The first of these alone gives them such an advantage that we cannot afford to let our phonetic alphabet fall behind them as regards (2) and (3), if we can avoid it.

Our alphabet is also a Roman one. It is based on the existing Roman letters, supplemented by turned, diacritic, and new letters, and by the utilization of existing superfluous letters such as **c**. To each letter we give a more or less definite value—as far as possible its original Latin or else its most general European value—but we allow each language in its practical notation to choose each letter for the nearest sound in that language, using up all the old letters before having recourse to new forms.

Our alphabet in its present state is, as has been repeatedly pointed out, a compromise between a practical and a scientific alphabet, a scientific alphabet being one in which the values of the symbols are fixed, and do not vary from language to language. I propose now to deal only with the former.

From this point of view many of our symbols and distinctions are superfluous. Thus I cannot imagine any language requiring **ʋ**: that is, I don't know any in which **ʋ, v, b, w**, are all required at once, or, in other words, in which **ʋ** cannot be replaced by one of the other three. So also one **r**-symbol is enough—at least in English, French, and German.

Many of our new letters are well suited for a scientific alphabet, where the letters can be written or drawn detached, but are out of place in a practical system, where all the letters must be as easy to write and join as possible. Nothing is more difficult than to invent a good script letter. And the number of available ones is limited. The following are as good as any of the old letters: **ɲ, ŋ, ʃ, ʒ, ð** (in its script form), **ɥ, θ, ɛ**. Many of them, indeed, are really old letters. **ə** and **ɔ** come next. And yet I find that even these cause some difficulty to the majority of my pupils. Nearly all our other new letters I should reject from any practical system of writing, either long or short hand. Such distinctions as **ɪn** and **m** are almost impracticable even in print.

Some of the script forms, too, are difficult to remember because of their want of resemblance to the printed ones. Another thing which people are sure to grumble at is having to write old letters in a not only unfamiliar but inconvenient way; which is the result of such differentiations as **ʋ, v** and **ɑ, a**.

The latter, it is to be observed, is made solely in the interests of French. The result is that no one can use these symbols without thinking phonetically in French, and that there is no practical symbol for the normal Italian and English sound.

The French, as opposed to the international basis, is also seen in the use of the antiquated ˊ as a mark of stress: it is quite inadequate for any other language, and is, besides, required for intonation.

It is, I think, generally admitted that our notation of quantity, stress, and intonation is unsatisfactory. Why not then leave this and other doubtful points open? Doubling of long vowels ought to be optional.

As regards English, I see no need for the unmeaning and unwritable **ʌ** for a vowel—or rather a variety of vowels—which is practically the short of **ɑː**. If we pair **i, ii**, we are bound to pair **ʌ, ɑ**. So also **e, ei** involves **o, ou**. **ɔ** is only required for the long sound in *all*, where the mark of length is superfluous. A further simplification would be to abolish **ɔ** and write **oːl** or **ool**; but I do not advocate this for obvious reasons. It seems clear that **ɵ** should be substituted for the ugly and unwritable **ø** and that **þ** should take its place. The last is written as a looped up *p*: there is no difficulty in keeping the two apart. I also prefer **wh** to the unfamiliar and ambiguous **hw** and the unwritable **ʍ**. I take the opportunity of remarking that all systems of writing, whether practical or scientific, must include digraphs; also that a really practical alphabet ought to give digraph alternatives for all new letters, such as **sh** = **ʃ**, **th** = **θ** (aspirates can be distinguished as **t-h** etc.), to be used in writing to newspapers and for similar purposes.

In French I would substitute **ɵ** for **ø** and **æ** for **a**, thus getting rid of an impossible script form, and utilizing an easily written old letter. The mark of nasality might be made into an upright modifier following the vowel. The familiar **ñ** might be substituted for **ɲ**, which is liable to be confused with **ŋ**.

For the open German **g** in *sagen* it seems most practical to utilize **q**, instead of wasting it on a variety of **k** and leaving the corresponding variety of **g** unprovided for. **c** is the natural symbol of the consonant in *ich*.

Of course I mean all these suggestions merely as examples of the way in which I think we ought to face the problem of popularizing phonetic spelling not among enthusiasts, but among the lazy and prejudiced majority.

'Simplified phonetic spelling', *Le Maître phonétique*, 1906, pp. 125–7

The Principles of Spelling Reform

Introduction. The absolute necessity of phonetic reform is now almost universally recognized, not by only practical teachers but also by scientific philologists. All the objections that prejudice and irrational conservatism have been able to devise have been successfully met, and the only question now is, What system shall we adopt?

The great difficulty of arriving at any agreement is the multiplicity of possible systems. Any system, however clumsy and arbitrary, which clears away only a portion of the irregularities of the existing spelling, is an improvement on it. Any one, for instance, if he likes, can drop the silent *w* in such words as *write*, and make *night* into *nite*, thus getting rid of a large number of irregularities at one stroke. In fact, given a hundred human beings of average intellect who can read and write, it would be perfectly easy to turn out a hundred different systems of spelling, all of them more or less an improvement on the existing one.

This was until lately the state of things—every man did what was right in his own eyes. But in the thirty years that have elapsed since Messrs. Ellis and Pitman first began to work [on ? *Ed.*] a phonetic alphabet, practically everything has been changed, especially within the last ten years. The labours of Messrs. Bell and Ellis have given us a thorough analysis of the sounds of English, the history of English pronunciation has been fully investigated by Mr Ellis, and a variety of spellings have been practically tested.

It is now possible from an examination of these various systems to deduce certain general principles, by which all reform must be guided. If there were no such principles, the problem would be a hopeless one. Nothing can be done without unanimity, and until the majority of the community are convinced of the superiority of some one system, unanimity is impossible.

No one is qualified to give an opinion on spelling reform who has not studied these general principles, and has at least an elementary knowledge of the formation of the sounds of the English language and their relations to one another.

The present remarks are intended to supply the necessary information in as clear and untechnical a form as possible, so as to enable the general reader to form an independent judgment without having to search through an indefinite number of scattered publications.

General Principles

Choice of Letters. The object of an alphabet being to represent to the eye the sounds of a language by means of written symbols, it follows that in a rational alphabet—

(1) Every simple sound must have a distinct symbol, and

(2) There must be a definite relation between each sound and its symbol.

These principles are carried out in Mr Bell's 'Visible Speech'. In this alphabet each letter symbolizes the action of the vocal organs by which it is formed, according to certain fixed principles. Thus, all consonants are symbolized by a curve, like a c, which is turned in different directions to indicate the place in the mouth where each consonant is formed. ʊ, for instance, indicates any consonant formed by the point of the tongue, such as **t**, **d**, or **l**; ɔ, one formed by the lips, such as **p**, **b**, or **m**. The different varieties of 'point-', 'lip-' etc. consonants are indicated by modifiers added to these fundamental symbols. A short straight line inside the curve converts voiceless (surd) consonants, such as **t**, **p**, **s**, into the corresponding voiced (sonant) consonants **d**, **b**, **z**, etc. A bar across the opening of the curve denotes a 'shut' consonant or mute. So that any one who knows the symbols for **t** and **d** is at once able to recognize the symbol of **b** if he knows that of **p**.

Such an alphabet is, to a great extent, *self-interpreting*. When the meanings of a few radical signs have been learnt, hundreds of letters are understood at once, without further explanation. It is also a *universal alphabet*, providing symbols not only for all existing, but also for all possible sounds.

The Roman alphabet, with which English and most other European languages are written, evidently falls far short of this standard. In the first place, its letters are formed quite arbitrarily, and bear no definite relation to the sounds they indicate. No one would infer, for instance, from the shape of the letters that **d** was nearly related to **t**, and that there was the same relation between **b** and **p**. Again, the Roman alphabet supplies an utterly inadequate number of symbols for the sounds of most languages. Although the original alphabet has been supplemented in modern times by the addition of such letters as *j*, *v*, and *w*, it is still very defective, and consequently distinct sounds are often confounded under one letter in many languages. The difficulty of learning the values of the different letters is also much increased by the use of capitals and italics, many of which, especially the capitals, have entirely distinct forms. Compare A, a, *a*, G, g, etc. Besides being inadequate for the representation of the sounds of each individual language, the Roman alphabet has also lost to a great extent its universal and international character, the same letters being employed to signify totally distinct sounds in different languages. Compare *ch* in the English *church* with the French *chat*, the German *ach*, etc. Even in a single language one letter or letter-group often indicates a variety of distinct sounds. This is carried to such a pitch in English that our alphabet really consists not of twenty-five letters (not including the divergent shapes of the capitals) but of more than two hundred letters and letter-groups, all of which have to be learnt separately.

With a rational alphabet like Visible Speech all this confusion is impossible; for the connection between each sound and its symbol is so intimate that the one can never be separated from the other, as in the Roman alphabet, where the association of sound and symbol is arbitrary and purely traditional. If Visible Speech were as perfect in its practical details as in its general theory the only adequate solution of the question of spelling reform would evidently be to adopt it instead of the Roman alphabet. Unfortunately, however, Visible Speech is dependent on our knowledge of the formation of sounds, and until our knowledge is perfect, which it is as yet far from being, we have no guarantee that further discoveries may not oblige us to modify the details of our symbolization. Until then Visible Speech must continue to be a purely scientific alphabet, which cannot be brought into general use till it is firmly based on a perfect and complete system of phonetic analysis, and has been tested thoroughly in practice.

The Roman alphabet, on the other hand, is quite independent of the scientific analysis of sounds. It has also been thoroughly tested in practice. Long experience and many experiments have selected the most legible and distinct types, and a script alphabet of the most practical character has been formed. In fact the difficulty of our present English spelling lies not so much in any of the inherent defects of the Roman alphabet as in our irrational use of it.

The immediate practical question of Spelling Reform resolves itself therefore into this—By what arrangement of the existing alphabet can the sounds of the English language be best represented?

The imperfections of the Roman alphabet may be remedied in various ways, but the fundamental consideration is whether to confine ourselves to the existing letters or to form new ones. The objections to the second alternative are evident. New types are costly; they disturb and complicate the existing founts; and there is often a difficulty in providing suitable script forms. If, on the other hand, we keep to the old types, we form our orthography without expense or disturbance of the existing machinery of the printing-offices, and what is of extreme importance, we are provided with a script alphabet of a thoroughly practical character. The practical experience of Mr Ellis is important on this point. After expending much time and money in elaborating a new-type alphabet—the 'phonotypy' of Mr Pitman—he has entirely abandoned the new-type principle as impracticable. He excludes even letters with accents and diacritics, which, being only cast for a few founts, act practically as new letters.

If then we exclude new letters as impracticable, we are obliged to fall back on digraphs, which are already largely employed by English and most other languages. The obvious objection to them is that they violate the natural principle of denoting every simple sound by a simple sign. In a rational alphabet such as Visible Speech, this principle is carried out consistently, the consonants of *she* and *the*, for instance, being denoted by single letters just as that of *see* is. But with the Roman alphabet, which does not claim to be rational and consistent, this principle cannot be carried out: our business is to make the best use of the materials we have, and if we can make a convenient and unambiguous symbol for a simple sound by joining two letters together, we are clearly right in doing so. In fact we may consider the *h* in *sh* and *th* simply as a diacritic written for convenience on a line with the letter it modifies. It would be possible to write and print the *h* above the *s* and *t*, or to make some kind of tag, but the expense of casting new types and the trouble of writing the new letters would not be repaid by any gain of ease or certainty in reading.

There is, however, one simple method of forming new letters without casting new types, which is often very convenient. This is by *turning* the letters, thus—ə, ɔ. These new letters are perfectly distinct in shape, and are easily written. The ə was first employed by Schmeller to denote the obscure *e*-sound in the German *gabe*, etc. Mr Ellis, in his 'Palæotype', uses it to denote the allied English sound in *but*.

A great improvement would be to do away with capitals entirely. They greatly add to the difficulty of learning the alphabet, have a disfiguring and incongruous effect among the lower-case letters, and serve no useful purpose whatever. Proper names are always recognized in speech by the context, and do not require to be marked in writing either, whose exclusive function is to give a faithful representation of the sounds of language. Whenever general distinctions are required, they can be indicated by the use of a larger or smaller fount, or by thick (Clarendon) or thin type.

We thus arrive at the general conclusion that a reformed alphabet must consist of the existing lower-case types, supplemented by digraphs, and, if necessary, by turned letters.

Employment of Letters. This problem may also be stated thus—what values must be assigned to the letters that they may be most easily learnt, read, and written? The obvious requisites are unambiguity and consistency, and that system which combines them in the highest degree (as far as the radical defects of the Roman alphabet will allow), while observing the practical considerations stated in the previous section, is the best.

It is clear that the defects of our present orthography are mainly due to the disregard of these fundamental principles.

Ambiguity is shown in the use of one symbol for several distinct sounds, as in *man*, *lane*, *ask*, *salt* or of different symbols for one sound, as in *why*, *wine*, *eye*, *lie*. This fault is a violation of the fundamental principle of all rational spelling, viz. that of representing every sound by an invariable symbol (which may, however, be either a single letter or a digraph).

An alphabet is inconsistent when it fails to construct and apply its symbols on definite and uniform principles. It is, for instance, self-evident that a rational alphabet will indicate diphthongs by the juxtaposition of their elements, as in the *oi* of *oil*, which is really composed of *o* and *i*. But in English this simple principle is not carried out with the other diphthongs. In *out*, for instance, there is not a trace of an *o*, nor does its second element in the slightest degree resemble the *u* of *but*. Again, *au*, which would be the proper symbol of the *ou* of *out*, does not denote a diphthong at all.

The practical effect of inconsistency is not only greatly to increase the number of arbitrary symbols, but also to make their acquisition more difficult, because of the conflicting associations of ideas thus engendered.

Before going any further it will be worth while to stop and consider what are the causes of the ambiguity, inconsistency, and complexity of the present English spelling. When we have a definite idea of the cause, we shall be better able to devise a cure.

Up to the sixteenth century English spelling was mainly phonetic, like the present German. At that time the words *man*, *lane*, *care*, *father*, *water*, were all written with the same vowel because their vowels all had the same pronunciation, viz. that of the Italian *a* in *father*. Similarly *wine* was written with an *i* because its vowel really was the long sound of the *i* in *win*, *wine* being pronounced as *ween* is now, which last again, had a pronunciation agreeing with its spelling. However, as literature developed, and the printing-press began to assert its authority, the spelling became more and more fixed, till at last it became entirely stationary, while the pronunciation went on changing without intermission, so that the *ee* of *ween* came to be the long sound of the *i* in *win*, while *wine* itself changed its long vowel into a diphthong, as in the present English. The *a* in *man*, etc. changed also in various ways without any corresponding change being made in the spelling. In short we may say that our present spelling does not represent the English we actually speak, but rather the language of the sixteenth century. In other words, the present confusion in our spelling is due to the abandonment of the original Roman values of the letters, chiefly in the long vowels.

The only way of curing these evils is evidently to return to the original Roman values of the letters. If the beginner has once learnt to pronounce *a*, *e*, *i*, *o*, *u*, as in *glass*, *bet*, *bit*, *not*, *full*, he simply has to remember that long vowels are doubled, as in **biit** = 'beat', and **fuul** = 'fool', and diphthongs formed by the juxtaposition of their elements, as in **boi** = 'boy' and **hai** = 'high', to be able to read at once the majority of the vowel symbols. Of the consonants, whose original values have been mostly preserved, little need be said at present.

Of course, the Roman alphabet requires to be supplemented, and this is a problem that requires much thought, in order to attain the maximum of consistency and simplicity, so that the new symbols may, if possible, suggest any relationship they may bear to other known ones. Thus **æ** as the symbol of the *a* in *man* at once suggests a sound intermediate between the true **a** in *father* and the **e** in *bet*, which the *a* in *man* really is. Further details must be reserved till we come to the analysis of the sounds of English, for, until we know what the elementary sounds really are, it is impossible to symbolize them intelligently.

Transition from and to the present Spelling. We have hitherto considered the question of spelling reform solely from the point of view of those who learn to read for the first time. But we have also to consider the question of the transition from and to the present orthography. The two points of view may be contrasted thus:

(1) Which system of spelling will be easiest learnt by a child learning to read for the first time?

(2) Which will come easiest to an adult who has already learnt on the received system?

The first of these two alternatives is, as we have seen, fully met by the simple principle of returning to the original Roman values of the letters. The second, on the other hand, requires that our new spelling should be based not on the original values of the letters but on some one of their present values. We may, then, distinguish two main classes of reformed spellings, (1) the Roman-value system, and (2) the English-value system. The only consistent and practical alphabet on the English-value system that has yet been produced is the 'Glossic' of Mr Ellis.

Glossic is based on the principle of retaining the traditional means of expressing the sounds of English, but selecting one among the many symbols of each sound, and using it invariably to express that sound, rejecting, of course all silent letters. Thus *ee* is taken as the sole representation of the sound of long **i**, being written not only in *feel*, but also in *reed*, *skeem*, = 'read' and 'scheme', *peek* = 'pique', etc. *ai* is written not only in *fail* but also in *naim* = 'name', *rain* = 'reign', etc.

It cannot be denied that from its own point of view this system has considerable advantages. It would certainly cause the adults of the present generation less trouble than any Roman-value spelling, for any one who has learnt to read on the present system can read Glossic at sight. Mr Ellis also thinks that those who had learnt Glossic would easily acquire the ordinary or 'Nomic' spelling, as he calls it. Before attempting to settle the relative merits of the Roman- and English-value systems, as regards ease of transition to and from the 'Nomic' spelling, it will be well to weigh the following considerations:

(1) In both systems a large number of words will retain their spellings entirely or almost unchanged. The following words, for instance, remain unchanged in both: *best, bend, desk, fed, let, men*; *if, hit, fish, wish, in, gift*; *on, hot, got, dog, pot*; *oil, boil, loin*, and many others.

(2) Many, indeed most of the remaining words, will undergo great alterations under both systems. Let us consider, for instance, that most of our written words are practically hieroglyphs, which we recognise individually by their consonant skeletons without thinking of the sounds they represent. Thus, if we substitute a (-) for the vowels in such words as *kn-ght*, *wr-ck*, *-n-gh*, we still recognise them without any difficulty, which would not be materially increased even by the introduction of different vowels. Now, on any system whatever of phonetic spelling, these words, which all contain silent consonants, entirely alter the shape of their skeletons, so that whether we write *nite*, *neit*, or *nait*, *rec* or *rek*, *inuf*, or *enəf*, the results are equally disguised to the eye, and can only be made out by an effort. Any possible superiority of one alphabet over another is thus very considerably reduced. To this may be added that, although in most cases where any superiority in point of resemblance to Nomic can be claimed by one system over the other, the advantage is naturally on the side of Glossic, yet the Roman-value system often has the advantage on its side. Thus *u* in 'full', 'pull', 'put', etc., and the *i* in 'pique', 'machine', 'marine', etc., are preserved unchanged in the Roman-value system while in Glossic *u* being used to represent the vowel in 'but' cannot be retained in 'full', and the *i* of 'pique', etc. must of course be written *ee*.

(3) Again, the very resemblance of Glossic to Nomic often causes very puzzling confusions. Thus 'latter', 'ridding', 'supper', become *later*, *riding*, *super*, while the Nomic 'later', 'riding', 'super(fine)', are represented by *laiter*, *reiding*, *seuperfein*. The Roman-value system, being more remote from Nomic, is much less liable to such cross-association. In fact, the relation of Glossic to Nomic is very like that of two closely allied languages, such as Danish and Swedish, or Spanish and Portuguese. Although Danes and Swedes soon learn to understand one another's languages they hardly ever, even after years of study, succeed in speaking each other's languages with real accuracy, the very nearness of the two languages, with their constant deviations from one another in matters of detail, causing constant confusion and cross-association.

The Representation of Sounds

Vowels. Vowels are formed by retraction of the *back* of the tongue, as in 'f*a*ther'; by advancing the *front* of the tongue, as in 'b*i*t'; or else they are *mixed*, as in 'b*ir*d', in which the tongue is in a position half-way between back and front. By height they are *high*, as in 'h*i*t', *mid*, as in 'h*a*te', or *low*, as in 'h*a*t'. The vowels of these three words are all front, but the distinctions of height apply to back and mixed vowels as well.

Thus the *u* of 'full' is high-back, just as that of 'hit' is high-front. All these vowels may be further modified by labialization, or *rounding*. Thus, if the *ee* of 'feel' is pronounced with narrowed lip-opening, we obtain the French *u* in 'lune'—the high-front-round. There are besides other modifications caused by the shape of the tongue itself.

Of the large number of possible vowels only a small proportion is employed in each language.

Again, among the special vowels of any one language we must distinguish between those differences which are *distinctive*, that is, to which differences of meaning correspond, and those which are not. Thus the first elements of the diphthongs in 'by' and 'out' vary considerably: some people sound them broad as in 'father', some thin, as in 'man', with various intermediate sounds. And yet the meaning of the words remains unchanged. The distinction between the vowels of 'men' and 'man' on the other hand, though really slighter than that of the different pronunciations of 'by' and 'out', is a distinctive one.

If often happens that two sounds, though formed in different ways, have nearly the same effect on the ear. Thus the English vowel in '*tur*n' is formed in a totally different way from the French one in 'p*eu*r', the former being an unrounded, the latter a rounded vowel, and yet they are hardly distinguishable by an untrained ear. The consequence is that two such vowels are never employed together in the same language to distinguish the meanings of words, and for practical purposes they may be considered as variations of the same vowel. Hence we have to distinguish not so much between *sounds* as between *groups of sounds*. One of the most important distinctions of these groups is that of 'close' and 'open', the open vowels being generally formed by a 'low' position of the tongue or by some other widening of the mouth passage.

Disregarding special exceptions in individual languages, we may assume the following as the chief distinctive groups in language generally:

A. *Unrounded*

(1) the dull-back, b*u*t.
(2) the clear-back, f*a*ther.
(3) the mixed,* t*ur*n, fath*er*, gab*e* (German).
(4) the high-front, b*i*t, b*ea*t.
(5) the close-front, *été* (French).
(6) the open-front, m*e*n, m*a*re, m*a*n.

*The vowel in 'turn' is open-mixed, that in 'gabe' close-mixed.

B. *Rounded*

(7) high-back,	f*u*ll, f*oo*l.
(8) close-back,	s*o* (German).
(9) open-back,	f*o*lly, f*a*ll.
(10) high-front,	l*u*ne (French).
(11) close-front,	p*eu* (French).
(12) open-front,	p*eu*r (French).

Of these groups the mixed (3) is, as remarked above, almost identical in sound with the close and open front (11, 12), with which latter the dull-back (1) is often identified, although in sound it is really intermediate between them and the clear-back (2). In practice, therefore, the symbols for 11 and 12 will also suffice for 1 and 3.

a, ***i***, and ***u*** at once supply symbols for 2, 4, and 7 respectively. For 10 we have only to restore ***y*** to its original Roman value, which it still retains in Danish and Swedish. If we assign ***e*** to the close-front (5) and ***o*** to the close-back-round (8), in accordance with the general European tradition, we must find letters for the corresponding open vowels. For the open-front (6) ***æ*** at once suggests itself, the *a* indicating openness. For the open *o* (9) there is no type ready to hand; I propose therefore to adopt the turned ***ɔ*** used by Mr Ellis in his Palæotype. This letter, which is really a turned *c*, is meant to suggest a turned *o*, which is impracticable. For the rounded ***e*** (11) the turned ***ə*** may be used, and for the open sound (12) ***œ***. We thus obtain the perfectly parallel forms ***i***, ***e***, ***æ***, and ***y***, ***ə***, ***œ***. The last two at the same time supply symbols for the special English *u* in 'but' (1) and 'turn' (3).

Diphthongs are, of course, symbolized by the juxtaposition of their elements. The following are the English diphthongs:

ai	as in	*ai*sle
au	,,	n*ow*
oi	,,	b*oi*l
ei	,,	v*ei*l
ou	,,	s*ou*l

Diphthongs in all languages vary greatly in their constituents, and the above combinations must be understood as simply denoting general tendencies. Thus ***ai*** does not literally imply a combination of the ***a*** in 'father' and the ***i*** in 'bit', but merely a movement in that direction. We may start, not with a full-back vowel, but with a mixed one, which may move towards ***i***, but without reaching it: in fact the commonest pronunciation of 'aisle' may be represented by ***əel***. In the same way ***ei*** only implies a front vowel moving upwards, and, as a matter of fact, the starting-point may be either close or open *e* or even the *a* of 'man'. Indeed ***ei*** often begins with a mixed vowel, in which case 'veil' is confounded with 'vile'.

Note that ***ei*** and ***ou*** in English supply the place of close long ***ee*** and ***oo***, which most English people are unable to pronounce.

ii and ***uu*** are often diphthongized in a peculiar way in English, by being made to end in the consonants ***y*** and ***w*** respectively, **wiin** 'ween' and **fuul** 'fool' becoming ***wiyn*** and ***fuwl***.

Having thus laid a general foundation, we may proceed to discuss some special modifications required in English.

As there is no short close *e* or *o* in English, it is superfluous to use *æ* and *ɔ* to denote the quality of sounds whose openness is always implied by their shortness. We can, therefore, discard *ɔ* altogether in English, and employ *æ* to denote the peculiar *a* in 'man', for which it would otherwise be difficult to find an appropriate letter.

The longs of *æ* and *ɔ* may be expressed, as with the other vowels, by doubling—***ææ***, ***ɔɔ***. But as this is inconvenient, and as *ɔ* is not used in English, it is better to denote the long of ***æ*** by ***ae***, the separation of the letters implying length. Long *ɔ* may, on this analogy, be denoted by ***ao***.

R and its modifications. The consonant *r* in English only occurs before a vowel, either in the same or the next word, as in 'erring' **eriq**, 'far off' **faar aof**. When not followed by a vowel, that is, either by a pause or a consonant, it is weakened into *ə*—the *er* of 'father'. After ***aa*** and ***əə*** the *ə* is absorbed, as in 'bar' **baa**, 'farther' **faadhə**, 'her' **hoe**, 'heard' **hoed**, the first two being indistinguishable from 'baa' and 'father'. *ə* is sometimes dropped after ***ao***, especially before a consonant, as in 'floor', 'floored', although the full **flaoə**, **flaoəd** are most usual in careful speech, especially when the *ə* is final. After other vowels *ə* is preserved throughout, also when the ***r*** is sounded as a full consonant: compare 'air' **aeə**, 'aired' **aeəd**, and 'airy' **aeəri** with 'far off' **faar aof**, 'her own' **hoer oun**, and 'flooring' **flaoriq**.

The following table will give a general idea of these changes:

faar aof	'far off'	**faa**	**faadhə**	'farther'
hoer oun	'her own'	**hoe**	**hoed**	'heard'
fiiəriq	'fearing'	**fiiə**	**fiiəd**	'feared'
aeəriq	'airing'	**aeə**	**aeəd**	'aired'
muuəriq	'mooring'	**muuə**	**muuəd**	'moored'
flaoriq	'flooring'	**flaoə**	**flaoəd**	'floored'
faiəriq	'firing'	**faiə**	**faiəd**	'fired'
flauəri	'flowery, floury'	**flauə**	**flauəd**	'flowered'

leiəriq	'layering'	**leiə**	**leiəd**	'layered'
louəriq	'lowering'	**louə**	**louəd**	'lowered'.

Note that ***eiə(r)*** and ***ouə(r)*** in rapid, especially in vulgar speech, often pass into ***aeə(r)*** and ***aoə(r)***.

When *r* is preceded by a short vowel, as in 'hurry' **həri**, 'merry' **meri**, no *ə* is generated.

Unaccented Vowels. The two chief unaccented vowels in English are *ə* and ***i*** together with the rare ***o***. The former may be regarded as a shortened ***oe*** as in 'her', into which it always passes when emphasized or prolonged, but it is really nothing but a voice murmur without any definite configuration. The ***i*** is an intermediate vowel between ***i*** and ***e***, and might as well be written ***e*** as ***i***. It may be regarded either as a very open ***i*** or a very close ***e***. The following are examples of *ə*:

ətemt 'attempt', **əpouz** 'oppose', **əpon** 'upon', **tədei** 'to-day'.
soufə 'sofa', **menshən** 'mention', **peishəns** 'patience', **kærət** 'carrot'.
faadhə 'father', **onə** 'honour', **mezhə** 'measure'.
faowəd 'forward', **shepəd** 'shepherd'.
feivərit 'favourite', **mezhəriq** 'measuring'.

ə is often dropped before ***l***, ***n***, and ***m***; always when the *ə* is preceded by ***t*** or ***d*** and followed by ***l*** or ***n***:

metl 'metal', **ĝaadn** 'garden', **ĝaadniq** 'gardening', **mətn** 'mutton'.
iivl 'evil', **loukl** 'local', **simbl** 'cymbal, symbol'.

When two or more unaccented *ə*'s or ***i***'s follow one another, one of them is often thrown out, as in—

hist(ə)ri 'history', **feiv(ə)rit** 'favourite', **vedzh**$\left\{\begin{matrix}\text{ə}\\ \text{i}\end{matrix}\right\}$**təbl** 'vegetable'.

i is less common than *ə*. It is most usual as a weakening of front vowels, especially when *i* or *y* is written:

piti 'pity', **məndi** 'Monday'.
divaid 'divide', **ditekt** 'detect'.
ræbit 'rabbit', **fishiz** 'fishes', **əbiliti** 'ability'.

It is the regular unaccented vowel before ***dzh***, even when ***a*** is written:

vilidzh 'village', **kæridzh** 'carriage', **kolidzh** 'college'.

In rapid speech ***i*** is apt to pass into *ə*, except when final.

Unaccented ***o*** in ordinary speech is simply *ə* rounded. When dwelt on it becomes ***ou***. Examples are:

pəteito 'potato', **folo** 'follow', **felo** 'fellow'.

In rapid speech this *o* passes into *ə*.

These vowels occur also in unaccented monosyllables. Compare 'a man' **ə mæn** with 'against' **əgenst**, 'to go' **tə gou** with 'to-day' **tədei**, 'for all' **fər aol** with 'forgive' **fəgiv**, 'of course' **əv kaoəs** with 'offence' **əfens.**

the and *to* have two distinct unaccented forms. Before consonants they both have *ə*, while before vowels they assume the fuller forms ***dhi*** and ***tu***:

> **dhə mæn** 'the man', **dhi enəmi** 'the enemy'.
> **tə gou** 'to go', **tu entə** 'to enter'.

It was, I believe, first noticed by Mr Ellis that 'that' as a demonstrative is always full ***dhæt***, while as a conjunction and relative pronoun it becomes ***dhət***: **ai nou dhət dhæt dhət dhæt mæn sez iz truu** 'I know that that that that man says is true'.

Consonants. As regards the use of the letters there can be no question about the value of the following: b, d, f, g, h, k, l, m, n, p, r, s, t, v, w, z.

This leaves *c*, *j*, *q*, *x* undisposed of. We also have ***y***, which is not required as a vowel-symbol in English. If we allow ***y*** to retain its present value, we can also retain ***j*** as a convenient abbreviation of ***dzh.*** For ***tsh*** we have ***ch***, which, by the omission of the superfluous ***h***, can be reduced to simple ***c***. We thus have ***c*** and ***j*** perfectly parallel. ***q*** may very well be taken to represent the back nasal *ng*, as Mr Ellis has done in his Palæotype. ***x*** lastly, if employed at all, must in consistency be extended to all ***ks***'s in the language, not only in such words as ***six***, but also in ***rex*** 'wrecks', ***cex*** 'cheques', etc.

These contractions fully counterbalance the necessity of retaining the digraphs ***th*** and ***sh***, to which must of course be added ***dh*** and ***zh.*** ***wh*** is very generally made into ***w*** in Southern English, but it is well to keep up the distinction on the chance of its being afterwards revived. The breath ***yh*** (= German 'i*ch*') sometimes occurs in such words as 'hue' **yhuu**, more commonly, however, pronounced ***hyuu***, with a separate ***h*** before the ***y***.

Consonants are often dropped in English. Thus the ***h*** of the personal pronouns is generally dropped when they come after a verb, and are unaccented, as in ***ai sao im*** 'I saw him'. *Saw her* and *soar* are both pronounced ***saoə***. The ***d*** of *and* is generally dropped before a consonant, as in ***kət n kəm əgen*** 'cut and come again', where the vowel is dropped also on account of the ***t*** and ***n***.

Assimilations also occur in rapid speech. Thus, many people who pronounce the ***q*** of 'going', etc. quite distinctly in most cases, regularly change the back into the point nasal **n**, when it is followed by a point consonant **t**, **d**, **n**, as in ***gouin tə*** . . . 'going to . . .'. In *I can't go* the ***t*** is generally dropped, and the point nasal is often assimilated to the ***g*** by being made into the back nasal ***q***—***ai kaaq gou.***

Accent and Quantity. The chief accent or stress in each word may be marked by (·) following the letter on which the accent begins: ***əg·enst*** 'against', ***fəg·iv*** 'forgive'. To indicate the secondary accent, when necessary, : may be used: ***i:nkənv·iinyəns*** 'inconvenience', ***dist:rəktəb·iliti*** 'destructibility'. These very convenient marks were introduced by Mr Ellis. In practice the accent need only be marked when it is on some other than the first syllable. Thus it need not be marked in ***foutogræf*** 'photograph'.

Unaccented vowels are always shortened. Thus ***hii*** in ***hii gouz*** 'he goes' is much shorter than in ***it iz hii*** 'it is he', but its vowel is quite distinct from the regular short ***i*** in 'hit'. As this shortening is always implied by the want of accent, it need not be marked: ***hi gouz*** would imply that the ***i*** was pronounced as in 'hit'.

Emphasis, or the accent of a word in a sentence as distinguished from that of a syllable in a word, is marked by a · before the word. Such subordinate monosyllable as 'he', 'she', 'it', 'and', 'if', 'to', 'for', etc., are assumed to be unaccented unless thus marked. We thus distinguish between ***hii gouz*** and ***it iz·hii***, between ***hii hæz mai buk*** 'he has my book' and ***it iz ·mai buk not ·hiz*** 'it is *my* book, not *his*'. Principal words, such as nouns, non-auxiliary verbs and adjectives, which regularly receive a full accent, may be marked in the same way whenever they are made exceptionally emphatic, thus ***ai ·fəg·iv yu*** indicates that the second syllable of ***fəg·iv*** is uttered with extra emphasis.

List of English Symbols. The following table gives a complete list of the English vowel symbols in the 'Romic' system I propose, together with those consonant ones which require elucidation, with examples.

A. *Vowels*

aa:	pap*a*, f*a*r, gl*a*ss, *a*fter, *au*nt. [Before ***s*** and ***f*** or before two (pronounced) consonants ***aa*** is sometimes shortened, and sometimes becomes ***æ***: ***glæs***, ***ænt.***]
æ:	m*a*n.
ae:	*ae*rate, b*ea*r, f*a*re. [Always followed by ə.]
ai:	Is*ai*ah, *ai*sle, w*i*ne.
ao:	extr*ao*rdinary, br*oa*d, m*o*re.
au:	F*au*st, n*ow*, n*ou*n.

e: red.
ei: they, veil, name.
i: ill, fishes.
ii, iy: machine, feel.
o: not, cloth, cross, soft. [Often becomes ***ao*** before ***th***, ***s***, and ***f***: ***klaoth***, ***kraos***, ***saoft***.]
oi: boy, boil.
ou: flow, soul, stone.
u: full, put, good.
uu, ***uw***: truth, rue, fool.
ə: up, come; father, here.
oe: her, turn, heard.

B. *Consonants*

c: church, catch.
dh: then, with.
j: judge, gentle.
q: sing, finger.
sh: fish.
th: think.
x: six, wrecks.
y: young.
zh: rouge, pleasure.

New Types. Although new types should be avoided at first, their exclusion is only a practical consideration, not a matter of principle, and there is no reason why they should not afterwards be introduced by degrees. Thus Mr Pitman's ŋ is unquestionably superior to ***q*** as a symbol of the back nasal *ng*, for its shape at once associates it with the other nasals ***n***, ***m***. Again the Greek θ and δ (or perhaps better the Anglo-Saxon ð) would do very well for ***th*** and ***dh***, both being easily written. The long *s* and tailed *z* of Pitman's Phonotypy are also excellent letters for ***sh*** and ***zh***. We should thus avoid the ambiguity of such words as ***pothuk*** 'pothook', which at present can only be avoided by writing ***pot-huk***.

Special Considerations

Varieties of Pronunciation. It is clear that as soon as spelling ceases to adapt itself to existing varieties of pronunciation—whether 'colloquialisms', 'vulgarisms', or 'provincialisms'—it ceases to be phonetic.

Spelling apart from the sounds it represents has, properly speaking, no meaning, no existence whatever. A picture of a man at once suggests the idea 'man' to any one, and the sounds represented by the letter-group *man* suggest the same idea to all English-speaking people, but the letters *m*, *a*, *n* only suggest sounds, not ideas. After a time, of course, we learn to associate ideas with letter-groups without thinking of the sounds, but this is necessarily a secondary process, although it may be carried so far that the connection between the letters and their sounds becomes to a great extent forgotten—till, in short, the spelling becomes *unphonetic*, as in the present English. The only way to cure these evils—which is the object of all spelling reform—is to restore spelling to its only legitimate function, that of symbolizing sounds.

It follows necessarily that if two people have different pronunciations, their spellings must also be different. If A, who pronounces ***glæs*** 'glass', ***gæl*** 'girl', ***iidhə*** 'either', is to be compelled to write ***glaas***, ***goel***, ***aidhə*** because B pronounces so, phonetic spelling becomes a mere mockery, and is really no more phonetic than the present system, which writes *knight* and *wright* because people pronounced so three hundred years ago, although half of the letters are absolutely unmeaning now.

As a matter of fact, these differences, which hardly ever cause the slightest difficulty even in the most rapid speech, and, indeed, generally pass quite unheeded, cannot possibly cause any difficulty to the reader, who has time to consider deliberately the meaning of any passage, if necessary. When divergences of pronunciation increase to such a degree as to make a faithful phonetic representation of them unintelligible, or nearly so, to those acquainted only with the standard form of speech, it is certain that the spoken pronunciation itself will prove still more difficult.

In fact, one of the worst features of a fixed orthography is that it loses all control of pronunciation, and thus indirectly proves the cause of such changes as have completely changed the character of English in the last few centuries. If those careless speakers of the seventeenth century who used to drop the initial consonants in such words as *write* and *know* had been obliged to omit them in writing as well as in speech, it is probable that the change would have been nipped in the bud, and people would have seen that uniformity of spelling is a delusion, unless based on a corresponding uniformity of pronunciation.

The history of ***h*** and ***r*** in modern times is an instructive instance of how pronunciation may be controlled by a changing spelling. It is certain that if English had been left to itself the sound ***h*** would have been as completely lost in the standard language as it has been in most of the dialects. But the distinction between *house* and *'ouse*, although in itself a comparatively slight one, being easily marked in writing, such spellings as *'ouse* came to be used in novels, etc. as an easy way of suggesting a vulgar speaker. The result was to produce a purely artificial reaction against the natural tendency to drop the ***h***, its retention being now considered an almost infallible test of education and refinement. The weakening of ***r*** into a vowel, and its absorption into the vowel that precedes it, although really quite as injurious to the force and intelligibility of the language as the dropping of ***h***, not being easily marked in writing, passes unheeded, and, indeed, few people realize the fact that they make no difference whatever between such words as *father* and *farther*. Indeed, if such a reformed spelling as Glossic is adopted, in which these trivial distinctions are still kept up, there is no reason why in the next half century ***r*** may not utterly disappear everywhere except initially; *hear*, for instance, becoming identical in sound with *he*.

If the high literary cultivation of the seventeenth and eighteenth centuries, and the consequent fixity of the orthography, not only failed to prevent, but positively encouraged the most sweeping changes in pronunciation, it is certain that the same effects will produce the same causes in the future. No one who has paid any attention to the tendencies of English pronunciation will deny that the following hypothetical changes of pronunciation in the next fifty or sixty years are all possible and some of them extremely probable (the pronunciations are given in the received spelling):

been	*becomes*	bane
bane	,,	bine
bine	,,	barn
boon	,,	been (*through* bün).

Indeed, many of these changes are already in progress. I have myself heard *take time* pronounced in a way which made it sound not very unlike *tike tarm*, and this from speakers who, although not very refined, certainly belonged to the upper middle class.

The result of these and similar changes will be that in another century any fixed scheme of reform adopted now will be nearly as unphonetic as our present Nomic spelling. It must also be remembered that by that time England, America, and Australia will be speaking mutually unintelligible languages, owing to their independent changes of pronunciation.

The only way to meet these evils is strictly to subordinate spelling to pronunciation. One very important result of this will be that instead of teaching spelling we shall have to teach pronunciation. Our maxim will be, 'Take care of the pronunciation, and the spelling will take care of itself.' If it is wrong to confound *father* and *farther* in spelling, it must be still more wrong to confound them in pronunciation. Then the question of restoring the consonantal pronunciation of *r* throughout will perhaps arise—certainly that of arresting further change will. School-inspectors will examine not in spelling but in pronunciation, elocution, and intelligent reading—subjects which are now absolutely ignored as branches of general education. When a firm control of pronunciation has thus been acquired, provincialisms and vulgarisms will at last be entirely eliminated, and one of the most important barriers between the different classes of society will thus be abolished.

It must, however, be remembered that these results are not to be attained by the adoption of any system indifferently that may be proposed. What is wanted is a simple, consistent, and above all *elastic* spelling, which, within certain practical limits, will adapt itself to every change of pronunciation. Changes of pronunciation cannot be controlled by any spelling based on the Nomic values of the letters. There is, for instance, no reason why *oo* should represent the sound of long **u** any more than that of long **i**, nor consequently why the **uu** of 'boon' should not change through **byyn** (with the French *u*) into **biin** without any change of spelling being thought necessary, and consequently without any control of such possible changes being exercised.

International Intelligibility. One very important result of a return to the Roman values of the letters would be the restoration of the original harmony of the English with the Continental values of the letters, which would much facilitate the acquisition of English by foreigners, and vice versa. At present, English people and foreigners have to learn each other's languages almost entirely by eye, unless thoroughly taught by a native, and consequently are utterly at a loss when brought face to face with the spoken language—in fact, they have to learn the same language twice over. Thus when a German sees the English written word *right* he easily associates it with his own *recht*, as also the English *name* with the German *name*, but when he hears the genuine **rait** and **neim**, he is thrown completely off the scent. Conversely, when an Englishman comes across the German *knie* for the first time, he at once thinks of his own *knee*, and naturally drops the **k** in the German word as well as in the English: if he were used to see the English word spelt ***nii*** he would never think of dropping the **k** in German.

It will, of course, be urged by the advocates of historical spelling that the silent letters in *right* and *knee* are really valuable helps in acquiring the language. All this really amounts to is, that sixteenth-century English bears a much closer resemblance to German than nineteenth-century English does, consequently that a German will learn the former more easily than the latter, and that an Englishman who knows sixteenth-century English will thereby learn German more easily. The practical result is, of course, that English has to be learnt twice over both by the English themselves and by foreigners. The worst of it is, that instead of learning the older stage of our language on an intelligent and systematic plan, we have it forced on us—whether we really want it or not—in the shape of a garbled and imperfect orthography, which, instead of giving us clear ideas of the language of the period it represents, only serves to hopelessly confuse our notions of our present language.

Of course the orthographies of most of the Continental languages require reform as well as English; French, especially, most urgently demands a thorough change. Indeed, there is no reason why foreigners should not learn French on a phonetic system, leaving the present French spelling to be acquired afterwards, even if the French themselves do not inaugurate a reform.

There are many significant facts in the pronunciation and spelling of English which show that the return to the Roman values of the vowels would not be by any means so violent a change as is generally supposed. Even without going beyond the commonest words in our vocabulary we have whole classes of words like *machine*, *marine*, *oblique*, *antique*, etc., in which long ***i*** retains its Roman value. In geographical names, such as *Alabama*, *Chicago*, *Granada*, *Medina*, *Messina*, the accented vowels all have the Roman values. In such names as *Isaiah*, *Achaia*, *Cairo*, the diphthong also has its strict analytical value. Indeed, the tendency is becoming stronger and stronger to retain as much as possible the native pronunciation of foreign names. The definite adoption of the Romic principle by the Indian government, and the reformed pronunciation of Latin, are all most important moves in the same direction.

History and Etymology. One of the commonest arguments against phonetic spelling is that it would destroy the historical and etymological value of the present system. One writer protests against it as a 'reckless wiping out of the whole history of the language', imagining, it appears, that as soon as a phonetic alphabet has once firmly established itself, the existing Nomic literature will at once disappear by magic, together with all the older documents of the language from Alfred to Chaucer. It need hardly be said that a few months' study of the language of Chaucer, or, better still, of the Anglo-Saxon Gospels, or, best of all, of both of them, would give what a life spent in the mechanical employment of our Nomic orthography fails to give, namely, some of the material on which a rudimentary knowledge of the history and etymology of the English language might be based.

As a matter of fact, our present spelling is in many particulars a far from trustworthy guide in etymology, and often, indeed, entirely falsifies history. Such spellings as *island*, *author*, *delight*, *sovereign*, require only to be mentioned, and there are hundreds of others involving equally gross blunders, many of which have actually corrupted the spoken language!

Even if we carried out—that is, if it were possible—the principle of etymological spelling consistently, by writing each word in its primitive Indo-Germanic form, writing, for instance, *klaipawardha* for *lord*, we should only be giving a portion of the materials of etymology. We should have to give in brackets or foot-notes to each word the Anglo-Saxon and Middle-English, together with the present English forms, the last *in phonetic spelling*, and, lastly, a brief abstract of the laws which govern the various changes of form and meaning. Even if we arbitrarily resolve not to trace our history further back than the sixteenth century we shall have to write each word twice over. It is absurd to say that the spelling *knight*, for instance, throws light on any word in the present English. Of course, the word meant is **nait**. But where do we find the existence of such a word even hinted at? All that the spelling *knight* tells us is that a word existed in a certain form in sixteenth-century English: it tells us nothing about its present form.

In short, historical spelling *destroys the materials on which alone history itself can be based.* This is the case in the English of the last few centuries. The word 'name', as its spelling indicates, was in Chaucer's time pronounced **naamə**, or something like it. It is now **neim** although still written 'name'. Now there must clearly have been several intermediate stages between **naamə** and **neim**—the one word certainly did not change straight into the other. If these changes had taken place in the period before Chaucer, we should have been able to trace their progress step by step in the changes of the spelling, which, as it is, not only fails to record these changes, but gives the false impression that the English language, in this word at least, has remained unchanged since the time of Chaucer. Hence the actual history of the English language since the invention of printing has to be investigated in a most laborious and uncertain way, quite independently of its written form, so far as the sounds are concerned. The investigations of Mr Ellis have proved that 'name' passed through the following stages: **naamə, naam, nææm** (long of æ in 'man'), **naem, neem, neim.** It is clear that if a consistent and etymological spelling had become fixed in the Indo-Germanic languages, there would have been no Grimm's law, no etymology, in short no philology at all possible.

The idea, too, that because etymology is an amusing and instructive pursuit, it should therefore be dragged into practical orthography, is about as reasonable as it would be to insist on every one having Macaulay's History of England permanently chained round his neck, because history is an improving study.

In conclusion, it may be observed that it is mainly among the class of half-taught dabblers in philology that etymological spelling has found its supporters. All true philologists and philological bodies have uniformly denounced it as a monstrous absurdity both from a practical and a scientific point of view.

Detailed Comparison of Glossic and Romic

The elementary vowel symbols of Glossic are contained in the following key-words:

gn*a*t, b*aa*, b*ai*t, c*au*l.
n*e*t, b*ee*t, h*ei*ght, f*eu*d.
kn*i*t.
n*o*t, c*oo*l, c*oa*l, f*oi*l, f*ou*l.
n*u*t, f*uo*t (for f*oo*t).

The only consonants that require notice (reserving *r* for the present) are:

*ch*est, *j*est.
*th*in, *dh*en (for *then*); ru*sh*, rou*zh*e (for *rouge*).

Glossic is an attempt to form a phonetic system of writing based on the present values of the letters. It is, therefore, necessarily a compromise. As Mr Ellis himself remarks, 'Combinations rather than separate letters have definite sounds. Thus *u* in *nut* has one sound, but the combinations *uo*, *ou*, *eu*, have no trace of this sound.' Of course, when the learner has once acquired these combinations he is taught to apply them consistently. In fact Glossic depends mainly on the *phonetic use of a limited number of unphonetic combinations* (that is, combinations whose pronunciation does not depend on that of their elements). In Romic, on the other hand, the combinations (diphthongs, etc.) are as phonetic as the actual words themselves, so that the learner of Romic only has to learn the values of six simple vowel-symbols, whereas the learner of Glossic has to master more than twenty, which are not only totally disconnected and arbitrary, but also suggest all kinds of puzzling cross-associations. Of course, even this is an enormous improvement on Nomic, in which there are more than two hundred combinations, many of which are employed almost at random.

The weakest part of Glossic is its treatment of *r*. *r* in Glossic is used both for the consonant and for the vocalized *r* (= **ə**), as in *peer* **piiə**, and hence must be doubled in *peerring* = **piiəriq**, the first *r* indicating the **ə**, the second the true **r**. **əə** in 'err', 'burn', etc., is written *er*: *er* = 'err', *bern* = 'burn'. Hence *deterring* = Romic **dit·oeriq**, on the analogy of *peerring*. But *er* before a vowel has the totally distinct value of Romic **er**, as in the word *ering* = 'erring' **eriq**.

Again, the conventional *ar* and *or* are retained to represent the same sounds as *aa* and *au*, *faadher* and *fardher*, for instance, being kept distinct, although their pronunciation is identical.

Here the phonetic character of Glossic entirely breaks down, for such distinctions as those last mentioned can only be taught by spelling lessons. This is equally the case with such spellings as those of the final vowels in *faadher* and *soafa* ('sofa'), where the same sound is represented in two distinct ways. Before the learner can decide whether to write *soafa* or *soafer*, he must stop and consider whether a following vowel would bring out the *r* or not.

These considerations show clearly at what a sacrifice of the most essential principles of phonetic writing Glossic retains its similarity to the existing spelling. Any attempt to make the writing of *r* phonetic could only produce such spellings as these, which would quite defeat the aims of the system: *peeu* = 'peer', *peeuring* 'peering', *sauu* 'soar', *faadha*, *faadhu* 'farther', *soafer* 'sofa', *ergenst*, *ugenst* 'against', etc.

In short, Glossic cannot be regarded as a consistently phonetic system even on its own principle of taking the values of combinations for granted.

The following tables have been prepared with a view to enable the reader to judge for himself on the relations of Glossic and Romic to one another and to Nomic. They consist of typical words chosen impartially to represent most of the more important values of the different Nomic letters and combinations, together with the Glossic and Romic spellings.

A. VOWELS

Nomic	*Glossic*	*Romic*	*Nomic*	*Glossic*	*Romic*
man	man	mæn	*saw*	sau	sao
lane	lain	lein	*ten*	ten	ten
hare	hair	haeər	*he*	hee	hii
ask	aask	aask	*where*	whair	whaeər
wall	waul	waol	*stern*	stern	stoen
salt	solt	solt	*see*	see	sii
nail	nail	neil	*sea*	see	sii
air	air	aeər			

Nomic	*Glossic*	*Romic*	*Nomic*	*Glossic*	*Romic*
bear	bair	baeər	*no*	noa	nou
earth	erth	oeth	*do*	doo	duu
head	hed	hed	*soon*	soon	suun
break	braik	breik	*good*	guod	gud
veil	vail	veil	*blood*	blud	bləd
key	kee	kii	*door*	doar	daoər
eye	ei	ai	*oath*	oath	outh
few	feu	fyuu	*oar*	oar	aoər
grew	groo	gruu	*woe*	woa	wou
in	in	in	*shoe*	shoo	shuu
myth	mith	mith	*oil*	oil	oil
wine	wein	wain	*boy*	boi	boi
first	ferst	foest	*out*	out	aut
pique	peek	piik	*soul*	soal	soul
thief	theef	thiif	*you*	yoo	yuu
lie	lei	lai	*four*	foar	faoər
on	on	on	*up*	up	əp
hole	hoal	houl	*tune*	teun	tyuun
none	nun	nən	*rule*	rool	ruul
more	moar	maoər	*burst*	berst	boest
word	werd	woed	*full*	fuol	ful

B. DROPPED CONSONANTS

Nomic	*Glossic*	*Romic*	*Nomic*	*Glossic*	*Romic*
debt	det	det	*hymn*	him	him
lamb	lam	læm	*psalm*	saam	saam
scene	seen	siin	*phthisis*	tizis	tizis
schism	sizm	sizm	*isle*	eil	ail
gnaw	nau	nao			
reign	rain	rein			

C. VARYING CONSONANTS

Nomic	*Glossic*	*Romic*	*Nomic*	*Glossic*	*Romic*
cat	kat	kæt	*see*	see	sii
cease	sees	siis	*as*	az	æz
ocean	oashen	oushən	*sugar*	shuoger	shugər
chin	chin	cin	*thick*	thik	thik
scheme	skeem	skiim	*this*	dhis	dhis
get	get	get	*Thames*	Temz	temz
George	Joarj	jaoj	*vex*	veks	vex
ghost	goast	goust	*example*	egzaampl	egzaampl
laugh	laaf	laaf	*Xerxes*	Zerkseez	zoexiiz
through	throo	thruu			

The results of a detailed study of this table may be conveniently, though somewhat roughly, summed up in the following lists, in which, however, only the commonest groups are given, each represented by its typical word:

I	II	III	IV
Unchanged in both	*Changed in both*	*Unchanged in Glossic*	*Unchanged in Romic*
(5)	(12)	(11)	(5)
ask[1]	lane	man	veil
ten	hare	nail	pique
in	wall	saw	soul
on	salt	(air)	full
oil	sea	(stern)	rule
	bear	see	
	head	few	
	wine	soon	
	hole	oath	
	none	out	
	good	up	
	blood		

We see that out of a total of thirty-three typical words more than a half either remain unchanged or else undergo equally violent changes *under any possible scheme of reform*. Also that only a third of the whole thirty-three remain unchanged in Glossic, from which the two in parentheses ought, strictly speaking, to be excluded, as their agreement with Nomic is obtained at a great sacrifice of phonetic consistency.

The results are, of course, rough. Mathematical accuracy would require that the number of words belonging to each group should be counted, and the relative importance and frequency of each word ascertained, all of which would be a very laborious work.

It is, however, clear that the ease with which Glossic is read by those familiar with Nomic is not inconsistent with considerable divergences between the two. It is, therefore, an important question to consider what would be the effect of the greater divergence between Nomic and Romic on the first attempts of a Nomic reader to understand Romic. If the difference between Glossic and Romic in ease of acquirement by a Nomic reader amounts, as it is possible it may, only to half-an-hour's preliminary study of the elementary symbols of the latter, and the principles of their combination, then it is a serious question whether it is worthwhile sacrificing the interests of future generations of learners to the half-hours of the comparatively few who have to make the transition from Nomic to Romic.

The Principles of Spelling Reform, Appendix to
A Handbook of Phonetics, 1877, pp. 169–208

[1] Sweet's Fn.: May be considered as practically unchanged.

C. PHONETIC NOTATION AND PHONETIC ALPHABETS

[The following section, in which there is inevitably a certain amount of overlapping interest and content with the previous section, contains not only accounts of Sweet's own systems of notation and their origins, but also much useful critical comparison of these systems with older systems such as Ellis's Palæotype and Lepsius's Standard Alphabet. There is also a statement on pp. 234–5 of the author's reasons for abandoning in his Revised Romic some of the digraphs adopted in the Romic of the *Handbook*, three years before. The details of this Revised Romic, together with Sweet's discussion of Bell's Visible Speech, and his argument in support of the revisions he made when composing his own Organic Alphabet, are set out in a separate sub-section.

There is further adumbration of the phoneme principle in the discussion of 'independently significant' sounds on pp. 230–1, and further expression of Sweet's objection to the mixing of capitals and lower case letters on pp. 237 and 245 (cf. previous section). *Ed.*]

One of Mr Ellis's most important contributions to practical phonetics is his adaptation of the ordinary Roman alphabet for the accurate representation of minute shades of sound, which is effected without having recourse either to new types or to those diacritics which made such systems as the well-known 'General Alphabet' of Lepsius impracticable for ordinary use.

. . . . .

The notation I have adopted is, like Mr Ellis's 'Palæotype', based on the ordinary Roman letters, which I have tried to employ more consistently than Mr Ellis has done, by utilizing the results of his manifold experiments and practical experience.

Preface to *A Handbook of Phonetics*, 1877, pp. viii, xi

Sound Notation. The notation of sounds is scarcely less important than their analysis: without a clear and consistent system of notation it is impossible to discuss phonetic questions intelligibly or to describe the phonetic structure of a language.

The only perfect alphabet would evidently be one in which every symbol bore a definite relation to the sound it represented. In the Roman alphabet these relations are entirely arbitrary, and an alphabet that has any claim to the title of 'rational' must therefore discard the Roman letters entirely. In Mr Bell's 'Visible Speech', accordingly, an entirely new set of symbols is used, which indicate the action of the organs in every case, all the symbols being made up of a few simple elements, which can be combined to any extent. If the phonetic analysis on which

Visible Speech is based were perfect, the alphabet itself might, with a few alterations, easily be made practically perfect, and capable of representing all possible sounds whatever with the minutest accuracy. But until phonetics are in a much more advanced state than they are at present, Visible Speech cannot be considered secure against the necessity of incessant alteration and correction.

The Roman alphabet on the other hand, not being based on a phonetic analysis, is not liable to be disturbed by any new discoveries. It has also the great advantage of having long been in practical use both in printing and writing.

The imperfections of the Roman alphabet may be remedied in four ways:

(1) by casting new types;
(2) by employing diacritics, such as grave and acute accents, etc.;
(3) by employing digraphs, such as *th*, *kh*, etc.;
(4) by employing turned letters, italics and capitals.

The same objection applies both to (1) and (2), when carried out to any extent, namely that a new system should utilize the means already existing before creating new ones, which involve expense and inconvenience of all kinds; and if we are to cast types, it would be simplest to discard the Roman alphabet altogether, and take a simplified form of Visible Speech, which would certainly be far easier to learn and use than any possible modification of the Roman alphabet. The practical experience of Mr Ellis is decisive on this point. He entirely discards such systems as Pitman's 'Phonotypy', and Lepsius's 'Standard Alphabet', the best known representatives of (1) and (2), and falls back entirely on (3) and (4), which employ only the ordinary resources of the printing-office. That it is possible with such means as these to form a practicable system, Mr Ellis has clearly shown in his 'Palæotype'.

The great defect of Palæotype, and the other systems contrived by Mr Ellis, is their unnecessary arbitrariness, especially in the vowels, which makes his symbols extremely difficult to remember.

In the present work a new system has therefore been constructed, in which the greatest possible regularity and consistency has been aimed at, as far as the radical defects of the Roman alphabet allow. Those who know palæotype will easily see how principles partly developed by Mr Ellis have been carried out consistently as far as possible.

Another defect of palæotype is the multiplicity of signs employed. Mr Ellis's principle of attempting to find a symbol for every sound that is possible, or has been described by others, seems out of place in any adaptation of the Roman alphabet, which can only be a temporary compromise. All that is necessary is to find signs for the fundamental distinctions, and the minuter or exceptional ones can easily be supplied by simple description. Thus if the reader is once told that the Danish **o** is formed by abnormal rounding, he simply has to remember this whenever he comes across a Danish word with **o** in it. If attention is to be specially called to any peculiarity, this can easily be done by putting a * after the symbol, to remind the reader that some modifier is understood.

This system, which I call 'Romic' (because based on the original Roman values of the letters), although probably the simplest possible for an accurate analysis of sounds generally, is too cumbersome as well as too minute for many practical purposes. (*Fn.*: This cumbrousness is inseparable from any attempts at extension of the radically defective Roman alphabet. In Visible Speech, on the other hand, the most minute synthetic distinctions can be symbolized without causing the slightest practical inconvenience.) In treating the relations of sounds without going into minute details, and in giving passages of any length in phonetic writing, and especially in dealing with a limited number of sounds, as in treating of a single language, it is necessary to have an alphabet which indicates only those broader distinctions of sound which actually correspond to distinctions of meaning in language, and indicates them by letters which can be easily written and remembered.

Thus, the innumerable varieties of diphthongs possible can all be classed under a few general categories such as **ai**, **au**, **oi** diphthongs, and if we simply provide unambiguous signs for these general categories, we can ignore the endless shades of difference within them, because these differences do not alter the meaning or application of the words in which they occur. Again, even if we confine our attention to definite distinctions, such as those of narrow and wide, close **e** and open **æ**, etc., which *may* correspond to differences of meaning, we find that each language utilizes only a few of these distinctions. Thus, in English, there is no distinction between narrow and wide in short vowels, most short vowels being wide only, while in French **i** and **u** are always narrow both long and short, ***i*** and ***u*** being unknown. In Danish, on the other hand, short **i** and ***i*** often distinguish words which would otherwise be identical. Icelandic only has ***i*** when short, but separates **iː** and ***i*ː** when long, often distinguishing words solely by the narrowness or wideness of the vowel. Danish has **iː** only when long, as in English also. We see from this that the distinction between **i** and ***i*** is a *significant* one in Danish and Icelandic; that is, one that corresponds to real distinctions in the languages themselves, while in French it does not exist at all. In English there is the distinction, but it is not an *independent* one, being associated with quantity. But to write **iɪ**, ***i*** in English would be superfluous, as length and narrowness, shortness and wideness go together, and if we simply write **iɪ** and **i** the quantity would always *imply* the distinctions of narrow and wide. Hence we may lay down as a general rule that only those distinctions of sounds require to be symbolized in any one language which are *independently significant*: if two criteria of significance are inseparably associated, such as quantity and narrowness or wideness, we only need indicate one of them.

What is wanted then is a general system which is capable of being modified on definite principles to suit the requirements of special languages. This general system should, of course, deviate as little as possible from the scientific one, and should be as little arbitrary as possible in its details. Like the scientific system it should be based on the original Roman values of the letters, supplemented by digraphs and turned letters.

Beginning, then, with the vowels, there is no difficulty in determining the general application of the elementary symbols ***a***, ***æ***, ***e***, ***i***, ***o***, ***œ*** (= Fr. 'p*eu*r'), ***u***, ***y*** (= Fr. *u*), but signs are required for the *u* in 'b*u*t' and the allied back and mixed vowels, the close French *eu*, in 'peu', and the 'open' *o*. For the open *o*, and for French *eu*, we can have little hesitation in adopting the *ɔ* and *ə* of the other system, and *ə* may be extended to the English *u* in 'but' and 'burn', and the German *e* in 'gabe', etc.

The following will then be the different values of each of the vowel signs in this system, which I will call 'Broad Romic', in apposition to the scientific 'Narrow Romic', as indicating only *broad* distinctions of sound.

a = a, *a*.
æ = *e*, æ, *æ*.
e = e.
ə = ʌ, ɐ, *ɒ*; **eh**, etc.; ə.
i = i, *i*.
o = o, **oh**, *o***h**.
ɔ = *o*, ɔ, *ɔ*, ɔ**h**, etc.
œ = *ə*, œ, *œ*.
u = u, *u*, **uh**, *u***h**.
y = y, *y*.

The diphthongs are expressed by **ai**, **au**, **oi**, **œi**, etc., minuter shades being disregarded. Long vowels are doubled. Broad Romic words or passages are written in bold type[1] or distinguished by (' '), not inclosed in [ ].

The consonant symbols will be the same as in Narrow Romic, except that all capitals are discarded, the front consonants being indicated

[1] Bold type has replaced Sweet's italics, and square brackets his parentheses [Ed.].

by **j**, thus—**lj**, **njh**, etc. The superfluous letters **c** and **x** will be employed as convenient abbreviations of digraphs in each language. Thus in English **c** may be used for **tsh**, in German for **kh**, in French for **sh**, and so on. Any letter which happens not to have a sound to represent in any language will be employed in the same way. Thus the vowel **y** is superfluous in English, and may, therefore, be used to represent the sound [**j**], **j** itself denoting **dzh**, parallel to **c** = **tsh**.

To prevent confusion in comparing different languages, it will often be advisable either to substitute the full spellings **tsh**, etc., for the contracted ones, or else to print the letters that are used in special senses in italics. Thus '**va*r***' in Danish would remind the reader that the Danish *r* is not the ordinary *r*, but a laryngal sound.

Whenever the 'broad' symbols are inadequate it is, of course, allowable to take others from the 'narrow' system. Thus **ih** = [**ih**] might be employed in Welsh, and [ʀ] might be introduced into Danish for special purposes. Capitals and italics, however, being inconvenient in rapid writing, it is best to form special combinations when such distinctions as those of narrow and wide are required, which is very seldom the case. Thus the wide [**i**] may be expressed by **ie**, as being intermediate in sound to **i** and **e**.

The main principle to be observed in all these contrivances is not to disturb the general associations of the letters more than is necessary, and never to lose sight of the importance of keeping up the international character of both the Narrow and the Broad system.

There now remains the question of synthesis-notation. After what has been said on the phonetic value of word-division no surprise need be felt at finding its abandonment advocated here. But, as I have remarked elsewhere [see p. 192. *Ed.*], the abandonment of conventional word-division by no means implies writing each sentence as an unbroken whole. We have already seen (see p. 144) that word-division serves, whenever it has any phonetic meaning at all, to indicate stress-division. If, then, we carry out this principle consistently, making each letter-division correspond with the beginning of a strong stress, as in [**henr*e***^{1} **keɪ*i*hm hoɪ*o***^{1}**m jestʌd*e***^{1}], we shall indicate the most important synthetical element of speech in the simplest and clearest way possible. The · otherwise required to mark the strong stress, will thus be available for the medium (secondary) stresses in each sound-group, as in [**tuɪw kænʌnb·ɔɪlz**], while, if placed at the beginning of a group, it will indicate very strong stress, the ordinary strong stress being implied by simple division, and weak stress by non-division. The : thus becomes quite superfluous, and four degrees of stress are expressed by a single sign. When a sound-group begins, as is often the case, on a weak stress, a special mark is required. The most convenient one is -, as in [**-dhʌmænɪdhʌtehih sɔɪ**]. When the sound-group begins on a secondary stress, : may be prefixed, as in [**:kɐm ɐp**], instead of - followed by ·, which would otherwise be required.

Tone would be indicated by -, ´ and `, etc., which would take the place of the ordinary marks of punctuation at the end of each breath-group, thus serving the double purpose of indicating breath-division and intonation. Marks of key, voice-quality, etc., would be prefixed to each group. There are of course various degrees of accuracy required for different purposes. For the purely practical applications of Broad-sign mere-stress divisions, with an occasional use of · when necessary, together with the simple tone-marks, are amply sufficient, and the - may be omitted whenever the syllable to which it is prefixed is one whose phonetic structure does not allow it to take a strong stress; thus, in **rə təən** = *return*, we see at once that **rə** cannot be an accented syllable because of the final **ə**.

Whenever word-division is indicated it must be understood to be something altogether extraneous and subordinate, just like indicating the substantives in German by capitals. Word-division is perfectly useless to those readers who are practically familiar with the particular language: they do not hear any word-division in rapid speech, and require it still less in slow deliberate reading. Whenever word-division is required it can easily be indicated in Broad Romic by italics or capitals, which otherwise are not employed at all.

A Handbook of Phonetics, 1877, pp. 100–8

My own views on the question of notation up to the time of the publication of my *Handbook of Phonetics* will be found stated in that work [see pp. 228–33. *Ed.*] and again, from the practical Spelling Reform point of view, in the Appendix [see pp. 204–27. *Ed.*]. The most important principles I then upheld (and still uphold) were that every alphabet, whether scientific or practical, must be based, as far as possible, on the original Roman values of the letters, that the letters must be applied with the minimum of arbitrariness, and that we require not only a minutely accurate symbolization, but also a less elaborate system marking only the broader distinctions of sounds, but so constructed as to be able to adopt more minute symbols from the other system if necessary, the two being harmonized as much as possible. I thus formed the two systems, *Broad* and *Narrow Romic*, mainly on the basis of Mr Ellis's *Palæotype*, from which the latter differs mainly in the values assigned to the letters. To the relations between my two systems corresponds that between Mr Ellis's *Glossic* and *Universal Glossic*, which are, however, based not on the Roman values of the letters, as is the case with Palæotype, but on an attempt to retain their present English value. In my Appendix [see pp. 224 ff. *Ed.*] I have tried to show that such attempts can only lead to a breakdown of the fundamental principles of phonetic writing, not only from a scientific, but also from a purely practical point of view, nor has the recent controversy in the *Academy* between Mr Ellis on the one hand and Mr Nicol and myself on the other done anything but strengthen my convictions.

The most important result (from the notational point of view) of the practical experience gained in the preparation of my *Handbook* has been the breakdown of digraphs in any minutely accurate system. In Mr Ellis's Palæotype the impracticability of any thorough-going system of digraphs is disguised from several causes. One of these is the connexion between his choice of letters and his theories about the originality of certain sounds. In this way he is enabled, for instance, to employ the unmodified **e**, **ee**, **o**, **oo** in denoting the pronunciation of Chaucer, but according to my views (which are those of many others besides) he would have to write **E**, ***ee***, **ɔ**, **AA**—all modified letters. Although digraphs are not employed here, these examples will show how a slight change of theory may seriously impair the convenience of a notation. Again, there are certain sounds which Mr Ellis does not seem to recognize practically, such as Bell's 'mixed' varieties of **o**. Thus he regards the French *o* in *homme*, *dot*, simply as the ordinary open 'back' sound, and writes it accordingly with his unmodified **o**. Bell, Storm, and myself, however, all agree in regarding it as a 'mixed' vowel, that is to say, as an approximation to the 'front' vowels in *peu*, etc. On this theory the French short *o* must be written **oh** in Palæotype. In my Narrow Romic I have carried out consistently the principle, initiated by Mr Ellis, of denoting all mixed vowels by an **h**. Hence the necessity of denoting the very common unaccented vowel heard in the second syllable of the German *gabe* by **eh** instead of Mr Ellis's simple **ə**, which on my principles has to denote a different sound. Now the more minute the analysis of vowels, especially in diphthongic combinations, the greater the number of mixed vowels that have to be recognized. Hence it is that the English diphthong in *wine*, which Mr Ellis writes with two letters, appears in my Narrow Romic with no less than four—***e*h*i*h**. In representing some simple sounds I have been obliged to have recourse to trigraphs, as in the Danish soft *d*, which I am obliged to write **dh*j*** to distinguish it from the English **dh** in *the*, with which it was formerly confounded. The result of all this is, as I stated at first, the practical break-down of digraphs (and trigraphs) for purposes of consistently accurate notation.

The fact is, that if we want minute accuracy, we must have new types. When we have availed ourselves of the resources offered by the utilization of otherwise superfluous letters, such as *c*, *q*, *x*, and by turned letters and the other devices employed in Palæotype, we must have new types for the commoner simple sounds, such as **sh**, **th**, **dh**. But we must not rush into the opposite extreme of banishing digraphs altogether. Digraphs can never be entirely avoided, as is sufficiently shown by the fact that even Visible Speech, which is entirely independent of the defects of the Roman alphabet, frequently employs them. Such general modifiers as ***j***, to indicate palatalization, etc., are absolutely required. All we require is to make digraphs *exceptional*—not to abolish them entirely—and to get rid of trigraphs. In fact we want *elasticity*, and not to require to cast a new type for every insignificant shade of sound. Marks of accent and quantity, etc., should be cast on separate types, to avoid such unpractical monstrosities as *ā́*, etc., necessitating as they do the cutting of a number of subordinate types for every new letter. Such combinations should be analysed into **aa´** or something of the kind. The objection to employing accents in the middle of a word as in **bev·´aara**, is pure prejudice, the result of habit and association. What types should be adopted is a question which I cannot go into now; it is, however, evident that the new letters must be such as to show most clearly the relations of the sounds they denote to those denoted by the old letters, and to admit of being easily written, besides having distinctive forms. These principles would exclude such letters as, for instance, the Old English *þ* and *ð*, the former being easily confounded with *p*, the latter troublesome to write.

For rougher phonetic notation, and for purely practical purposes, digraphs are perfectly admissible, as is shown both in Mr Ellis's Glossic and in my Broad Romic. There can, however, be no doubt that here also they will be gradually superseded by new types.

'English and Germanic Philology', Presidential address to the Philological Society, 1878, in *Collected Papers of Henry Sweet*, 1913, pp. 117–20

The problem of sound notation is as old as civilisation itself, but it is only of later years that that of *scientific* sound notation has become urgent. There is now a general conviction among philologists of the necessity of a general alphabet, but with utter discord of opinion as to the means of attaining it. Most hold with some modification of the Roman alphabet, each phonetician employing a modification of his own. Of *organic* alphabets, which are based on a physiological analysis of the actions of the speech-organs, Brücke's and Merkel's may be said to have come still-born into the world, while Bell's *Visible Speech* attracted great attention at the time, although still little known, except by name, outside a small circle of his own pupils.

My objects here are (1) to consider what is the best possible modification of the Roman alphabet, (2) to show that such an alphabet is inferior to Bell's, and (3) to describe an improved and extended form of both.

Modifications of the Roman Alphabet

Of the two fundamental defects of the Roman alphabet, namely the arbitrariness of its symbols and their limited number, it is the latter which most imperatively calls for reform. The former, indeed, being inherent in the alphabet itself can only be remedied by abandoning that alphabet altogether—a contingency which, till comparatively lately, has hardly been taken into account at all, and is still ignored by most phoneticians.

The Roman alphabet can be supplemented in five distinct ways:

(1) by adding new letters—ʒ, ɫ, þ.
(2) by diacritics—ā, ä, ñ.
(3) by turned letters—ə, ɐ, ɔ.
(4) by italics and capitals—*a*, ᴀ, *ə*.
(5) by digraphs—th, dh, n*j*.

Of all these expedients, the first is the one which has always been the most obvious and popular. Pitman's Phonotypy even goes so far as to provide simple signs for diphthongs, such as the English 'long *i*', and consonant-groups, such as tʃ. As a general rule it may be said that the more inexperienced and ignorant the reformer is, the more reckless he will be in adding new types. The main objection to new types is, of course, the trouble and expense, except in those cases where the new letters are already provided in the printing-office. There is also the difficulty of applying uniform modifications to a variety of letters, some of which, such as g, are already cumbrous enough.

The same objections apply also, though in a less degree, to diacritics, which, as Mr Ellis says, 'act as new letters'. The best known of the diacritic alphabets is Lepsius's *Standard Alphabet*, thus criticized by Bell (*Visible Speech*, p. 99): '(It) consists of Roman and Greek letters, varied by the addition of diacritic marks. Seventeen diacritics are used above, and fourteen are used below the body of the letters; so many as three diacritics being in some cases applied to a single body. The number of lower-case letters thus employed exceeds 280, and of these above 200 require to be cut for every fount used.' A special objection to diacritics is their want of compactness, and they are always troublesome to write (though not more so than many of the new letters that have been proposed), as we see in our ordinary dotted *i*'s. They have, however, the great advantage over new letters of giving uniform modifications of a variety of letters, and also of being more accessible in an ordinary printing-office.

The third way, that of *turning* the letters, which has been largely developed in Ellis's *Palæotype*, gives new letters without trouble or expense. Such forms as ə and ɔ are, indeed, infinitely superior to many of the monstrosities that have from time to time been proposed as new types. But it is limited in its application.

The use of *italics* and *capitals* has many of the advantages of turning, but makes writing troublesome, and small capitals are not always accessible.

Digraphs, lastly, have nothing but convenience to recommend them. They are sprawly, especially when in minutely accurate writing of sounds they develop into *trigraphs*, and are sometimes ambiguous. A digraph is, however, generally written easier and quicker than a new type, and is often read as easily.

It is evident that all these expedients fall under two main heads:

(1) those which require new types to be cut;
(2) those which require only the old types;

and that if the question of reform is to be mainly guided by considerations of typographical convenience, only those modifications can be adopted which fall under the second head, namely, the last three of those first enumerated, together with a few out of the first two classes of letters. That it is possible to frame a minutely accurate alphabet without exceeding the resources of an ordinary printing-office has been conclusively shown by Ellis's *Palæotype*, on which my own *Narrow Romic* is mainly founded. We may in short say that the main result of the manifold experiments made in England up to the publication of my *Handbook of Phonetics* was the rejection of the new-type and diacritic systems, or, in other words, the subordination of compactness to general accessibility. Whatever may be said against the English systems, they at least provided every writer and printer with the means of representing the minutest shades of sound with the least possible delay, trouble, or expense. The importance of this becomes evident when we consider that it was mainly the typographical difficulties of the 'Standard Alphabet' which caused its disuse by missionaries and travellers, for whom it was specially intended. Palaeotype and Narrow Romic still continue to be the only approach to a universal alphabet with Roman letters.

However, these principles have met with no favour out of England, and the latest Continental alphabet—the Swedish, noticed in my last Address (*T.P.S.* 1877–9, pp. 396 foll.)—follows directly opposite ones, being supplemented entirely by new types, diacritics being employed only for quantity, tone, etc., and consisting entirely of italics. Although this alphabet is intended only for the Swedish dialects, it employs no less than eighty-eight elementary letters, and as a large number of diacritics are required, the number of types runs up to several hundred. If this alphabet were extended to all languages, and its principles were carried out rigorously and minutely, the number of letters would rise to as many thousands.

In my *Handbook* the old-type principle was more severely tested than in Mr Ellis's works (see p. 234), the result of which was 'the breakdown of digraphs in any minutely accurate system'. But, as I have also said, (see p. 235. *Ed.*) we must not rush into the opposite extreme of banishing them entirely. It is quite visionary to attempt to have a new letter for every minute shade of sound, which is not attempted even in Visible Speech. The radical defects of the Roman alphabet are so incurable that any extension of it must necessarily be a very unsatisfactory compromise, although all beginners think they can turn out a perfect scheme by rigorously applying some one principle. It seems to me that, putting all our experience together, the following is the only practical compromise:

(1) abolish the present use of capitals, as is done in Bell's and the Swedish alphabet;
(2) after determining the values to be assigned to the existing letters, supplement them,
(3) by turned letters,
(4) by new types, beginning with those already provided, and always reserving the right of employing digraphs occasionally;
(5) denote general modifications, such as nasality, by italic letters;
(6) mark quantity, stress, etc., by separate signs on a line with the other letters.

Thus, I would denote mixed vowels by two dots instead of the **h** employed by Mr Ellis and myself, using **ë** for **eh**, **ü** for the Swedish *u*. Even if we adopted only those dotted letters which are in common use, retaining the digraphs **ɔh** and some others, the Narrow Romic vowel-notation would become practically almost as manageable and compact as can be expected from any modification of the Roman alphabet. In the consonants **ʒ** and **ð** would be substituted for **gh** and **dh**, etc. Nasalization and palatalization would be indicated by ***n*** and ***j***, quantity by a simple upright stroke (provisionally by ɪ), stress by a point. This method is in every way preferable to the ordinary one of placing these marks as diacritics above and below the letter modified, which it is besides impossible to carry out consistently and minutely in practice. Even if we allow only two degrees of quantity and stress, and four tones, which is utterly inadequate, we get eight diacritics, with a large number of special combinations. The attempt to form new letters for every variety of nasalized, etc., sounds, is equally visionary, and if italics were limited to the function of general modifiers, such digraphs as a*n*, s*j*, etc., would not cause the slightest inconvenience, and s*j*, at least, is less clumsy and scarcely less compact than any of the attempts I have seen to combine *s* and *j* into one letter.

There is, however, a fatal obstacle to the general adoption of such an alphabet for international scientific purposes, namely, the impossibility of an agreement as to its details. It is a natural consequence of the fundamental arbitrariness of the Roman alphabet, whose elementary symbols have no definite relations either to one another or the sounds they represent, that the values of these symbols vary almost indefinitely in different languages, and consequently that any general system stands in a very different relation to each national orthography, which approaches it with special associations of its own. Hence such irreconcileable contrasts as the 'Roman' and 'English' values of the vowels and the impossibility of agreeing on a basis even for the rough practical system required for spelling reform purposes. The ridicule which phonetic spelling invariably excites in uneducated minds, and the dislike with which every phonetician regards all phonetic notations except the one evolved by himself, are simply the result of an instinctive and rational protest against cross-associations, or, in other words, against the Roman alphabet itself.

. . . . .

Every new book brings a new alphabet. As phonetics is studied more and more, so will the number of books increase, each with its own notation, these notations becoming more and more complex, till at last comparative phonology will become a sheer impossibility, as, indeed, it nearly is already.

Even if the impossible were to happen, and such a general alphabet were accepted, its essential complexity and arbitrariness would make it very difficult to learn, and it would be impossible to secure it against misinterpretation. The temptation to avoid inconvenient symbols in writing each language would also infallibly lead to inaccurate compromises and substitutions.

It is, in short, clear that the question of introducing an entirely new organic alphabet is not a mere theoretical consideration, but is of vital practical importance. Such an alphabet, formed by the systematic combination of a few fundamental signs denoting the elementary actions by which all sounds are formed, would be free from the defects of any possible modification of the Roman alphabet. As its letters would all stand in a definite relation to one another and to the sounds they represent, they would be learnt with ease, and as every stroke of them would have a meaning, their number might be extended almost indefinitely without taxing the memory, just as the nine digits of arithmetic may be combined indefinitely. These qualities would also secure it against arbitrary misapplication. There would be no cross-associations with the ordinary Roman orthographies. It would also be perfectly impartial, every simple sound having a simple sign, so that the English *th* and the German *ch* would be put on a perfect level with *k*, *s*, etc. The value for scientific purposes of an alphabet in which every letter would be practically a diagram of the actions by which the sound is produced would be incalculable, and the different varieties of such a vowel as **a**, for instance, would appear in their true light, namely, as perfectly distinct sounds, hitherto confounded simply by an accident of defective notation. The rationale of sound-change would then become self-evident in most cases by the mere juxtaposition of the symbols.

The objection oftenest urged against the adoption of such an alphabet is, that being based on a physiological analysis of the actions of the organs of speech, each advance in our analysis and each correction of earlier errors, will involve a modification or enlargement of the alphabet. The natural answer to this is that perfection in all practical matters can never be reached without repeated trial, and that long experience is required to determine what are the best shapes of the letters—the simplest and most distinct, how the words are to be divided, and many other similar questions. Also that an alphabet in which the facts already established were embodied on a systematic and consistent plan would itself be a most powerful instrument of progress. The question is not whether we have arrived at an absolutely perfect and final analysis of speech-sounds, but simply whether we have a sufficient number of firmly established results to form the basis of an organic alphabet which for scientific purposes is an improvement on any possible modification of the Roman alphabet. I answer confidently, Yes. An alphabet which could stand such tests as *Visible Speech* was subjected to by Mr Ellis and other eminent phoneticians (*V.S.*, pp. 23 foll.), an alphabet too whose very structure makes it capable of indefinite expansion and elaboration, must yield at least a solid foundation.

. . . . .

If we impartially survey the whole field of phonetic knowledge, we shall see that the great majority of the facts are really as firmly established as anything can well be. It is, for instance, absolutely certain that *p*, *b*, and *m* are all formed by the lips, and that *k*, *g*, and *ng* are all formed by the back of the tongue, also that *p*, *b*, *k*, *g* are formed by complete stoppage, that *m* and *ng* are nasal, and so on. These are certain results which no amount of physiological, acoustic, or any other kind of scientific investigation can possibly modify, at least as far as their symbolization is concerned. Again, it is by no means certain that our present views on the formation of voice are final, but there is no doubt that there is such a thing as voice, that it is inherent in *b*, *m*, *g*, etc., and that *b* stands in the same relation to *p* as *g* does to *k*, as regards the presence and absence of this element. Even if we knew nothing more than this parallelism, without having any idea of the real nature of voice, and denoted *b* and *g* by an arbitrary but consistent modification of the signs for *p* and *k*, we should attain a practically permanent result. The vowels have always offered greater difficulties, but many of the main divisions of palatal, labial, high and low, etc., have been agreed on long ago. As a matter of fact, Bell's analysis of the vowels is so perfect that after ten years' incessant testing and application to a variety of languages, I see no reason for modifying its general framework.

'Sound Notation', *T.P.S.* 1880–1, pp. 177–235, in *Collected Papers of Henry Sweet*, 1913, pp. 285–93

Sound-notation. The traditional or 'nomic' orthography of English, as of most languages, is only imperfectly phonetic. The divergence between sound and symbol which makes English spelling unphonetic is in most cases the result of the retention of phonetic spellings after they have become unphonetic through changes in the pronunciation of the words which they represent. Thus such spellings as *knight* and *wright* were still phonetic in the time of Chaucer; for in the Late Middle English of the fourteenth century the initial consonants of these words were still pronounced, and the *gh* still had the sound of *ch* in German *ich.* So also we write *see* and *sea* differently, not for the sake of making an arbitrary distinction, but because they were pronounced differently till within the last few centuries, as they still are in the English spoken in Ireland.

In dealing with the sounds of English it becomes necessary therefore to adopt a phonetic notation. It is now generally agreed that the best way of constructing such a notation is to give the letters of the Roman alphabet the sounds they had in the later Latin pronunciation, with, of course, such modifications as seem to be improvements or otherwise desirable, supplementing the defects of the Roman alphabet by adding new letters when required. This is the 'Romic' or international basis.

This basis may be used to construct either a 'broad' or a 'narrow' system of notation. A broad notation is one which makes only the practically necessary distinctions of sound in each language and makes them in the simplest manner possible, omitting all that is superfluous. Letters and words in Broad Romic are enclosed in ( ), when necessary to prevent confusion with the nomic spelling. Thus in English Broad Romic we distinguish the present pronunciation of *knight* and that which it had in the time of Chaucer as **nait** and **kniçt**. But these spellings, though accurate, are not minutely accurate. Thus **ai** is the symbol of any diphthong beginning with a vowel resembling the 'Italian *a*' in *father*, and ending in an approximation to the *i* of *it*. Of course, if the **a** is definitely broadened into **o** or thinned into the **æ** of *man*, then we write it **oi** or **æi**, as the case may be. But minuter shades of vowel-pronunciation can be disregarded for ordinary purposes, just as in writing **nait** we do not generally consider it necessary to show that the two consonants are formed on the gums, and not on the teeth, as in French.

But in comparing the sounds of a variety of languges or dialects of a language, and still more in dealing with sounds in general, we require a 'narrow', that is, a minutely accurate notation covering the whole field of possible sounds. Such a Narrow Romic notation, in which each symbol has a fixed, definite value, serves as a key to the exact pronunciation of the vaguer symbols of the Broad Romic notations of each language. Narrow Romic are distinguished from Broad Romic symbols by being enclosed in [ ]. Thus *i* **i** = [*i*] means that the vowel in *finny* is 'wide', not 'narrow' as in the French [**i**] in *fini*. In the Broad Romic notations of both languages **fini** is written for *finny* and *fini* alike. So also the English and French **n**'s are in Narrow Romic distinguished as [**n˧**] and [**n˫**] respectively. Such distinctions may, of course, be introduced into the Broad Romic notation of any language when there is any practical advantage to be gained thereby.

The 'International Alphabet' of *Le Maître phonétique*, the organ of the International Phonetic Association of Paris, is based on the English romic systems. It is a compromise between a broad and a narrow notation, being an attempt to make a special adaptation of the romic principle to the needs of French into a general notation for all languages.

. . . . .

When sounds are symbolized, not isolated, but joined together in words and sentences, it is often necessary to add marks to show the quantity or length, the stress (comparative force or loudness), and intonation (comparative pitch or height) of sounds and syllables.

In English Broad Romic it is only necessary to distinguish *long* from *short* vowels by doubling the former. **ɔ** is not doubled because it does not occur short. Repeated vowels can be distinguished from long ones by inserting a hyphen as in **hæpi-ist** *happiest*.

. . . . .

In English it is necessary to distinguish four degrees of stress: *weak* -, *medium* or half-strong :, strong ·, *extra strong* or emphatic ;. The last is only occasionally required. These marks are put before the symbol of the sound on which the stress begins, so that they serve at the same time to indicate the syllable-division: **·dount :kontrə·dikt -im** *do not contradict him*. But strong stress need not be marked in monosyllabic words, or when it falls on the first syllables of longer words whose other syllables have weak stress, as in **veri wel** *very well*. If a monosyllabic word has weak stress, it must be marked by prefixing **-**. But if the weak-stressed monosyllable contains an **ə**, it is not necessary to mark the stress, as this vowel occurs only in weak syllables: **ə mæn əv onə** *a man of honour*. If only one strong or emphatic stress is marked in a polysyllable, all the other syllables are assumed to have weak or medium stress; in which case the often doubtful distinction between medium and weak stress need not be marked. Hence the sentence first given may be written more simply **dount kontrə·dikt -im** or **dount kontrə;dikt -im** according to the degree of emphasis.

It is sometimes necessary to distinguish weak vowels and syllables as 'pre-tonic' and 'post-tonic' according as they occur before or after a strong- or medium-stressed syllable; thus in **əmerikə** *America* the first **ə** is pre-tonic, the second post-tonic.

As regards intonation, we distinguish the following tones: *level* ˉ, which hardly ever occurs in English; *rising* ˊ, as in **whotˊ** *what?*; *falling* ˋ, as in **nouˋ** *no!*; *falling-rising* or compound rise ˇ, as in **teik ˇkeə** *take care!*; *rising-falling* or compound fall ˆ, as in **ˆou** *oh!* as an expression of sarcasm. The tone-marks may be put either at the end of the sentence or before the word on which they fall, as is most convenient. If no tone-mark is added, a comma or ? implies a rising tone; a full stop, colon, or semi-colon a falling-tone.

The Sounds of English, 1908, pp. 9–13

Phonetic Notation. One of the greatest difficulties in the study of general phonetics is the diversity of notations employed not only by different writers, but often also by one and the same. This diversity is not solely the result of caprice and the striving after cheap originality, but is to some extent the inevitable result of certain fundamental divergencies in the objects and uses of sound-notations, of which there are three kinds:

(1) Arbitrary alphabetic, in which there is no consistent association between sound and symbol: the Roman alphabet is a familiar example.

(2) Symbolic alphabetic, in which there are definite relations between sound and symbol, which relations may be either organic or acoustic, or a mixture of both of these, it being now generally admitted that a scientific symbolic alphabet must be organic, while a popular one must be partly acoustic: the best example of a scientific symbolic alphabet is Visible Speech, of which the Organic Alphabet is the revised and supplemented form.

(3) Analphabetic, in which each sound is represented by a group of symbols resembling a chemical formula, these symbols being generally either numbers or Roman letters, or a combination of both with, perhaps, other characters as well. Jespersen's Analphabetic Notation is the best known and most fully worked out of these.

It is evident that the notations which fall under (3) are of such limited application that they may be ignored from the point of view of practical phonetics, useful as they undoubtedly are from a theoretical point of view, even if we regard them only as temporary substitutes for an ideal scientific alphabetic system.

When we say 'alphabetic', we mean only alphabetic basis. The maxim 'one single symbol for each sound' is all very well in theory, but impossible to carry out in practice. The number of possible distinctions is so great that no notation can do more than provide symbols for groups of sounds, each of which sounds must be further differentiated when necessary by modifiers such as 'inner' and 'outer', and marks of rounding, etc. No system of writing can dispense with digraphs and even trigraphs; in fact, the more scientifically minute a notation is, the more it approximates to the analphabetic principle.

Whatever alphabet is adopted—whether an arbitrary or a symbolic one—it must be capable of modification so as to supply the want of (1) an international scientific 'narrow' notation, in which all possible shades of sound can be expressed with minute accuracy by symbols of fixed values, and (2) an indefinite number of national 'wide' notations, each of which selects the minimum number of simplest letters required to express the practically necessary sound-distinctions of the language in question, ignoring those that are superfluous, so that all the national systems appear as modifications of a common basis, each diverging from it only as far as is made necessary by considerations of simplicity and ease of printing and writing both in long and short hand.

As regards the distinction between the last three, it is to be observed that in printing the complexity of the letters does not necessarily affect speed or ease; so that the number of possible forms is infinitely greater than in writing, which has a comparatively very limited number of simple, joinable forms to choose from. Hence the printed forms are generally more distinct than the written ones, as we see by comparing, for instance, the capital and lower-case Roman A, a with the italic *a*. As it is desirable to have as few types as possible, most phonetic systems founded on the Roman alphabet discard altogether the use of capitals as such, using small capitals, if at all, only to supplement the lower-case alphabet, the capitals acting thus as new letters. As the capitals have no convenient script forms, this use of them is confined to scientific notations.

Some transcriptions consist entirely of italics, the idea being to make the printed and the written characters the same as far as possible, and also to make the phonetic symbols stand out distinctly on a page of Roman type. But as italics are required for a variety of other purposes as well, it is better to make the more legible lower-case letters the basis, and use italics for supplementary purposes—of course, only in scientific notations.

The Roman alphabet is in itself unscientific and imperfect, but it has the great advantage of being the result of a long series of experiments, besides being in universal use. Its foundation ought to be left untouched, for any attempts at radical reform would simply result in the substitution of a totally different alphabet—which will no doubt come to pass sooner or later.

In adapting the Roman alphabet to phonetic purposes the first thing is to utilize all the available existing symbols: to give phonetic values to *c*, *q*, *x*, settle what is to be done with the italic and capital letters, and so on. The next step is to supplement it. There are many supplementary devices—such as the use of italics and capitals—which, as we have seen, are admissible only in a scientific notation where speed and ease are not indispensable qualifications of a working alphabet. In a practical broad system, on the other hand, the first thing to be considered in a new letter is whether it can be written and joined easily. The best new letters are those which are the result of utilizing duplicate script forms, as in the use of the otherwise superfluous long forms of **s** and **z**—**ʃ**, **ʒ**. Such new letters as **ə**, **ɔ**, **ŋ** are also unexceptionable in every way. But to make italic *a*, *g*, *v* into Roman letters distinct from **a**, **g**, **v**, by printing them upright instead of sloping, as is done in the alphabet of the Association Phonétique, is an illegitimate extension of the principle. The inevitable result is that new script forms have to be invented to take the place of the old *a*, *g*, *v*, which latter are perfect for the purpose. The natural further result is that most of these new script forms are not used at all, their place being taken by laborious detached facsimiles of the printed forms.

The most objectionable class of letters in a broad alphabet are diacritical ones. In their printed forms they are practically new letters; and in writing they involve not only a break, but a further waste of time and effort in the movements of the pen from the line of writing to the diacritic and back again, as we see in the letter *i*. Of course, when diacritic letters already exist, they may be utilized, especially in a scientific notation.

But every modification of such a basis as the Roman alphabet must necessarily be an unsatisfactory makeshift—repulsive to every one but the inventor, who is generally not an inventor at all, but simply a reviver of devices which have been tried and rejected over and over again. To the general public all systems of writing which clash with the associations of the traditional printed and written nomic orthography are ugly and ridiculous—whatever their intrinsic merits may be.

But in spite of all diversity there is also much agreement: there is already a rudimentary public opinion, sometimes in the principles, but oftener in the details of phonetic notation. It is therefore better to leave disputed and doubtful points to be settled by experience, to trust to the survival of the fittest, rather than make the vain attempt to enforce one uniform system of notation while the very foundations of phonetics are still under discussion.

The adoption of a uniform phonetic notation for exclusively scientific purposes will, of course, be highly desirable when our knowledge of sounds is fairly complete, and there is agreement among experts on the principles of phonetics. But such rigid uniformity is not desirable, or indeed possible with a practical alphabet, which, as we have seen, must necessarily differ in its details with each language to which it is applied.

It must be observed that the distinction between 'narrow' and 'broad' is not an absolutely definite one. There are degrees of broadness. The extreme of simplicity with which an easily accessible modern European language can and should be written would be out of place in the representation of the necessarily more or less conjectural restoration of the pronunciation of Chaucer or Shakespeare: here we naturally expect a more minute notation—a compromise between narrow and broad.

Such a compromise must not be confounded with a dilettante notation. The former adopts the minuter distinctions of the scientific alphabet only when they are practically useful from its special point of view; the latter is a compromise in a more literal sense: it is not accurate enough to be really scientific, and yet too complicated and cumbrous for ordinary practical use. Not that it is to be condemned on these grounds; on the contrary, a dilettante phonetic notation has the same justification as the dilettante conception of phonetics of which it is the expression. It is better that people should frankly acknowledge that the distinction of narrow and wide vowels or the discrimination of five degrees of stress is too much for them and ignore them accordingly in their transcription than attempt to use a notation involving distinctions which they are unable to make.

The great disadvantage of the use of the Roman alphabet in phonetic notation is the inevitable confusion between the associations of phonetic and nomic spelling, not to speak of the endless confusions which arise in passing from one phonetic notation to another.

For this reason some will perhaps find it desirable to avoid the cross-associations between the broad and narrow Romic notations by discarding the latter in favour of the Organic alphabet—especially in dealing with the vowels. The confusion is much less with the consonants. On the other hand, it is necessary to have a narrow Romic notation for convenience of use by those who have not access to the Organic symbols; and also because to many a totally new notation like Visible Speech or the Organic Alphabet is—or seems to be—a more formidable obstacle than the cross-associations of a Romic system.

The Sounds of English, 1908, pp. 112–17

Sound-notation: Spelling Reform. Next to the analysis of the sounds themselves, the most important problem of phonetics is their representation by means of written and printed symbols. The traditional or 'nomic' orthographies of most languages are only imperfectly phonetic. And, unfortunately, of the languages in most general use, two are exceptionally unphonetic in their orthographies, French showing the greatest divergence between sound and symbol, while English shows the maximum of irregularity and arbitrariness. The German orthography is comparatively phonetic: it has hardly any silent letters, and it generally has one symbol for each sound, each symbol having only one value, the exceptions falling under a few simple rules, which are easily remembered. There are other languages which have still more phonetic orthographies, such as Spanish, Welsh and Finnish. But even the best of them are not perfect: even when they are not actually misleading, they are always inadequate. On the other hand, no system of writing is wholly unphonetic. Even in French and English there are many words whose spelling not even the most radical reformer would think of altering. In fact, all writing which has once emerged from the hieroglyphic stage is at first purely phonetic, as far as its defective means will allow. The divergence between sound and symbol which makes spelling unphonetic is the result of the retention of phonetic spellings after they have become unphonetic through changes in the pronunciation of the words themselves. Thus, such English spellings as *knight* and *wright* were still phonetic in the time of Chaucer: for at that time the initial consonants of these words were still pronounced, and the *gh* still had the sound of *ch* in German *ich*. So also *see* and *sea* are written differently, not by way of arbitrary distinction, but because they were pronounced differently till within the last few centuries—as they still are in Irish-English.

Where there is no traditional orthography, as when Old English (Anglo-Saxon) was first written down in Latin letters, spelling was necessarily phonetic; but where there is a large literature and a class of professional scribes, the influence of the traditional orthography becomes stronger, till at last the invention of printing and the diffusion of one standard dialect over a large area occupied originally by a variety of other dialects make changes of spelling as inconvenient as they were once easy and natural. The ideal orthography for printers is one which is absolutely uniform over the whole territory of the language, and absolutely unchangeable. In such orthographies as those of the present English and French there is no longer any living correspondence between sound and symbol: they are, in intention at least, wholly unphonetic; they are preserved by graphic, not by oral tradition.

But unphoneticness has its practical limits. A purely unphonetic degradation of an originally phonetic system of writing—one in which there is absolutely no correspondence between sounds and letters—could not be mastered even by the most retentive memory: it would be even more difficult than the Chinese writing. Hence a phonetic reaction is inevitable. In the middle ages the spelling was periodically readjusted in accordance with the changes of pronunciation—as far, of course, as the imperfections of the existing orthography would allow. This adjustment went on even after the introduction of printing. In fact, it is only within the last hundred years or so that the orthographies of English and French have become fixed.

One result of this fixity is that any attempt to continue the process of adjustment assumes a revolutionary character. When, in 1849, the pioneers of the modern spelling-reform movement—A. J. Ellis and I. Pitman—brought out the *Fonetic Nuz*, few of those who joined in the chorus of ridicule excited by the new alphabet stopped to consider that this uncouthness was purely the result of habit, and that the Authorized Version of the Bible in the spelling of its first edition would seem to us not less strange and uncouth than in the new-fangled phonotypy of

Messrs Ellis and Pitman. Nor did they stop to consider that phonetics and phonetic spelling, so far from being innovations, are as old as civilization itself. The Alexandrian grammarians were not only phoneticians—they were spelling-reformers; they invented the Greek accents for the purpose of making the pronunciation of Greek easier to foreigners. The Romans, too, were phoneticians: they learnt Greek by phonetic methods, and paid great attention to niceties of pronunciation. The Sanskrit grammarians were still better phoneticians.

As a matter of fact, English spelling was still phonetic as late as the time of Shakespeare—in intention, at least. But although people still tried to write as they spoke, the inherited imperfections of their orthography made it more and more difficult for them to do so. Hence already in the 16th century a number of spelling-reformers made their appearance, including classical scholars such as Sir John Cheke, and A. Gill, who was head-master of St Paul's School in London. Gill has left us extracts from Spenser's *Faerie Queene* in phonetic spelling: but, strange to say, nothing of Shakespeare's, although he and Shakespeare were exact contemporaries. But Gill's and the other alphabets proposed were too intricate and cumbrous for popular use.

Nevertheless, some important phonetic reforms were successfully carried through, such as getting rid of most of the superfluous final *e*'s, utilizing the originally superfluous distinctions in form between *i* and *j*, *u* and *v*, by using *i*, *u* only as vowels, *j*, *v* only as consonants, instead of at random—a reform which seems to have begun in Italy. Another important reform was the introduction of *ea* and *oa*, as in *sea* and *boat*, which had hitherto been written with *ee* and *oo*, being thus confused with *see* and *boot*.

All these were as much phonetic reforms as it would be to utilize long *s* and tailed *z* ʃ, ʒ to denote the final consonants in *fish* and *rouge* respectively; a reform first suggested by A. J. Ellis, who was himself the first to call attention to the works of these early phoneticians and to utilize them in the investigations enshrined in his great work on *Early English Pronunciation.*

With all its defects, the present English spelling is still mainly phonetic; we can still approximately guess the pronunciation of the vast majority of words from their spelling. So when we say that English spelling is unphonetic we merely mean that it is a bad phonetic spelling; and all that spelling-reformers aim at is to make this bad into a good phonetic spelling, that is, an efficient and easy one. But the difficulties are great; and the more we know of phonetics, and the more we experiment with different systems of spelling, the more formidable do they appear. One of the difficulties, however, that is commonly supposed to stand in the way of spelling-reform is quite imaginary: namely, that it would destroy the historical and etymological value of the present system. Thus E. A. Freeman used to protest against it as 'a reckless wiping out of the whole history of the language'. Such critics fail to see that historical spelling, if carried out consistently, would destroy the materials on which alone history can be based: that these materials are nothing else but a series of phonetic spellings of different periods of the language, and that if a consistent historical and etymological spelling could have been kept up from the beginning there would have been no Grimm's Law, no etymology; in short, no comparative or historical philology possible.

The advantages of beginning a foreign language in a phonetic notation are many and obvious. In the first place, the learner who has once mastered the notation and learnt to pronounce the sounds the letters stand for, is able to read off at once any text that is presented to him without doubt or hesitation, and without having to burden his memory with rules of pronunciation and spelling. Another advantage of phonetic spelling is that when the learner sees the words written in a representation of their actual spoken form he is able to recognize them at once when he hears them. And if the learner begins with the phonetic notation, and uses it exclusively till he has thoroughly mastered the spoken language, he will then be able to learn the ordinary spelling without fear of confusion, and quicker than he would otherwise have done.

Spelling-reform may be carried out with various degrees of thoroughness. After the failure of many schemes of radical reform, an attempt was made to begin with those numerous spellings which are both unphonetic and unhistorical, or are against the analogy of other traditional spellings. Accordingly, in 1881 the Philological Society of London 'aproovd (*sic*) of certain partial corections (*sic*) of English spellings', which were also approved of by the American Spelling-reform Association, and a list of them was issued jointly by the two bodies, and recommended for general adoption. A similar movement has been started in France. But the general feeling appears to be that it is better to keep the ordinary spelling unchanged, and wait till it is possible to supersede it by one on a more or less independent basis.

If the existing Roman alphabet is made the basis of the new phonetic notation of any one language, the most obvious course is to select one of the various traditional representations of each sound, and use that one symbol exclusively, omitting, of course, at the same time all silent letters. A. J. Ellis's *English Glossic* is an example of such a phonetic spelling on a national basis. The following is a specimen:

Ingglish Glosik iz veri eezi too reed. Widh proper training a cheild foar yeerz oald kan bee redili taut too reed Glosik buoks.

But a system which, like this, writes short and long vowels with totally different symbols (i, ee) is only half phonetic: it is phonetic on an unphonetic basis.

A fully phonetic system, in which, for instance, long vowels and diphthongs are expressed by consistent modifications or combinations of the symbols of the short vowels, and in which simple sounds are, as far as is reasonable and convenient, expressed by single letters instead of digraphs such as *sh*, must necessarily discard any national basis. The best basis on the whole is obtained by giving the letters their original common European sounds, i.e. by returning to the Late Latin pronunciation, with such modifications and additions as may be advisable. As regards the vowels at least, this Latin basis is very well preserved in German and Italian. In French, on the other hand, the Latin tradition was greatly corrupted already in the earliest period through the rapid changes which the language underwent. Thus when the Latin *u* in *luna* assumed the sound it now has in French *lune*, the symbol *u* was still kept; and when the sound *u* afterwards developed again out of the diphthong *ou*, this digraph was used to denote the sound. So when the French system of spelling came into use in England after the Norman Conquest these unphonetic symbols were introduced into English spelling, so that such a word as Old English and Early Middle English *hus*, 'house', was written *hous* in the Late Middle English of Chaucer, although the sound was still that of Scotch *hoos*, *ou* (*ow*) being also used to denote a true diphthong **ou** in such words as *knou*, *know*, from Old English *cnāwan*.

By returning, then, to the original values of the letters we get the 'Romic' or international (Continental) basis as opposed to the Glossic or national basis. Thus the passage quoted above appears as follows in Sweet's 'Broad Romic' notation:

iŋǵliʃ ǵlosik iz veri iizi tu riid. wið propə treiniŋ ə tʃaild fɔə jiəz ould kən bii redili tɔt tu riid ǵlosik buks.

Another important general distinction is that between 'broad' and 'narrow' systems of notation. A broad notation is one which makes only the practically necessary distinctions in each language, and makes them in the simplest manner possible, omitting all that is superfluous. From a practical point of view the necessary distinctions are those on which differences of meaning depend. A distinction of sound which is significant in one language may be unsignificant in another. Thus the distinction between close *é* and open *è*, *ê* is significant in French, as in *pécher*, *pêcher*; so if in French phonetic writing the former is denoted by **e**, it is necessary to find a new symbol **ɛ** for the open sound. But in languages such as English and German, where the short *e* is always open, there is no practical objection to using the unmodified **e** to denote the open sound, even if we regard **e** as the proper symbol of the close sound. And in those languages in which the short *e* is always open and the long *e* always close it is enough to make the distinction of quantity, and leave the distinction of quality to be inferred from **e**, **ee**. In such a case as this it is, of course, possible to apply the principle of ignoring superfluous distinctions in the opposite way: by writing the long and short vowels in such a language **e**, **ɛ**, leaving the quantity to be inferred from the quality. But the former method is the more convenient, as it does not require any new letter. The 'broad' principle is especially convenient in writing diphthongs. Thus in English Broad Romic we write the diphthongs in *high* and *how* with the same vowel as *ask* **hai**, **hau**, **aask**, although all these **a**'s represent different sounds in ordinary southern English pronunciation. But the pronunciation of these diphthongs varies so much in different parts of the English-speaking territory, and the distinctions are so minute that it would be inconvenient to express them in writing; and as these distinctions are non-significant, it would be useless to do so. **ai** and **au** are symbols, not of special diphthongs, but of two classes of diphthongs: they can stand for any diphthongs which begin with a vowel resembling the Italian *a*, and end with approximations to *i* and *u* respectively. Theoretically it would be just as correct in English and German to write these diphthongs **ae**, **ao**. But these notations are misleading, because they suggest simple sounds.

In comparing the sounds of a variety of languages, or of dialects of a language, and still more in dealing with sounds in general, we require a 'narrow', that is a minutely accurate, notation covering the whole field of possible sounds. It is evident from what has been said above that such a universal scientific alphabet is not suited for practical work in any one language. But the symbols of such a notation as Sweet's 'Narrow Romic' are of the greatest use as keys to the exact pronunciation of the vaguer symbols of the Broad Romic notations of each language.

To prevent confusion between these two systems of notations Broad Romic symbols are enclosed in ( ), Narrow Romic in [ ], which at the same time serve to distinguish between phonetic and nomic spellings. This in English *i* (**i**) = [*i*] means that the English vowel in *finny*, is the 'wide' sound, not the 'narrow' one in French *fini*, although in the Broad Romic notations of both languages **fini** is written for *finny* and *fini* alike.

Narrow Romic was originally based on A. J. Ellis's 'Palaeotype', in which, as the name implies, no new letters are employed. The symbols of Palaeotype are made up, as far as possible, of the letters generally accessible in printing-offices, the ordinary Roman lower-case letters being supplemented by italics and small capitals **i**, ***i***, ɪ and turned letters ə, ɔ, many digraphs **th**, **sh** being also used. This notation was a reaction from Ellis's earlier phonotypy, in which a large number of new letters were used. Some of these, however, such as ʃ = **sh**, ʒ = **zh**, were afterwards adopted into Broad and Narrow Romic. In his Palaeotype Ellis also discarded diacritical letters, which, as he rightly says, are from a typographical point of view equivalent to new letters. In Narrow Romic a certain number of diacritical letters are used, such as **ñ**, **ä**, most of which are already accessible. Palaeotype is a Roman-value notation, the main difference as regards the values of the symbols between it and the later systems being that it is more complex and arbitrary. Ellis afterwards had the unhappy idea of constructing a 'Universal Glossic' on an English-values basis, which is even more cumbrous and difficult to remember than Palaeotype.

Sweet's Romic systems were made the basis of the 'International' alphabet used in *Le Maître phonétique*, which is the organ of the International Phonetic Association, directed by P. Passy. Although this system is at the present time more widely known and used than any other, and although it is constructed on the international Romic principle, it is not really an international system. It is rather an attempt to make a special adaptation of the Romic basis to the needs of the French language into a general notation for all languages. But the phonetic structure of French is so abnormal, so different from that of other languages, that the attempt to force a Broad Romic French notation on such a language as English is even more hopeless than it would be to reverse the process. Although well suited for French, this alphabet must from a wider point of view be regarded as a failure: it is too minute and rigid for practical, and yet not precise enough for scientific, purposes. In short, although it has done excellent service, and has helped to clear the way for a notation which shall command general acceptance, it cannot be regarded as a final solution of the problem.

Of the numerous other notations now in use, some still adhere to the diacritic principle of Lepsius's *Standard Alphabet* (1855), intended for missionary use, but found quite unfit for that purpose because of the enormous number of new types required. Most of them prefer to use new letters formed by more or less consistent modifications of the existing italic letters. A. J. Lundell's Swedish dialect alphabet and O. Jespersen's Danish dialect alphabet are good specimens of this tendency. In the latter Roman letters are used for special distinctions, just as italic letters are used in the Romic systems.

But in spite of all diversity, there is much agreement. As regards the vowels, the following approximate values are now pretty generally accepted:

a	*as in*	father.	**i**	*as in*	it.
ai	,,	time.	**o**	,,	beau (Fr.).
au	,,	house.	**œ**	,,	peur (Fr.).
æ	,,	man.	**ɔ**	,,	fall.
e	,,	été (Fr.).	**oi**	,,	oil.
ei	,,	veil.	**ou**	,,	soul.
ɛ	,,	there.	**u**	,,	full.
ə	,,	further.	**y**	,,	une (Fr.)

Vowel-length is in some systems denoted by doubling **aa**, in others by special marks (**a:** etc.), the diacritic in *ā* being used only in the nomic orthographies of dead and oriental languages.

The only consonant-symbols that require special notice are the following:

c	*as in*	tyúk (Hung.).	**ŋ**	*as in*	sing.
ç	,,	ich (German).	**ʃ**	,,	fish.
ð	,,	then.	**þ**	,,	thin.
j	,,	you.	**w**	,,	we.
ɟ	,,	nagy (Hung.).	**x**	,,	loch.
ñ	,,	ogni (Ital.).	**ʒ**	,,	rouge.

All the systems of phonetic notation hitherto considered are based on the Roman alphabet. But although the Roman alphabet has many advantages from a practical point of view, it is evidently impossible to build up a consistent and systematic notation on such an inadequate foundation of arbitrary signs. What is wanted, for scientific purposes especially, is a notation independent of the Roman alphabet, built up systematically—an alphabet in which there is a definite relation between sound and symbol.

This relation may be regarded either from the organic or the acoustic point of view. The tendency of the earlier attempts at an a priori universal alphabet was to symbolize the consonants organically, the vowels acoustically, as in E. Brücke's *Phonetische Transcription* (1863). It is now generally acknowledged that the vowels as well as the consonants must be represented on a strictly organic basis. This was first done in A. M. Bell's *Visible Speech* (1867), which appeared again (1882) in a shorter form and with some modifications under the title of *Sounds and their Relations*. Bell's pupil, H. Sweet, gave a detailed criticism of Visible Speech in a paper on *Sound-notation* (Trans. of Philological

Society, 1880–1881) [see p. 257 ff. *Ed.*], in which he described a revised form of it called the *Organic Alphabet*, which he afterwards employed in his *Primer of Phonetics* and other works. Sweet's Narrow Romic notation already mentioned is practically a transcription of the Organic Alphabet into Roman letters.

Such notations are alphabetic: they go on the general principle of providing separate symbols for each simple sound. But as the number of possible shades of sounds is almost infinite, even the most minutely accurate of them can do so only within certain limits. The Organic Alphabet especially makes a large use of 'modifiers'—characters which are added to the other symbols to indicate nasal, palatal, etc., modifications of the sounds represented by the latter, these modifiers being generally represented by italic letters in the Narrow Romic transcription; thus **l*n*** = nasalized **l**.

In the Roman alphabet such symbols as *f*, *v* are arbitrary, showing no connection in form either with one another or with the organic actions by which they are formed; but in the Organic symbol of *v*, for instance, we can see the graphic representation of its components 'lips, teeth, voice-murmur'. By omitting superfluous marks and utilizing various typographical devices the notation is so simplified that the symbols, in spite of their minute accuracy, are often simpler than in the corresponding Roman notation. The simplicity of the system is shown by the fact that it requires only about 110 types, as compared with the 280 of Lepsius's very imperfect Standard Alphabet.

All the systems hitherto considered are also alphabetic in a wider sense: they are intended for continuous writing, the more cumbrous 'narrow' notations being, however, generally employed only in writing single words or short groups. An 'analphabetic' basis was first definitely advocated by Jespersen, who represents each sound by a group of symbols resembling a chemical formula, each symbol representing not a sound, but an element of a sound: the part of the palate, tongue, etc., where the sound is formed, the degree of separation (openness) of the organs of speech, and so on. The two great advantages of such a system are that it allows perfect freedom in selecting and combining the elements and that it can be built up on the foundation of a small number of generally accessible signs.

As regards Jespersen's scheme, it is to be regretted that he has not worked it out in a more practical manner: that in his choice of the thirty odd symbols that he requires he should have gone out of his way to mix up Greek with Roman letters, together with other characters which would be avoided by any one constructing even a scientific alphabetic notation. And his use of these symbols is open to much criticism. In fact, it cannot be said that the analphabetic principle has yet had a fair trial.

'Phonetics', in *Encyclopædia Britannica*, 11th Edn., 1911, pp. 459–62

Bell's Visible Speech, the revised Organic Alphabet, and revised Romic

[This section begins with Sweet's statement in 1880, that in the year or two since the publication of the *Handbook of Phonetics* he had come to believe that the Romic system there advocated should be superseded 'for scientific purposes' by a reformed organic alphabet—such as the one subsequently used in the *Primer of Phonetics* and other works. The considerations that led to this view are largely set out in the preceding section. The present section is devoted to Sweet's detailed account of Bell's Visible Speech; his comments and criticisms, which generally appear in parentheses, with the consequent revision of Bell's system in his own revised Organic Alphabet; and, finally, Sweet's statement of revised Romic, with his own table giving the Organic equivalents. *Ed.*]

Of course, such an alphabet as Visible Speech has to be learnt, but this really involves only learning the meaning of a few fundamental marks and the principles of their application, which can be acquired by any one in a few hours. To read such an alphabet fluently requires, of course, considerable practice, but the student will acquire a perfect command of it long before he has mastered the actual facts of phonetics embodied in it. The real difficulty is *the thing itself*, namely, the facts of phonetics, whose difficulties are largely increased by a bad notation like the various make-shift Roman-letter ones, and are simply reduced to their natural proportions by a rational notation. If non-Sanskritists will take the trouble of learning the enormously complex Sanskrit alphabet, which gives the key to only one language, merely for comparative purposes, the comparative phonetician cannot grudge the trouble of attaining the phonetic key to all languages, which is besides in itself the easiest of all possible alphabets.

These views are not the result of desultory theorizing, but of the practical experience of myself and my fellow-worker, Mr H. Nicol. We both studied practically under Mr Bell himself, and have worked with his alphabet ever since, employing it exclusively in our private memoranda and correspondence with one another. We had, however, till lately no intention of advocating its general use among philologists, thinking that a general Romic system would excite less prejudice and do well enough for a time. However, the considerations set forth have made us change our minds during the last two years, and we have been driven by sheer necessity to have types cut for a reformed organic alphabet for our own use. The expense of the undertaking has been shared equally between us, but the use of the new types will be free to any member of the Society who wishes to employ them in any paper printed in our Transactions.

As I have had more leisure and opportunity for phonetic work than Mr Nicol, most of the modifications of Bell's original alphabet have been devised by myself, but they have all been subjected to Mr Nicol's criticisms and approval before final adoption, as also to the criticisms of Mr Ellis and Dr Murray.

Bell's Visible Speech. As Bell's book (*Visible Speech*, by Alex. Melville Bell, Inaugural Edition, 1867) is now practically inaccessible to ordinary students, and as the want of key-words makes it difficult of comprehension to the untrained reader, I have tried to make the following abstract of it full and clear enough to supersede reference to it for ordinary purposes, and at the same time as brief as possible, by omitting detailed explanations of universally accepted facts of phonology. Wherever Bell's views are obscure, or diverge from my own or those of others, I have quoted his own definitions.

Bell's complete alphabet is shown in the annexed table (see p. 258), reproduced by Mr Ellis's permission, from the one in his *Early English Pronunciation*, Part I.

For the sake of convenience, I shall in my exposition employ the new letters whenever they agree with Bell's. For many of the symbols peculiar to Bell I have been able by Dr Murray's kindness to make use of his set of types. Where these failed, I have been obliged to refer to the table.

Symbols marked * are those which have been modified or discarded in the revised alphabet.

General Principles

All the consonants and vowel-letters are formed by the combination of the following elements, some of which are also used as independent letters. They are all, as far as possible, pictorial of the actions or positions of the organs.

o. Open glottis, or *breath.* A segment of this, c, is the foundation of *primary* (my *open*) *consonants*, the same indented, ε, of *divided* consonants.

ɵ. 'Contracted super-glottal passage', or *whisper.*

I. 'Glottis contracted to a narrow chink', or *voice.* Foundation of all vowels, such as ſ i. Incorporated in voiced consonants, as in ϵ ʒ.

	1	2	3	4	5	6	7	8	9	0	
a	C	∩	∪	Ↄ	I	1	I	ɪ	O	'	*a*
b	C꞉	Ω	ʊ	Ↄ꞉	ƨ	]	l	[	()	ł	*b*
c	Ɛ	ɷ	ω	3	ʎ	J	I	ι	χ	'	*c*
d	Ɛ꞉	ɷ꞉	ω꞉	3꞉	ɣ	1	T	ɾ	ʃ	,	*d*
e	ɑ	ɑ	ʊ	ɒ	ʔ	ɉ	ɿ	ɩ	ʗ		*e*
f	ɑ꞉	ɑ꞉	ʊ꞉	ɒ꞉	>	J	I	ι	⬭	<	*f*
g	Є	ᘉ	ω	∋	Ɨ	ɨ	Ɨ	f	ʒ	>	*g*
h	Є꞉	ᘉ꞉	ω꞉	∋꞉	ƨ	}	ŧ	ɟ	θ	<	*h*
i	ɛ	ɷ	ω	3	ʎ	ɟ	ɪ	ɩ	}	c	*i*
k	ɛ꞉	ɷ꞉	ω꞉	3꞉	¥	ɨ	Ŧ	f	{	ɔ	*k*
l	ɘ	ɑ	ʊ	ɵ	ƻ	ɉ	ŧ	ɟ	Λ	‖	*l*
m	ɘ꞉	ɑ꞉	ʊ꞉	ɵ꞉	ɸ	ɟ	Ɨ	ɩ	V	°	*m*
	1	2	3	4	5	6	7	8	9	0	

ʃ. *Nasality*; pictorial of the pendulous soft-palate.

Dot. *Narrowness*-definer, as in ɾ **i.**

Hook. *Wideness*-definer, as in ɾ ***i.***

Cross-stroke. *Rounding*, as in f **y.**

Upright-stroke. *Stopping*, as in ɑ **k.**

There are other elementary signs which are employed only as modifiers.

The *place* where each sound is formed is shown by the *direction* in which the symbol is turned. Thus ɑ = **k**, ɒ = **p**, ʊ = **t.**

The following is the complete alphabet of types.

16 *Consonants*

o	θ	c	c꞉	ɛ	*ɛ꞉	ɑ	*ɑ꞉
χ	θ	є	є꞉	ɛ	*ɛ꞉	ɘ	*ɘ꞉

20 *Vowels*

7 *Glides*

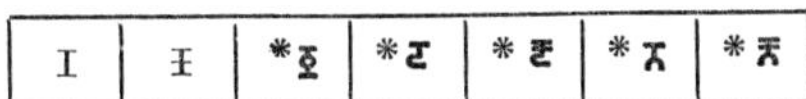

14 *Modifiers*

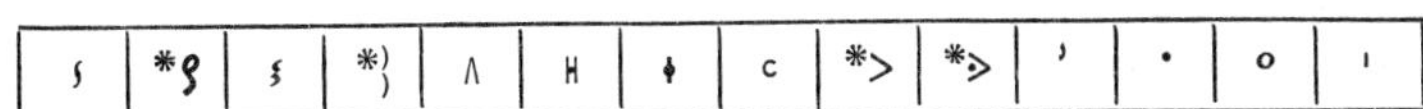

4 *Tones*

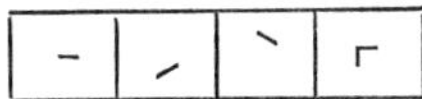

The types are reversible, and the consonant ones, being square, can be turned in any direction, so that, for instance, c, ɔ, ∩, ∪ are all printed from one type. The complete alphabet of 119 single letters is, therefore, printed from the above 61 types.

Certain typographical modifications proposed by Mr Bell himself, and adopted in our revised alphabet, will be described hereafter.

We can now proceed to the detailed descriptions of the separate symbols.

Rudimentary Symbols

These are defined by Bell as 'those which represent the elements of interjectional or inarticulate utterance.'

1. o. When the glottis and the super-glottal passage are perfectly open, the breath creates no sound in its emission. A moderate degree of expulsiveness to render the 'aspiration' audible is implied. (Bell uses this letter throughout as the symbol of the various **h**-sounds in language, not knowing that they are (apparently) always accompanied by glottal narrowing (see pp. 153–4). He was, on the other hand, aware of the glide-nature (see p. 154) of **h** (*Fn.*: Written H in the *Handbook*), and it would have been more consistent to denote it by > (No. 12), as was afterwards done by Mr Nicol and myself.)

2. ɪ. When the glottis is contracted to a narrow chink, the breath in passing sets the edges of the orifice—the 'vocal ligaments'—in vibration, and creates sonorous 'voice'. (The description is not absolutely correct: see p. 47.)

3. o. When the glottis is open, and the super-glottal passage is contracted, the breath creates in the latter the non-sonorous rustling or friction which is called 'whisper'. (This is a description, not of ordinary whisper, but of the wheeze ɹ̣ (see p. 49). Bell was not aware that the former is produced by simple narrowing of the *lower* glottis.)

4. ɵ. Compound of o and ɪ, and denotes whisper and voice heard simultaneously. (Here, of course, the o can only denote super-glottal action.)

5. x. Glottal 'catch'.

6. ʃ. Nasality.

7. *9e. Compound of ʃ and o, and denotes guttural contraction with nasality, as heard in the French sounds *in*, *on*, etc. In these elements there is a gliding semi-consonant effect in the throat as well as nasal modification. (See p. 50. French nasality seems to be only a stronger development of the preceding one, due to further lowering of the uvula.)

8. ʆ. Trill.

9, 10. ʌ, v by themselves, refer to the aperture of the mouth as affected by the close (ʌ) or open (v) position of the jaws. Following other symbols, ʌ denotes configurative compression, with consequent percussion on leaving the configuration; and v denotes configurative openness or organic laxity. Thus:

oʌ. An exhaustive aspiration from upward pressure of the diaphragm;—a wheeze. (Hardly correct: a wheeze seems to require super-glottal contraction.)

ov. A gentle inaudible aspiration.

xʌ. Glottal closure with distention of the larynx from pressure on the confined breath, and percussive emission on opening the passage;—a cough.

11, 12. <, >. Whisper or voice may be produced by air going inwards (<) or by breath coming out (>). All symbols except < and · imply emission. Symbol > is used to denote a transitional emission from the symbolized configuration in passing from one position to another. The effect is different from the throat-aspiration, o. Thus from the shut position of the glottis (x) we may either open sharply upon an utterance of voice (xɪ) or we may *ease off the pressure* of the 'catch' by interpolating a 'breath-glide' (x>ɪ). (This makes > practically identical with my **h**, both before and after vowels (see pp. 153–5) and in aspirated stops (see p. 162).)

13. *·. Signifies that the organic separation or recoil from any symbolized position—which is always implied in final elements when the 'stop' is not written—does not take place. Thus x· is an unfinished 'catch', in forming which, the impulse ceases with the *closure* of the glottis. The effect of organic 'stop' is implied between elements in verbal combinations, such as *tl* in *outlaw*, *td* in *outdo*, etc.; where, necessarily, the *t* is not followed by organic recoil, as it would be at the end of a word. In these cases, of course, the 'stop' does not require to be written. (These two cases are distinct. The latter is simply one of absence of glide (*breath*-glide in the two words cited). The former means cessation of out-breathing before the recoil, not *absence* of recoil. A stop maintained indefinitely without recoil would cause suffocation.)

14. *ʾ. In verbal combinations of elementary sounds, each element is inseparably joined to the succeeding one. When any element, except the last in a combination, is finished independently of what follows, the sign of 'hiatus' (ʾ) is used. The effect of ʾ will be understood by pronouncing the word *bedtime*, in which the *d* and *t* are not disjoined, in contrast with the separate pronunciation of the two words '*bed*, *time*'. Symbol > is an *aspirated* hiatus; symbol ʾ is non-aspirated—a mere *interval*. (This symbol is practically a breath-glide (see p. 160), and is superseded when we have proper signs for the various glides. For glideless combinations see p. 165.)

15. *ʿ. Denotes a very 'abrupt' utterance, shorter than ordinary 'short quantity'. The latter is implied in all symbols where no sign of quantity is written.

16. ɫ. Sign of long quantity, or 'holder'. Extra prolongation may be denoted by ɫɫ.

17. *ı. The sign of 'accent' or *stress* distinguishes the syllable in a word, or the element in a combination, which receives the principal impulse. The mark is placed *before* the accented syllable. (No sign provided for secondary stress.) This sign inverted is used to mark *emphasis* or sentence-stress. (This is superfluous, as the distinction between stress and emphasis is only logical, not phonetic.)

Consonants

The separate symbols are c (primary), ɛ (divided), ɑ (shut), **ɑɜ** (= ɑʃ) (nasal), together with the corresponding voiced ϵ, ɛ, ɘ, **ɘɜ**. The place of the sound is indicated by the direction of the curve, thus: c back x, ∩ front ç, ∪ point ṛ, ɔ lip ɸ. Curves of different direction are united in one symbol to show simultaneous action, as in ɞ ʍ = ɔ+c, ɕ **xv** = c+ɔ, the large curve showing the preponderating element. Voiced consonants are distinguished by the insertion of the voice-symbol: ɷ **j**, ɘ **g**.

Other positions are expressed by the modifiers *} (inner), *{ (outer), ᶜ (inverted), ᵓ (protruded): ʊ} **ṯ**, ʊ{ **t̨**, ʊᶜ **t↓**, ʊᵓ **t↑**.

Other modifiers are: ʌ (closeness) and v (openness), as in ɔʌ (blowing to cool) and ɔv (expressive of faintness, or want of air); ʃ (nasality), as in ɷʃ **jn**; ʃ (trill), as in ωʃ **rr**.

The following are applied to stops:

*>. Emission stopper. Organic separation without emission. The 'stop' (·) shows that the action is conjunctive only; and the 'emission-stopper' signifies that the organs are separated after contact, but that the breath is retained. (There is no reason why this modifier should not be applied to other sounds as well as stops. In fact, Bell himself says, after treating of Consonant Suctions, under the head *Consonant Actions without Breath*: 'All the consonant configurations of every kind—primary and divided as well as shut—may be formed without either emission or suction. If the breath within the mouth be compressed behind the articulating organs while an inner closure is held, a distinct, and in some cases, a powerfully percussive effect will be produced on the abrupt separation of the organs. The signs > and < represent the two modes of this mere motion of the organs of speech.' Bell apparently means to include both the reaction just described (>) and the clicks (<) under the designation 'mere motion of the organs of speech'.)

*<. Suction stopper. Suction and organic separation without inhalation. The formation of the shut consonants by suction (<) gives rise to a peculiar class of elements. The lip-shut symbol followed by the sign of suction (ɒ<) represents a sound interjectionally expressive of sudden pain; but there may be suction during the organic contact and separation of the organs without ingoing air. For this effect the special sign 'suction stopped' is provided. The lip-, point-, and front-shut actions performed in this way, and the point-shut with side termination (ʊʜ), produce a series of sounds or 'clicks' which are very common in interjectional or inarticulate utterance, and which are elements of ordinary speech in some African languages. Compare also note on the Zulu clicks. (This method of symbolizing the clicks is very ingenious. The air is sucked from between the tongue and palate from behind, so that its movement is necessarily inwards, which is expressed by the <, the (·) showing that this inward movement is not obtained by ordinary inhalation.)

ʜ Side opener. Lateral or 'divided' termination instead of organic recoil.

ᵘ Unilateral. Opening of a single lateral passage. (This modification can be applied also to unstopped consonants and vowels.)

Bell remarks: 'When a shut consonant precedes a nasal one of the same organic formation, the oral organs are not disjoined, but the nasal valve is simply opened, as in *pm* (ɒʊ) in *chapman*, etc. The independent completion of the shut consonant in such cases would be inconsistent with the law of coalescence, which requires all the elements of a word to be joined together without *hiatus*.' He then proceeds to symbolize the 'nasal termination' of a final shut consonant by ɒʃ: it would be more consistent with the foregoing to write ɒɒ, as also ʊω, ʊωᵘ instead of his ʊʜ and ʊᵘ. There is no reason why these combinations should be only final.

A few of the consonant-symbols require special discussion.

o, ◊ and ◊ have been noticed above (pp. 259–60).

x{. There can be no inner variety of the catch, but an outer formation, or closure of the super-glottal passage, yields a distinct percussion, which is very common in Chinese and many other languages. The closure is effected by depression of the epiglottis, as in the act of swallowing. (I never succeeded in acquiring a definite idea of this sound.)

*ʊ (s). Front-mixed. The front and the point of the tongue both raised, so as to bring the convex surface of the tongue close to the front of the palatal arch, and the point of the tongue, at the same time, close to the upper gum.

*ʊ (ʃ). Point-mixed. The point and the front of the tongue both raised —the latter to a less degree than for ʊ—bringing the front surface of the tongue near the rim of the palatal arch. (This can only represent a voiceless palatalized ω, **rj**, which is quite distinct from ʃ.)

*ʊ (þ). Front-mixed-divided has its centre check at the *tip* of the tongue, and its apertures between the edges of the flattened point and the teeth or the upper gum, the front of the tongue having considerable convexity within the arch of the palate. (See *Handbook* where **þ** is described as simply breath directed on to the teeth by (flattened, or even concave) tongue. The convexity of the tongue described by Bell would convert the English **ð** into the Danish **ðj**. Lastly, division could only produce some variety of **l**. If we take the symbol literally as ω+υ, it can only mean a voiceless Italian *gl* modified by **ṛ**. ω, the point-divided, is described by Bell as '(having) its apertures over the sides of the middle of the tongue, the point being in contact with the upper gum; the front surface of the tongue is flattened or slightly concave, so that the apertures are large and productive of but little friction or sibilation'.)

*ꙍ. Point-mixed-divided has the apertures of ω ꞁ narrowed by convexity of the tongue, and the breath is in consequence strongly sibilant. (This is, according to Bell, the Welsh *ll*, usually identified with ωᵘ, and the Zulu *hl*. The voiced sound he identifies as the Zulu *dhl*. It is not clear in what way the sound is supposed to differ from the preceding one. The Welsh *ll* certainly has a strong sibilant effect, but this can be effected by spreading out the lateral edges of the tongue, as well as by convexity of its front, and I conjecture that the Zulu *dhl* is simply such a (buzzed) ω. Taken literally ꙍ ought to represent **lj**—the ordinary French *l* in *belle*.)

ɜ (**f**). Lip-divided is formed by placing the centre of the lower lip on the edges of the upper teeth, while the breath hisses through the interstices between the teeth or between the teeth and the lip. A similar effect of divided formation results from placing the lower on the upper lip, instead of the teeth, and directing the breath over the corners of the lips. This peculiarity would be represented by the modifier (ↄ) 'to lip' after the lip-divided symbol ɜↄ. (Bell's own analysis contradicts his symbolization of **f** as a divided: the true lip-divided is the sound he writes ɜↄ.)

These errors of symbolization are evidently due to the attempt to uphold the symmetry of the system, even where its ground-plan is defective. It certainly is a defect that there is no sign for the teeth-position, which would enable **þ** and **f** to fall into their natural places 'point-teeth' and 'lip-teeth' respectively. **s** and **ʃ** are more difficult to deal with. It may be noted that Bell's providing a sign **l***k* for the very rare **l̂***v*, while leaving the frequently occuring **s***j*, **ʃ***j*, **ʃ***v*, **j***v* unsymbolized, is also due to the exigencies of symmetry, which allows only *opposite* curves to be united in one symbol, and hence excludes ∩+ↄ, Ω+∩, etc. The way in which the revised alphabet meets these difficulties will be seen hereafter.

The following is Bell's 'General Scheme of Consonants':

Voiceless

Throat	o	ᴑ	..	..	x	..
Back	c	*ɕ	ε	*ε̤	ɑ	*ɑ̤
Front	∩	*Ω	ɱ	*Ω̤	Ω	*Ω̲
Point	∪	*ʊ	ω	*ω̤	Ʊ	*Ʊ̲
Lip	ɔ	ɔ̤	*ɜ	*ɜ̤	ɒ	*ɒ̤

Voiced

Throat	..	ɵ	..	..	..	..
Back	є	є:	ɛ	*ɛ̈	ɑ	*ɑ
Front	ɒ	*ɒ:	ɒ	*ɒ	ɒ	*ɒ
Point	ɯ	*ɯ:	ɯ	*ɯ	ɯ	*ɯ
Lip	ɜ	:ɜ	*ɜ	*ɜ	ɑ	*ɑ

In Bell's nomenclature the *place* is named first and *voice* last: ɑ lip-shut-voice. Consonants of two curves he calls 'mixed', thus :ɜ is 'lip-mixed', є: 'back-mixed'. It seems simpler to name both organs: lip-back, back-lip. Bell calls ɑ, etc., 'shut' consonants, instead of the more usual 'stop'. I have also substituted 'open' for his 'primary'.

Glides

Bell's symbolization of the non-syllabic vowels with which diphthongs are formed is the one general feature of his alphabet which has met with least approval among phoneticians.

'The primary consonants are formed by the breath or voice issuing with a degree of friction, sibilation or buzzing, through a narrow passage over the back, front, etc., of the tongue, or between the lips. When the configurative channel is so far expanded as to remove compression or buzzing from the voice, a series of semi-consonant, semi-vowel sounds results, which we call "glides". These elements are only *transitional* sounds. If they had a fixed configuration, they would be vowels, and would form *syllables*; as even the closer consonants do when their configuration is held.

'The glides being thus intermediate to consonants and vowels, are appropriately represented by the organic consonant curves joined subordinately to vowel-stems; thus ⊼ (from ∩). The glides unite with vowels to form diphthongs, or double sounds with a single syllabic impulse. The vowel-stems ɪ, ɪ̵ are now specifically employed by themselves to denote *non-syllabic* vowel murmurs.'

He thus describes a vowel:

'A vowel is a syllabic sound moulded by a definite and momentarily *fixed*, or tense, configuration of the free channel of the mouth, and creating no oral sibilation or friction in its emission. A vowel without a fixed configuration loses its syllabic effect and becomes a glide; and a glide with sibilation or friction in the oral channel becomes a consonant.

Consonants, like glides, are merely transitional sounds; but their configurations may be held so as to receive syllabic impulse, in which case a consonant without a vowel has the effect of a syllable. All vowels make syllables.'

This view of 'glides' being intermediate to consonants and vowels is the result of confusion between two distinct divisions of sounds, namely, that of syllabic and non-syllabic and that of consonant and vowel. The latter is entirely the result of the *position* of the organs, while the former is purely relative, dependent mainly on stress, secondarily on quantity (see pp. 137–8, 142–3). Any sound, whether consonant or vowel, may be either *syllabic*, that is, a syllable-former, or the contrary. *Any consonant whatever*, not merely **l**, **n**, etc., may constitute a syllable, and any vowel may be made non-syllabic without the slightest modification of the position with which it is formed. Bell's intermediate symbols would be defensible only if glides were formed with a degree of friction or closeness intermediate to that of consonants and vowels, which is not the case. It is also clear that there must be as many glide- as there are vowel-symbols, but Bell provides only eight glides to represent the thirty-six vowels. Thus, the six vowels ſ, ſ, [, [, ʅ, ʅ are all represented by the single glide ⊼. Some vowels, such as Ĩ, have not even an approximate glide to correspond.

The remaining glide-symbols are really weakened consonants, such as ¥, which is a weak ɷ **r**.

The following is a complete list of the glide-symbols. Bell's key-words are given by him on p. 94 of his book:

* > Breath glide. A transitional aspiration of organic quality corresponding to that of the adjoining elements, = a soft effect of ᴄ, ᴖ, etc. (See p. 261 above. Bell's key-word is the Irish *p'aper*.)

ɪ Voice-glide. Vocal murmur, = a non-syllabic effect of ʅ. (Non-syllabic ʅ ë implies a definite position—the mid-mixed-narrow, but it is also possible to make a voice-murmur in passing from one position to another, of so transient a character that it cannot be said to have any definite configuration. ɪ ought to be used to denote this sound only. Key-word, the English *va'ry*.)

ɪ Round-glide. Rounded murmur, = a non-syllabic effect of ʅ ö. (Compare the remarks on ɪ. Key-word, American and Cockney *now*. This is rather the ordinary English pronunciation.)

*ɪ Throat-glide. A semi-vowelized sound of ɵ ɹ, resembling the vowel ȷ *ɒ*. (This comparison is misleading, as there is no throat action in ȷ. The key-word given is a 'peculiar' pronunciation of *are*. Bell told me that my own pronunciation of the vowel *r* in *hear*, etc., was this throat-glide, but I believe it is simply a glide-ɪ *ä*.)

*ʑ Back-glide. A semi-vowelized sound of ϵ ʒ, resembling the vowel] ɐ or 1 ɯ. (Key-word, *are* = smooth burr.)

*ʑ Back-round-glide. A semi-vowelized sound of ϵ ʒ*w*, resembling the vowel } o. (Key-word, *our* = smooth burr labialized.)

*ӿ Front-glide. A semi-vowelized sound of ɷ j, resembling the vowel ʃ i. (Key-words, English *die*, *day*. The sound here is, of course, a glide-ʃ, not ʃ.)

*ӿ Front-round-glide. A semi-vowelized sound of ɷ with lip-modification, resembling the vowel f y. (Key-word, North Irish *new*.)

*ɤ Point-glide. A semi-vowelized sound of ω r, resembling the vowel ɪ ä. (Key-word, English *are*. This seems to be a compromise between Bell's half-Scotch, half-elocutionary pronunciation of the English vowel-*r* as ωv (without trill), and the ordinary glide-ɪ or ɪ pronunciation.)

*ɤ Point-round-glide. A semi-vowelized sound of ω, with lip-modification, resembling the vowel ɪ ɔ̈. (Key-word, English *our*.)

*ƨ Lip-glide. A semi-vowelized sound of ɜ β, resembling the vowel ɪ ü. (Key-word, French *lui*.)

*ƨ Lip-round-glide. A semi-vowelized sound of ɜ w, resembling the vowel ɪ u. (The combination of 'lip' and 'round' is, strictly speaking, a tautology: by 'rounding' Bell here implies *inner* rounding (see pp. 62–3). Key-word, English *now*, which seems to be generally pronounced with glide-ɫ or ɪ, Bell's ɪ.)

In Bell's nomenclature *glide* comes last: ƨ, lip-round-glide.

Vowels

Bell's definition of a vowel has been quoted already (p. 265).

Primary (my *narrow*) vowels are those which are most allied to consonants, the voice-channel being expanded only so far as to remove all fricative quality. The same organic adjustments form *wide* vowels when the resonance-cavity is enlarged behind the configurative aperture—the physical cause of wide quality being retraction of the soft palate, and expansion of the pharynx. (See pp. 50–1 where the distinction of narrow and wide is shown to depend on the shape of the *tongue*, and to apply to consonants also. The narrowing of *back* sounds appears, however, to be due to tension and consequent advancing of the uvula, often with a simultaneous sympathetic retraction of the tongue. The flexible soft palate has, therefore, the same function in the back of the mouth as the flexible front of the tongue has in the front of the mouth.)

The vowels are divided into three classes of palato-lingual formations, according as the oral cavity is moulded mainly by the *back*, the *front*, or the *mixed* (back and front) attitudes of the tongue.

The symbol of voice (I) is the basis or 'stem' of all the vowel letters. To this stem a *primary* or *wide* definer (p. 258 above) is joined, to the *inner* side for back, to the *outer* for front, and to *both sides* for mixed vowels.

Three degrees of elevation of the tongue in its back, front, or mixed attitudes are discriminated by the position of the definers on the vowel-stem. Thus:

	Primary			*Wide*		
	back	*mixed*	*front*	*back*	*mixed*	*front*
high	˥ ɯ	Ꭵ ï	ſ i	˥ *ɯ*	Ꭵ *ï*	ſ *i*
mid	] ɐ	ɭ ë	[e	] a	ɭ *ë*	[*e*
low	ȷ ɒ	ɪ ä	ɩ æ	ȷ *a*	ɪ *ä*	ɩ *æ*

(These) lingual positions yield another series of vowels when the voice-channel is 'rounded' and the apertures of the lips contracted. The mechanical cause of round quality commences in the super-glottal passage, and extends through the whole mouth-tube, by lateral compression of the buccal cavities and reduction of the labial aperture. The last—lip-modification—being the visible cause of round quality, is assumed as representative of the effect. The amount of lip-modification corresponds to the degree of elevation of the tongue: high vowels have the narrowest, low the broadest, and mid an intermediate aperture.

The lips are drawn *across the aperture* of a lingual vowel in order to round its quality; and the resulting effect is symbolized by a short line drawn *across the vowel-stem.*

	Primary			*Wide*		
	back	*mixed*	*front*	*back*	*mixed*	*front*
high	ƭ u	Ŧ ü	f y	ƭ *u*	Ŧ *ü*	f *y*
mid	} o	ƚ ö	{ ə	} *o*	ƚ *ö*	{ *ə*
low	ɟ ɔ	ɟ ɔ̈	ƫ œ	ɟ *ɔ*	ɟ *ɔ̈*	ƫ *œ*

The effect of rounding, not being dependent on the lips alone, is producible—with some peculiarity—without contraction of the labial aperture. The sign of 'inner' formation may be used to denote this mode of pronunciation. Thus ƭ} = *oo* rounded without the lips.

Other faintly different shades of vowel-sound are possible; as, for instance, from giving a greater or less than the ordinary or *symmetrical* degree of lip-modification. Even these delicate varieties may be perfectly expressed by the modifiers 'close' (∧), 'open' (∨), 'inner' (;), 'outer' (;), or by 'linked' symbols.

In naming the vowels height comes first, rounding last: ʅ mid-mixed-wide-round.

Linked Symbols

Peculiar oral combinations may be indicated at pleasure by writing two organic symbols with a 'link' (∘) between them, to show that they are to be pronounced simultaneously, not in succession. Thus, ω∘ɔ labialized *r*, ω∘c gutturalized *r*, etc. Any two elements may be thus linked, where a single symbol does not express the whole mechanism of a peculiar sound. Thus the low-back vowel linked to the lip-consonant (ɪ∘ɔ) would show close labial modification of a sound which, when normally rounded, is associated with a broad aperture of the lips.

Governing Signs

A pair of linked symbols within parentheses may be used as governing signs to denote *habitual* peculiarities of any kind, and thus save the writing of the latter at every instance of their occurrence. Thus the nasal sign or back consonant linked to any element will show a general nasalizing or gutturalizing of that particular sound, as (ω∘ʃ:) *l* nasal, (ω∘c:) *l* guttural.

A more general indication of such peculiarities, without reference to any specific element, will be furnished by writing the link before the nasal, etc., sign by itself, within parentheses, as (∘ɔ∧:) close lips, (∘ʃ:) general nasal quality.

Tones

– Level tone.
ˊ Simple rising inflexion.
ˋ Simple fall.
∨ Compound rise—falling and rising with a single impulse of voice.
∧ Compound fall—rising and falling with a single impulse of voice.

In the notation of tones no more is aimed at than the discrimination of the radical varieties. The types for tones being, however, reversible, may be used to indicate relative *pitch* as well as inflexion. Thus:

ɪˊ High-pitched rise.
ɪˏ Low-pitched rise.

Modulation or change of key, is symbolized by

⌐ Key elevated.
⌟ Key depressed.

Other Signs

ɵ Whistle.

Other alphabetic forms may be introduced to show the combinations cᵒɑ, cᵒʋ, etc., with excess of either element. The sign of trill, inner or outer formation, etc., may be similarly combined, by superposition, or otherwise, with the letter to which they refer.

Revised Organic Alphabet

General Principles

In the above exposition I have abstained as far as possible from criticism, only pointing out the more obvious errors of Bell's analysis for the reader's guidance. It will now be necessary to carry out our criticism in detail, in order to justify the alterations proposed. These alterations are of two kinds, (1) those which deal with the *shapes* of the letters, (2) those which are the result of difference of *analysis*.

Before entering on the details of the former class of alterations, it will be as well to make a few remarks on the principles of sound-symbolization from a purely graphic point of view. It is evident that the two main requisites are *distinctiveness* and *simplicity*, which are, to a certain extent, opposed to one another, this opposition becoming more and more marked as the number of letters increases. The co-existence of such letters as I l i in the Roman alphabet, and, to a less extent, of o c e, is a sin against distinctiveness, while such letters as g, Sanskrit ओ = *o*, or almost any one of the German capitals, are equally objectionable from the second point of view. The complexity of the Roman alphabet is enormously increased by its often having perfectly distinct forms for the same letter according as it is lower case, capital, or italic—a A *a*, g G *g*. It is evident that no forms can be more distinctive and, at the same time, simpler than those on which Visible Speech is mainly based—| ᵒ. The distinctiveness of Visible Speech is, however, limited by its principle of indicating the relations of the sounds by a corresponding resemblance between their symbols, so that, of course, the more closely allied two sounds are, the slighter will be the difference between their symbols. It has, for instance, been urged as an objection to Visible Speech that its distinction between narrow and wide is too minute. I do not believe that it is, but if it were—if the distinction between ſ and ſ were one which might easily escape a cursory reader—it is of little importance, the distinction not being meant for cursory readers, and the objectors forgetting that in ordinary Roman spelling, as in the English words *pick* and *pique*, the difference between narrow and wide is left absolutely unmarked.

The Roman alphabet has reached its present high standard of simplicity and clearness by a gradual process of wearing down and elimination extending over thousands of years, and it is interesting to observe that Visible Speech, although an independent and a-priorily constructed system, has many letters which are, as regards the elements they are composed of, identical with Roman ones. Thus the following Roman letters reappear almost or quite unchanged in Visible Speech: o c f *f* J I l *x*, while others contain the same elements: j e D U.

An objection which generally suggests itself to those unacquainted with Visible Speech is that the repetition of the same symbol turned different ways is confusing. To this it may be answered that exactly the same thing occurs in Roman, where b, d, p, q are distinguished solely by the direction of one and the same combination, which only requires to have its stem shortened to become the Visible Speech symbol of a stopped consonant.

If experience shows that any of the letters are not distinctive enough, it will be easy to add marks or make slight modifications, as long as they do not obscure the groundwork of the symbol. This is in fact already done in such pairs as ω, ɷ, where the divided consonant is beaded, to distinguish it still further from the open one.

We will now proceed to details, beginning with the purely formal alterations.

The most important and general one consists in a return to Bell's original plan of casting the consonants on oblong instead of square bodies, which requires twelve additional types, and making the vowels ascend and descend above and below the line, high vowels ascending, low descending, and mid both ascending and descending, which makes the vowel-symbols more distinctive, and, at the same time, informs the eye of the number of syllables in a letter-group. This naturally suggests a further reform, namely, to abolish Bell's vowel-glides, and make non-syllabic vowels of the same height as the consonants: thus ɑ]ɾ **kui**,]ɾ ***ai***, [ɪ **æu.** ɪ and ɪ̵ are retained.

Glide consonants are indicated by a following), thus ω) is a glide **l**, and ɷ) is exactly equivalent to ɾ. Glideless combination is indicated by ‿, thus ɑ‿ω is **kl** without any glide between the **k** and **l.**

In the consonants it has been found impossible to work with Bell's nasals, on account of the difficulty of distinguishing them from the corresponding stops, especially on a small scale. The difficulty lies in combining the three elements cıʃ in compact and distinctive symbols, allowing also for the addition of the voice-stroke. After many trials the simple remedy suggested itself of omitting the c altogether, combining the ı and ʃ, and indicating the place of the nasal by the direction of the ʃ, thus: ⅃ **q**, ⅃, **ɥ**, ⅂ **ṇ**, ⌐ **ṃ**, the voice-stroke being added thus: ⅃, ⅃, ⅂, ⌐. These forms are less elegant than the original ones, but are as simple, distinctive, and self-interpreting as is possible.

We now turn to those modifications and additions which have been made necessary by divergent analysis and increased knowledge.

In the consonants a special symbol for 'teeth' has been adopted, namely ∨, the angle being pictorial of the edges of the teeth. The other organs concerned in the production of a teeth consonant are indicated by the direction in which the symbol is turned: ∨ point-teeth **þ**, > lip-teeth **f**. To indicate the 'blade' position (see p. 39) the form s has been adapted from Bell's script, being regarded as a special combination of ∩ and ∪, implying an intermediate position. s being taken as blade, is reversed to symbolize blade-point: s **s**, s **z**, ꙅ **ʃ**, ꙅ **ʒ**. Those who disagree with Bell's analysis must regard s as a purely conventional and arbitrary sign, taken direct from the Roman alphabet, and ꙅ as an arbitrary modification of it.

The only one of Bell's 'mixed' consonants that has been retained is ɔ (and ɕ). The others have been superseded by the introduction of uniform modifiers, formed from segments of the curves for back, front, etc.: (back, ⟍ front, ⟍ point,) lip, ɒ lip-back, (ɕ back-lip), as in ω⟍ ***rj***, ⋒) ***jv***. The principle of providing modifiers for all the fundamental actions has been carried out consistently, the following being the remaining consonant-modifiers: ʂ blade, ı stop, ıı open, ɪ glottal stop. The first is formed from s, the last from x, while ıı is formed on the analogy of the existing ʜ (divided). ɪ after a consonant denotes simultaneous closure of the glottis ('implosion', see p. 162).

Bell's signs for inner and outer being liable to confusion with the nasal sign ʃ, ⊣ and ⊢ have been substituted, which are also turned upwards and downwards ⊥ and ⊤ to indicate raising and lowering, for which Bell has no sign, thus [⊣ inner **i**, [⊥ raised **i**.

Bell's symbolization of breath, whisper, and voice is in some respects rather arbitrary, and requires extension. This has been effected by various modifications of the o. o itself has been taken to signify breath without any oral modification, the breath-glide being symbolized by a smaller circle, thus ɑ° = Danish **kh**. When the breath-glide is simply a gliding devocalization of a following vowel, the same smaller circle is placed on a glide-vowel stem, thus ʂ] = ordinary **ha** (pp. 153 ff., 159 ff.). ° is a *stress*-glide (or aspiration), and to denote the ordinary stressless glide in English ***ka***, etc. which only requires to be written in very minute notation, a still smaller circle is used, as in ɑ°] (p. 160). The corresponding stressless voice-glide is symbolized by ˈ, a shortened voice-symbol, as in ɑˈ] (p. 160), ɐˈ]. These last two doubled, ꞉ˈ, are employed as modifiers, thus ʃ𝟹 voiceless **i.** From ɵ is formed the whisper-glide ◊ on the analogy of ᵒ, and the modifier ᴅ, thus ʃᴅ = whispered **i.**

The signs for in- and out-going breath, < and >, have been retained, but only as modifiers, Bell's breath-glide being expressed by ᵒ. Instead of Bell's dot it has been thought simpler to extend the ı to breath-stoppage also: ▹ emission-stopper, ◃ inhalation-stopper ('click').

The signs for closeness and openness, ʌ and v, have also been retained, but only in their strict applications. From them, the marks of syllabic stress have been formed, ^ and ˅, the latter signifying weak stress, the former strong. ^ is, for convenience, shortened into a simple point, as employed by Mr Ellis, (˙) being used for strong, (˙˙) for extra strong, (:) for half stress. To indicate non-syllabic force on an isolated element, these signs are lowered, ɑ‸J, the (‸) being employed in order to prevent confusion with the ordinary full stop. Lastly, from ^ and ˅ are formed modifiers ⩓ and ⩔ to symbolize narrowness and wideness respectively, ɜɔ⩓, for instance, being narrow **w.**

The holder ɫ is shortened (ˌ) to denote half-length, and this latter inverted (ˏ) is the sign of shortness, instead of Bell's arbitrary (ʿ).

⌣ between two symbols denotes absence of glide, and) shows that the preceding symbol is a glide. At first the plan of enclosing the symbol in ( ) was tried, but this was found cumbrous, and only the second half was retained.

As Bell's link is appropriated for breath, the sign + has been introduced to denote simultaneousness. * is used as a general modifier to indicate that the preceding symbol is not to be read literally, but with some implied modification.

The following are the main principles that have been followed in the above alterations and extensions: (1) to avoid isolated symbols, as in the abandonment of Bell's breath-glide and mark of shortness; (2) to provide separate modifying-symbols for all the organic actions; (3) to make the modifiers thinner than the corresponding full symbols; (4) glides, etc., being made into modifiers by doubling.

Other symbols (especially those whose adoption requires further consideration) will be described hereafter.

In the present imperfect state of our knowledge of intonation, Bell's symbols will suffice for general purposes.

Detailed List of Symbols

General Symbols

Modifiers naturally *follow* the letter they refer to. An exception may often be made in the case of *tones*, which generally apply to groups of sounds, not merely to single ones. When several are applied to one letter, that one which is associated most intimately with it comes first. Thus the symbols of quantity and stress come after the more special ones of rounding, closeness, elevation, etc., as ത)ɫ, ωʃ˙, ωʃʌɫ˙, stress-marks following those of quantity. When modifiers are applied to *groups* of sounds, such as a sentence or paragraph, they must be written before them, either in the way indicated above (p. 269), or else simply by prefixing the symbol, which must then be separated a little from the first letter of the group it modifies. Thus the sentence *come up!* might be written ʃ ɑ]ꟳ]ɒ, ɫ ɑ]ꟳ]ɒ, according as it is uttered with nasality, slowly, quickly, energetically, etc. If the prefixed modifier is meant to apply only to a *portion* of the group, the point where its application ceases can be marked by repeating it with the stop-symbol after it, thus ʃı would indicate cessation of nasality.

* *general modifier*. (See p. 273.) Used wherever a special modifier is not provided or is inconvenient, or else to indicate doubtful or imperfectly analysed modifications. Thus ᴗ* = any variety of English **þ**, such as the Danish ᴗ\, Jʃ* ***a*** with some peculiar form of nasality. Retained in Romic.

+ *link* denotes simultaneity. Thus ω+ത palatalized **r**. Not much required in the revised alphabet, which provides special modifiers, the above sound, for instance, being written ω\. The final consonant in English *open* (p. 165) is ꟳ+ꞁ, which with the modifiers would be written ꞁ+)ɒꞁ)ı. Retained in Romic.

ɫ ɫ ɫ *quantity*. ɫ = full, ɫ half length, and ɫ ordinary shortness, usually left unmarked. Extra length or drawl is indicated by ɫɫ, extra shortness or abruptness by ɫɫ, intermediate quantities by ɫɫ between full and half, ɫɫ between half and short, etc. In Romic **ɪ** may be used, but as this is liable to confusion with *i*, a simple stroke is better, which may be cut in two, and inverted, just like ɫ: it may be regarded as the stroke of *ā*, etc. written separate. (*Fn.*: In this paper I have temporarily used the Organic stop-symbol ı.)

˙ ˅ ˄ ˅ *force*. Only a few of these are required in ordinary writing: (˙) strong stress, (:) half-strong or medium, and (˙ ˙) extra-strong. Intermediate degrees can be indicated by (˙:) between strong and medium, (:˅) between medium and weak, etc. Very weak (evanescent) would be indicated by (˅˅), (˅), weak being hardly ever required. All these denote *syllabic* stress, the mark being placed immediately after that member of the syllable on which the stress begins, as in Iꞁ˙[Iꟳ 'a name', Iꞁ[˙Iꟳ 'an aim' (p. 144). Of the corresponding marks of absolute, or non-syllabic force, (˯), weak, is hardly ever required, and (˰) not very often.

The latter might be employed in monosyllables, and also in polysyllables, to show that one member of a syllable is uttered with exceptional force, but without altering the general force of the whole syllable as compared with that of the other syllables in the group. In Romic (.) must be used for (˄), the negative degrees (˅ ˬ) being left unmarked.

‿]) *glides* (retained in Romic). ‿, denoting glideless combination, is required in such words as the English ꞁɑ‿ʊ *act* as distinguished from the normal ꞁɑʊ = ꞁɑ°ʊ, which is the French pronunciation. In such combinations as ɔʊ **nd**, ɷʊ **ld**, the glidelessness is implied in the juxtaposition of the elements. In the vowels it has been found necessary to distinguish syllabic (such as ɽ) from the non-syllabic or glide-vowels (such as ɾ). The term 'glide', as applied to the second element of such a diphthong as]ɾ **ai**, is not absolutely correct, for the ɾ can be lengthened indefinitely, if only the continuity of stress is observed (p. 155), and it is not till we begin a new stress on the second element that monosyllabic]ɾ becomes dissyllabic]ɽ. The rigorously correct definition of ɾ is, therefore, *non-syllabic* vowel, implying weak stress, and generally also shortness and transitional configuration, on which latter the term 'glide-vowel' is founded. A consonant is generally non-syllabic, hence ɱ˕ is practically identical with ɾ. Many of the combinations in which consonants appear as 'syllabics' do not require any special marking, as in ɑꞁʊɷ *cattle*, which can be pronounced only in one way. Sometimes, however, a 'syllabic-former' is required. For this purpose] may be used, to be regarded as a special modification of the vowel-stem ɪ, a syllabic consonant being an approximation to a vowel. Thus in ꜰɱɷɑ *milk* either of the two liquids might take the syllabic stress and become syllabic, but the actual pronunciation is ꜰɱɷ]ɑ. (I used to analyse this word as ꜰɱꞁɷɑ **mj*u*lk**, misled by the frequent rounding of the liquid, which is often ɷɒ **l*w***.) Practically, however, this word is unambiguous, because ꜰɱ]ɷɑ would naturally be written ꜰɽɷɑ, or, at most, ꜰɽʌɷɑ, if the consonantal narrowing were very marked. When it is necessary to emphasize the gliding, non-syllabic character of a consonant, the 'glide-former' or non-syllabic modifier) is used. Thus the English *try* is strictly ʊʋ)ɷ˥ɾ. This sign may be usefully employed to distinguish between the length of a diphthongic vowel and the length of the transition between the preceding full vowel and it. Thus]ɾ· denotes actual lengthening of the second element, while]ɾ·) implies that the transition or glide between the two positions is made slowly. It will be observed that these symbols do not distinguish with absolute strictness between non-syllabicness and gliding, which it is, indeed, often very difficult to do. The distinction could be made, if necessary, by retaining) in the former value, and indicating glides in the strict sense by smaller sizes of the non-syllabic vowels and of the ordinary consonants. At present it is safer to err on the side of vagueness.

> (!), < (¡), ▹ (?), ◃ (¿), *breath-directors.* Of these the out-breather or expiration-sign > is hardly ever required, being implied in ordinary writing. The in-breather or inhalation-sign < must, of course, be written when required. ▹ ◃ imply respectively outwards and inwards motion of the air in the mouth without out- or in-breathing. The latter is the click-sign, as in ʊ◃, the ordinary *tut!* ▹ denotes what Mr A. G. Bell (*Visible Speech*, p. 126) calls an 'expulsive' click. Thus ɑ▹ would imply **k**-position with shut glottis and throat-contraction, and consequent percussive escape of the squeezed air when the ɑ is relaxed. All these signs are modifiers.

Cessation of breath is indicated by the breath-glide followed by the stop symbol, °ı, which, if necessary, may be combined in one symbol. Thus ʖɑ°ı **ak** without 'recoil'.

∧ ∨ (^{1} ₁), *close, open.* These signs must be carefully distinguished from those of force. A **j** formed with the front of the tongue as near the palate as possible, ɷ∧, may be uttered with any degree of force, as also the relaxed ɷ∨, which is practically equivalent to ɾ **i** or ɾ ***i***. Closeness and openness, are, on the other hand, closely related to raising and lowering respectively, ɷ∧ being practically equivalent to ɷ⊥. In the case of the back sounds they are generally more nearly related to retraction.

∧̂ ∨̌ (^{11} ₁₁), *narrow, wide.* Occasionally required for consonants. Thus ɜ∧̂ = the consonantized ʇ or ʇ, in French *oui*, ɜ∨̌ = English *w*. Also occasionally required for the glides ɪ (ʌ) and ɪ (ʌ*w*), whose narrowness is generally left undecided.

⊥ ⊤ (^{1} ₁), *raised, lowered* ⊣ ⊢ (, ͺ) *inner, outer.* [⊥ raised Danish **e**, ʖ⊢ advanced Danish **a**. The normal positions may be emphasized by employing both signs of either pair, thus [⊥⊤ the normal French **e**. The vertical and horizontal modifiers can be combined, thus [⊥⊣ **e** raised and retracted at the same time. These combinations could be effected by making the horizontal stems of ⊣ and ⊢ point obliquely upwards or downwards to indicate simultaneous raising or lowering.

ᴄ ɔ (ɟ ɫ), *inversion, protrusion.* ʊᴄ inverted (cerebral) **t**, ʊɔ **t** formed on the lips. With a lip-sound ɔ may be used to indicate lip-pouting, thus ʇɔ Scotch or German **u**. Different degrees may be distinguished by doubling the symbols or combining them with ⊣ and ⊢.

(\ \ ) ɒ (*x, j, ɟ, v, w*), *back, front, point, lip, lip-back modifiers.* The last is exactly parallel to ɜ, implying inner rounding. ɯ(gutturalized **l**, ɯ\ palatalized **r**, ʖ) muffled **a**, distinct from ʇ = ʖɒ. A special application of) is to denote abnormal degrees of vowel-rounding. Thus the Swedish **o** may be written ʇ), implying one degree more of rounding.

Further distinctions may be made by doubling the) or adding ʌ or v. Observe that) is written, not ⟩, because the inner rounding is implied in the vowel symbol itself. Defective rounding is symbolized by adding ⟩ to the symbol of the unrounded vowel, thus l⟩ = l with low-rounding = Swedish short *u*. Absence of inner rounding may be emphasized by writing)⊦, and varieties of inner rounding by)⊣, ⟩⊣, ⟩⊦. The point-modifier is required in writing vowels into which an inverted **r** is incorporated (see p. 69), as in the Kentish *sparrow* = SDJ⫲ɩc.

ʂ (*s*) *blade-modifier*. A **t** formed by stopping an **s** would be written Ʊʂ, a position intermediate to **s** and **ʃ** would be written Sʂ. In Romic it could be expressed by *ʃs*.

ɪ ǁ ʜ ᵘ (ɥ, ʎ, §§, §) *stopped, open, divided, unilateral modifiers*. ᵘ is applied to vowels as well as consonants, as in Ɪᵘ, where it implies unilateral rounding. The other modifiers are not much required, being incorporated in the ordinary symbols. Ʊʂ might also be written Sɪ. ɪ is also used without ambiguity in a wider sense to denote cessation of breath, etc. (pp. 274, 276). ǁ may be applied to vowels to denote the converse of rounding, [ǁ for instance = **i** with spread lips, the neutral English vowel being emphasized by writing [ǁ).

ʃ ʂ (*n*, *r*) *nasal, trill modifiers*. The strong French nasality can be distinguished as ʃv. According to Storm (*Englische Philologie*, p. 36) the nasal vowels in Polish assume before dentals a dental, before labials a labial character, as in *pęnta Dąbrowski*, which can be indicated by writing ʃ\, ʃ).

o ᵒ ° ϱ ꞉ (**h***h*, **h**, **h**, **h**, *h*) *breath-consonant, strong breath-glide*, or *aspirate, weak breath-glide, vowel breath-glide, breath-modifier*. See p. 272.

I Ɨ ˈ ⁝ (ʌ, ʌ*v*, ', ɑ) *voice-glide, voice-glide round, weak voice-glide, voice modifier*. See p. 272. ⁝ may be used to express various degrees of vocality, as in C⁝, Є⁝, as opposed to the normal Є or Є⁝꞉.

X ʎ (; ,·) *throat-stop, throat-stop modifier*. See p. 272.

O Ө ᴏ D (ɹ̣, ɹ, '', ') *throat-open cons., throat-open voice, whisper-glide, whisper-modifier*. See p. 273. ' is added to the voice symbol, thus **n**' = ꓶD. It does not seem possible to reproduce the distinction between ᵒ and ° in the voice and whisper series, on account of the obstruction of the breath and consequent difficulty of differentiating the force of its outgoing. The voiced whisper-glide ᴏ⁝, if pronounced strongly enough to be distinguishable from simple ˈ, becomes practically equivalent to the full consonantal Ө, and hence no special symbol has been provided for it.

It will be observed that O and its modifications are ambiguous, being, in fact, general signs for all throat-actions except those which produce voice. The difficulties of practical discrimination make it safest to retain Bell's comparatively vague symbols for the present.

Vowels

ʅ ɯ high-back-narrow. Armenian ʅs *the*.

ʅ *ɯ* high-back-wide.

] ɐ mid-back-narrow. English *up*.

] a mid-back-wide. English and Italian *a*. The English sound is nearly]ɪɪ: the evanescence of the glide-vowel may be expressed by writing]ɪɪ).

ɹ ɒ low-back-narrow. Vulg. London *park*, Dutch *land*.

ɹ *a* low-back-wide. Sc. *man*, Fr. *â*, ɹʃ Fr. *an*.

ɪ ï high-mixed-narrow. Russian *y*, Welsh *u*, Sw. dialectal *i* in *Viby*, all fall under this vowel, the first two being apparently identical. The last is apparently retracted ɪ˧, the *y* in *Viby* being ɪ˧), with outer rounding only, distinct from ɪ. But I cannot speak with certainty about these Swedish sounds, for which see Lundell, *Landsmålsalfabetet*.

ɪ *ï* high-mixed-wide.

ʅ ë mid-mixed-narrow. American ʅɾʋ *earth*. Bell writes this American diphthong with ɪ, but repeated hearing has convinced me that he is wrong. German, etc., unacc. *e* in *gabe* is, perhaps, sometimes ʅ, its shortness making recognition difficult.

ʅ *ë* mid-mixed-wide. E. ʅɾ˕ *eye*.

ɪ ä low-mixed-narrow. E. ɪɪʋ *earth*.

ɪ *ä* low-mixed-wide. E. ƨɪɪ *how*. South German *käse*, etc., seems to have this vowel (ɑˈɪɪs) rather than ɪ.

ɾ i high-front-narrow. Fr. *fini*, Sc. *sick*. ɾʃ Portug. *sim*.

ɾ *i* high-front-wide. E. >ɾɔɾ˕ *finny*.

[e mid-front-narrow. Fr. *été*. [˔ Danish *se*.

[*e* mid-front-wide. E. *pen*. Fr. père.

ɩ æ low-front-narrow. Sc. *men*. ɩʃ Fr. *vin*.

ɩ *æ* low-front-wide. E. *man*.

ɫ u high-back-narrow. Fr. *sou*. Sc. *book*. ʅ) Sw. *kung*. ɫʃ Port. *um*.

ɫ *u* high-back-wide. E. *book*.

} o mid-back-narrow. Fr. *beau*. }) Sw. Dan. *sol*. }˔) Norw. *sol*.

} *o* mid-back-wide. E. *owe*, *boy*. Fr. *or*. North G. *gott*. }ʃ Fr. *on*.

ɟ ɔ low-back-narrow. E. *law*, almost ɷɟɪɪ. ɟ) Norw. *så*. ɟ)ᐯ Dan., ɟ)ʌ Sw. *så*.

ɟ ɔ low-back-wide. E. *not*. ɟ) Sw. *hopp* (?).

ɪ ü high-mixed-narrow. Norw. *hus*. ɪ˫ Sw. *hus*.

ɪ *ü* high-mixed-wide. Vulg. E. ʊɪɪɪ) (two).

ɫ ö mid-mixed-narrow.

ɫ *ö* mid-mixed-wide. Fr. *dot.*
ɪ̶ *ɔ̈* low-mixed-narrow.
ɪ̶ *ɔ̈* low-mixed-wide. Sw. dialectal *son.*
f y high-front-narrow. Fr. *lune.* ʃ) Sw. *y.*
f *y* high-front-wide. Germ. *hütte.*
ɟ ə mid-front-narrow. Fr. *peu.*
ɟ *ə* mid-front-wide. Fr. *peur.*
ɪ œ low-front-narrow. Sw. *höra.* ɪʃ Fr. *un.*
ɪ *œ* low-front-wide.

Glide-vowels

ɪ ʌ voice-glide. E. ϱʃɪɪ *here.*
ɪ ʌ*v* voice-glide-round. E. ϱɪɪɪ *how.*

These symbols imply a transitional murmur without fixed configuration. In deliberate utterance the above words might be written ϱʃɪɪ, ϱɪɪɪ. ɪ might be written in the slurred pronunciation of *against*—ɪɑʃɜsʊ.

The other glide-vowels being simply the full vowel symbols shortened, do not require to be enumerated.

Consonants

o ɹ throat (-open-breath). oʃʌ = Arabic *hha* (?).
ɵ ɹ throat-voice. ɵɔ = Dan. *r.* ɵʃʌ = Arabic *ain* (?).
x ; throat-stop (glottal catch). Danish 'stödtone'.
c x back. Sc. and Germ. *loch.*
є ʒ back-voice. Middle Germ. *tage.* є(*s*) = Germ. *r.*
ი ç front. Sc. *hue.* Germ. *ich.* ი) Germ. *züchtig.* ი+ɔ South Sw. *skepp.*
ന j front-voice. E. *yes.*
ʊ r̥ point. ʊʃ = Icel. *hr.*
ω r point-voice. E. *red.* ωʃ = Sc. *red.* ω\ Russ. *rĭ.* The Sw. 'thick' *l* (p. 167) may be symbolized by ωcн, implying an attempt to combine ωc and ω. The Japanese *r* (p. 167) is ω)ω.

s s blade. E. *hiss.* sʃ is apparently the German *s* in *stein.* s\ Russ. *sĭ.* sc Sw. *kors.*

ꞩ z blade-voice. E. *is.*
ꝛ ʃ blade-point. E. *fish.* ꝛ) Germ. *sch.* ꝛ\ Polish *ś*, Norw. *sjæl.*
ꝛ ʒ blade-point-voice. E. *measure.*
ᴗ þ point-teeth. E. *thin.*
ᴗ ð point-teeth-voice. E. *then.* ᴗ\ Dan. *gud.*
ɔ ɸ lip. Romaic *ϕ* (?).
ɘ β lip-voice. Middle and South Germ. *w.*
> f lip-teeth. >\ Russ. *krovĭ.*

ɜ **v** lip-teeth-voice.
ɛ **ɫ** back-divided.
ɛ **ɫ** back-divided voice. Russian and Polish guttural *l.*
ɞ **l̥** front-divided.
ɞ *l* front-divided-voice. Italian *gl.*
ω **l̥** point-divided. Icel. *hl.* ω Welsh *ll.*
ω **l** point-divided-voice. English *l.* ω(Dutch *l.* ω\ French *l.*
ɜ **ɸ*** lip-divided.
ɜ **β*** lip-divided-voice.
ɑ **k** back-stop. ɑ\ older E. *kind.* ɑ Russ. *komnata.*
ɑ **ǵ** back-stop-voice.
ɑ **c** front-stop. ɑ = Russian *tĭ.*
ɑ **ɟ** front-stop-voice. ɑ = Russian *dĭ.*
ʊ **t** point-stop. ʊ Fr. *tête.* ʊ Sw. *kort.*
ʊ **d** point-stop-voice.
ɒ **p** lip-stop. ɒ Germ. *p* in *pfund.*
ɒ **b** lip-stop-voice.
ɹ **q̥** back-nasal.
ɹ **q** back-nasal-voice. E. *sing.*
ɭ **ŋ̰** front-nasal.
ɭ **ñ** front-nasal-voice. Ital. *gn.*
ʇ **n̥** point-nasal. Icel. *hn.*
ʇ **n** point-nasal-voice.
ɼ **m̥** lip-nasal.
ɼ **m** lip-nasal-voice.
ɕ **x*w*** back-lip. Germ. *auch.*
ɛ **ʒ*w*** back-lip-voice. Germ *auge.*
ɔ **ʍ** lip-back. E. *wh.*
ɔ **w** lip-back-voice. E. *w.*

Revised Romic

The general principles of the Revised Romic notation here employed have been already indicated in outline.

The main distinction between this notation and the older one used in my *Handbook* is the introduction of diacritical letters and new types whenever they are already in existence, italics being restricted as much as possible to the function of modifiers, which are made as complete as possible, so as to facilitate the symbolization of new sounds. Capitals have been eliminated entirely, because they are often not provided for several founts, and because they do not readily admit of diacritical modification; but they may, when convenient, still be employed to denote special sounds. When italics fail as modifiers, punctuation and other marks are employed, as by Mr Ellis, though necessarily with frequent deviations from his usage.

The main improvement in the vowels has been the consistent symbolizing of the mixed vowels by two dots above the corresponding front open, and back round vowels, **ä** and ***ä*** being for the sake of convenience used instead of dotted **æ** and ***æ***. A single dot may be used to denote intermediate positions, thus **ȧ** =]ʜ. **ʌ** and **ᴀ** have been superseded by **ɯ** and ***ɯ***, which at once suggest relationship with **u** and ***u***.

In the consonants the use of **β**, **ç**, **ð**, **ʒ**, **ɫ**, **ñ**, **ɸ**, **ʃ**, **þ**, **ʒ**, taken from the Anglo-Saxon, Greek, and various European alphabets, and from Pitman's Phonotypy, is self-evident. **x** is used in preference to **χ**, as its italic ***x*** gives the necessary back-modifier. For the fronts the **c** and **ç** of Sanskrit transliteration recommend themselves, while the turned **ɟ** is convenient for ɷ, being readily associated with **j**. The voiceless and front liquids and nasals offer great difficulties, which have been more or less successfully overcome by a combination of turning and dotting, the latter being familiar in Sanskrit transliteration. It was impossible to carry out either of these methods exclusively, because some liquids, such as **w**, are not provided with dots, while **n** cannot be inverted. ɷ and ɷ offer the greatest difficulty, and the only resource has been to fall back on italics.

Details will be best seen in the following (as near as possible) alphabetical list, in which turned follow unturned, italic unitalic, modified unmodified, and foreign the nearest native letters. When a turned letter, however, suggests associations with some other letter, it follows that letter; thus **ɔ** follows **o**. The organic equivalents are not repeated where symbols are identical in both systems. The forms in brackets are optional ones.

a =]
ɐ =]
a = ȷ
ɒ = ȷ
æ = ɩ
æ = ɩ
ä = ɪ
ä = ɪ
b = ɒ
β = ɜ
c = ɑ
ç = ɑ
d = ʊ

ð = ᴗ [δ]
e = [
ə = ɛ
e = [
ə = ɛ
ë = ɭ
ë = ɭ
f = >
ġ = ɑ
ʒ = ϵ [ɣ]
h = °, ♀
h = ჵ
h*h* = o [H]

ʎ = ‖
i = ſ
i = ſ
ï = ɪ̈
ï = ɪ̈
j = ⊂
j = \
ɟ = ⊂
k = ɑ
ʞ = ı
l = ω
l = ω
l̥ = ω
l̥ = ω
ɫ = ɛ
ɫ̥ — ɛ
m = ꟻ
m̥ = ɼ
n = ʒ
n = ʃ
n̥ = ʒ
ñ = ɩ
ŋ = ɩ
o = ʒ
ɔ = ɟ
o = ʒ
ɔ = ɟ
œ = ɬ
œ = ɬ
ö = ɬ
ɔ̈ = ɟ [ɔ̈]
ö = ɬ
ɔ̈ = ɟ [ɔ̈]
p = ɒ
ɸ = ɔ
q = ɟ
q̥ = ɹ
r = ω
r = ʃ
ɹ = ɵ
r̥ = ʊ
ɹ̥ = ɵ

s = s
s = ʃ
ʃ = ɛ [ʃ]
t = ʊ
t = \
þ = ∪ [θ]
u = ɫ
u = ɫ
ü = ɫ
ü = ɫ
ɯ = 1
ɯ = 1
v = ɜ
ʌ = ɪ
v =)
ʌ = ¦
w = ɜ
ʍ = ɔ
w = ɒ
x = c
x = (
y = f
y = f
z = ɜ
ʒ = ɛ
(a)ı = ♦ [aa, aɪ]
a·
a. = ʒ^
a:
a, = ʒ˧
aˌ = ʒ˫
(') = ˈ
z' = sɒ
; = χ
,· = χ [:]
! = ˃
¡ = ˂
? = ▹
¿ = ◃
)
]
‿

*	a_1 =]ᐩ
⸸ = c	j_{11} = ⅏ᵥ̌
† = ɔ	r+*j* = ω+⅏
§ = ꟷ	= (See p. 132)
§§ = H	<
a^1 =]⊥	>
j^{11} = ⅏̂	

General List of Symbols

Vowels and Glide-vowels

ʅı ɯ	Ɪɪ ï	ʃɾ i	ʅı *ɯ*	Ɪɪ *ï*	ʃɾ *i*
]ɔ ɐ	ʅı ë	[c e	]ɔ a	ʅı *ë*	[c *e*
JJ ɒ	ɪɪ ä	ʅɩ æ	JJ *a*	ɪɪ *ä*	ʅɩ *æ*
ıŧ u	Ŧŧ ü	fŧ y	ıŧ *u*	Ŧŧ *ü*	fŧ *y*
}ɟ o	ŧŧ ö	fŧ ə	}ɟ *o*	ŧŧ *ö*	fŧ *ə*
JJ ɔ	ɪɪ ɔ̈	ŧŧ œ	JJ *ɔ*	ɪɪ *ɔ̈*	ŧŧ *œ*

General Symbols

*	+	ɸ	ɵ	ɋ	•	:	ᵛ
ᴧ (.)	ᵛ	=	<	>	‿	]	)
> !	< ¡	▹ ?	◃ ¿	∧ (¹)	∨ (₁)	⩓ (¹¹)	⩔ (₁₁)
⊥ (¹)	⊤ (₁)	⊣ (,)	⊢ (‘)	c ⸸	ɔ †	(*x*	∖ *j*
∖ *ɟ*	) *v*	ɞ *w*	ʂ *s*	ǀ *ʞ*	ǁ *ʎ*	H §§	ꟷ §
ʃ *n*	ʂ *r*	∘ h	♀ h	∘ h)	⸰ *h*	I ʌ	
Ŧ ʌv	ˈ (’)	¦ *ɑ*	⟩ ,·	◊ (‘’)	▷ (‘)		

Consonants

ɵ ɹ̣	c x	∩ ç	∪ ṛ	∪ þ	s s	ƨ ʃ	ɔ ɸ	ɜ ʍ	> f
o h*h*	ε ɫ̣	ɷ *l̩*	ω l̥	ω l̥,			з ɸ*		
χ ;	ɑ k	ɒ c	ʊ t	ʊ t,			ɒ p		
	ɹ q̣	ɩ ŋ̰	ɿ ṇ	ɿ ṇ,			ɼ m̥		

ɵ ɹ	ϵ ʒ	ⴰ j	ɯ r	ɯ ð	ȣ z	ɛ ʒ	ɘ β	ɜ w	ɜ v
	ɛ ɫ	ɷ *l*	ω l	ω l,			з β*		
	ɑ g	ɒ ɟ	ϖ d	ϖ d,			ɒ b		
	ɹ q	ɩ ñ	ɿ n	ɿ n,			ɼ m		

All the organic symbols are printed from the following types:

40 *Vowels and Glide-vowels*

lı	Iɪ	ʃɾ	]ɔ	ɭı	lı	Iɪ	ʃɾ	]ɔ	ɭı
łɨ	Ɨɨ	ʄɟ	]ɜ	ɬɨ	łɨ	Ɨɨ	ʄɟ	]ɜ	ɬɨ

39 *General Symbols*

*	+	ɸ	ɨ	·	:	(ᵛ)
(ᵥ)	‿	]	)	>		
▹	∧	^̬	⊥	⊣	c	(
\	ɔ	ʂ	ǀ	ǁ	ʜ	ɥ
ʃ	ʒ	o	Ω	°	⸰	I
Ɨ	ˈ	⁝	⟩	◊	ᴅ	

30 *Consonants*

o	ɵ	c	∩	∪	s	ƨ	ꝯ	›
ɛ	ɷ		χ	ɑ	Ω	ɺ	ɭ	
	θ	ϵ	ʘ	ψ	ꞩ	ɞ	ꝯ̵	⋝
ɛ̵	ɷ̵			ɑ̵	Ω̵	ɺ̵	ɭ̵	

109 types in all, from which 177 single characters are printed.

'Sound Notation', *Transactions of the Philological Society*, 1880–1, pp. 177–235; in *Collected Papers of Henry Sweet*, pp. 294–330

Symbol Index

Organic symbols

A comprehensive index of these will be found on pp. 278–85.

Romic symbols

In the following index of Romic symbols, the order of the entries largely follows Sweet's own conventions (see p. 281): modified letters follow unmodified, double follow single, turned follow unturned, italic follow roman, capitals follow italics, new or foreign letters (e.g. Greek) follow the nearest roman letters.

The abbreviations used are: HB = *Handbook of Phonetics*, SN = 'Sound Notation' in *TPS* 1880–1, HES = *History of English Sounds*, PSE = *Primer of Spoken English*, PP = *Primer of Phonetics* (usually the 1906 edition), NEG = *New English Grammar*, PSL = *The Practical Study of Languages*, HL = *The History of Language*, SE = *The Sounds of English*, EB = 'Phonetics' in the *Enc. Brit.* of 1911, MP = articles in *Le Maître phonétique*, (BR) = Broad Romic, (NR) = Narrow Romic. In the abbreviated descriptions of vowels h = 'high', l = 'low', f = 'front', b = 'back', n = 'narrow', w = 'wide', r = 'round', o = 'out-shifted', i = 'in-shifted', m = 'mid' if in first place, 'mixed' if not in first place, e.g. m.m.n. = 'mid-mixed-narrow'. The following abbreviations are used in the examples: Ar. = Arabic, Dan. = Danish, F. = French, G. = German, Ice. = Icelandic, Ir. = Irish, It. = Italian, MG. = Middle German, N. = Norwegian, NG. = North German, Ru. = Russian, Sc. = Scotch, SG. = South German, Sp. = Spanish, Sw. = Swedish, Vulg. = 'vulgar'. IPA = the International Phonetic Alphabet.

a	HB, EB f*a*ther, SN m.b.w.; elsewhere b*u*t
ä	SN, HES, PP, SE s*ir*
a^{2} / **a**^{ɔ}	PP, SE m.o.b.n.
ä$_{2}$ / **ä**^{c}	PP, SE l.i.m.n. (Ir. s*ir*)
aa	f*a*ther (BR)
ae	*ai*r (BR)
ai	h*i*gh, *wi*ne (BR)
ao	HB f*a*ll (BR)
au	n*o*w, h*ou*se
ɐ	HB, SN, NEG, b*u*t; HES, PP Cockney p*a*rk; SE occ. F. p*a*s
ɐ^{2} / **ɐ**^{ɔ}	PP, SE l.o.b.n.
a	HB Sc. f*a*ther; SN Sc. m*a*n; elsewhere f*a*ther
ä	SN, HES, PP, SE h*o*w
a^{2} / ***a***^{c}	PP, SE m.b.o.w. (*u*p, *e*ye)

Symbol	Use
ä$_2$ / *ä*^{c}	PP, SE l.i.m.w.
aq	HB F. *en*
ɑ	MP as in IPA
ɒ	HB l.b.n.; SN Cockney park; HES Sw. m*a*t; PP Dan. m*a*t; SE F. p*as*
ɒ^2 / ɒ^ɔ	PP, SE l.o.b.w. (Dan. m*a*ne)
ᴀ	HB h.b.w. (superseded by ɯ in SN, and elsewhere by ʌ)
ᴠ	HB h.b.n. (superseded by ɯ in SN, and elsewhere by ʌ)
æ	*ai*r, Sc. m*e*n, Sw. l*ä*ra (NR); m*a*n (BR)
æ$_2$ / æ^c	PP, SE l.i.f.n. (Sw. l*ä*r)
æh	HB b*ir*d
æ*n*	HL F. v*in*
æ*q*	HB F. v*in*
æ	m*a*n
æ$_2$ / *æ*^{c}	PP, SE l.i.f.w.
*æ*h	HB l.m.w.
*æ*hoh / *æ*hʌ*w*	HB h*ow*
b	*b*ee
bh	HB SG *w*ie, Sp. sa*b*er (later β)
bh*j*	HB palatalized **bh** F. l*u*i
bh*r*	HB lip-trill
β	SN SG *w*
β*	SN lip-divided
β*j*	NEG F. h*u*it
c	HB *ch*ur*ch* (BR); HES, EB Hu. *ty*úk; MP suggested for G. i*ch*
ç	SN, EB G. i*ch*
[ɔ	after o]
d	*d*ay
dh	HB *th*en (later ð)
dh*j*	HB palatalized **dh**
ᴅ	HB Hu. Ma*gy*ar (later ɟ)
ð	*th*en
δ	variant of ð
dzh	HB *j*u*dg*e (later dʒ)
dʒ	*j*u*dg*e
e	F. *é*t*é*; m*e*n (BR)
ë	HES, PP G. gab*e*; SE Sc. b*e*tter

Symbol	Use
ẽ	PSL F. vi*en*s
e^I	HB **e** with raised tongue
ë$_2$ / ë^c	PP, SE m.i.m.n.
eh	HB G. gab*e*
ei	HB f*ai*l (BR); PSE, PP, SE, EB s*ay*, v*ei*l
e*i*h	HB f*ai*l (NR)
eə	PP, SE *care*, *air*
ə	HB F. p*eu* (NR), b*u*d (BR); SN, HES, PP, SE F. p*eu* (NR); PSE, PP, PSL, HL, SE, *to*geth*er*, sof*a*, *u*pon (BR); EB f*ur*th*er*
ə$_2$ / ə^c	PP, SE m.i.f.n.r. (Sc. g*ui*d)
əə	b*ir*d (BR)
əi	PSE twil*igh*t
əu	PSE comp*ou*nd
e	HB Dan. tr*æ*; SN, HES, PP, NEG m*e*n
ë	HES *eye*, bett*er*; PP, SE bett*er*
e$_2$ / *e*^{c}	PP, SE m.i.f.w.
ë$_2$ / *ë*^{c}	PP, SE m.i.m.w.
*e*h	HB m.m.w.
*e*h*i*h	HB *eye*
ə	HB NG sch*ö*n; SN, HES F. p*eu*r; PP m.f.w.r.
ə$_2$ / *ə̈*^{c}	PP, SE m.i.f.w.r.
ɛ	PSL F. pl*ai*t; EB th*ere*
ɛə	PSE, PSL *care*
f	*f*i*f*e
ɟ	SN front-stop-voice; HES, EB Hu. *gy*
g	*g*o
gh	HB G. ta*g*e
gh*r*	HB F. '*r* grasseyé', Northumbrian *r*
gh*w*	HB G. zu*g*e (labialized **gh**)
g*j* / ɢ	HB palatalized **g**
ɣ	SN 'variant of ʒ'; HL G. sa*g*e
ʒ	SN, HES, NEG G. ta*g*e
ʒ*w*	SN G. au*g*e
h	*h*ouse; HB (i) breath-modifier (BR), (ii) mixed

Symbol	Meaning
	vowel sign; SN breath-glide, the aspirate
h*h*	SN breath consonant
ɥ	MP as in IPA
h	HB, SN, SE breath-modifier (NR); HES, NEG mark of voicelessness
H	HB the aspirate
[H]	HB breath-glide
Hh	HB breath, open glottis
i	F. *fini* (NR); b*i*t (BR)
ĭ	PSE cit*y*
ï	Welsh *u*
i_2, iᶜ	PP, SE h.i.m.n. (Gael. *ao*)
ih	HB Welsh *u* (later ï)
ii	f*ee*l, s*ee*
ij	f*ee*l, s*ee* (NR)
iy	f*ee*l, s*ee* (BR)
iə	PSE h*ere*
i	HB, SN, HES, PP, SE *it* (NR)
ï	SN, PP, SE h.m.w; HES, HL pretty
i_2, *iᶜ*	PP, SE h.i.f.w. (pr*e*tty)
$ï_2$, *ïᶜ*	PP, SE h.i.m.w.
*i*h	HB pr*e*tty, j*u*st (= 'jist')
I	MP *i*n
j	*y*ou (NR); *j*udg*e* (BR)
j	HB, SN front modifier
jh	HB G. i*ch*
jh*w*	HB labialized **jh**
j*n*	HB nasalized **j**
k	*c*ome
ḳ	HB Ar. *kaf*
kh	HB lo*ch*; SN aspirated **k**
kh*r*	HB back (uvular) trill
kh*w*	HB G. au*ch* (labialized **kh**)
k*j*, K	HB palatalized **k**
kH	HB aspirated **k**
ʞ	SN stopped modifier
l	*l*ook
l̩	MP syllabic **l**
ḷ	SN Welsh *ll*
ɫ	SN back-divided voice; HES It. *gl*
lh	HB Welsh *ll*, F. tab*le*
l*h*	HES voiceless **l**
ɪ	PSE Ru. pa*l*ka
ɫ̥	SN back-divided-breath
ɭ*h*	HES back-side-voiceless
ɟ*h*	HES front-side-voiceless
l	SN It. *gl*
ḷ	SN front-divided-breath
L	HB It. *gl*, Sp. *ll*
Lh	HB front-divided-breath
ꞁ	HB back-divided-voice (guttural **l**)
ꞁh	HB back-divided-breath (voiceless ꞁ)
m	*m*an
m̥	SN lip-nasal-breath (voiceless **m**)
mh	HB lip-nasal-breath
m*h*	HES voiceless **m**
ɯ	SN h.b.n.
ɯ	SN h.b.w.
n	*n*i*n*e
n̥	SN Ice. *hn*
ñ	SN, HES, EB It. *gn*
n⊥	HB cerebral **n**
nh	HB Ice. *hn*
n*h*	HES Ice. *hn*
ñ*h*	HES voiceless **ñ**
ɥ̃	SN front-nasal-voice
n	HB, SN, NEG, SE nasal modifier
N	HB F. Boulo*gn*e (palatal **n**)
ɲ	MP palatal nasal
ŋ	si*ng*
ŋ*h*	HES voiceless **ŋ**
o	F. *beau* (NR); n*o*t (BR)
ŏ	PSE *O*ctober
ö	SN, HES, PP, m.m.n.; NEG *O*ctober
õ	PSL F. *on*
o¹	HB **o** with narrowed lip-opening
o_2, oᵓ	PP, SE m.o.b.n.r.
$ö_2$, öᶜ	PP, SE m.i.m.n.r.
oh	HB m.m.n.
oi	HB, PSE, PP, SE, EB b*oy* (BR)
o*i*h	HB b*oy* (NR)
ooᴵ	HB n*o* (NR)
ou	n*o* (BR)
ŏu	PSE, SE foll*ow*
öu	NEG fell*ow*
o	HB NG. st*o*ck; SN *o*we, b*o*y; HES b*o*y, G. st*o*ck; PP, SE b*o*y

ö	SN F. d*o*t; HES F. h*o*mme; PP Du. bet*e*r
o^2, $o^ɔ$	PP, SE m.o.b.w.r. (foll*ow*)
$ö_2$, $ö^c$	PP, SE m.i.m.w.r.
oh	HB F. h*o*mme
oq	HB F. *on*
ou	NEG n*o*
ɵ	MP suggested as substitute for **ø**
ø	MP as in IPA
ɔ	s*aw*; NEG n*o*t (BR)
ɔ̈	SN, HES, PP l.m.n.
$ɔ^2$, $ɔ'^ɔ$	PP, SE l.o.b.n.r.
$ɔ̈_2$, $ɔ̈^c$	PP, SE l.i.m.n.r.
ɔɔ	HL f*a*ll
ɔh	HB l.m.n.
ɔə	SE b*oa*, *oar*
ɔ	n*o*t (NR)
ɔ̈	HES, PSE l.m.w.; PP Sw. *u*pp
$ɔ^2$, $ɔ^ɔ$	PP, SE l.o.b.n.r.
$ɔ̈_2$, $ɔ̈^c$	PP, SE l.i.m.n.r.
***ɔ*h**	HB l.m.w.
œ	HB, PP, SE, EB F. p*eu*r; SN, HES Sw. h*ö*ra
$œ_2$, $œ^c$	PP, SE Sw. g*ö*r
œœ	PSL F. coul*eur*
œ*q*	HBF. *un*
œ	HB, SN l.f.w.; PSE, PP G. g*ö*tter
$œ_2$, $œ^c$	PP, SE l.i.f.w.r.
p	*p*ay
p‡	HB 'kiss'
ph	HB lip-open-breath (later **ɸ**)
ph*j*	HB palatalized **ph**
ph*r*	HB lip-trill-breath
pʜ	HB aspirated **p**
ɸ	SN lip-breath
ɸ*	SN lip-divided-breath
q	HB, SN si*ng* (later **ŋ**)
q̦	SN back-nasal-breath
qh	HB back-nasal-breath
q	HB sign of French nasality
r	*r*ed
r̥	SN Ice. *hr*
r⟊	HB inverted **r**
rh	HB voiceless **r**
r*h*	HES Ice. *hr*
rh*r*	HB Ice. *hr*, F. théât*re*
r*j*	HB palatalized **r**
r*r*	HB trilled **r**
ɹ	SN, PP Ar. *ain*; SN Dan. *r*
ɹ̣	SN Ar. *hha*
ɹ*h*	HES Ar. *hha*
r	HB, SN trill modifier
ʀ	HB Dan. *r*
ʀh	HB 'wheeze', voiceless **ʀ**
ʀh*r*	HB Ar. *hha*
ʀ*r*	HB Ar. *ain*
s	*s*ay
sh	HB fi*sh* (later **ʃ**)
s*j*	HB palatalized **s**
sh*j*	palatalized **sh**
sh*w*	HB G. Fi*sch* (labialized **sh**)
s	SN blade-modifier
ʃ	fi*sh*
t	*t*en
t‡	HB 'tut!'
th	HB *th*in (later **þ**)
tʜ	HB aspirated **t**
tsh	HB *ch*ur*ch* (later **tʃ**)
tʃ	*ch*ur*ch*
ɟ	SN point-modifier
ᴛ	HB front-stop (later **c**)
þ	*th*in
θ	MP as in IPA
u	F. s*ou* (NR), f*u*ll (BR)
ŭ	PSE, SE val*ue*
ü	SN, HES N. h*u*s; NEG val*ue*
u^2, $u^ɔ$	PP, SE h.o.b.n.r.
$ü_2$, $ü^c$	PP, SE h.i.m.n.r.
uh	HB Sw. h*u*s
uu	f*oo*l
uw	f*oo*l
uə	PSE, SE p*oo*r
u	b*oo*k (NR)
ü	SN Vulg. tw*o*; HES val*ue*
u^2, $u^ɔ$	PP, SE h.o.b.w.r. (val*ue*)
$ü_2$, $ü^c$	PP, SE h.i.m.w.r.

_u_h	HB Sw. *u*pp
v	*v*iew
‘v	HB whispered **v**
ʌ	HB voice; SN voice-glide; HES Gael. l*ao*gh; PP, SE h.b.n.
ʌ^2, **ʌ**ᵓ	PP, SE h.o.b.n.
‘ʌ, **ʌh**	HB whisper
ʌ_v_	SN voice-glide-round
_v_	SN lip-modifier
ʋ	MP as in IPA
w	*w*e
ʍ	SN, HES *wh*at
wh	*wh*at
w_h_	NEG *wh*at
_w_	SN lip-back-modifier
x	HB glottal catch (NR), si*x* (BR); elsewhere lo*ch*
x_w_	SN G. au*ch*
_x_	SN back-modifier
y	F. l*u*ne (NR), *y*oung (BR)
y$_2$, **y**ᶜ	PP, SE h.i.f.n.r.
_y_	HB, SN, G. sch*ü*tzen; HES Dan. l*y*st
_y_$_2$, **_y_**ᶜ	PP, SE h.i.f.w.r.
ʎ	SN open modifier
z	*z*eal
zh	HB rou*ge* (later **ʒ**)
ʒ	rou*ge*

Modifiers

>	HB out-breather
<	HB in-breather
‘	HB breath; SN whisper
ɪ	length mark
’	SN weak voice-glide
!	SN out-breather
¡	SN in-breather
?	SN expulsive click
¿	SN click sign
‡	HB click sign
•	strong stress
:	medium stress
..	very strong stress
-	weak stress
;	SN throat-stop (glottal catch); PSE emphatic stress
,˙	SN throat stop modifier
’	SN whisper-glide
‿	glideless combination
]	syllabic former
[ ]	glide
┌	high key
└	HB low key
┘	PP low key
┌└	HB middle key
┌┘	PP middle key
–	level tone
ˏ	rising tone
ˎ	falling tone
∨	compound rising tone
∧	compound falling tone
=	level force
<	increasing force
>	diminishing force
ˏ	inner modifier (away from the teeth)
ˎ	outer modifier
⸸	inverter
†	protruder
ᵓ	out-shifter
ᶜ	in-shifter
˔	raiser
˕	lowerer
˧	retracter
˫	advancer
˫˔	forward raiser
˧˕	backward lowerer
˫˕	forward lowerer
˧˔	backward raiser
§	unilateral modifier
§§	divided modifier
^{1}	close modifier
^{11}	narrow modifier
$_{1}$	open modifier
$_{11}$	wide modifier
^{2}	in-shifter
$_{2}$	out-shifter

Topic Index

PRINTED IN GREAT BRITAIN
AT THE UNIVERSITY PRESS, OXFORD
BY VIVIAN RIDLER
PRINTER TO THE UNIVERSITY